# *Education and Employment in the European Union*

# *Education and Employment in the European Union*

## The Social Cost of Business

DIMITRIS N. CHORAFAS

GOWER

Published by
Gower Publishing Limited
Wey Court East
Union Road
Farnham
Surrey
GU9 7PT
England

Gower Publishing Company
Suite 420
101 Cherry Street
Burlington
VT 05401-4405
USA

www.gowerpublishing.com



**British Library Cataloguing in Publication Data**
Chorafas, Dimitris N.
Education and employment in the European Union : the social cost of business.
1. Business and education--European Union countries.
2. Employability--European Union countries. 3. Human capital--European Union countries. 4. Manpower policy--European Union countries. 5. Pension trusts--European Union countries. 6. Pensions--Government policy--European Union countries.
I. Title
331.1'094-dc22

ISBN: 978-0-566-09201-5 (hbk)
978-0-566-09202-2 (ebk)

**Library of Congress Cataloging-in-Publication Data**
Chorafas, Dimitris N.
Education and employment in the European Union : the social cost of business / Dimitris N. Chorafas.
p. cm.
Includes index.
ISBN 978-0-566-09201-5 (hbk.) -- ISBN 978-0-566-09202-2 (ebook)
1. Labor supply--Effect of education on--European Union countries. 2. Manpower policy--European Union countries. 3. Education--European Union countries. 4. Business and education--European Union countries. I. Title.
HD5764.A6C56 2010
331.11'423094--dc22

2010030731

MIX
Paper from responsible sources
FSC
www.fsc.org
FSC® C018575

Printed and bound in Great Britain by the MPG Books Group, UK

# Contents

# List of Figures

# List of Tables

# List of Tables

# Foreword

This stimulating book draws the reader's attention towards a critical problem of today's world: the attitude of states and people towards educational and employment issues confronting our society. Despite alarm bells ringing all over and a widespread bitter projection of what the future may bring, little or nothing has been done to confront this problem.

Yet, we are approaching a crisis of worldwide dimensions. On the one hand, governments are failing to make drastic changes in social policy by revising the status of the 'state supermarket', as well as that of its contributors and beneficiaries. On the other hand, people are unwilling to change their current mindset; they passively wait for solutions to materialize without effort or, even worse, expect to live their lives forever on charitable handouts.

Part One focuses on a basic contradiction in the European Union's current learning system in which, in Dimitris Chorafas' words, 'education, including university education, is paid by the government. At the same time, however, governments are chronically short of funds, which explains the state of many schools and universities.'

Substandard funding is made worse by the expansion in the number of colleges and in the learning population – a phenomenon which become dominant during the second half of the twentieth century. This educational boom resulted in the dilution of higher education system standards, leading to the dilemma: 'Quantity or quality in undergraduate studies?'

Dr Chorafas discusses this issue from various angles, one of which centres on the organization of university degrees after the Bologna Initiative. Concepts such as 'learning how to learn' and the 'beautiful faculty of thinking' are elaborated with the help of quotations from great thinkers who distinguished themselves through the centuries.

Research, development and innovation are keywords of Part Two; they are also the road leading from education to employment. In a modern society the need for scientific research and development is present in practically all industries, from manufacturing to banking and insurance. Even when times are hard and there is a profit squeeze, no industry sector (or company) can allow itself to fall behind in R&D, because eventually this leads to oblivion.

Two key concepts in the globalized market are: making knowledge work productive and internal discipline. Both are discussed through practical examples taken from lessons learned in different markets – for instance, R&D successes from South Korea's breakthrough to global standing and the many start-ups collectively known as Silicon Valley companies. Then, the reader's attention is driven towards managing and financing R&D in the European Union.

That part of the analysis is focused on the evolution of EU research funding, starting from the First Framework Programs for Research and Development launched with the objective of coordinating national research policies. Dr Chorafas's opinion is that this did not lead to flourishing research, development and innovation within EU, one reason being the 'state supermarket' culture which led to a genetic mutation of researchers into bureaucrats.

Part Three is devoted to employment. The reader is presented with a number of reflections revolving around the fact that employment means different things to different people – from having a job to demands for higher wages and salaries, with ambitious plans running into reality and being followed up by a search for miracle solutions. The bottom line is that while many sociologists say that all people have the 'right to work' and this should be guaranteed by the state, it is not the state's business to find everyone a job.

The love of the status quo, coupled with a continuous search for solutions coming straight from heaven, leads to a serious lack of opportunities. This is true not only in regard to employment but also in connection with the urgent need to restructure endowments that have become unsustainable – the theme of Part Four.

The downslide of the welfare state goes back to over a century ago, when the first pension systems were introduced. Originally, state-sponsored retirement was designed for people whose age surpassed the life expectancy of the time – namely, for a limited number of individuals. Nowadays, not only is retirement for everyone, but it also runs as long as 20 years or more, bringing social security to an impasse.

Another factor that creates serious economic imbalances is that nowadays people look to the government (i.e., the taxpayers) as the source of not only their pension, but also security, healthcare, education, unemployment benefits, protection from poverty, housing and a growing shopping list of other entitlements. The author uses the term 'state supermarket' to denote this type of nanny state which endeavours to cover all the wants and risks of an ever larger population.

Alongside social insurance and its consequences, the book discusses the demography and social costs associated with longevity and healthcare. Although the ratio of retired people to those contributing to social security has been totally destabilized due to the increasing size of the elderly population, governments, desperately eager to please their people with all sorts of goods on offer, have continually delayed crucial decisions on the restructuring of social services in order to make them:

- efficient and
- affordable.

This book stimulates deep reflection on our society.

Professor Sergio Bittanti
Politecnico di Milano

# *Preface*

Several salient problems haunt, all at once, the 27 member states of the European Union. One of them is that most of the newer accession countries have been ill-prepared for EU membership. Another is that the euro is a currency without a country, which is a reason for instability in good times and might lead to euroland's break-up in bad times. Still another is the mixing of business and politics which has always characterized European public life. Three of the most vital issues presently confronting the European Union, as well as America, are:

- education,
- employment and
- pensions.

The three correlate among themselves as well as with other factors, such as slow economic growth, runaway healthcare expenses and demographics. All of them are socio-economic processes crying out for inquiry and investigation, which has to be performed rigorously and lead to reform and new policy guidelines in the European Union.

This is one of the issues to which this book is directed. Many claims have been made about reform, but none has been thoroughly researched or verified from a twenty-first-century perspective, let alone tested for effectiveness. The text rejects the hypothesis that the all-knowing welfare state, which I term the 'state supermarket', has the answers. What the politicians say in haste must be questioned. The world is rarely, if ever, what the authorities may think, or even suggest, and their conventional wisdom must therefore be challenged.

Defying the 'obvious' is not something that everybody is able or willing to do. The situation of an unchallenged authority prevailed in the Middle Ages, when it was dangerous to put the Church's claim of an earth-centred universe to question. Standing in contrast to that sort of medieval experience was the spirit of the Renaissance, a time when science and discovery flourished and modern civilization took off.

This spirit of questioning is at the core of this book. The text has been written for business practitioners, managers of industry, commerce and banking, consultants and government officials, as well as for academia, particularly for faculty and graduate students – both in the European Union and in North America.

Indeed, the same questioning spirit has guided the whole research project which led to this book. In meeting with cognizant people in every one of the arenas under examination – from education to R&D, employment and pensions – a focal point has been that of worst-case analysis: precisely what might develop in a troubled future. As Murphy's Law states, 'If something can go wrong, it will'.

However, the outcome does not need to be the worst-case disaster. The goal of this book is to come up with eye-opening findings arising from a focused, clear and calm investigation. It is, in essence, a most necessary *qualitative analysis* which both complements and helps in interpreting *quantitative statistics*. Cold numbers can be widely misleading without an associated qualitative examination.

- Analysis gives form to the formless, and
- the question, 'What is truth?' is answered – up to a point – through eager and unbiased investigation into the nature of goals, policies and results.

All things have to be examined by calling them into question, and there should be no limits set to thought. The participants in these research and analysis meetings – which provided food for thought for this book and its readers – have been encouraged to think aloud about the strengths and weaknesses of the subject under discussion.

The spirit of questioning included the consequences of current problems left unattended, and the way to solve these problems (if there is a way). While statistics have been respected, the key aim of the aforementioned exercises was to freely formulate thought. 'A slave is he who cannot speak his thought,' said Euripides. It was true in Antiquity, and it is true today.

Chapter-by-chapter, *Education and Employment in the European Union* examines the positive and negative aspects of each one of the themes that it tackles. This includes current policies and the results these have had in education, innovation, employment and pensions – particularly in light of EU experiences. It also questions whether or not current practices have produced the required social cohesion.

This strategy of challenging the 'obvious' has been chosen as the best way of identifying the salient issues that confront people who are engaged in each of the targeted domains. It is nobody's secret, for example, that, from primary schools to universities, current European educational standards leave much to be desired. Graduates don't have the necessary skills and know-how to live and work in a knowledge economy, and Part One suggests what needs to be done to upgrade present-day educational standards. These are the facts:

- University degrees are less meaningful because the mass education system has awarded more and more of them.
- The wall dividing education from business and industry in the European Union penalizes practical experience in the name of theoretical achievements which are not called for.
- Free higher education for all, financed by the state supermarket, is starving EU universities, making it impossible to create academic powerhouses with mighty reserves of money and talent.

We are all responsible for what has happened, and continues to happen, because we have expanded mass education from primary schools to universities, without paying due attention to maintaining quality. Suddenly, mediocrity became an option and even illiteracy has been allowed to spread among the young. It is time for a change. Mediocrity should not be permitted to gain the upper ground.

We can get the engines of our educational system working again *if* we cease to bend over backwards in order to accommodate the lowest common denominator. Teaching and research must be recombined, and academic credentials should become subject to accreditation. We can and should make education rewarding for our students – and for society – by transforming the classroom experience:

- from passive reception of information

- to active inquiry into the sense of knowledge and skills needed for professional life.

This should definitely include the all-essential ability of *learning how to learn*, which the current drifting of education has left by the wayside. Students must regain back their self-respect and respect for their teachers, for ethics and for society – and they should become accountable for mastering their subject at a level attained by the best artisans and professionals.

There is no better domain for testing educational achievements than research and development – the theme of Part Two. This is also where a person's qualifications for employment are appraised and assessed, because research and analysis oblige people to think.

Research is a process of solving problems. Its deliverables are new knowledge and innovation. By all accounts, new knowledge is the motor behind society's development, from intellectual proficiency to a good standard of living and better health. As for innovation, it is one of the most profitable investments.

Research is as well a testbed for evaluating, synthesizing and structuring management problems. As a thinking process, it assists people in developing the critical judgement and understanding needed to operate in a range of human undertakings. Therefore, it is most regrettable that the European Union has not found its way in bringing together universities and industry for excellence in research and development (R&D).

This has evident after-effects over and above those already discussed in connection with cradle-to-grave education. Combined with slow economic growth, the new generation's lack of qualifications – particularly in analytics – has a negative impact on employment because it diminishes career openings and associated opportunities for a better life. This is the subject of Part Three. Also working against employment are structural factors, ranging from inflexible labour laws to heavy social costs which penalize EU companies and discourage hiring.

Careers are not made by looking into the future through the rear-view mirror. Neither is staying in one place or in one job for one's whole life a way of growing in terms of experience and expertise. Moving ahead and taking chances has been the concept which inspired the Spanish *conquistadores* – and it served them well.

To survive in today's global society, with competition coming from all sides, people need to change their career three or four times in their lifetime. Failing to do that condemns them to oblivion and unemployment, as documented by the examples and case studies presented in this book. The best way to promote one's personal well-being and employment opportunities is by being:

- imaginative,
- risk-taking, and
- productive.

'Choose a job you love,' said Confucius, 'and you will never have to work a day in your life.'[1] The state supermarket bought the people's future through entitlements, swamped imagination and downsized the pleasure of work. For many people, today's

1 Unfortunately, this proverb can only apply to a few individuals who have created their good fortune through *their own* initiative. The majority is not using imagination, as this is not required (even less, desired) in the state supermarket which bets on widely distributed mediocrity. Besides, somewhere along the line, we lost sight of the fact that *progress* is not synonomous to *civilization*.

employment is like *a rite of passage*, replacing other rituals like national service in the army (which, in many countries, belongs to the past).

From science to finance, through practically any walk of life, there is little that can be accomplished without occasional venture or risk. Risk events are uncertain in the sense that they do not have a well-defined or sure outcome. Events which are certain, on the other hand, coagulate and offer no new opportunities.

With regard to the third bullet point, growth in productivity is one of the most important measures of a person's deliverables and of an economy's health. Improvements in efficiency of labour and capital reflect themselves in living standards. Numbers alone, however, can be tricky.

According to figures published in early November 2009, output per work-hour in America increased 4.5 percent year-on-year. The reason was big job cuts; not investments. By contrast, labour productivity for the whole of Euroland, in all sectors of the economy, shrank by 4 percent[2] because many workers remained in the labour force, even if semi-employed. As this example documents:

- Numbers talk, but sometimes their message is unsatisfactory because it may hide qualitative facts.
- It is always perilous to try to compress complex problems into statistics which, unexplained, may present a distorted message.

Precisely for these reasons this book seeks to explain what lies behind statistical facts and figures. By and large, this is the after-effect of a mass society and of the state supermarket, both of which oblige people to grapple with new orthodoxies they do not understand or appreciate. This is further complicated by the fact that each of the three main themes – education, employment and pensions – finds itself at an inflection point.

Part Four examines the future of pensions. Deliberately, it does not follow the mainstream but takes a polyvalent approach which includes savings, investments, state pensions and company pensions, as well as the pensions' alter ego – healthcare.

The news is not particularly good. Some of the current pension schemes are only marginally functional, because of demographics; others are handicapped by a lack of abundant investment opportunities, risks that are higher than in the past, and pension money melting away in economic crises. Precisely because the risks associated with pensions are rising, past solutions are no longer able to deliver.

Just as the state supermarket cannot afford to guarantee free education from cradle to grave, despite its promises, the present social security system is unable to provide lifelong support in pensions and healthcare. Demographics on the one side and mismanagement on the other make these and other heralded endowments unaffordable and unsustainable. Nor is it feasible to effectively separate the problems confronting pensions from those confronting healthcare.

- For both, the unsurmounted issue is who is going to pay for them, and,
- Of the two, healthcare is and will continue to be the more money-hungry.

2 European Central Bank, *Monthly Bulletin*, October 2009.

Modern solutions for education, research, employment, pensions and healthcare should be self-supporting – which means that they should promise and deliver a level equivalent to the contributions they receive from the people who benefit, or will benefit, from them. Taxpayers' money should not be spent to cover their ever-growing deficits. This is important, because the list of 'must dos' confronting the state supermarket is without a visible end.

In addition, one of the more recent revelations of our society's weaknesses is its lack of expertise (and sometimes of will) in dealing with twenty-first-century financial crime. Closely connected to this is the inability of politicians and regulators to get tough. (This is not the present book's subject,[3] but it ranks high in the list of reasons why the status quo is far from being satisfactory.)

Let's face it. From education, to research, employment, pensions, healthcare and the ability to keep crime of all sorts – including financial – under lock and key, our society is not short of problems requiring urgent attention and effective solutions. Regional and global political 'summits' are a dime a dozen these days, but for any practical purpose they are a monkey house.

Careful observers of political decisions, and of their lack of focus, have come to the conclusion that it is almost impossible to get any sense of direction from the frequent gatherings of heads of state and prime ministers. The only thing that can be said for sure is that this 'summit tourism' is expensive and a vast waste of time. None of these gatherings is addressing the most vital issue, namely how to:

- confront a modern society's salient problems in an able manner, and
- prevent the world's social and financial system from looting and total collapse.

This is written on the understanding that both the European Union and America (though not yet Asia) have by now all the ingredients they need for a debacle of tremendous proportions. This book presents the evidence. It also suggests what is needed to start redressing the balance, before *déclinisme* reaches the point of no return.

* * *

I am indebted to a long list of knowledgeable people, and of organizations, for their contribution to the research which made this text feasible. Also to several senior executives, university faculty and other experts for constructive criticism during the preparation of the manuscript, most particularly to Dr Heinrich Steinmann, Dr Nelson Mohler and Eva-Maria Binder.

Let me take this opportunity to thank Martin West for suggesting this project, Gillian Steadman for seeing it all the way to publication, and Linda Cayford for the editing work. To Eva-Maria Binder goes the credit for compiling the research results, typing the text and making the camera-ready artwork and index.

Dr Dimitris N. Chorafas
Valmer and Vitznau

3 Energy and environmental protection are also important subjects – the themes of the next research.

# PART I

# The European Union's Educational Challenge

# CHAPTER 1 Education in the European Union

## 1. Learning Defined

Mahatma Gandhi said: 'Live as if you were to die tomorrow. Learn as if you were to live forever.' In a few words Gandhi defined the process of *learning* as well as its further implications in the realm of a knowledge society.

'The laws of education are the first we receive ... they prepare us to be citizens,' advised Montesquieu (1689–1755), the French writer and philosopher, 'If the nation in general has a principle, then the parties composing it – which means the families – will also have one.' He also pointed out that 'we have three educations which are different or contrarian to one another. Those of

- our fathers,
- our teachers, and
- of the world.'[1]

Anthropologists say that what distinguishes man from other animals is his tools and his ability to keep on developing them. Though true, this statement goes only up to a point because it does not place enough emphasis on the tool called *learning* – since, without learning, man would have been unable to engage in any significant effort, including *self-development*.

The tools themselves provide an example. Most types of stone tool unearthed by archeologists are still being made in the bush, and there are also older tools believed to belong to pre-human times.[2] Better and better tools, however, would not have come without paying attention to:

- what was right and wrong with those already existing, and
- learning how to make improvements which increase their effectiveness.

Sociologists suggest that the sophistication of tools increased with warfare and in hunting less intelligent animals, because it required a matching of wits not needed in agriculture. A predatory animal does not ordinarily tackle an adversary much larger than

1 Montesquieu *'De l'Esprit des Lois'*, Classiques Garnier, Paris, 1961 (author's translation).

2 Such as pebble tools and choppers excavated in a site east of Lake Turkana (formerly Lake Rudolf) in Kenya, dated as having been made and used about 2.5 million years ago by man-like creatures which had not yet attained the size and status of brain attributed to *Homo sapiens*.

itself.[3] But, owing to the combination of his learning ability and his weapons, man attacks both

- larger animals and
- other men, who fight back.

There is a widespread opinion that, over the 200,000 year-long history of *Homo sapiens*, big game hunters and war-makers have been distinguished by the respect and rewards they received if they survived the task they thrust upon themselves, no matter if it were fundamentally destructive. Many of them, however, have been distinguished for their learning, their courage and their appreciation that:

- true learning involves pain.

Much of what we learn demolishes what we already 'know' and is part of 'us'. Albert Einstein spoke of common sense as 'the collection of prejudices acquired by age eighteen'. The act of cutting something out of ourselves (and out of our beliefs) and replacing it with something better is bound to be painful. In addition,

- learning requires discipline – self-discipline above all – which itself has to be learned. But there is also discipline by the family, which is a prerequisite to self-discipline but has unfortunately disappeared because families have disintegrated and the mass society[4] no longer permits disciplining children. Lenient morals have discarded the advice given by the old French adage: 'He who loves well punishes well.'

Equally important is school discipline which is also on the wane. School discipline has melted away partly because the prerequisite of self-discipline is utterly lacking, and partly because when the teacher disciplines pupils he or she is shown no respect and can sometimes be physically attacked – even knifed – by pupils.[5] Being obliged to work under lamentable educational standards, underpaid and unappreciated, the teacher no longer cares.

This is a pity because learning leads to knowledge, whether this is the result of formal teaching (more on this later) or of acquiring experience by osmosis in the family, in school, in society, and on the job. On-the-job learning is *tacit knowledge*, and (to a significant degree) it contrasts to *articulate knowledge* which comes from schooling and from reading books.

Socrates said 'I learn as long as I live'. Some people are particularly able to capitalize on tacit knowledge. In the seventeenth century there were two military commanders who proved their value at the age of 20. One was Louis-Antoine-Henri de Bourbon-Condé, duc d'Enghien; the other Lennart Torstenson who had learned the military arts by osmosis by serving as a page to Gustav-Adolph, King of Sweden.

---

3 This is true even of lions, tigers and bears.

4 Read: the socialist society or, more precisely, the culture of the state supermarket.

5 A recent example of pupil violence, reported in the French TV news media, is the 13-year-old who on 15 May 2009 in the Collège François Mitterrand tried to cut the throat of his teacher with a kitchen knife 'because she punished him for not having done his homework'. The teacher suffered an internal haemorrhage and had to undergo an emergency operation.

In 1624, ready to attack the Lithuanian army in Livonia, Gustav-Adolph sent Torstenson with his orders to his commanders. But the Lithuanians had moved in the opposite direction to that which the king had thought. Torstenson saw this. When Gustav-Adolph became aware of the Lithuanians' change in battle plans he was in despair. 'Sir,' said the page, 'please excuse me. Having seen the enemy making the opposite movement, I gave the opposite order.' The same evening the page was invited to eat with the king, the next day he commanded a company and, immediately after that, a regiment.[6]

Tacit knowledge can imprint virtue in a person's mind. Socrates said that *virtue* is knowledge which cannot be taught. It might be acquired by living in a virtuous society, just as skills are transferred by observing the master and learning from osmosis. Human interaction and the observance of facts and events are excellent mechanisms of learning.

The reason why tacit knowledge cannot be easily articulated is that it reflects subconscious judgement, based on a growing body of wide-ranging experience. This is the know-how which a person bent on learning picks up as he walks through life. There are two challenges connected to this way of increasing one's virtue and wisdom:

- First, not everybody has the will and method to learn after leaving school.[7]
- Second, the opportunity to follow the footprints of tacit knowledge may well be lacking.

For many people, 20 years' experience is nothing more than one year repeated 20 times. History books say that people residing in certain nations are *fortunate* because they are in the middle of learning and action. Living near centres of thought and of science helps, but these centres have been developed by people – while other people, because of custom, religion, inertia or other reasons,

- have been adverse to learning, and
- have therefore fallen behind in personal development.

*If* just by living near a centre of civilization was enough by itself and personal initiative in learning was secondary, *then* North Africans in France, Pakistanis in Britain, Turks in Germany, Indonesians in the Netherlands and Moroccans in Belgium and Spain should be way ahead in culture. But they are not. They don't capitalize on the centuries-old cultural environments of their new countries to get ahead.[8]

In total contrast to this policy directed against learning, knowledge and personal development[9] is the philosophy which embodies the famous dictum by Louis Pasteur, the famous French chemist, '*Chance favours the prepared mind*'. Getting prepared takes self-discipline, concentration and hard work. It also requires forward thinking and an open mind. In 2006 the World Economic Forum, in Davos, included an unprecedented 22 sessions on *innovation*. Themes were:

---

6 Voltaire *Le Siècle de Louis XIV*, Flammarion, Paris, 1966.

7 Provided that he or she has the will to learn while in school, which is not self-evident.

8 In medieval times when most of Europe was in the dark ages, North Africans in Spain had developed a great civilization. But then, as it so often happens with centres of learning, it collapsed.

9 Typically promoted by religious fanatics because illiteracy makes people weak and unstable – hence easy prey.

- building a culture of innovation
- making innovation real, and
- what creativity can do for you.

The common ground behind the three bullets is *learning* as well as *thinking as a way of living*. This is an old concept dating back to the civilizations of China, India, Mesopotamia and ancient Greece. More recently, it has underpinned the knowledge society, reflecting the fact that people, companies and nations cannot generate value by looking backwards. Education and innovation have become the pillars of the future.

Victor Hugo, the nineteenth-century French writer, said: 'He who opens a school door closes a prison.' That's true in regard to education at its best, and, for this to happen, the teacher:

- must have plenty of authority and
- very few reasons to exercise it.

This climate of school discipline existed in Hugo's time, but it is only a memory today because the authority of both the school and the family has been greatly diluted. It is easy to invoke 'children's rights' and other reasons in order to escape discipline and put numerous constraints on educating and learning.

## 2. A Knowledge Economy Cries Out for Excellence in Education

These have been ill-advised measures because the basic characteristics that distinguish winners from losers in the twenty-first century are learning, knowledge, innovation, productivity, willingness to take risks and the ability to keep a close watch over these risks. A *knowledge economy* is driven by brilliant service ideas. Google, Apple, Microsoft and Amazon.com, for example, have based their success on the imagination of people able to look into the future and capitalize on its opportunities.

- Innovation creates plenty of favourable circumstances, and
- what it produces amounts to a fast-growing share of gross domestic product (GDP).

Favourable circumstances have to be caught in the right way in the net of a person's daily, even hourly, activities. 'Effectiveness is a habit,' said Peter Drucker. But 'luck' is what happens when preparation meets opportunity. The broader a person's knowledge base and the greater his or her willingness to act the more successful will be his or her career.

It is not for nothing that L.M.K. Boelter, my dean at the Department of Engineering, UCLA, in the 1950s insisted that to enlarge their knowledge base engineers must learn the humanities. 'Who knows only his own generation remains always a child,' said George Norlin, former president of the University of Colorado. Learning is a multi-dimensional enterprise extending both

- in the depth of time, and
- through the breadth required to respond to the challenges of a globalized society.

The trouble is that today's mass society is betting on quantity not on quality as it was in Antiquity and should be the case today. No wonder that, despite all the rhetoric that accompanied the adoption of the UN's 1999 'Education for All' goals, progress has been patchy at best.

The larger the number of school-age children the lower the level of education they get. In addition, attending school is only the first step towards education, and just spending time in school does not guarantee a good outcome. The way an article in *The Economist* had it, in Ghana 'sixth-graders sitting a simple multiple-choice reading test scored on average the same mark that would be gained by random guessing'.

These facts and trends affect both individual lives and the different nations' development. A January 2010 study by the Organization for Economic Cooperation and Development (OECD)[10] provides evidence of the link between educational attainment and prosperity, by comparing international data on 15-year-olds' cognitive skills – that is:

- how they apply their science, maths and reading ability, and
- how they contribute to their countries' economic growth by means of their education.

The study further shows that good examination results tend to be followed, a few years later, by small but measurable improvements in economic growth. That is reasonable, because, like it or not, ours is a knowledge economy, and less developed countries cannot pull themselves up by their shoestrings. They have to depend on their human capital.

A knowledge economy needs human capital of a high calibre. Sound management and financial resources are next in line of priorities – because, to continue growing, a modern economy requires sustained investments. Money alone will not tip the scales, but it has to be available. Just prior to the economic crisis of 2007–2011, an article in *Business Week* suggested that America was investing \$1.5 trillion per year in the moving gear of the knowledge industry, measured by budgets for:

- education and
- research and development (R&D).[11]

Who is contributing this significant amount of capital? *Business Week* said that \$1 trillion comes from businesses, investing in R&D and education; \$0.25 trillion from the government's sponsorship of R&D and education; and \$0.25 trillion from households – invested in education of the young and lifelong learning of the parents.

There has been practically no counterpart for this quarter–trillion-dollar contribution by households in continental European countries as everything, including university education, is paid for by the government (read: the state supermarket).[12] At the same time, however, governments are chronically short of funds, which explains the sorry state of many schools and universities in the European Union (EU). It is wrong to think that students can continue getting something for nothing, but this is a generalized belief.

10 OECD, *The High Cost of Low Educational Performance*, January 2010.

11 *Business Week*, 13 February 2006.

12 Although, in Britain, students pay tuition fees and get loans for subsistence which they then pay back.

To better appreciate the impact of investment in education, research, development and innovation on a nation's future, we should grasp the fact that what we call *human ability* is a social product. Each person's ingenuity, imagination and power to deliver must be developed in multiple ways, starting with the family and proceeding with schooling. Human ability depends a great deal on:

- educational opportunities,
- lifelong learning programmes,
- research activities, and
- the skill to put research results to practical use ahead of others.

Here is what an article in *The Economist* wrote about educational opportunities:

> *Until the 1970s South Korea was about as prosperous as Brazil but, helped by its superior school system, it has leapt ahead and now has around four times the national income per head. World domination, even the friendly and non-confrontational sort Brazil seeks, will not come to a place where 45 per cent of the heads of poor families have less than a year's schooling.*[13]

Getting ahead of everyone else is not a question of throwing money at the problem, but of exercising organization and discipline. Mexico invests 5.3 per cent of GDP on education, Brazil 4.2 per cent and Argentina 4 per cent. South Korea invests 'only' 4.2 per cent of GDP in education, but in terms of results it shines compared to the Latin Americans.[14] The difference is made by:

- clear goals and
- better organization.

It is normal that there is a difference between EU jurisdictions regarding the money invested in knowledge industries – higher education, research and development, and software production. But such differences should not be king-size. When they are, they demonstrate that the policies of some countries are wanting. To right the balances, they have to question everything.

France provides an example of a university system in distress, because an expansion to 82 universities[15] has unavoidably resulted in lack of funding. These 82 French universities are catering to over 1.5 million students who have enrolled without a screening examination. Fitness for higher education left aside, that's twice the number of students a quarter-century ago – accompanied by an increase in drop-outs, and hence spoilage of precious resources.

- All French universities are public.
- All faculty members are civil servants.
- All institutes of higher education are barred from selecting undergraduates at entry.
- So, as can be expected, the attrition rate is high.

---

13 *The Economist*, 6 June, 2009.

14 Statistics from: http://www.nationmaster.com/graph/edu_edu_spe-education-spending-of-gdp.

15 With about a quarter of them being, more or less, in a state of permanent student strikes and discontent.

Enrolment fees amount to just €200 a year, with practically all tuition being paid for by the state. The country's elite keeps its children out of the university system, sending them to the *grandes écoles*. These cater for just 4 per cent of the total student population, but the quality of learning is much higher because the rules are different.

Shanghai's Jiao Tong University, which publishes an annual world ranking of universities worldwide, has no French university in its top-20 list. Only Paris VI, the better part of the old and famous Sorbonne, qualifies (in 45th position) among the world's top 50. Moreover, the 'in' subjects at these 82 universities are soft themes, like social science, which are not in demand by French industry. Anecdotal evidence suggests that some 45,000 study a subject called 'sports science'.

Underfinanced, with underpaid faculty staff, with popular subjects like 'social pseudoscience' and 'sports pseudoscience', higher education in the EU is in full retreat. Seventeen of the top 20 universities in the world are American (again according to Shanghai's Jiao Tong University) while only two are European (Cambridge and Oxford). But two Swiss universities show up in the top 30: ETH in Zurich and EPFL in Lausanne.[16]

The rating of European universities suffers for precisely the same reasons why the primary and secondary education are unwell: the majority of students don't care to learn; there is inertia in revamping curricula; faculties and laboratories are underfunded; and all this is topped by overgenerous and unrealistic educational promises made by governments – which, as everybody knows, cannot be kept.

- 'Numerus clausus' would have limited the number of university entrants by accepting only the best,[17] but the state supermarket decreed 'higher education for all'.

Consequently, in some universities up to 46 per cent of all new students drop out, while other universities seem to have turned themselves into a sort of left-wing institutions specializing in social unrest, rather than focusing on learning and professional training.

- The state supermarket also decreed 'free-of-charge university studies', no matter how many years a student takes to finish – if he or she ever 'finishes'.

The OECD, a richer nations club, assesses primary and secondary education by testing randomly chosen groups of youngsters from each country in reading and mathematics. It also samples university students to see what they have learned. It would be wise as well to take peer opinions from academics and from employers on what the graduates are worth (a subject treated in Chapter 3 under the heading 'Promoting the process of accreditation'[18]).

Peer-to-peer evaluation is highly relevant because quality counts for much more than quantity. Since students choose where to spend their time and money in the global education market, ambitious university bosses want a sharper competitive edge for their institution; and employers who are worth their salt value the graduates' critical thinking

16 Both federal technical universities.

17 By setting an upper limit to the number of students being admitted commensurate to their qualifications and available facilities at the university site.

18 Accreditation reflects factors such as the number and quality of staff, including: prizes the professors win and how many books and articles they publish; quality of students; state-of-the-art labs; research projects; and more.

and analytical capabilities. The latter is promoted by fields of study like mathematics, physics, engineering, economics and finance – not by the pseudosciences.

## 3. In the EU, Engineering Education is in Regression

The member nations of the European Union and the major engineering universities are facing a common problem. They are simply not attracting sufficient young people into the sciences, and formerly flourishing engineering companies (as well as their suppliers) are being confronted by a scarcity in recruiting. Behind this is the simple truth that if Europe's universities are not turning out enough engineering graduates this is because students and would-be-students:

- don't want to put the necessary effort into the sciences, and
- they fail to appreciate that in one stroke they also kill their opportunity for interesting work and a good career.

Different studies show that engineering is unpopular among undergraduates. True enough, along with medical students, physicists and biotechnologists, engineering students work harder and in a more structured environment than in the (incorrectly called) 'social sciences'. In return, however, few professions offer the deep satisfaction of turning designs into reality – and, at the same time, contribute to society far more than what the 'soft sciences' can offer.

A recent letter from the president of *Science* magazine had an interesting opinion on this malaise in the study of hard sciences, which is hitting both sides of the North Atlantic:

> *In today's economic crisis, the disinterest of [our] youth in scientific careers and the public's poor understanding of science greatly threaten [our] future at a time when science and logical problem-solving skills are critical. Yet the performance of [our] young people on science tests … is barely average, and many students leave middle school being illiterate in science. Moreover, the content of science education is often questioned and even disparaged.*[19]

- The European Union and the United States are not alone in the mire of problems which plague their educational systems, and most particularly science learning.
- In this modern age, what students *should* learn to get ready to compete in the global economy is not the same as what they want to learn – to take it easy and relax.

Lack of coordination is another major problem. In the EU, the educational system is run by its 27 member states and each one has its own baffled policy-makers. In the US, with 50 states, discord is just as great. For example, Mississippi has different expectations for pupils than California or New York. In a ranking of 15-year-olds in 30 industrialized

19 The quotation comes from an article written by Pierre Lena of the French Academy of Sciences ('Europe Rethinks Education', *Science*, 23 October 2009) to express his frustration about the failure of education systems.

countries in 2006, American teenagers came a dismal 21st in science and 25th in maths.[20]

Opinions are divided as to the reasons why the young generation in Europe and America turned away from the 'hard sciences'. Some say that the students themselves don't want to put up the effort, having been spoiled in their upbringing by their parents and by society at large.[21]

Other people think that most of the fault is to be found with the high-school teachers. A 2007 study by McKinsey, the consultancy, pointed out that countries whose students perform well recruit teachers from the top of the class.[22] In contrast, a British report by Politeia, a think-tank, said that, by international standards, the bar for getting into teacher training in England is unusually low.

- Trainee teachers can resist basic literacy and numeracy tests as often as they like, and
- year in and year out some 1,200 pupils – a third of the population – finish their studies at the lowest level of the class from which they graduate.[23]

That's not good news for teachers, their pupils or students, parents and society at large. As an article in *The Economist* noted, the result is a general sense that the country's teachers have been scraped from the bottom of the barrel.[24] This is not just a British phenomenon. It is widespread in Europe.

Still other people say that this refusal of the young generation to base their careers on the 'hard sciences' is a failure of the engineering companies themselves to communicate the creative excitement of the profession and to describe the excellent career paths that go with it. There are plenty of things to be explained to Europe's (and America's) young people, long before they get to the point of choosing academic courses which will help define their future.

'Choose a job you love,' said Confucius, 'and you will never have to work a day in your life.' Work can be pleasure, but this is rarely accounted for in career planning. The 'normal' exercise of educational and career choices is often implemented by public opinion. In our mass society 'the law of public opinion' has become the universal law of gravitation in the way careers go (and not only careers).

- Explaining and persuading is not incompatible with a liberal regime, but it is often taken as coercion, and
- careers are not being carefully planned to parallel the market's demand for knowledge and services, way before reaching high school.

---

20 *The Economist*, 21 November 2009.

21 According to this opinion, today's young have, at the age of 23, the level of maturity to decide about their future that 17-year-olds had at the end of World War II.

22 'What Works in Education; The Lessons According to McKinsey', *The Economist*, 18 October 2007.

23 *Teachers Matter: Recruitment, Employment and Retention at Home and Abroad*, The Report of the Politeia Education Commission, Politeia, London, July 2009.

24 *The Economist*, 1 August 2009. 'Teach First', a program founded in 1989 that trains 4,000 teachers a year, aims to reverse this vicious cycle by creating a route into teaching for high-fliers. However, the same article also makes reference to a participant in that programme who was about to start teaching mathematics to 15-year-olds who have had *22* maths teachers *over the past three years*. No wonder that pupils have become maths-illiterate.

The wrong career orientation is amplified by the lack of appropriate learning (read: basic literacy) at primary and secondary schools (section 4) and the choice of soft subjects at university level. Matters for all students are made even worse by the 'right' which the state supermarket has given to near-drop-outs to enter the university system and spoil its resources.

The end result is that those penalized are the students who go to university to learn and make a career, rather than to kill their time or for reasons of prestige. Professional maturity and career openings are not necessarily what the majority of students are after. In terms of career planning and job opportunities, it is more rational to study engineering, physics and mathematics.

- Unsurprisingly, graduates in 'soft' subjects find their degrees worthless in the job market.

The spoilage of resources matters greatly in terms of future deliverables. The fact that universities are obliged to offer subjects that EU industry does not need correlates with unemployment among university graduates.

- Curiously enough, even graduates with more serious degrees want to become civil servants; they don't take risks by being enterprising.

Unexciting specializations and dull careers point to a decline of the middle class in the EU – because, all things considered, the middle class has been promoted by learning and therefore it is committed to education. Analyses about economic growth stress the importance of what economists call 'human-capital accumulation'. This involves, among other things:

- higher educational qualifications, starting at primary school,
- a steady process of adult lifelong learning, and
- healthier lives, including the way in which people live and behave.

Human capital is needed to man, promote and watch over the processes of wealth creation – and this invariably means more designers, better logistics experts and, generally, an improved breed of professionals. Industry is not going to financially sponsor schools whose products are low-quality or out-of-date.

Part of the reason for wrong study choices lies in the fact the students are not paying their dues. With the possible exception of Britain, where a few years ago the law changed, all European universities, aw well as primary and secondary education, are on tight budget. Through making too many *unaffordable and unsustainable promises*, the state supermarket has run out of money. Take France as an example. Statistics from *Business Week* say that the country devotes only 1.1 per cent of its GDP to university education, versus an average of 1.4 per cent in western Europe and 2.5 percent in the US.[25]

'Free higher education for all', for those who are qualified and those who are not, results in spoilage. Year in and year out, the French university system ejects 100,000

25 Which in a way is understandable because there are so many competing public services for state funding – and, as Jacques Chirac used to say, 'Too many taxes kill the tax intake'.

students without a degree. Back in September 2006 Dominique Strauss-Kahn, a former minister of finance (currently managing director of the IMF) and one of the few brainy Socialist Party leaders, asked for this system to be dynamited by:

- establishing entry examinations,
- ending the unique university degree and
- providing universities with administrative independence.

The concepts behind all three bullets make sense. Three more issues should be added. The first is pan-European educational standards, from primary to secondary and tertiary education. This is in no way offered by the so-called Bologna Initiative (see Chapter 4) which is, at best, a light opera's *libretto*.[26] The second is the promotion of private universities to give the rusty, backwards-looking state universities some badly needed competition. The third is the aforementioned peer-to-peer and professionally-motivated accreditation of universities, both the public universities currently in existence and the new private ones (see Chapter 3).

There are some green sprouts about private institutions of higher education in continental Europe. On 2 June 2008 in Toulouse, before a crowd of international economists and French business chiefs, Valérie Pécresse, the then universities minister, inaugurated the Toulouse School of Economics (TSE) – a graduate institution of the University of Toulouse. The institution's English name and English-only teaching are matched by the fact that its financing comes from companies – not from the government. To start with, it raised €33 million from private sponsors such as AXA, Total and BNP Paribas. Pécresse said that she will match every euro raised with the equivalent in public money. Jean Tirole, the new school's director, called it the 'realization of a dream'.[27]

The second novelty with TSE is that it plans to kill the sacred cow of 'equal treatment', which is the state supermarket's credo: that everybody should have a full share in whatever happens. Valérie Pécresse explicitly blessed competition, which is a great start. But students in some 20 out of France's 82 universities took to the street in protest against efforts to establish private universities. (The same sort of black reaction also occurs in Greece and elsewhere in the EU.)

These two novelties are the good news. The bad news is that the TSE is an exception, all the way to its curriculum. Companies may be happy to support economics or science, but they would not spend more on abstract sociology, psychoanalysis and other fields whose 'skills' contribute nothing to human capital and to the economy. To fulfil their social contracts, universities should also be

- freed from meddling bureaucrats,
- made more accountable for their products, and
- allowed to develop curricula reflecting what the labour market requires.

Plenty of attention must also be paid to career development, otherwise some of the best graduates will leave to work abroad. Many continental EU countries, including France

26 Theoretically at least, this involves the harmonization of European degrees into a 'bachelors, masters and doctorate' structure as in America and Britain. Practically, it is a fiat of tunnel visions in education.

27 *The Economist*, 7 June 2008.

and Germany, suffer from brain drain rather than enjoying a brain gain. By contrast, for years America has been benefiting from huge inflows of human capital, estimated by *Business Week* to be worth about $0.2 trillion per year. Many young graduates from the educated elite of countries around the globe flock to America to make a career.[28]

## 4. In Europe Illiteracy Starts at the Primary School

Asked what condition of man he thought deserved the most pity, Benjamin Franklin answered: 'A lonesome man on a rainy day who does not know how to read.' This is the best possible way to describe the importance of books and the ability to read and understand them. Literacy goes much deeper than having a school system and libraries of good books that will never be read.

There are many levels of literacy, but fundamentally the term stands for the ability to read, write and understand what one reads. It is a gateway to culture, though human development is also linked to many other issues presently troubling our society. Problems connected to rising illiteracy are deep and growing.

- They start at very early age in the life of the new generation.
- They remain practically unattended at all ages of society.
- They deconstruct the West's knowledge economy brick-by-brick.

Some people say there is no reason to worry. On the surface, at least, things look fine, Yes, but only on the surface. Every September, laden with heavy backpacks, children file back to school. Very few parents, however, ask themselves: 'Are they ready for the education system?' and 'Is the education system ready for them?'

Given the old primary and secondary European education's reputation for rigour and secular egalitarianism, the answers should have been positive; but they are negative. What went wrong? The best response is contained in a 30-page 'Letter to Educators' published by Nicolas Sarkozy in September 2007, in his first year as president of the French Republic. This letter pointed out not just French but also pan-European and American problems:

- too many school drop-outs,
- not enough respect or authority in the classroom,[29]
- too little value placed on the teaching profession,
- too much passive learning in the curriculum, and
- too much theory and abstraction.

Britain, Germany, Italy, Spain, the Netherlands and practically all other European countries are facing similar problems. The statistics vary from one jurisdiction to the next, but the trend is towards 30–40 per cent of pupils leaving primary school with serious learning gaps in basic reading, writing and arithmetic.

28 Note that during the last decade this includes many young French who finally overcame the language barrier and are now finding top jobs in Britain, Canada and the US.

29 Nicolas Sarkozy, 'A letter to educators', 4 September 2007. English translation at: http://www.ambafrance-uk.org/President-Sarkozy-writes-to-French.html. Pupils, Sarkozy correctly says, should stand up when the teacher enters.

Under this perspective should be seen the initiative by Angela Merkel, the German chancellor, who in late October 2008 gathered the premiers from all of Germany's 16 states for an 'education summit' in Dresden. Its goal was to transform Germany from a mediocre performer into an *education republic*. Merkel's initiative is welcome, but whether in Germany or elsewhere it is neither easy nor likely to be achieved very soon.

However, the goal is attainable, although the general opinion is that the chances of achieving it are limited. Almost half the children in some German cities come from immigrant families – Turkish by majority – who still speak mainly their mother tongue at home. These immigrant children are only slightly worse than those from France and America:

- Between 8 per cent and 10 per cent of all 16-year-olds are school drop-outs.
- They are hardly the sort who could ever pursue professional education or develop a challenging career.

In France, one in five pupils finishes secondary school with no qualification at all. Even the *baccalauréat* is becoming an unreliable degree. The 2007 pass rate of 83 per cent was up from just over 60 per cent in the early 1960s not because student quality had improved but because the de Villepin government suddenly became extra-lenient.[30] The *bac* is worth absolutely nothing, asserts Jean-Robert Pitte, president of the Sorbonne University of Paris IV.

The president of the Republic is worried, and for good reason. In a conference he gave on 24 April 2008 Sarkozy said that 15 per cent of kids who finish primary school don't know how to read and write. And one out of two who get their *baccalauréat* does not come up to the level that characterized these graduates in the past. Other statistics document that today 5th class (primary school) pupils have the same level of learning as 3rd class pupils a short 30 years earlier.[31] That's a 40 per cent decline in learning in a short timespan.

In Britain, too, literacy and numeracy standards in primary schools have flattened out and are somewhat in decline, even if national strategies introduced in 1998 (for literacy) and in 1999 (for numeracy) produced some improvements. In the early years of this century the Labour government said that learning standards had risen, but independent observers suggest that much of the initial rise was illusory, a consequence of:

- grade inflation and
- pushing children towards easier subjects.

The British state school system is particularly weak. The estimated 7 per cent of British children who go to private schools account for more than 40 per cent of the intake at Oxford and Cambridge. Students at private schools comprise a fifth of the school population taking A-levels, which are essential for getting into famous universities.

Research by the British Institute of Education, published on 21 April 2009, looks at those corners of the state-education system where some parental choice does exist.

---

30 Ironically, the rate of those who passed the *bac* exam soared the very year high-school students lost three months of their education demonstrating in the streets against the de Villepin government.

31 Author's own research.

Even there, it turns out to be neither unleashing competition nor raising standards.[32] Money thrown at the educational problem has been part of the state supermarket's larger problem – not of the solution.

That much was foretold on 30 June 2009 in the education White Paper published by the Labour government.[33] The taxpayer will finance parents who demand catch-up tuition for their lazy children, as well as challenging lessons for their gifted ones. And parents will be informed by new school report cards that set out exam and inspection results, as well as sport and healthy eating issues.[34]

The British government doubled spending on education between fiscal years 1999 and 2007. The irony is that this spending surge coincided with a dramatic decline in Britain's position in the OECD's ranking of educational performance.[35] This and similar findings in other countries are another reminder that:

- throwing money at the problem makes matters worse, and
- much more than budgetary increases is needed to build up human capital.

The silver lining of this waste of public money seems to be that, according to the White Paper, naughty children will be (supposedly) tamed by forcing parents to sign agreements to make them behave. (Also, theoretically, teaching will be transformed by relicensing teachers every five years. That's the second try since the government has already blown £2 billion ($3.2 billion) on micromanaging teachers to little effect.[36]

In total contradiction to the government's self-congratulation, an article in *The Economist* stated that:

> *Since Labour came to power in 1997 proclaiming education its priority, one grand policy after another has foundered. Schools were told to run themselves – but forbidden to do the things that matter most, such as paying good teachers more.*[37]

According to the same article, while parents were encouraged to choose schools, there have been too few attractive ones to choose from, and many pupils have been rejected by the schools their parents selected. To remedy the situation, parents were urged to lobby local government for new schools, but they were largely ignored when they did so. That says much about the *parent-promoted* schools policy.[38]

In my experience, the essential difference is not just in educational budgets, but also, and mainly, in the way money is managed to produce high-quality education. Currently, results are substandard. As the British, German and French examples demonstrate,

32 Reported in *The Economist*, 25 April 2009.

33 Department for Children, Schools and Families, *Your Child, Your Schools Our Future: Building a 21st Century Schools System*, Cm 7588. Available at: http://publications.education.gov.uk/eOrderingDownload/21st_Century_Schools.pdf.

34 That's what parents who care about their kids should be keen to find out by themselves, at home and by regularly visiting the school – not through the report cards.

35 This input comes from meetings with people knowledgeable about educational policies and their deliverables.

36 *The Economist*, 4 July 2009.

37 *The Economist*, 26 September 2009.

38 In fact, up to the end of the third quarter of 2009, which practically means over a dozen years of Labour government, only two 'parent-promoted' schools actually opened in Britain. However, since these lines were written, the new Conservative-Liberal Democrat coalition government has changed its policy on education, taking down barriers to parent-run schools.

problems with education, from teachers to students, are widespread in the EU. Where northern and southern Europe differ is in terms of the way in which teachers and students express their anger and frustration.

- In Britain and Germany they don't take to the streets in fruitless demonstrations.
- The street circus is Mediterranean countries' speciality, and it makes a bad situation even worse.

The more their learning is wanting, the more the French and Greek students run wild, with the result that they cry more and learn less. (See also the case of persistent street demonstrations against the CPE in Chapter 9.) It needs no explaining that students' number one priority should be their learning, not a perpetual carnival.

- This irrational and destructive behaviour is being promoted by different socialists, who have been proved wrong six times out of six,[39] and
- the students' demonstrations are spreading both to the earlier years of secondary education and to countries far away from the EU, like Chile.

An irony with Chile is that schoolchildren took to the streets in protest under the government of Michelle Bachelet, herself a socialist. Back in June 2006, after Bachelet took over, pupils at the country's secondary schools came out on strike marching in the streets and occupying schools for three weeks at a time. Their frustration, it was said, was shared by their parents over:

- the generally low quality of education and
- the alarming deficiencies of state schools.

Like their French and Greek peers, Chilean pupils and students have also questioned the government's insistence on tight spending. Their demand for 'better education' not only interrupted Bachelet's supposed idyll with the electorate, but also exposed apparent inconsistencies in the promises with which the socialists had wooed the country. Still:

- Chile is one of the countries which, in terms of education, is doing best in Latin America, and
- students and their parents should not be eager to destroy that record, because it is *they* who will ultimately pay the damages.

In conclusion, improvements in primary and secondary education require better curriculums, trained teachers and a change of attitude of pupils and parents (see also section 7). Governments should spread that message to families, schools and society at

39 In Greece, George Papandreou, son and grandson of prime ministers, when he was leader of the socialist opposition called on Greek students to imitate the French and take to the streets. It's like ping-pong; socialists in France likewise prod the students to imitate the Greeks. George Papandreou, incidentally, had to find a remedy to deal with the troubles he promoted while in opposition – when he became prime minister in late 2009. The wild and highly irrational demonstrations in the streets continued, and they intensified in early 2010 after the announcement of austerity measures.

large. If we are to solve the learning problem in our society we need to raise everybody's awareness about responsibilities and accountabilities. The free lunch has ended.

## 5. Illiteracy Also has a Ball in the United States

Existing evidence on the education of the young generation is just as dismal in other Western countries. In America an estimated 30 million people, nearly 10 per cent of the population, have serious literacy problems and roughly one in three pupils drop out of school in their early teens. Statistics also show that as many as 75 per cent of juvenile offenders have trouble reading.[40]

- Many American workers do not have the education and necessary skills to keep pace with technology, and
- US companies are facing rougher and tougher competition from abroad because the productivity level of the workforce is falling behind that of other countries.

While the American university system is tops, critics say that primary and secondary education are limping. One of the background reasons is that, against all logic, American children have it 'easier' than most other youngsters – and in the final analysis this is to their disadvantage.

The US features the shortest school years anywhere, a mere 180 days compared with an average of 195 for OECD countries and more than 200 for East Asian. Over 12 years of primary and secondary schooling, a 20-day deficit means American children lose out on 240 days of learning, equivalent to more than an entire school year.

The curriculum, too, leaves much to be desired. In the early 1980s Ross Perot, of EDS and GM fame, was named head of the Texas Governor's Select Committee of Public Education. Having established the system's weakness, Perot prodded the legislature to enact a 'no pass, no play' rule for high-school athletes.

- Students are in school to learn, he said, and
- football was interfering with that basic mission.

The outraged chairman of the board of education called Perot a 'dangerous man'. Others branded him 'un-American'.[41] But, as Perot saw it, schools were wasting billions in tax dollars. 'At a time when we are losing to international competition,' he said, 'why do we spend all our time worrying about how much we play?'

As if this spoilage of time by giving priority to football (Oh! pardon, I should have written *sports science*) was not enough, American children also have one of the shortest working days, with schooling adding up to 32 hours a week.[42] By contrast, the school week is 44 hours in Belgium, 53 in Denmark and 60 in Sweden.

---

40 Too often, the frustrated teenager who can't read well enough to keep up in school becomes the drop-out selling drugs.

41 Michael Meyer, *The Alexander Complex*, Times Books, New York, 1989.

42 Even better than the French workers' and employees' 35-hour week (see Chapter 9).

To his credit, Barack Obama has urged school administrators to rethink the school day, saying that 'we can no longer afford an academic calendar designed for when America was a nation of farmers who needed their children at home ploughing the land at the end of each day'.[43] But, for the time being, a critical review and revamping of the school system is on hold.

One, but only one, of the factors that works against higher educational standards is so-called *home schooling*. Its opponents argue that it is socially divisive, it is regulated lightly or not at all, and it is hard to tell whether children being taught at home are receiving adequate knowledge even by public school standards.

The pupils' parents may even have the best intentions, but most of them don't have the wide-ranging knowledge a modern society requires, let alone the teaching methodology. The bad news for American society is that home schooling is becoming a trend. Instead of sending their children to a public or private school, parents teach them at home.

- Up to the 1980s home schooling was rare and, in many states, illegal.
- Today, by contrast, there is an estimated 1.5 million to 2 million home-schooled pupils in America – a number that has doubled in a decade.[44]

The reasons vary widely, and they are largely inconsistent. The majority of home-schooling parents say that their local public schools are unsafe, drug-ridden or unwholesome in some way. Others complain of poor educational standards. Still others say that one of their children has a physical or mental problem that the local school cannot or will not accommodate. The opposite argument is also present: some parents teach at home because their children are brilliant, and public schools don't cater for their exceptional skills.

All this, of course, does not add up, and many experts think that the real reason is that parents want to instil their own religious or moral values in their children. Several parents admit that much, and peer examples see to it that their numbers have risen over the last decade. What they fail to consider, however, is that their kids are hit by a double whammy:

- a lower level of education[45] and
- absence of social interaction, which is one of the major contributions of schooling.

It is only evident that, in a way similar to that of the EU, poor educational performance is weakening America's economy. Research by McKinsey, the consulting company, discussed in one of the meetings which led to this book, shows that the lagging performance of America's schools, particularly among poor and minority children, has wreaked more devastation on the economy than the 2007–2011 deep recession.

America also faces a legacy problem which EU nations have been silly enough to emulate. The best way to describe that challenge is through the example of two school

43 Quoted in *The Economist*, 13 June 2009.

44 To roughly 3–4 per cent of the school-aged population.

45 This in no way means that public schooling is great. As a recent article had it, from 2006 to 2008 fewer than 3 per cent of pupils met Illinois's meagre standards of achievement. (*The Economist*, 3 October 2009). But missing even the little that public education offers is even worse.

districts: Jefferson County, Kentucky, and Seattle, Washington. Both of them deliberately balance each school's racial mix through firm quotas.

Parents of white children complain that, because of their skin colour, they cannot get a fair shot at admission into the public schools they want. Ironically, both those for and against firm school quotas for pupils claim to have the US Constitution's Fourteenth Amendment on their side.

- This was ratified after slavery ended, and
- it granted everyone equal protection under the law.

While deliberate discrimination is no longer an issue, demographic trends and the flight to the suburbs keep pushing in the direction of a *de facto* segregation of schools.[46] Bureaucrats who want lots of integration try to achieve it with a strong hand, which is undemocratic. They do so by insisting that 15–50 per cent of each school's students be black.

- This ends by being not equal opportunity but *inverse segregation*, and
- it is happening daily not only in education, but also in jobs – the 'best one wins' is no longer the top slogan.

With inverse segregation having a field day, sometimes judges play politics. A famous mid-2009 case was that of the Supreme Court ruling that New Haven, Connecticut, was wrong to deny promotion to white firemen because no blacks had scored high enough marks in a qualifying exam to warrant advancement.[47]

Illiteracy and inverse segregation create a *compound effect*.[48] So-called 'equal opportunity' sees to it that more than half of American industries report that they have problems with analphabetism among workers, affecting the quality of labour. The welfare rolls bulge with people who would like to work, but who cannot read or write well enough to get or keep a job.

Hailed as the great factor of civilization, personal computers and the Internet have become part of the problem. About half of all American children use PCs at home or school; and 40 per cent of American adults use computers at work. Is this 'good' or 'bad'? In November 2007 the US National Endowment for the Arts released a devastating report on reading trends in America – comparing the current quantity and quality of reading by different age groups, and these with results from earlier decades.

- The most dramatic declines have been among teenagers, but all age groups have shown declines.

46 'Discrimination' might have been a better term, but 'segregation' and 'inverse segregation' are those typically used by the press and politicians in the US.

47 This case attracted a lot of interest because one of the judges on the Federal Appeals Court panel that saw its previous decision in the lawsuit overturned was Sonia Sotomayor. She was Barack Obama's nominee to the US Supreme Court.

48 Compounding describes a situation in which the overall risk is greater than the sum of individual risks, measured separately.

- The reasons include not just school quality, but also time spent on playing video games, instant messaging, social networking chatrooms, and other endlessly time-consuming distractions (television included).[49]

The bad news does not end there. As the study by the National Endowment for the Arts points out, there is a general decline in reading among teenage and adult Americans, with both reading ability and the habit of regular reading sliding among college graduates. This has social, civic, economic and cultural implications.

- Because they read less well, they have lower levels of educational achievement,[50] and,
- with lower levels of reading and writing ability, people fare badly in the job market, earn lower wages, and have fewer opportunities for advancement.

That's real life, no matter what the 'affirmative action' theorists and proponents say.[51] Neither is this twenty-first-century news. Back in 1990 *Business Week* published an article which included, among other references, an interview with a 29-year-old high-school drop-out who could not read. He spoke of the frustrations of illiteracy and said that he could not:

- decipher some road signs,
- make out directions on shipping manifests, or
- read children's books to his four-year-old daughter.

*Illiteracy* is an enormous problem in the US, the *Business Week* article stated. Of the 1 million or so people living in Detroit proper, 200,000 told census-takers in 1980 that they couldn't read. In 1982 researchers testing for the US Education Department estimated that 11 per cent of Michigan's 6.6 million adults, aged 20 and over, were illiterate in English.[52]

The situation is by no means better in Britain. In January 2008 the Labour government commissioned Jim Rose, a former chief inspector of primary schools, to trim ten existing 'required subjects'. The aim was to give 'extra space' to computing skills and accommodate a foreign language, as well as integrate into the curriculum the then optional 'personal, social, health and economic education'.

That curious Russian salad of 'optional issues' included eating fruit and vegetables, refraining from hitting one's classmates and much more – the sort of stuff parents should have taught their kids while they were growing up. In December 2008 the Rose interim report proposed merging the then compulsory subjects with history and geography to become 'human, social and environmental understanding' – a new Russian salad. The Rose recipe was:

- merging reading, writing and foreign languages into 'understanding English, communication and languages', and

---

49 National Endowment for the Arts Office of Research and Analysis, *To Read or Not To Read: A Question of National Consequence*, Washington, DC: NEA, 2007.

50 65 percent of college freshmen read for pleasure for less than an hour per week or not at all. By contrast, 15–24-year-olds spend 2 to 2½ hours per day watching TV – as this same study points out.

51 See also in Chapter 10 the discussion of the destructive power of 'affirmative action' at the social level.

52 *Business Week*, 16 July 1990.

- integrating physical education with a little bit of science and various odds and ends into 'understanding physical health and well-being'.[53]

Does this sound ridiculous? It is. The Labour government's high priests were honouring the state supermarket by destroying the middle class. They were trying to achieve that goal by doing away with learning and knowledge altogether. Since the education programme is going to lose rigour, there is no longer a reason for teaching basics. According to the reorganizers, to please those who don't want to learn, and not to hurt their feelings, everybody should become a drop-out.

## 6. Education is the Middle Class's Castle

According to Socrates, tragedy and comedy are essentially the same thing and should be written by the same authors. Today the tragedy in Western countries is growing illiteracy. The gears of culture have been put in reverse by second-raters who thought that the best way to roll in the mass society was to reduce everyone's literacy quotient.

The statistics we saw in section 5 about America and Britain are in line with prevailing trends worldwide, because illiteracy, too, has been globalized:[54] 25 per cent of people in this world are fully analphabetic and an estimated 60 per cent of these analphabets live in Africa. In fact,

- *Functional analphabetism*[55] has become global licence, and
- it is currently standing at about 50 per cent worldwide.

It is as if governments and the media put up a goal of destroying the middle class through lowering the standards of education which is the gate to the middle class's castle (see also Chapter 8). As results of the American tests, referred to earlier, have shown:

- the majority of illiterate people live around cities, and
- an alarming number are under 40, despite the fact that younger generations generally have more schooling than their elders.

True enough, statistics from the American tests date back to 1990, but 20 years down the line these numbers have also become a European nightmare. Dismal news is coming from the *banlieux* of Paris and those of other major cities in the EU. Governments are at a loss, even in deciding what the school system should teach.

Lost in the socialist mania of the middle class's destruction in Western countries is the role of human capital as basic indicator of economic strength. In mid-2009, for example, economists predicted that Spain would be one of the last Western countries to emerge from the deep recession that began in 2007 because: some 30 per cent of children leave

53 *The Economist*, 13 December 2008.

54 Though there are some exceptions. See D.N. Chorafas, *Globalization's Limits: Conflicting National Interests in Trade and Finance*, Gower, Aldershot, 2009.

55 This means that the individual does not have the appropriate linguistic qualifications for the job he or she is doing.

school without qualifications; only 5 per cent of exports are high-tech; research spending is feeble; and a large part of the workforce is protected by armour-clad contracts, which adds to the woes of lack of qualifications.

Europe's current educational comedy and tragedy is that, after a 30-year civil war (1914–1945), its society finds it difficult, if not outright impossible, to decide which should be the new generation's future. This involves not only the quality and content of schooling, but also many other issues whose weight counts a great deal in defining 'tomorrow', These range:

- from employment (Part Two),
- to social values (including discipline) and standard of living,
- to retirement and state-supported healthcare (Part Three).

The authors of this comedy and tragedy are the second-raters the West has as politicians. Whoever thought that the new generation would breed some leaders worthy of talking about with some measure of respect has been deceived. When the World War II generation passed away, political leadership took a long-lasting leave, and it has not yet come back from retirement.

The losers have evidently been society's values – human, political, economic and cultural – in short, the pillars on which civilization rests. Culture does not have to be uniform, nor should it be so. Quite to the contrary, cultural development requires the *biological richness* that resides in a population's genetic heritage, but

- biological richness and *cultural richness* are twins, and
- cultural richness has to be planned in the right way.

'If you plan for a year, plant rice. If you plan for ten years, plant trees. If you plan for a hundred years, educate people,' says an old Chinese proverb – and proverbs are long experience expressed in a short sentence. 'Our future is already written on our wall, but who takes any notice of it?' asked the American evangelist Jim Feathers.

Some countries do take notice by learning from other countries' mistakes. India, for example, has correctly placed education high on its list of middle-class values. Parents save to send their kids to school. As in America of the good old days.

- the middle class invests more in the next generation than do either the poor or the rich, and
- middle-class parents are also more likely to let their children stay on at school as teenagers, especially if they live in cities.

By contrast, Western countries seem to have abandoned this educational wisdom, as society's tolerance for school drop-outs (and for their guilty parents) indicates. The tragedy written on the wall says that western Europe and America, focused on ephemeral well-being, are both unwilling and unable to take their future into their own hands.

There is also folklore. Signitia Fordham, an anthropologist, conducted a study at a high school in a low-income neighbourhood of the District of Columbia that is 99 per cent black. The study concluded that many black students limit their academic success so that their peers will not think they are 'acting white'.[56]

A similar case exists with the children of legal and illegal immigrants in the EU – and more generally with kids who are afraid of being called 'brainiac', Washington's street term for academic achievers. Hence, they voluntarily choose to remain illiterate and therefore unemployable.

Natural selection based on educational achievements is no racism, but this does not mean that racism does not exist. Racial tensions in society have, among other roots, historical reasons. 'Outsiders' – for instance, Koreans in Japan and Turks in Germany – were brought in as labourers. This stage-hand status

- qualified them as second-class citizens, and
- the stigma remains, because few among the stage-hands put in the effort to come up from under.

This is a mistake with grave consequences, which truly industrious people avoid. In Malaysia, the British owners of tin mines, rubber and tea plantations imported Chinese and Indian workers. Expatriate Chinese, however, excelled in commerce, and Indians gravitated towards education and the professions.

In many places in Asia, when the Dutch and the British left, the original population suddenly (and resentfully) found itself working for the former immigrants and their children. *Education made the difference.*

Indeed, many of the Chinese have been in Indonesia and in Malaysia for four or five generations. The same is true of Indians. Chinese and Indians are the pillars of Malaysian economy even if ethnic Malays comprise 95 per cent of the population and have the political power that goes with those kinds of numbers. Interestingly enough, one use the ethnic Malays make of their political power is to pressure the ethnic Chinese to take Malayan Islamic names or to convert outright to Islam – which is *religious racism* of the worst kind.

- Combined with religion and politics, racism can be explosive.
- We saw it in the 1930s in Nazi Germany. It may happen again inside different country borders, and all over the world.

The Taliban provide an example. In mid-May 2009 they attacked a girls' school not far from Kabul, in Afghanistan, with explosives and chemicals. Interviewed by the media, a captured Taliban said that 'it is written in the Koran women should not be educated'. That's a false statement. It is not the religious scripts which led the Taliban's hand, but the political interest of those who want to keep people illiterate, because then they can use them as slaves and cannon fodder.

## 7. The Need to Change Mental Models

When it comes to a policy of reversing the current decadence in learning and knowledge, the need to change mental models starts in the family, not at school. That's where the

56 From a meeting attended by the author.

frontline of a reversal of the disastrous current trends lies. Unfortunately, the second-raters at the vertex of the EU bureaucracy in Brussels are bent on continuing along the wrong path.

In mid-2008 a new EU directive forbade parents to slap their children, even for disciplinary reasons. Market research carried out by the EU executive (as if it had nothing better to do) found that 87 per cent of the parents interviewed had slapped their children's backsides, and the Brussels bureaucrats don't permit this. According to them, slapping has the very negative effects of:

- blocking the children's learning capability, and
- creating psychological damage and other horrible but unnamed effects.

Hence, the new EU slogan and *diktat*: 'No slapping.' In my opinion, psychological damage is not going to be found in the children but among the bureaucrats who do anything silly to justify their salaries[57] and try to micromanage the way parents bring up their children without assuming any responsibility for the results. This is another 'museum piece' (see Chapter 2, section 7) among the so many irrelevant and counterproductive EU policies and directives.

School learning, too, has had its share of negative bureaucratic interference. For three decades, from 1957 to the late 1980s, there existed, for all practical purposes, an artificial division of teaching duties in the EU, with *training* being distinct from *education*. As a term,

- training was used in its most limited form, implying basic preparation for a job, and
- education was given a broader non-vocational connotation.

This fuzzy distinction has to do not only with the bureaucratic mind, but also with the national cultures of EU member states and their aversion to delegating broader integrative approaches to the EU Executive in regard to educational initiatives. A better solution was developed by the 1992 Maastricht conference and subsequent meetings of EU heads of state: to make the EU citizen more aware of the role of education *and* training in their professional life.

But, even after 1992, Community funds allocated to education and training have been small, and sponsored projects like Comet, Erasmus and Lingua did not distinguish themselves in terms of excellence. The latter two were superseded by another, Socrates, and supplemented by yet another, Leonardo (for R&D projects sponsored by the EU see Chapter 6). Basically, these EU educational programmes concerned themselves with:

- cooperation between universities and private enterprises,
- student exchanges between universities in the EU, and
- improving students' language skills by contributing to member-state budgets assigned to that purpose.

The Socrates project focused on initiatives connected to higher education, but no outstanding results have been obtained. Critics say the reason is that most emphasis was placed on *mainstreaming*, a term used in connection to a policy of 'equal opportunity' in

57 In this case, overimplementing the UN Human Universal Declaration of Human Rights.

the employment of graduates, rather than to raising the standards characterizing higher education in the EU. That's the classical case of:

- the average being taken as preferable to the best and
- quantity becoming a goal which overwhelms quality.

The EU countries of Eastern Europe provide an example of the first bullet. In Poland, Romania, Bulgaria and the Baltic states, state-financed higher education has been remarkably resistant to reform. Universities are run as 'fiefs' where innovations such as teaching by outside practitioners are strongly resisted. In addition, the higher demand for graduates tends to result in:

- corruption in entrance requirements and
- a drop in standards, rather than better teaching.

This does not mean that matters are so much better in western Europe. The idea of getting pupils and students excited about the process behind problem-solving instead of rushing into an answer is typically unheard of. Studying is usually fragmented, and those who are supposed to be learning are frantically trying to memorize things, with no attention paid to understanding the context.

Good teachers, of course, try to make traditional learning interactive. But good teachers are rare, particularly those who know how to:

- develop the students' critical thinking skills,
- guide the students on applying them to different situations,
- help students develop supporting evidence, and
- test the reasons for a conclusion they are reaching.

Failures in education planning and career development are inexcusable because people able to see further out into the future have warned the different EU prime ministers and heads of state about the demands of the knowledge society. In a 1943 speech at Harvard University, Winston Churchill observed that 'the empires of the future will be empires of the mind'. Nearly seven decades, or three generations, later we see that Churchill was right:

- The greatest asset of an individual and of our society is the asset of talent, and
- the balance of brains has become as important as what used to be called the 'balance of power'.

The demand for brains and talent continues to increase at a time when, ironically, the average quality of human capital has fallen. In 2006 the Washington-based Corporate Executive Board (CEB), a business research and executive education entity, conducted research among an international pool of senior human resources managers; 75 percent of them said that 'attracting and retaining talent' was their number one priority. This survey of some 4,000 hiring managers concluded that:

- the average quality of candidates had declined by 10 per cent since 2004, and

- the average time to fill a vacancy had increased from 37 days to 51 days, because of the difficulty in finding qualified candidates.[58]

In a globalized economy, to be ahead and stay ahead, people, companies and countries need an increasingly business partner-centric methodology for managing their future. These business partners, evidently, are employers, employees and customers. Responding successfully to this need requires *changing mental models* as part of a strategy of business transformation through a social culture which:

- welcomes competition and
- views it as prerequisite to further development.

The planning, execution and delivery of educational and R&D output is an integral part of changing mental models. In 2005 Booz Allen Hamilton (BAH), the consultancy, made a comprehensive study assessing the influence of R&D on corporate performance. BAH concluded that there is little relationship between R&D spending and the primary measures of economic or corporate success. What matters most is not how much money is spent on R&D, but *how* it is spent.[59]

A different study carried out in 2006 by the European Central Bank (ECB) came to the conclusion that an indicator of technological advances is provided by *R&D intensity*. This is calculated as spending on R&D expressed as a percentage of value added in the manufacturing sector of the economy. R&D intensity is at:

- 5.8 per cent in the EU and
- 8.5 per cent in the United States.[60]

R&D is propelled by educational achievements; but its goal must also be to launch new products, processes and services as quickly as possible, ahead of competition. Therefore, merely paying lip-service to research is not enough. The most important criterion is the deliverables – the design-based visible and tangible results of R&D investments, and their effect on the global market (more on this in Chapter 5).

58 'A Survey of Talent: The Battle for Brainpower', *The Economist*, 5 October 2006.

59 'Does R&D Spending Deliver Results?', *Business Week*, 11 October 2005.

60 European Central Bank, *Monthly Bulletin*, July 2006.

# CHAPTER 2 Back to Basics: What it Means to Educate People

## 1. Emphasizing the Role of the Individual

When King Ferdinand of Spain visited the conservative University of Cervera, the rector proudly reassured the monarch with the words: 'Far be from us, Sire, the dangerous novelty of thinking.' Yet thinking is what distinguishes people from other animals, and thinking is also what education is all about.

In his visit to ancient Egypt, Solon (c.630–c.560BC), the law-maker of ancient Athens, was received by an old priest to whom he spoke with pride about his country of origin. The host interrupted him: 'Greeks are like kids; there are no old people in Greece.'

'What do you mean?' asked Solon.

'You are young in spirit,' responded the Egyptian priest, 'because you have no really old traditions, no concepts withered by the sun.'

The old Egyptian priest was right. Time had sharpened the spirit of that country's philosophers and sages. If we take Pericles' time (the high-water mark of ancient Athens) as a reference, there is as much chronological distance between that period and ours as there is between Pericles' time and ancient Egypt's Pharaoh Djoser with his pyramid of Saqqara. When Herodotus visited the Nile Valley some 450 years BC, the Pyramid of Cheops (Khufu) (2589–2566BC) was already more than 21 centuries old.

All this is highly relevant because, as Homer's *Iliad* has shown, history is vital ingredient in cultural development. But, at the same time, a community cannot survive on history alone and on what it remembers. It will persist and prosper because of what it affirms and believes, as well as on how it educates its new generations:

- in thinking and
- in delivering results.

The key to both thinking and delivering results is education emphasizing the role of the individual in society, which in turn requires an inner force characterizing the individual's behaviour. Some societies approach this issue in a way that is peculiarly logical; others direct their attention to a person's soul.

That's not necessarily a religious rite. Musashi was a well-known Japanese samurai whose techniques are inner-directed, speaking to the soul of an individual. Study, meditation, and mental preparation constitute the Musashi approach to life (as well as the Buddhist principle of cultured individuals).

'My way of strategy is the sure method to win when fighting for your life, one man against 5 or 10,' says *A Book of Five Rings*.[1] In this, Musashi talks of a *culture*, not just of individual behaviour. To a large extent this approach reflects the fundamental notions underpinning professional life in the early part of the twenty-first century – provided the illiteracy hurdles discussed in Chapter 1 are overcome.

These illiteracy hurdles, most unfortunately, are present and real all the way to higher education. University heads increasingly complain about students being totally unprepared for their studies. At the other end of the line, employers are unhappy about the lack of well-trained and skilled manpower. As we have seen in Chapter 1,

- in many Western countries proficiency in academic literacy is wanting, and
- matters become much worse in respect of quantitative literacy because school graduates are lacking the fundamentals of mathematics.

Although the above two bullet points describe accurately enough the situation in Western countries, both academic and quantitative literacy are at even worse status in developing countries – and the population explosion is one of the key reasons, if not by far the most important. The school intake is simply too big, the goals ill-defined, the teachers poorly trained, and the educational system itself too poor to provide the needed *cultural dimension*. In turn, this absence leaves no hope for coming up from under.

Many philosophers and plenty of educators have underlined the existence of a cultural dimension in any meaningful effort towards self-reliance. The late Peter Drucker once said that the company of the twenty-first century would be rich in professionals and thin in managers. In a way, it will resemble an orchestra with 300 professionals and one conductor.

- An orchestra does not have sub-conductors, in the way industrial and financial organizations are built today.
- But it has a first violin, a top professional who distinguishes himself by being a *virtuoso*.

Contrary to what the rector of University of Cervera said to the visiting King Ferdinand, the secret of being a virtuoso is thinking, and that's where university teaching should excel. To gain insight we must challenge the 'obvious'. Nothing should escape scrutiny or questioning. Neither should people be afraid of self-criticism and soul-searching:

- What are the broader implications of a decision or claim I make?
- Which is its upside? Its downside? Its more distant consequences?
- How could the same evidence on which I am basing my decision or claim be interpreted differently?

Quite often, these critical queries remain unanswered – or are not even asked because thinking fails. Most people are not being taught *how to think*, yet, without thinking, the only profession in which they might succeed is in becoming bureaucrats (see Chapter 8), pushing paper and blocking the advancement of others.

1 Myamoto Musashi, *A Book of Five Rings*, The Overlook Press, Woodstock, NY, 1974.

Thinking is the fundamental ingredient of what we call 'brains' (the high professionals, Drucker's virtuosi). Thinking promotes skills and feeds know-how. The requirement to hire the best brains exists all over government and industry (see section 5), but the more sophisticated the task, the higher the know-how sought by employers. 'The ability to recruit senior guys is one of the things you expect senior people to be able to do,' said Michael C. Ruettgers, executive chairman of data storage EMC Corporation.[2] The challenge is:

- to find the best skills available,
- to steadily grow these skills, and
- to use them in an effective way throughout people's careers.

Plenty of post-mortems and walkthroughs have documented that the size of contribution made by human resources can only be judged through deliverables – and these are not always forthcoming. In his book *Legacy of Ashes*, Tim Weiner points out that the CIA failed to warn the White House of the first Soviet atom bomb (1949), the Chinese invasion of South Korea (1950), anti-Soviet risings in East Germany (1953) and Hungary (1956), the dispatch of Soviet missiles to Cuba (1962), the Arab–Israeli war of 1967 and Saddam Hussein's invasion of Kuwait in 1990. Not a good record.

While its primary function of intelligence gathering went unattended, according to Weiner, the CIA had plenty of extra-curricula activities. In Japan, France and Italy it sought to protect democracy by buying elections. It sponsored coups in Guatemala, Iran, Syria and Iraq, where a Ba'ath Party leader boasted in 1963, 'We came to power on an American train.'

Dwight Eisenhower called what the CIA had brought to the office of the president 'a legacy of ashes', and Richard Nixon derided the agency's analysts as clowns reading newspapers.[3] This is not the sort of skill an organization needs. May be the CIA did not take care to hire the best. A 2001 study at MIT came to the conclusion that, in terms of deliverables, the difference between hiring the best and getting an average person can be a factor of 50 to 1. The best person will:

- have a broadly-based background,
- be flexible and adjustable,
- be innovative and imaginative,
- challenge what he sees and hears,
- have a deep sense of planning and control (see section 2).

Companies must be very careful to hire 'the best' not only because in the short term the results will be so much better, but also because in the longer term the new hires will probably reach the top of the organization. The quality of senior management plays a vital role in terms of an entity's survival. In the late 1960s Standard Chartered and the Hong Kong & Shanghai Banking Corporation (HSBC) had roughly similar

- geographical reaches,

2 *Business Week*, 11 March 2002.

3 Tim Weiner, *Legacy of Ashes: The History of CIA*, Doubleday, New York, 2007.

- balance sheets,
- market capitalizations,
- profit figures, and
- staff numbers.

Why is it, then, that Standard Chartered has so dismally underperformed its rival emerging-markets bank ever since? The answer can be found in HSBC's culture, strategy, professional skill and management quality. Their compound effect was business plans which have been effectively executed, as well as management controls exercised at the right time and in the right place.

## 2. Learning How to Manage Time and How to Plan

The aim of this section, and more generally of this chapter, is not one of presenting the specifics of a given discipline in higher education, but of highlighting important issues valid for all disciplines. Leadership is evidently one of the most important general issues, but so much is written on leadership that I have deliberately chosen to leave it out of this text. Instead, emphasis is being placed on planning and the management of time.

- Planning and time management are two of leadership's basic ingredients,
- yet very little attention is paid to them in current university curricula.

*If* an institute of higher education aims to build human resources for any profession other than the bureaucracy, *then* among its foremost preoccupations should be to teach how to manage time. The paradox of time is that nobody seems to have enough of it, yet everyone has all the time that is available.

- All of us have 24 hours a day, seven days a week.
- *Time management*, however, is a question not of how many hours we have, but of how well we use them.

Time is a unique resource. It cannot be accumulated like wealth, yet without it we can accomplish none of our tasks. Shakespeare said there are three things that don't return in life: An opportunity that has been lost, a word that has been spoken and time that has passed by.

We are forced to spend time, whether we choose it or not, though few people know how to spend it in an able manner. Of all our resources it appears to be the least understood and most mismanaged, despite the aphorism 'Time is money'. Time is money because:

- it is a strategic factor in enterprise, and
- it is nearly impossible to recapture the time lost through indecision or waste.

If the steam engine was the prime mover of the industrial age, the measurement of time (invented in the first millennium in Byzantine monasteries) is central to the post-industrial society. Although, for everybody, each hour has 60 minutes of 60 seconds, mental productivity is measured by the way we use time.

The secret of mental productivity is that time moves at faster rate for those who are better organized, concentrate in their thinking and work faster. This concept is known as *intrinsic time*. Time moves faster in New York's financial market because American traders don't interrupt their trading for lunch; the traders take sandwiches and they eat them at their desks while working. Time moves more slowly in Tokyo because the Japanese traders go to a sushi bar and wait to be served.

Because time moves faster for those who work more steadily, people with higher intellectual productivity accomplish more in the same amount of clock time than people who work at a so-called normal pace or slower. This is one of the challenges associated with time. The other, even more important, challenge has been highlighted by Siegmund G. Warburg, the banker, who used two Greek words to distinguish between:

- *chronos*,[4] the longer time perspective and planning horizon, and
- *kairos*, the short timespan which is dominated by the clock.[5]

*Chronos* can also be seen as the *arrow of time*. As far as daily work is concerned, *kairos* seems (but only seems) to hold the upper ground over *chronos*. Events ripple forward, but the size of the ripple diminishes until, so to speak, it vanishes. Eventually, *chronos* wins, which is another way of saying that the longer term is a pattern of the shorter terms.

- The present often influences the longer term and it may lead to change of plans because of events which are overwhelming.
- But, in terms of overall progress or regression, what counts is *chronos* rather than the ripples of *kairos*.

This talks volumes about the impact of *planning*. 'The plan is nothing; planning is everything,' Dwight D. Eisenhower once said. Effective plans require perspective and the ability to tear them to pieces in order to ascertain how well they can withstand stress. Big plans are not small plans thrown together. As Harry Truman stated, 'You can always amend a big plan, you can never expand a little one.'

Plans must be challenged, and those which don't pass stress-testing should be sent back to the drawing board. The people responsible for them should be asked to come up with new proposals or be replaced. Students must learn that human resources that do not perform and deliver should be weeded out of the organization – a basic principle in staffing. Along this frame of reference, in 2002 IBM instituted a personnel strategy which rests on a rigorous grading system:

- Employees rated '1' are those who obtained results beyond their set goals. Typically, they are few in number.
- Those getting a grade of '2' attained the objectives set for them, but had no exceptional performance.
- Employees rated '3' only met some of their goals. They are required to improve their know-how and performance through formal training.

---

4 Named after the god of gods who ate his children. Metaphorically speaking, according to some historians, in ancient Greek thinking *Cronos*, the father of Zeus, was indeed *Chronos*.

5 Cited in Jacques Attali, *Sigmund Warburg: Un homme d'influence*, Fayard, Paris, 1985.

People rejected by the grading system get a '4'. They have not met the company's standards, their deliverables are below average, their ability to develop their skills is questionable, and therefore they are the first to be let go. This gives an opportunity to renew the human capital without increasing the head-count, and without loss of time.

Few people and companies appreciate that the able management of human resources is one of the best examples that can be found on how pragmatic management's plans must be.

A realistic approach to resource planning has two prerequisites:

- learning how to plan and how to control the plans being made,
- paying attention to the practical essentials, rather than filling one's mind with theories disconnected from real business.

In his excellent book, *Adventures of a Bystander*, Peter Drucker mentions a story about Henry Bernheim, the man who started from nothing and, at end of the nineteenth century, built one of the most important merchandizing chains in the United States. Bernheim had sent his son to the then brand-new Harvard Business School to learn the secrets of management.

'But father,' said the son when he returned from higher education, 'You don't even know how much profit you are making.'

'Come along my boy,' answered Henry, and he took his son on an inspection tour, from the flagship department store's top floor to a sub-sub-basement, which was cut out of bedrock. There, at the rock's edge, lay a bolt of cloth.

Contrary to what business schools teach, there were no statistics around, no balance sheets and no income statements. Just the bolt of cloth.

'Take away all the rest,' said the father, 'It's the profit. This is what I started with.'[6]

Henry Bernheim had a strategic objective, a plan to see through, and the will to get results. Hence, his was a success story.

The message these references convey are that prudent planners look far ahead and they bet on *chronos*, not on *kairos*. They do not limit themselves to the near future. Moreover, they ask themselves probing questions about products, processes, business realities, market reactions and their own (as well as their company's) ability to face future competition:

- Which will be *our* strategic products in ten years, 15 years hence?
- Are we capitalizing on our strengths in developing them? If not, what do we need to do?
- Are we swamping our weaknesses and rebuilding our human resources?
- Can the products we have in the pipeline respond to coming market requirements?
- Where should our further-out innovation drive be directed? Our new effort in research?

A precondition to responding to the queries is close coordination between planning, engineering, production and marketing, because the products we develop must have market punch. There should be handholding between product planning and marketing

6 Peter Drucker, *Adventures of a Bystander*, Heinemann, London, 1978.

from the level of market research to that of product development, product pricing and product launch. There is synergy between design and sales. All this rests on the ingenuity of the leader and his immediate assistants – on tacit knowledge (Chapter 1).

In conclusion, there are no 'Ten Commandments' in time management and in planning. Tacit knowledge can be transmitted in a university setting by professors with deep experience and with the sense of the salt of the earth. In the early 1950s at UCLA I was lucky to learn under people who were not only highly knowledgeable, but also knew how to transfer knowledge and how to motivate. Admittedly, not all faculties have these qualities.

## 3. The Building of Trustworthy People

A primary responsibility of the university system, on a par with improving the students' knowledge base, is to build up their character and their trustworthiness. We don't blindly admire progress for the sake of progress or growth for the sake of growth. But we should admire a professional person's, and anybody else's, honesty and character.

Siegmund Warburg gave a good example of how trustworthy people are brought up, taking as reference his mother's family. When his mother was young her father had advised her: 'My child, if you need to choose between two courses, ask yourself first of all which is the most difficult – because that's the one which will prove to be the better one of the two.'[7]

Obstacles and adversity, but also the will to overcome them, build up people like they build up nations. The fast-moving Asian countries, collectively known as Asian Tigers, show few doubts about the roots of their success: it was sheer necessity and adversity. This has been the position taken by K.T. Li, the veteran cabinet minister who was a scientist in Cambridge before he helped to organize Taiwan's economic planning. 'Our adversity,' he said, 'can build a nation.' They had, he explained, to choose the right policy at the right time, moving from agriculture to industry, to electronics and high technology.

The Asian Tigers appreciated in time that in the post-World War II world, with Pax Americana, economic interdependence would grow – and economic performance rather than military power would increasingly be the index of national power, with trade wars replacing wars with weapons systems. Having done so, they used the intelligence of their people to position themselves against the future.

In general, people are either very much demanding of themselves or satisfied with themselves. The first are those who, like the citizens of the Asian Tigers, contribute to progress. Those who face great challenges are the real winners in life. 'Most of the triumphs of people faced with adverse conditions are won by the person's character rather than his intelligence,' Warburg advised his customers, associates and assistants, adding that: 'High-quality people find it easier to pardon others than to pardon themselves.'

Universities would be well advised to put these 12 words in golden letters at the entrance of their main buildings. Equally vital is Warburg's warning that: 'The worst that can happen to any organization is auto-satisfaction, because it leads to negligence and to lack of interest in what one does.' (The reference to IBM's rating, in section 2, should be seen in this perspective.)

---

7 Jacques Attali, *Un Homme d'Influence: Sigmund Warburg*, Fayard, Paris, 1985.

J.P. Morgan, another person who left a great name in financial history, used very similar words to describe trustworthiness and character when he said in his 1912 deposition to the House Banking and Currency Committee that *the basis of credit is character* (a principle that has been unfortunately forgotten by bankers, politicians and nearly everyone else).

'Is it not commercial credit based primarily upon money or property?' Samuel Untermyer asked.[8]

'No sir. The first thing is character,' Morgan replied, 'Because a man I do not trust could not get money from me on all the bonds of Christendom.'

Morgan was renowned for his ability to know each major client personally, thus judging character and performance. This can be done only with great difficulty, if at all, in the globalized financial marketplace, which is another reason why university education should have a top responsibility in building up students' characters. (As the sub-prime crisis demonstrated, the relegation of creditworthiness to rating agencies has yielded dismal results.)

That sort of teaching is not happening today. Instead, from primary to university education, many curricula concentrate on trivia and on psychological issues. Elias Canetti, who received the 1981 Nobel Prize in Literature sharply criticized Sigmund Freud for focusing on emotional disorders of the individual. Canetti thought that the central psychological problem of the twentieth century:

- was not the individual,
- but *society*, and most particularly the mass movement.

Mass movements, Canetti predicted, would dominate the twentieth century, and this would lead to lots of trouble.[9] Indeed, this is precisely what happened, spilling over into the twenty-first century. José Ortega y Gasset, a Spanish social philosopher and writer, came to the same conclusion, as revealed by his monumental work, *The Revolt of the Masses*.[10]

Contrary to what Morgan and Warburg have advised, but as Canetti and Ortega have predicted, trustworthiness has taken a vacation and ethics went along too, with neither of them hinting if and when they might return.

White-collar crime has graduated from being the province of petty thieves and has reached the level of professionals, on a massive scale. Backdated share options, unjustified king-size bonuses and Ponzi schemes provide three out of many examples. Corporate America has never seen anything quite like the carnage caused by these scandals. Bernard Madoff is just one example. On 8 October 2010 it was stated on Bloomberg News that the FDIC may seek $1 billion from more than 50 bank executives suspected of wrongdoing.

When a market-wide options scam first hit the public eye, in mid-2006, over 100 companies were known to be under investigation for backdating options in order to value them at low points in their share prices; and several hundred more have come since then

8 During the 1912 investigation on the Money Trust, by the US House Banking and Currency Committee, whose special legal counsel was Untermyer.

9 Elias Canetti, *Crowds and Power*, Continuum, New York, 1960.

10 José Ortega y Gasset, *The Revolt of the Masses*, W.W. Norton, New York, 1932.

under suspicion.[11] The backdating scandal was triggered by several academic papers that identified suspiciously favourable patterns in the timing of option grants.

Yet, there existed laws and rules forbidding that practice. For instance, the Securities and Exchange Commission's (SEC) rule 10b5-1 is designed to assure that company executives do not take advantage of insider information to generate suspiciously high returns. Those who engaged in such unethical practices and rip-offs of their shareholders

- shamelessly answered that backdating itself is not illegal,
- but this weak argument forgets that a lack of accurate disclosure may well be fraud.

All this has been particularly prevalent among high-tech companies, employing plenty of graduates, though all organizations are open to that kind of abuse. Universities have failed to teach that scientists can at no time abstract themselves from concerns about honesty and trustworthiness. Nor about truth when dealing with the public. Honesty is a fundamental responsibility for the scientific community.

It is time to return to the basics, and to the Morgan and Warburg behavioural model. In a book they published in 1990, James Patterson and Peter Kim offer plenty of evidence that people today are materialistic and shallow. A quarter of those surveyed said they would abandon their families for $10 million, and 23 per cent responded they would become a prostitute for a week for the same sum. In follow-up interviews, that price falls, until it drops below $2 million.[12]

In other interviews conducted by Patterson and Kim, workers admitted they spend more than seven hours of the working week goofing off – malingering, drinking, using drugs, or calling in sick when they are not. This happens even though most believe that America's economic power matters more than military might. In addition:

- only one-tenth of the respondents were satisfied with their jobs, and
- half of them believed that one gets ahead by playing office politics and cheating, not by hard work.

A couple of problems underlie the reference made in the above two bullets. One is that creativity is not really taught in schools; another is that students choose trivial subjects and the easiest possible way to learning, with the result that they then have to do odd jobs to make a living. Furthermore, neither their families nor the school system teach them about ethics and trustworthiness. Hence, they play politics in order to survive.

## 4. Imagination Must Be the Keyword for Higher Education

The themes of the previous two sections have been planning and time management, and trustworthiness and the ambiguities surrounding its underlying concept respectively. Two other fundamental subjects that higher education institutes should teach in all their faculties and departments is:

---

11 *The Economist*, 21 October 2006.

12 James Patterson and Peter Kim, *The Day America Told the Truth*, Prentice Hall, New York; 1990; and *Business Week*, 3 June 1991.

- how the students can cultivate their imagination, and
- how they can rid themselves of prejudices in their profession and in their daily life.

Against this advice works the fact that our social and political goals are ill-defined; the views we take of many issues are too narrow-sighted; religion teaches us to believe but not to search and discover; our priorities are not properly sorted out; self-conflicting aims abound; and, more or less generally conformism not imagination is the game. In short, students are not taught how to use their intelligence.

George Bernard Shaw maintained that people thought that he was intelligent because he used his brains twice a week. Few people are using their brains for thinking, and even less for penetrating into a subject to discover and innovate. To make matters worse, pride associated with the work one is doing is a rare bird indeed because, whether in the family or in school, having pride in one's work is not being taught.

When, in the battle of Blenheim, Marshal Tallard, the commander of the French army, was taken prisoner by the Duke of Marlborough, the former said to the latter: 'Vous venez, Milord, de battre les meilleurs troupes de l'Europe.' 'Exceptez toujours celles qui les ont battues,' replied Marlborough.[13] That's pride.

Few professional people today feel pride for the work they are doing, and this works at the expense of both initiative and experience. Not only is professional pride not taught in schools and universities, but the policy followed by governments (particularly in the EU) is to buy out one new generation after another through subsidies instead of job opportunities, in a senseless effort to avoid social troubles without having to create jobs.

This is, of course, totally nonsense. Rather than buying out the new generation with unemployment subsidies, a sound policy would be to open the gates to individual initiative and lower the barriers to the entry of new enterprise (see also Part Two). In one shot, this will:

- provide a taste of freedom and adventure to build up careers, and
- will do away with a rebellion against the dull, monotonous, conventional life usually looked upon as the result of forced retirement at age 25[14] through government subsidies.

Imagination, discovery, and creation are what make life worth living. Instead, many university students are conditioned to look at a job with the government as their ideal after graduation. In one of the numerous demonstrations by university students in the streets of Paris, a journalist asked a sample of students what they were looking to obtain after graduation. Three out of four answered 'a government job'.[15]

Invariably known as 'Chinese mandarins,' 'Byzantine logothetes' or simply bureaucrats, these are the people Lawrence Sperry, the young and resourceful inventor, deeply hated. For him, the term Byzantine logothete[16] reflected his own impatience with

13 'My lord, you have beaten the best soldiers of Europe,' to which Marlborough answered, 'The best, except for those who have beaten them.'

14 That's the age in France when young unemployed start getting government subsidies.

15 As reported on French TV.

16 A Greek word which stands for 'one who fixes the word (logos) or the rules' – a fine definition for do-nothing bureaucrats.

bureaucratic bumbling. (There are 37,000 Byzantine logothetes in the EU's headquarters in Brussels, and 15,000 lobbyists, often ex-logothetes.)

Lawrence Sperry's formative years, in 1898 when he was six, were influenced by a 59 year-old man who taught moral precepts about investing one's talent and not hiding one's light in the dark. His teacher's name was John D. Rockefeller who had retired from Santa Oil and taught young people how to become men (not scrambled eggs) at the Euclid Avenue Baptist Church, in New York.

That teaching opened the young Sperry's mind. One of his many inventions was the so-called 'aerial torpedo' (today's missile). The bureaucrat of the US government, and chief of the Engineering Division, supposed to approve the agreed-upon bonus became jealous: '... I have investigated that matter and believe that the bonus payments would be illegal under the terms of the contract, as it was not contemplated that radio be used. The contract only stipulated that the engine shall function in flight test *without manual control.*'

'Radio control is not manual control,' Lawrence Sperry told the chief of the Engineering Division, 'Try to get that simple idea fixed in your little bureaucratic mind.'[17]

One of the hurdles open minds have to overcome in using their imagination is that of resistance to change and renovation. First resistance comes from those who stand to lose significant advantages from abandoning the status quo and from ironing out the inefficiencies of the current system. But failure to change condemns a person, a company and a nation to decay. Take Silicon Valley as an example. Not long ago a study showed that:

- to survive, a technology company must reinvent itself every 2½ years, and
- the same is true of university education and of the institutions themselves.

This is one of the reasons why doing sponsored research is a necessary path to reinventing higher education. It takes the best of current scientists to teach those who would be tomorrow's best scientists, and there is no way to avoid that fact. The opposite is also true. Most of what is done in reinventing university today is done under the pressure of business which depends in a most significant way on a vibrant higher education system for its future.

Business is increasingly dependent on technical knowledge and the ability to put it in practice. The extent to which this is true is documented by the fact that about some 85 per cent of all the high-growth enterprises created in America in the past two decades were launched by college graduates with fertile imaginations. University research departments have helped drive innovation in everything from design to entertainment and have kept open the channels needed to circulate ideas, helping turn them into practical new products.

The way an article in *The Economist* has it, British executives 'lament the country's educational standards and complain that many universities disdain collaboration with industry.' The fact that things are improving at slow pace is spurring companies into looking for solutions in America. In Virginia, the offer to Roll-Royce included state investment in education at all levels to help provide a skilled workforce. This should have been offered in Britain, but it is difficult to:

- overcome inertia,

17 William W. Davenport, *Gyro! The Life and Times of Lawrence Sperry*, Charles Scribner, New York, 1916.

- challenge the status quo, and
- induce the best and brightest to study the subjects that high-tech manufacturing demands.

According to the same source, moreover 'Rolls-Royce executives say that the (British) pool of experienced engineers, process managers and skilled workers from which the company can recruit is shrinking. Many of these people used to come from carmakers or other industrial firms. But a once-steady flow is now a trickle.'[18]

## 5. Principles of Talent Management Technology

In nearly all major EU member states there is confusion in the minds of the people, and of those governing them, about the fortunes of the post-industrial society in which we live and of their future. Uncertainty and its accompanying destabilization find their origin in the nineteenth-century Industrial Revolution, the class struggle which followed it, the socialist manifesto, and the fact that freedom, democracy and equality may be good guideposts but are not well defined.

When uncertainty about a society's future affects a great number of individuals, it leads to general defensiveness and nostalgia for an epoch which is long past or outright utopian. This prevents people from appreciating that, since the early 1980s globalization, deregulation, technology and innovation have changed the world in which we live, work and invest. Examples are innovation in:

- financial instruments,
- modes of payment, and
- ways of managing new forms of wealth.

Innovation means *change* and it affects employment all the way from opportunities to risks. Gone is the time when somebody entered a company, or any other organization, and stayed with it until retirement. Gone, too, is company paternalism by which, in return for its employees' loyalty, the company would look after them and their families, and care for them as a good father would.

Inequality in professional life differentiates those people who are dynamic, active, motivated by knowledge and the drive for results from those who are weak, dumb and lazy – waiting for the state to find them a job or, even worse, pay them unemployment benefits.

To survive and prosper in the post-industrial society, people must not only have knowledge assets, but also make sure that these are properly used and regularly renewed. They must also exhibit flexibility, adaptability and a motivation to change careers several times over their working lives. Yet, to the majority of people this truth is by no means self-evident, because:

- politicians seem unable to explain the new realities, and
- the education system itself does not teach the very basic concepts of multiple careers as the best way to assure employment.

18 *The Economist*, 10 January 2009.

Closely connected to all this is the lack of a drive for achievement in *à la* Lawrence Sperry, as described earlier. When employed by a company an individual – and most particularly a professional – must distinguish himself or herself by deliverables that contribute substantially to the company's profits, rather than being uninterested in output or behaving in a miserable and antagonistic way.

- Design, production and marketing, the three main phases of the product development and sales cycles, have become unstuck.
- They can be outsourced, with *innovation* and *cost* deciding whether the company and its people will prosper or go bankrupt.

A globally recognizable brand and low-cost price tags are the two predominant assets in global marketing. Label and novelty correlate. But nobody can sleep on his laurels because there is always a challenger ready to come up from under and overtake people and companies that are tired of their profession (and quite often of life) or asleep at the wheel.

In addition, salaries and wages in the West (compared to developing countries) see to it that for anything other than the most recent innovations and high technology, production has become secondary. China provides the manufacturing platform – but not only China. In Europe, Switzerland and the Czech Republic both have an educated and motivated labour force, but the hourly cost in Czech Republic is about 13 per cent that of Switzerland. Guess where companies establish production facilities.

- The knowledge economy and post-industrial society brings along with it inequality, not equality as people like to think.
- The impact of this inequality is widespread, and its after-effects are highly significant, to personal careers, companies' survival and countries' stability.

There are plenty of opportunities for professionals who want to live according to the times, but to capture them they should follow the advice of Sun Tzu (the great Chinese statesman and general, c. 500BC): 'A victorious strategist only seeks battle after the victory has already been won, whereas he who is destined to defeat first fights and afterwards looks for victory.' In a knowledge society, to be victorious, careers must be planned – and that's the individual's job, not the government's. Six principles distinguish those who have learned how to live in their epoch:

1. 'The president can tell me to leave every morning, and I can take my hat and leave on my own every afternoon.'

That's what John Connally said after being appointed US Treasury secretary by Richard Nixon in response to a journalist's question about the nature of his contract with the president.[19]

19 This comment attracted my attention. It is a basic principle of success because between the lines it conveys a message that if you want to write your own contract it matters little if you are fired because there is a queue of offers waiting for you.

2. 'In today's globally competitive world you cannot survive, let alone thrive, without satisfied customers.'

This statement is attributed to Andrew Grove, the former CEO of Intel, who also said that in the high-technology industry only the paranoid can survive.

3. 'Globalization accelerates the arrival of entirely new markets, and turns the mass market into a "mass of niches".'

That's the motto used by intensively market-oriented companies like Toyota, in tuning their marketing strategy and in offering their customers the possibility of choosing their new car's characteristics, for delivery in a few days.

4. 'To succeed, companies need employees loaded with talent, imagination, energy and passion for work.'

This statement comes from the president of a well-known university in a meeting aimed at defining how a dynamic curriculum can be established and steadily revised to meet educational needs.

5. 'Employee loyalty and societal virtues go out of the door with lifetime employment.'

That's the opinion expressed, in a personal meeting, by the CEO of a firm which began life as a start-up and became one of the best known in its field of business activity.

6. 'The best people are those happy to stay and ready to leave for another job.'

These were the words of Jack Welch, the former CEO of General Electric, when he was defining the human resources policy adopted by his firm.

Together, these six statements constitute the pillars of a modern *talent management technology* – embracing properly managed careers progressing in accordance with carefully thought-out *personal* strategic plans. Lifelong learning matters a great deal (see section 6), but just as valuable is a sense of self-confidence and the drive to get the best out of oneself, in marked contrast to the bigotry of low expectations.

At the same time, of course, when compared to the average, a high-flying career might be called a 'positive' example of inequality – but there is no greater injustice than to reward in an equal way unequal efforts, drives and capabilities. Equality in careers always was, and remains, a castle in the sky. The key players in talent management are:

- the graduating students themselves and
- the companies employing them, which must manage scarce talent in a very effective way.

To avoid any misunderstanding, let me add that there also exist negative examples of inequality. One confronting practically everybody is huge discrepancies in pay scales. In the early part of the twentieth century J.P. Morgan, the banker, used to say that he would give no loan to a company where the pay ratio president-to-worker was greater than 20, because such company was heading for trouble. More recently, in the 1980s and early 1990s the president-to-worker pay ratio had risen to 40, as Peter Drucker noted in one of his lectures. It was irrationally high, but not outright ridiculous. Today this ratio is 480, bigger by 2,400 per cent in comparison to Morgan's time. This is absurd; it is also the ingredient for a social debacle of tremendous proportions.

## 6. Learning How to Learn

What the six principles of talent management technology essentially suggested is the degree to which knowledge and self-confidence must be built into the human brain. The main contributors are the family, early schooling, higher education, on-the-job experience and steady effort by the person him- or herself. Learning is both the journey and the reward; it is a journey without end. Young people should appreciate that, because their minds will become the pillars of tomorrow's society,

- *if* their learning is soft,
- *then* society itself will warp and decline.

Culture cannot survive without top performers. What distinguishes an average person from a virtuoso is that the latter has learned how to learn. Top performers spend many more hours than the average person practising their craft. They also concentrate on what they are doing, and they enjoy doing it.

Behind the genius of Mozart was his ability to focus for long periods of time on improving his skills. Getting down to basics, the ability to concentrate and focus, along with a propensity for hard work, is the celebrated, but misunderstood, ingredient of talent. Other important personal contributions are the ability to:

- pay attention to detail and
- adapt without delay to changing situations.

Top performers also appreciate that continuing research and education are exercises that make them fit. According to a study published by the Geneva Association, individuals with lower levels of education are 70 per cent more likely to be physically inactive and 50 per cent more likely to be obese than those with higher levels of education.[20]

Let me add another analogy which helps in better evaluating not only what has just been said, but also where we may be going in the coming years. Machines propelled the nineteenth-century Industrial Revolution, but brains are the motor power of the knowledge revolution which specifically requires *lifelong learning*, not just a one-off educational effort, even if it lasts for several years.

Lifelong learning is vital in providing hope for a better future, mastering fear of the unknown and eradicating the backwater conditions existing in some segments of society. When asked by parents what kind of advice he had for their sons and daughters, Andrei Gromyko, the former president of the Soviet Union and prior to that foreign minister for a couple of decades, answered: 'Tell them to learn how to learn.'

20 'SHARE: Survey of Health, Ageing and Retirement in Europe', *The Four Pillars*, No. 44, March 2009, p. 5.

Learning how to learn is one of the most fundamental requirements for a successful (and for an effective life, as well), but it is not achieved by running wild and protesting in the streets. Therefore, students who do so, as happens so often in France, Greece and other EU countries, are men and women against themselves. Whether they understand it or not, they are being used as bait by *agents provocateurs* and commit professional suicide rather than investing their time in developing their brains. It makes no sense for young people to go to school or university if they don't fulfil their mission of:

- getting the most out of their education and
- taking the greatest care to ensure that they are able to live and work in a knowledge society.

Following Gromyko's advice about learning how to learn is part of the personal responsibility and accountability of every citizen, because, without the fruits of lifelong education, a country will never be able to compete for the increasingly sophisticated and demanding jobs of this century. Several of the member states of the European Union are anyway in decline. There is no reason to make it worse by 'going down the street' with banners, crying, demonstrating and burning other people's houses.

(When at the end of 1944 Winston Churchill was attacked in parliament by the Labour party and other fellow travellers for having sent British troops to save Greece from falling slave to Tito and the communists, he answered: 'Democracy is no whore to be picked up in the street by a man with a tommy gun.'[21] The same is true of learning: 'Education is no whore to be picked up in the street by youngsters with banners.')

It is a crime against democracy, liberty and culture that since the end of World War II weak governments all over the EU have bent to the wild cries in the streets and the writing on the banners. Inevitably, this has led to a decline of personal initiative as people learned that by protesting and showing their anger they can:

- milk the state supermarket and
- scare its guardians into subservience.

Economists talk of Japan's 'lost decade' in reference to the period after the 1990–91 bust that followed its boom years of the 1980s, (Essentially there is not one but two lost decades. Both the 1990s and first ten years of this century have been miserable for Japan, Inc.). Something similar can be said about the *two lost generations* in the European Union (from the 1960s to today) in regard to:

- education and
- career development.[22]

21 Winston Churchill, *The Second World War*, Volume 11: *The Tide of History*, Cassell, London, 1954.

22 A most trusted advisor to the publisher commented that this is one of a number of places where I express the view that the soft or social sciences are generally of no value. He added that he entirely follows the underlying point about the relative worth of these and the hard sciences in relation to the needs of employers and economies, but wonders whether the tone is rather too utterly dismissive and that it would be good if somewhere in the text I acknowledged that some people benefit from a social science-oriented education and find that it has equipped them to do something useful. I fully agree with the advisor if instead of 'social sciences' (an ill-defined mismatch of soft disciplines), we speak about *humanities*. Humanities should be taught in primary and secondary school and be part of technical education at, say, a 15 per cent

The last 40 years of the twentieth century and the first decade of the current century have not really seen many top performers. Consequently, self-respecting EU companies are now looking at kindergartens (nurseries) to find their engineers, scientists and managers of tomorrow. This is also motivated by the shortage of engineers which has become acute because (as already noted) so many young people study subjects that have absolutely no market value.

Well-known industrial firms such as Siemens and Bosch are among hundreds of companies giving materials and money to kindergartens to try to interest children, as young as three, in technology and science. Although many European countries, ranging from Switzerland to France, suffer shortages of engineering graduates, the problem is especially acute in Germany, renowned as a land of engineering.

As of 2008 German companies had 95,000 vacancies for engineers, with only about 40,000 being trained in universities. Said Wolfgang Malchow, board member for human resources at Bosch, 'We are working with kindergartens. This is our future and we need to seize it.'[23] Chief executives of other companies which are strong in forward planning are also setting their sights on selecting the best children before they enter primary school. They want to wake children up to technology from an early age.

Siemens has provided thousands of 'discovery boxes', filled with science experiments suitable for three to six-year-olds, at a cost to the company of €500 a piece. Other German engineering firms train kindergarten teachers, as well as sending their apprentices to kindergartens to explain what they do at work and then later inviting the tiny pupils to look around the company. Franz Fehrenbach, Bosch's CEO put his thoughts in these terms: 'Germany is based on innovation, and that needs people.'[24]

Bosch and other companies are also increasingly looking abroad – from Ireland to China – to get their message across to the kindergarten generation. This is a fantastic idea which should have been picked up by the universities. Globalization being what it is, spreading the gospel of education in engineering, physics, biology, biochemistry, biotechnology, mathematics and other sciences should start at kindergarten, with the message:

- Work is pleasure.[25]
- Learn how to learn.
- Remember that experience really does count.

When later on in life – maybe two decades down the line – these kids become professionals they will remember these three points as the signposts that changed their life. Once they have learned how to learn, their skills will never become obsolete.

As a final piece of advice, to survive in an interdisciplinary world in which so much is changing at the same time, they must learn to think in parallel – and universities should help them in doing so. While the large majority of *Homo sapiens* have been taught to think and operate sequentially, *genuine creativity* is really a parallel process. Mozart

---

share of the curriculum. But just graduating in soft 'social sciences' is no good way to find employment, or contribute to the society's wealth (material as well as cultural).

23 *Financial Times*, 17 June 2008.

24 Lewis Page, 'Bosch, Siemens: Vorsprung durch Kinder und Technik', 17 June 2008, at: http://www.theregister.co.uk/2008/06/17/german_kinder_v/.

25 As the careful reader will recall, Confucius said so.

claimed: 'Nor do I hear in my imagination the parts successively, but I hear them, as it were, all at once.' Imagine! A whole symphony, all at once.

## 7. Reinventing Ulysses to Avoid the European Union's 'Museification'

Like *déclinisme*, a term coined to mean the unstoppable decline of a society and of a civilization, *museification* is a new word in the French vocabulary and, by extension, in the English. It describes something like a city, a region, a country becoming nothing else than a big museum and was first coined a couple of years ago with regard to what Paris has to offer nowadays – museum pieces.

The term is thought-provoking, but the museification of Europe will be confirmed if things continue to go downhill. *If* we don't bend *déclinisme's* curve, *then* eventually the reason for going to one of the EU capitals – from London to Paris, Rome and Athens – would be to visit its museums. The whole European Union faces this risk of museification.

Critics say that:

- *if* democratic rule is indeed something better than an EU museum piece,
- *then* EU enlargement, approval of the EU Constitution, joining the Euro and plenty of other important issues should have been confirmed by public vote in *every one* of the EU's member states.[26]

What particularly interests us in this chapter, however, is not the EU Constitution,[27] but the contribution to the European Union's museification made by students who mix with undesirable elements to fight the police. Neither their parents nor their teachers seem to have explained to them that even 'free' education, with all expenses paid by the state, requires effort and discipline on their part. Learning is a *rewarding*, but *painful*, exercise.

- Lack of discipline leads nowhere, and,
- when chaos reigns, it becomes a one-way street to disaster.

Students who mix with undesirables to fight with the police (as happened on 28 June 2006 in Athens), set fire to the Law faculty, burn cars or damage and loot shops – no matter what might be the reason for their 'anger' – are part and parcel of the generation of future *unemployables* (more on this in Chapter 10). They also stand a good chance of becoming outcasts of society, living on handouts from the state supermarket.

Whether organized or spontaneous, these revolt by students against themselves are the best assurance of a bleak future. They also bear witness to the existence of a twist in the students' reasoning. Speaking about the irrationality of such sort of demonstrations, a French weekly paper highlighted a two-way miscomprehension.

- Plenty of faculties and students have a bad opinion of companies,

---

26 As an example, just as Dutch and French voters refused to endorse the EU Constitution, German citizens, had they been given a voice, would have probably vetoed the abolition of the Deutschmark in favour of the Euro.

27 A theme treated in D.N. Chorafas, *The Business of Europe is Politics*, Gower, London, 2009.

- but business managers also don't trust the campuses which they consider to be badly disposed towards enterprises[28] and the spirit of *enterprise* as a whole.

All this 'effort' towards an acceleration of museification is happening at a time when the demand for talent-intensive skills is rising and, with it, the value of intangible assets. (The importance of intangible assets, which include everything from skilled workers' know-how to patents, has gone from 20 per cent of the value of companies in the S&P 500 index to nearly 70 per cent.)

To fill the needs created by this fast-rising demand for highly qualified people, the educational planning of society – and, clearly, of the universities – should focus on creating open minds, because coping with radical novelty in business and industry requires *new thinking* and *new departures*. It also calls for countries, companies and individuals to reinvent themselves. The people we employ in our firms:

- should use their brains every day, and
- whatever becomes routine must be handled by computers.[29]

To describe the innovator, thinker and risk-taker in the most vivid terms, Homer wrote the story of Ulysses (Odysseus) as an allegory. Ulysses is a character of charm and great fascination. He is also a popular figure, because his daring epitomizes the minds of many ancient Greeks. It is therefore wise to pay attention to Homer's story; Ulysses should be every young person's role model in the twenty-first century.

At the beginning of Homer's great work, which was the first text of ancient literature to include, plenty of heroes, each with different characteristics, the character of Ulysses is embedded in a general chorus of actions, some major and others minor. Among the major, he has the merit of finding Achilles, hidden in the island of Skyros, and persuading him to sail for Troy with 12 ships.

- Achilles is the handsome, rich and powerful hero who, with his own strength and honour, fights heroically against his enemies.
- But the person who courageously overcomes every kind of difficulty, not so much with sheer might but with intelligence and astuteness, is Ulysses.

Under the magic baton of Homer, Ulysses' personality gradually takes shape, starting with his quarrel with Palamedes, following with the artefact of the Trojan horse, and ending with the long odyssey. Everything included in that text is innovation in action. No two days are the same. Examples are:

- Ulysses' meeting with the Cyclop,
- his stay with Circe,
- his passage between Scylla and Charybdis,
- his encounter with the Lotus Eaters and Laestrygones.

---

28 *Le Canard Enchainé*, 11 October 2006.

29 This in no way downgrades machine intelligence, but expert systems are not part of this text so I do not explain what they can and cannot do.

The rich scenario Homer wrote for Ulysses includes many novel events worthy of a Greek tragedy. Among plenty of examples are his moments with the sirens, his time in the arms of Calypso, and his return to his homeland. There, disguised as a beggar, he wins the show of strength designed to permit his wife Penelope to choose among her suitors.

Part and parcel of a myth full of innovative encounters is how Penelope faithfully awaits him, passing her days by weaving the legendary web. As in the tragedies of Aeschylus, Sophocles, Euripides or Shakespeare, every figure that becomes the stuff of a legend, or steps on to the stage of history to popular acclaim, is bound to encounter a horde of opponents and of serious problems on the way. This is precisely why Homer's *Odyssey* is a great guide for today's young generation.

This array of serious opponents whose schemes are aimed at destroying Ulysses, combined with renewed waves of adversity, prompt the listener to (or reader of) Homer's poem to:

- think about risk and reward,
- raise the question, 'What's in it for me?', and
- search for an answer which may even surpass that of Ulysses in terms of ingenuity.

In the more recent history of Europe, the quest to come up from under was part and parcel of the fifteenth and sixteenth centuries with the great explorers; of the seventeenth century with the Age of Enlightenment; and of the nineteenth century with the Industrial Revolution. It also showed up in the twentieth century with nuclear research and the computer era, but by the end of that century it waned, and what has been left is the nightmare of museification.

It takes conceptual skills to plant the seeds of a new epoch – skills enriched with analytics, steady learning and experience – in short, what we call wisdom. There are good reasons why stoic philosophers considered Ulysses the prototype of a wise man, and politicians praised him as great leader and a man of action. Greek tragedians like Pindar and Euripides dwelt not on Ulysses' astuteness but on his foxiness, but foxiness, too, is part of real life. Outwitting an opponent is better than being dragged under because of laziness, lust and greed – which end in looting rather than in creating new wealth.

# CHAPTER 3 A Sense of Leadership in Education

## 1. The Beautiful Faculty of Thinking

Chapter 2 made the point that *thinking* must be part of everybody's education. One of the world's most resourceful businessmen, Thomas J. Watson Sr, came up with the corporate slogan 'THINK' and saw it become almost synonymous with his company, IBM. In his Cambridge lecture on 31August 1837, Ralph Waldo Emerson said: 'In the distribution of functions the scholar is the delegated intellect. In the right state, he is *Man Thinking*'.[1]

Niels Bohr, the nuclear physicist, was teasing his peers and his students by telling them: 'You are not thinking, you are only being logical.' Great thinkers in history have always appreciated that thinking means challenging the 'obvious', and therefore doubting and experimenting. Because it is based on thinking, experimentation is the mother of all sciences.

Thought should be guiding young and aspiring students when deciding on their first big investment: higher education. An ambitious young person about to take the first steps towards his or her professional life should reasonably examine, indeed speculate, about what sort of qualities the future employer might be looking for:

- when he hires the new generation of employees, and
- when he promotes people to senior positions.

Is there a particular specialization or domain of future excellence one should try to adopt or avoid? Moreover, if one is aiming high, one ought to study the profiles of past and current leaders in professional and business life. What jobs did they hold on their way up the social ladder? What was the special line of learning through which they entered their professional career? What kinds of decision were crucial?

Advancing in one's career requires not only theoretical but also practical knowledge, as well as breadth of know-how: What are the specific ingredients of the future professional's success in the marketplace of ideas? A university degree is important not just as a vocational licence, but as a message that its holder is able to continue educating himself or herself (more on this later).

There is a particular sense in the demands by business and industry for both specific knowledge and the candidate's ability to learn on the job. Skills acquired on university courses may not be directly applicable to one's first job. But if the student has *learned how to learn*, then the time spent in schooling is fully compensated. This requires:

- learning how to explore things in depth and detail,

1 From: http://www.vcu.edu/engweb/transcendentalism/authors/emerson/essays/amscholar.html.

- having the patience to study different levels of complexity and subtlety of a subject, and
- appreciating that while one does not know every issue, one must have the motivation to fill one's gaps.

There are two ways of achieving the goals set by these three bullets and they are complementary, not alternative, to one another. The one is to read the biographies of people who left a mark on their time. Well-written biographies contain profiles of scientists, engineers and executives, mostly of private-sector companies but also of non-business organizations which are set up as endowments later. Andrew Carnegie, for example, belongs in both classes.

What is instructive about biographical studies and notes is the extraordinary variety of personalities, backgrounds and decisions that, over the years, has led to professional success. No doubt it helps to be visionary, creative and entrepreneurial; but what else is also vitally important? The most critical factors are:

- the will to succeed
- learning ability
- hard work
- leadership style
- key strengths
- best and worst decisions
- lessons learned in business or in science.

Biographies should not be read as if one is watching a film. The reader should stop and think practically at every paragraph, understand the meaning of references being made and take notes. This is a simulated way of gaining experience.

The other (and complementary) way is to examine what the labour market is asking for, both now and in the future. Smart young people are doing so well before reaching a decision about their future profession. In the 1950s it was electronic data processing, and was later called information systems (IS) in the US and information technology (IT) in Britain.

- Being ahead of the crowd meant to belong to a small group of top specialists residing at the number one spot.

After the novelty of, and demand for, IT specialists began to wane, it was overtaken by other fields like telecommunications, robotics, biotechnology, nanotechnology and more. In the coming years, sought-after professionals will be those able to study and solve water and energy shortages, climate challenges, pollution problems and more.

Parents who let their kids drift into the 'soft sciences' because they find it easier and they don't have to think so much are greatly damaging their future. Indulgence always damages the other party's future. This is not written in the sense that higher education is the only future and that society should become more meritocratic. Rather, it is a reflection of the fact that:

- we live in a knowledge economy, and

- employers are becoming increasingly interested in the educational qualifications of their new hires, not just in a piece of paper which poses as a degree.

A corollary to this statement is the fact that a great deal of the job of higher education is to send a signal to employers that the student not only has a specialization that his company needs, but also has learnt to observe, understand, think, develop, persevere and present ideas. This runs contrary to current practices, so the problem young people face is threefold:

- They have not been taught to evaluate future employment opportunities and decide on potential job offers.
- They have been featherbedded by the family, the state and society at large for too long – hence the effort required by *real learning* looks mountainous.
- As the supply of university graduates grows, and the quality of teaching in crowded universities declines, the value of a higher education degree shrinks.

There are also reasons other than supply and demand for that shrinkage. Education is supposed to make young people articulate, confident and smart. But mass education is far from fulfilling this requirement. Add to this the fact of graduates having chosen soft subjects as majors, it is understandable that employers tend to pay little attention to higher educational degrees.

In its Spring 2004 issue, *UCLA Magazine* focused on preparation for higher learning. Interviewed on how this issue might regain its former glamour the then chancellor Albert Carnesale said:

> *At research universities like UCLA, we believe it is our obligation to produce informed citizens. We prepare leaders and well-trained professionals who will shape our shared future ... Moreover, as the workplace becomes increasingly complex, and as careers shift over time, we find that adults are pursuing further study through venues like UCLA Extension or our Executive Education programs.*[2]

Carnesale's reference to extension programmes and executive education brings up another crucial subject which is not given the attention it deserves in other universities (and most particularly in Europe). The time is long gone when what a student had learned in his or her higher education remained more or less valid for the rest of his or her career.

- Science and technology now move so fast, that there is now an unprecedented degree of obsolescence in know-how.
- Though important in themselves, general concepts like a good level of literacy, numeracy and reasoning are not enough to fill the gaps when one's skills in one's profession decay.

*Lifelong learning*, discussed in more detail in section 6, is 'education at the next step', and it can be sustained only through a steady effort that requires both formal training

2 'The education imperative', interview with Albert Carnesale, *UCLA Magazine*, Spring 2004, pp. 1–3. Available at: http://magazine.ucla.edu/year2004/spring04_01.html.

and personal research throughout one's career. It takes all sorts of personalities to make a company (as well as society at large), and all sorts of career paths to get to the top of one's profession. But falling behind in science and technology is pure recklessness.

## 2. Facing the Enemies of Higher Educational Standards

Obviously what was written in section 1 about *thinking* as key factor of personal and professional success also applies to those entrusted with planning, managing and controlling the institutes of higher education. Innovation, business transformation and social development are not going to come about through ill-focused university projects prepared by politicians or bureaucrats who repeat past errors or just want to show they are doing something. Typically, the large majority of these projects:

- burn their timetables,
- consume a multiple of their budgets and
- never yield tangible results.

Critics say that since the Second World War most European universities have been reduced to a level of *educational socialism* which goes from nowhere to nowhere. Part of this wrong policy is the underutilization of graduate students' skills, which is to everybody's detriment. For an example of the contribution graduate students make, read this quotation from a letter written in mid-July 2009 by Gene D. Block, chancellor of UCLA, to the university's alumni:

> *During the same period (2008–09) faculty won more than $966 million in research funding through competitive contracts and grants. This is a record for UCLA and keeps us ranked among the nation's top universities in this arena.*

Dr Block is right to be proud of UCLA's research accomplishments, because this is the result of long years of effort. But where is the industry which will trust and finance R&D in a system whose main characteristic is *mass higher education*?

Mass and quality are not just incompatible. They are each other's worst enemy. After the end of World War II students flocked to American universities from Europe because the US institutes of higher education were leaders in learning (see section 5), in research and in terms of testing the students' quality.

The testing process continues to be good. An example is the Graduate Record Examination (GRE) required by American universities. This gauges students' analytical, verbal and quantitative skills as well as their personality traits. Unavoidably, however, the explosion of registration has a triple negative aftermath – namely:

- spreading the faculty too thinly,
- reducing individual contact time and thus students' best learning opportunities and
- escalating costs, as universities desperately try to preserve the quality of education despite the explosion in student numbers.

'No one should go broke because they chose to go to college,' said Barack Obama in his January 2010 State of the Union address, but he failed to explain how to square the circle made by these three bullets. American college students worry that they might go broke because of fee increases at technical colleges and universities, which became necessary to compensate for the reduction in state funding and to maintain quality of education.[3]

In California, some public colleges and universities increased fees by more than 30 per cent, and cut back on their offerings as the state's financing shrank because its budget is fully in the red. Another 38 states in the US have decreased their funding for public colleges and universities (though less than in California) and imposed corresponding increases in tuition charges.[4]

In an effort to rein in runaway budgets, and in a reversal of past trends, several higher education institutions have started to cut the number of students they enrol. This helps save money but also, in conjunction to the 2007–2011 severe economic crisis, provides evidence that the wild growth of university education is unaffordable and unsustainable.

America is not alone in this explosion of the tertiary sector of education. In the mid-1960s Britain had 32 universities – a legacy from the pre-World War II years – and 220,000 full-time students. By the end of the twentieth century it had some 80 universities and over 1 million students. Both the number of universities and the number of students per school had exploded.

- Quantity is the public enemy of quality in higher education.

In the 1990s alone, British student numbers rose by almost two-thirds, with the proportion of 18-year-olds who proceeded to university studies zooming from 19 per cent to 32 per cent. This educational boom has been a quantitative bust. It was not planned way ahead, and it therefore resulted in dilution of standards. Yet, many people who foresaw the coming events warned about the serious implications of expansion for the higher education system. Three stood out:

- the experience and quality of faculty staff, which establishes the university hierarchy,
- funding the new facilities, as well as their future evolution and
- faculty advisory facilities for students – undergraduate, graduate and postgraduate.

The result has been spoilage of financial and human resources, including in the latter the faculty's time and the student's misdirection. The British version of the educational state supermarket paid no attention to the fact that the greatest asset of American universities, ranking even higher than their faculties which in many cases are worth a great deal, is their graduate students and the research work they perform under the faculty's guidance.

- Graduate students cannot be attracted in large numbers unless the faculty is first-class, and research projects are available to support them.

3 On 4 March 2010 students and disgruntled faculty staff staged protests at around 100 campuses in over 30 states, calling on state legislators and university administrators to put a halt to recent tuition hikes and funding cuts.

4 Peter Henderson, 'Students Protest Fee Hikes at Universities', 4 March 2010, at: http://www.reuters.com/article/idUSTRE62312E20100304.

- But rich research contracts will not come to universities whose faculties are underpaid, whose students spend more time demonstrating in the streets than learning (albeit not in Britain), and whose culture is against enterprise.

The second bullet describes the state of some European universities. In France, about a quarter of the 82 universities are 'occupied' by their students, who learn nothing more than how to strike and keep others out of work. When both faculty and students descend in anger to the streets and squares, they are simply ridiculing themselves by demonstrating in the manner of a provincial circus – becoming, in one go, higher education's number two enemy.

- Sometimes it is the faculty (claiming higher pay or shorter working hours) which is pushing the students to the forefront.
- In other cases, it is the students (for whatever reason hits their fancy) that pull the faculty, and their own parents, out into the streets.

While the number of universities reached for the stars, the quality of education went south. France's educational standards have been upheld by the *Grandes Ecoles*, which include the Ecole Polytechnique and Ecole Normale Supérieur. These are the country's most prestigious schools of higher education and until 2010, despite several socialist governments having tried to change the rules, they held their own. Admission continued to be based on entry exams which:

- screened the applicants and
- retained only the best.

This has abruptly changed. In January 2010 a new government decree mandated that 30 per cent of entry places will be on a 'fixed quota' reserved to poorer students from poorer backgrounds who have not made it in school and are deficient in scholarship – but still want to get a *Grandes Ecoles* diploma. This quota will be filled by students who are largely non-qualified. So they will simply sit the entry exams; the grade they attain will be of no consequence.

Unsurprisingly, the French academic community is in revolt against such a massive destruction of academic credentials. Faculties particularly object to the government forcing the doors open by political means to disqualified individuals, while qualified applicants are left out in the cold – for centuries the sole criterion for entry into a *Grande Ecole* has been the candidate's academic qualifications and learning ability.

## 3. The Challenge of Private Universities in the EU

Matters are not that much better in other EU countries. In Greece, for instance, universities, banks, agricultural people and the transportation industry don't think twice before going on strike. Many university strikes are due to the fact that, in the various state-supported institutes of higher learning, the faculty reacts negatively to the idea of private universities authorized by the government because this has become an EU objective.

As Chapter 2 pointed out, it is difficult to see what is wrong with competition in education. In principle, competition is a policy that raises educational standards. There is always the possibility that private universities will not succeed because success depends on many factors but, if so, they should be free to fail. The state supermarket's *university monopoly* is also an enemy of higher education.

One of the silly arguments put forward by embedded interests against private universities is that what choice and competition really do is serve to increase social differentiation between schools. Parents are known to compete to get their children into the most successful institutions, and they do so from the level of primary school onwards. This argument is wrong-headed and self-defeating. While *we want* all universities to be equally successful, we also know that some will be better than others – and that the quality of students these universities have is just as important as their faculty and their labs. There are only two ways of finding out which are the best, and they complement one another:

- Let the universities compete for faculties, students and end results and
- *accredit* them, based on examination of their faculties, labs, libraries, curricula and students.

International evidence tells us that the most effective way of upgrading educational standards is to raise the quality of teaching and learning – a long-term effort which has its enemies. Educational excellence will not come to pass just by preaching equality at the lowest common denominator.

*If* private universities can provide high-quality education, *then* so much the better for everybody. Why not? Without private university initiatives there would have been no Harvard and no Stanford University, to give just two examples.

It is definitely wrong to erect legal and bureaucratic obstacles which end up damaging the country's educational standards. Much worse is students taking to the streets in bitter demonstrations against private universities. These are definitely *students against themselves*.

The Japanese, who have been investing heavily in an 'intelligent society', offer an example of what it takes to raise the standard of higher education. They see their competitive advantage from a perspective expressed in terms of:

- highly qualified people who have a diverse range of skills and
- the steady upgrade of the profile of the *knowledge worker* – the right person in the right environment, supported the right infrastructure.

That's how a country could flourish in the globalized twenty-first century. By contrast, student and faculty strikes topped up by street demonstrations are the policy of decay. Just as bad is the spreading practice of failing the exams and being allowed to repeat the years of non-learning forever, at the expense of the taxpayer.

This chronic failure complex is another enemy of higher education – a major issue that the state supermarket has allowed to balloon. It's exacerbated by weak government and socialist ideas. One of the reasons for unrest in Greek universities has been a government decree that students who do not complete their degree within a couple of years beyond the normal length of study will be no longer be permitted to register.

- This has been a part of long overdue changes in higher education, proposed by a panel of Greek academics.

- The academics also recommended a change to the law banning police from entering university grounds without permission.[5]

However, other measures in Greece, France, Germany and practically everywhere in the EU have been compromises rather than radical departures aimed at putting higher education back on its feet. As a result, these countries failed to eradicate the problem of students taking a free ride at taxpayers' expense by:

- extending their studies indefinitely,
- overcrowding the universities and
- costing lots of money while producing nothing.[6]

The panel of Greek academics also said that there should be no more than 80 students in a lecture hall, or teaching room, at any one time. I look at this self-imposed ceiling as being two-and-half times higher than the maximum admissible if students are to learn anything from their professors. Even so, the students took to the streets, thinking that (for unidentified reasons) the proposed measure was too tough.

Similarly there has been a very negative ongoing student reaction in France since Valérie Pécresse, the minister of higher education, brought forward the law on university autonomy in July 2007. The enemies of higher education (including the labour unions, which try to find any excuse to demonstrate they are still alive) interpreted autonomy as opening the door to the privatization of the university system.

In conclusion, after the end of World War II, weak governments appealed to the general public by instituting 'free education' from cradle to university – without attaching to it any quality standards to be met by the faculty or qualifications by the students. Any change to that rotten state of affairs has become the public enemy to vested interests who (by omission or commission) fail to understand the need to restructure university education to make it more flexible and adjustable to the changing economy – as well as more effective.

## 4. Institutes of Higher Education and Their Management Plans

Let's start with a fact on which (I hope) we might all agree. A university is not a cemetery. It is a dynamic enterprise whose process is knowledge discovery through research, knowledge transmission by the faculty and knowledge acquisition by the students. This acquired knowledge will assist the graduates in finding employment and in having a better life. But, to do so, it has to be in tune with:

- what the economy requires to match its social goals and
- what companies need in order to compete in the markets where they sell their products and services – thereby enabling themselves pay their employees.

5 Which had turned some universities into hideouts for anarchists.

6 In 2005 there were some 144,000 Greek students who had extended their studies, compared to 171,000 who finished them within the prescribed length of their course. In other words, nearly 46 per cent of the 325,000 students were loafers or nearly so.

Neither of these two objectives is currently satisfied by the university system in any one of the EU countries. Some 20 years ago, an unpublished survey by the London Business School suggested that firms do not want the sort of academic specialists that business schools tend to produce under the vague label of MBAs. They want graduates with a broad range of management skills, who know how to apply them to real business problems,[7] and this is not being done.

This failure of university output to meet industry standards poses a critical question: does the aim of 'higher education for all' justify taxpayers funding 100 per cent of the budget? Put differently, how favoured should higher education be in the scramble for cash when compared to demands posed by other public services?

- The choices are to a very large extent political, and universities are popular with the electorate.
- But the same can be said of nurseries, lower schools, retirement benefits, health services and more.

It needs no explaining that, with so many goodies displayed in the racks of the state supermarket, funding is problematic. Within the university setting itself, plenty has to be covered – not only its premises, labs, faculty, administration and maintenance, but also (under the prevailing regime) student financial support for fees and living quarters. Logic suggests that support should be granted on a performance basis – that is, to the best students, not to the loafers.

There is also China's model of financing students' study, which should not be discarded outright. Graduates who take up jobs in poor, remote areas of western China get their university tuition fees refunded by the government. They are also promised preferential treatment after three years in the countryside when applying for civil service jobs or for places in a graduate school.[8] But university education per se is not free of charge to the student.

Universities should also be keen to become more cost-effective without compromising the quality of education. Cutting costs in university education is not a daydream. Lecture rooms can be open longer – including in the evenings, with courses benefiting from visiting faculty staff who have direct and practical experience. Procurement costs (a major expense item) can be reduced by smaller universities acting together to increase their negotiating clout through:

- standardization and
- collective purchasing.

The local business community should also be put to task. A 2007 study by the University of California, in Los Angeles, has shown that for every dollar taxpayers invest in UCLA, the university generates almost $15 in economic activity. This is largely spent in the community around the campus.[9] It is only reasonable that the community returns part of that favour through sponsorships.

---

7 *The Economist*, 20 April 1991,

8 *The Economist*, 11 April 2009.

9 *UCLA Magazine*, October 2007.

In terms of administration, much can be done to improve end results without large outlays or, alternatively, to cut he budget while keeping quality of education steady. (Don't try to do both cost-cutting and quality improvement in one shot.) Specialization is one of the answers. Universities cannot be all things to all people.

- The educational challenges of the future must be met effectively.
- But the better way to proceed is to achieve distinction in one domain, rather than following a 'me too' approach all over the educational business.

This is not precisely what happens today – for instance, with MBAs. There are some 200 schools and colleges in Europe producing 'masters of business administration', a line of skills characterized by oversupply – and, in many cases, by underperformance. In a way, this resembles the blind policy of Detroit in designing and producing big cars whose market ceased to exist.

Indeed, because they rarely get what they want in terms of skills, many companies have set up in-house business schools to produce the sort of managers they need. This leaves the wheels of the universities' MBA production turning in a vacuum, and it is only one example of misdirected effort. Another, even worse, is the massive production of 'sociologists', arts majors, film studies specialists and other fiefs characterized by two complementary factors:

- they are easy to study and
- they are directed to a market in which demand is soft and job opportunities are limited.

Although students choose their subject, what the universities offer weighs a great deal. British research published in early December 2008 demonstrated that many students may have chosen the wrong subjects and, by so doing, have damaged their chances of finding employment.

It looks *as if* British students and their parents are not wise to the unwritten distinction between 'hard' and 'soft' A-levels. Research-intensive universities offer more science and language degrees, and fewer in media studies and the like. Researchers at Durham University compared the relative difficulty of every subject and found that some subjects really did turn out to be much harder than others.

- Applicants with 'A' grades in sociology and similar subjects may be bright,
- but those with 'A's in physics are pretty sure to be so,[10] and they are much more in demand.

A challenging issue behind these findings is the return on investment of higher education to society and the *intrinsic value* of the university years to the graduating student. The first question is whether these years have opened the graduate's mental horizon; the second, whether he or she learned how to learn; the third, how much a university education improves the graduate's chances of finding employment and boosts his or her income.

10 *The Economist*, 20 December 2008.

These are highly pertinent questions for both students and institutions when managing their destiny by planning the right way for the future. The students are planning their career. Universities are engaged in long-range planning when they:

- select and define educational objectives,
- determine the means required for achieving them, and
- prepare for the systematic achievement of goals within stated periods.

Management practice teaches that the long-range plan itself is an opportunity for adaptation and restructuring. Five years ahead is often regarded as the minimum period to qualify as 'long-range', but 10-, 15- and 20-year ranges are more appropriate. Projections, as well as assumptions, must be made, and these should be made on the basis of much more than occasional brainstorming sessions or periodic weekend retreats.

As in every enterprise, the success of a restructuring plan will be conditioned by the deliverables, which will not come just by chance. To maintain themselves in a competitive market universities require first-class plans, akin to those of the best managed companies. To do so, they have to explore both policy and tactics, answering questions such as:

- What decisions have to be made for the longer term?
- Who is supposed to make them? (A tough question for state-supported institutions.)
- In what order of priority should they be made?
- What information is necessary in order to reach them? To document them?
- Which criteria should be used in reaching critical decisions?

As all this suggests, the institutes of learning, too, need management and restructuring. If they fail to take command of evolving educational needs, including adaptation in a changing environment, then not only their students, but also the universities themselves will have failed in their fundamental mission.

## 5. Learning from the Leadership of the American University System

The heavy hand of the state supermarkets, overexploitation of 'free education', professors and students on strike, absenteeism for different reasons, obsolete curricula and lack of money for salaries and labs are negatives which have seen to it that, since the end of World War II, Europe has progressively surrendered its pre-war lead in high education. As the careful reader will recall from Chapter 1, today America has 18 of the world's top 20 universities (according to a widely used global ranking by the Shanghai Jiao Tong University). Moreover,

- American universities currently employ 70 per cent of the world's Nobel Prize winners. The University of California System alone features 55 Nobel Prize winners in its faculty, and
- this faculty publishes 30 per cent of the world's output of articles on science and engineering, as well as 44 per cent of the most frequently cited articles.[11]

---

11 This correlates with the fact that accreditation examines the faculty's list of publication of books and articles (see section 6).

The best public higher education in the world is to be found at the University of California, as claimed by Shanghai Jiao Tong University in its worldwide ranking. The Berkeley campus of the University of California ranks third behind two private universities, Harvard and Stanford. Several of the other ten campuses, like UCLA and San Diego, are not far behind.

Reaching the top of a classification list is never happens by accident. As far as its finances permitted, the state of California had the ambition to educate as many of its young citizens as possible. This was put into effect through a three-tier system:

- The best students were admitted by the University of California.
- The next lot entered the Californian State University.
- And the others went to community colleges, with the possibility of trading up.

To reach the goal of excellence, successive presidents of the University of California attracted the best academics (and Nobel Prize winners) through a steady talent–scouting process. In return, the university's campuses collectively produced more Nobel Prize laureates than any other institute of higher education in the world.

Academic excellence was the goal in this course of events; and the goal was attained. But the 2007–2011 deep economic crisis hit the finances of the state of California like a hammer blow. In the aftermath, attracting and keeping academic superstars, and the research dollars that follow them, has become much harder.

Still, this is a good case study on how, in the second half of the twentieth century, many American universities became the cream of higher education worldwide through an ambitious plan and steady effort. 'One day you and I will not be here, but the university will be,' Dean Boelter told me when I gave a young student a higher grade than I should have given.[12] Speaking from personal experience at UCLA, I can attest that the role of the university:

- went beyond helping young people to understand the world around them, and
- extended to making the students understand themselves and their responsibilities.

Upgrading is a lifelong ambition or there is none of it. Leadership in higher education provides an irrefutable example. Richard D. Richardson, Jr, the biographer of Ralph Waldo Emerson, writes that in the nineteenth century 'the image of Germany that filtered back from Göttingen was bookish and learned'. In a letter to William Waldo (the writer) Emerson called it 'the paradise of dictionaries and critics'[13] – of university education as well. By contrast, in 2009:

- only six German universities have been among the top 100 in the Shanghai ranking, with Munich the highest at 55th position, and
- only a meagre 21 per cent of each age cohort gets a degree[14], against an OECD average of 37 per cent – which itself is too low.

---

12 Since then (1955) I have never given to a student, employee or colleague a single notch more than he or she was worth.

13 Robert D. Richardson Jr, *Emerson. The Mind on Fire*, University of California Press, Berkeley, CA, 1995.

14 *The Economist*, 27 June 2009.

Times have changed, and not for the better. What most European governments fail to appreciate is that well-run universities, with grade 1 faculties and students who really want to learn, dispose immense intellectual resources. These are being released by research projects, but also through start-ups in which faculty and students collaborate. An example is Intelligence Alley, just across the river from MIT. This helps the economy twice over because:

- without practical implementation of research results, university teaching will tend to be too detached from real life, and
- properly managed research, development and implementation contribute to the economy by directly promoting novel industrial activities, and indirectly promoting employment opportunities.

Both the above points highlight an added advantage of American universities, which was termed in Chapter 2 a *talent management technology*. A further aim of university–industry collaboration in research (which is looked down on in Europe, a relic from socialist regimes) is to raise productivity by managing talent in an effective way.

It must be stated to their credit that some European universities are aware that faculties and students have been indulged too far. Cambridge is considering a foundation year for students who show potential but are ill-prepared. Other universities, too, try to help students – at least those who are willing and able – to close the gap.

Also under discussion in British higher education institutions is a review of the government-imposed cap on tuition fees (more on this in Chapter 4). It is good to see that at least some administrations are beginning to actively renew the crumbling structure – as they appreciate that 'Bay of Pigs' type fiascos come to life when well-meaning people become dominated by outworn concepts that make them incapable of:

- checking out facts,
- challenging assumptions,
- exploring new options,
- risking arguments,
- correcting errors and
- changing their culture and methods.

Apart from faculty decisions on new orientations, a great deal depends on the subjects that students study, (as discussed in section 2), since this shapes their minds and future careers. As I will never tire of repeating, soft subjects are offer no professional future, and the choice of such subjects is therefore a spreading disease in European education.

Science and technology is a very important domain which does not attract the growing number of students it should appeal to, both in the EU and in America. To the contrary, science and technology – particularly engineering – are very popular in China and India.[15]

As if this turning away from real science studies was not enough, the subjects being taught in engineering and other fields have remained unchanged for years. By contrast, the themes in American university curricula are dynamic. Sometimes, I left a course for

15 D.N. Chorafas, *Globalization's Limits: Conflicting National Interests in Trade and Finance*, Gower, Aldershot, 2009.

next semester, only to see it disappear from the teaching schedule. In addition, because European university faculties have little intercourse with business and industry, training in higher education is often based on:

- too much theory and
- not enough practical advice on how to deliver results.

Three things are necessary to close this gap. First, European academia and industry must be brought closer together, using EU seed money. This was intended to happen with ESPRIT (European Programme on Research in Information Technology) and other EU projects aiming at cross-country collaboration among scientists, but, as we will see in Chapter 6, the results have not really been satisfactory.

Second, the quality of education should be given a much higher priority over quantity. The way to correct overcrowded lecture halls, crumbling buildings and the chaotic conversion from the traditional diploma to a European two- or three-tier degree system (see Chapter 4) is not by developing larger and larger unmanageable campuses, but by:

- screening students at entry into the system and
- putting in place strict grading associated to exams.

As the reader is already aware, European universities are underfunded by international standards though the state is not a delinquent financier. What are direly missing are private contributions, the *endowments* (see Chapter 4) which, in America, account for nearly 2 per cent of GDP per year – versus 1 per cent contributed by the states.

Germany wants to create nine universities with 'promising future concepts', but the policy followed by the government points the other way.[16] Instead of bracing for an influx of 275,000 extra students, as current plans indicate, the federal states and Berlin should focus on *upgrading* the faculties, labs and student bodies.

- The dismal 21 per cent who get a degree at the end should be doubled to 40 per cent as a start.
- This can be done by toughening up admission criteria, proceeding with accreditation and instituting a quarter or semester system ,with exams serving for screening.

Both the government and the university system should give every student a clear message that university halls are not for loafers. Mediocrity has no business on a campus. The University of California System, which is currently facing a severe funding crisis, offers an example. System-wide the deficit is $800, and it cannot be subscribed by the state. To cover it,

- student fees have gone up,
- the student body is scheduled for downsizing, and other cost cuts are planned,

16 One of the major contradictions in the German government's policy in higher education is the spending of €1.8 billion ($2.52 billion) on revamping the pre-World War II IG Farben building to provide classrooms for more thousands of students. Quantity not quality seems to hold the upper ground.

- but quality of education and of research will be upheld, because 'mediocrity is not an option'.[17]

Third, there should be instituted lifelong learning programmes for university professors and teachers, interleaved with practical industrial experience. The best policy is to train the faculty at all levels of education: primary, secondary and tertiary. OECD's education experts think that part of the reason why pupils in East European countries do so well in international tests, despite fairly modest educational spending, is that these countries have effective teacher-training programmes.

Critics also point out that the European Commission has totally failed in educational matters, which is particularly visible as individual EU governments don't take the initiative to shake up the curricula. Added to this is the fact that some subjects in the curricula of European universities have become sacred cows.

It matters little that, in some of their interminable 'summits' (which come ten a penny) and Lisbon meetings, EU officials proclaim their intention to turn the old continent into the world's premier 'knowledge economy'. The thinking behind this grand declaration is muddled at best. Glorious words have short legs. Things being what they are, Europe's only chance of preserving its living standards lies in working smarter than its competitors in the global market. This requires:

- the proper setting of priorities and
- a clear plan of action, backed by appropriate human and financial resources.

The European Commission, however, has failed to sort out its priorities, and it has been too timid to ask individual governments to provide the critical support necessary to see the different grandiose education plans through. A self-imposed 2012 target for the educational revolution has turned into a non-event – one of those initiatives lacking body and soul. *If* there was life left in it, *then* the first step would have been pan-European university accreditation. The next section explains what this means.

## 6. Promoting the Process of Accreditation

Let's start with the facts. Without a system which rates quality of education and research – hence what can be expected in terms of deliverables – any processes will run out of control. The existence of a quality rating system is therefore critical, whether we talk of engineering, medicine, physics, mathematics, finance or any other field of activity.

- Measurement is one of the foundations of science, and
- *accreditation* measures the quality of higher education at delivery.

The way it is practised in the United States, university accreditation is simple and straightforward. Committees from professional associations of electrical engineers, mechanical engineers, chemical engineers, accountants and other bodies periodically visit

17 Quoting from a mid-July 2009 letter by the UC Board of Regents.

all universities in order to audit their educational standard in the relevant disciplines. The examiners look individually into:

- the background and experience of each faculty member;
- the faculty's publications of books and articles, and their citations;
- the faculty's involvement in research projects, as well as patents and prizes;
- the composition of the curriculum, its currency, and pertinence to the faculty's specialization;
- undergraduate students and their study;
- graduate students, their quality and involvement in research projects;
- who is sponsoring these projects and how important each sponsorship is;
- the quality of and technology in, the university's laboratories';
- the quality and breadth of the university's library, and much more

Note that this is a peer-to-peer examination, and the results of the accreditation are dear to colleges and universities because they significantly affect both its intake of students – therefore future income – and its reputation in the academic community. No institute of higher education can afford to take the accreditation process lightly.

The students themselves pay attention to the accreditation of the university to which they will enrol. Other things equal, the salary offered to a graduate of an accredited American university is 20–25 per cent higher than that offered to a non-accredited university's graduate. In my experience, this process of accreditation is done in a fairly objective manner. The members of the committee (made up of selected members of professional societies) who visit the universities take their role very seriously when they:

- examine the curriculum,
- interview the faculty to ascertain the professors' know-how,
- take a close look at the student body,
- evaluate the installation's infrastructure and laboratories and
- use quality criteria of professional correctness to confirm or cancel the school's accreditation.

In its way, this process resembles a credit rating, but with educational professionalism in mind. It is a go/no-go result – hence a test by attributes rather than by variables (say from 1 to 10). The certification of quality of education ensures that students want to be graduates of accredited US universities, and not, as it happens in some EU countries, of universities which are always on strike.

A significant number of students from abroad attend American universities. According to the OECD, over 40 per cent of the 160,000 foreign students in the country during the 2007–2008 academic year came from just three Asian countries: China, India and South Korea.[18] Overall, numbers could be broken down as follows:

- 24,000 from China
- 10,000 from India
- 10,000 from South Korea

---

18 *The Economist*, 19 December 2009.

- more than 5,000 from Japan
- 5,000 from Germany
- a little under 5,000 from Canada
- 4,000 from France.

These statistics on foreign students flocking to American universities are followed by smaller numbers of students from Italy, Britain, Spain and Brazil. It is impressive that foreign students, in several fields such as engineering, physics and information technology, now dominate doctoral programmes in the US. Quality of learning is the top reason for students who go on to earn American PhDs.

Everyone has to gain by keeping universities, faculties and students on the run to fulfil the requirement of preserving (or, alternatively, regaining) their accreditation. It is nobody's secret that the quality of education varies tremendously from institution to institution – and sometimes between regions in the same country. Rating, however, is both:

- a penalty for drifting and
- a chance for those who need a push to come up from under.

Drifting can go all the way to the abyss. Southern Italy presents an example. Its educational quality standards are much lower than in the north. A ranking by Shanghai's Jiao Tong University put only three southern institutes of higher education among Italy's top 20, which are themselves hardly world-class. 'It is not just that the image of the *mezzogiorno* has deteriorated nationally and internationally. There also has been a loss of self-confidence,' says Alessandro Laterza, head of the local branch of Confindustria.[19] Regaining accreditation will boost confidence.

EU accreditation would also be instrumental in policing, cross-border, the behaviour of some university faculties, so that recent scandals will not be repeated. One of them, unearthed in August 2009 in Germany, involved the acceptance of bribes by university professors – to the tune of euro €4,000–20,000 – to help students complete their doctorate degrees.[20]

There is also the case of 436 Chinese students who entered the University of Toulon in an irregular way (to say the least). In some of this French university's faculties 30 per cent of the students are Chinese – an abnormal number, which roused suspicions. Allegedly the price paid to an intermediary to obtain admission was €3,000 ($4,500).[21] Yet, it is the French taxpayers who pick up the tab since, after admission,

- the Chinese students pay a tuition fee of €460 ($690) per year,
- whereas in an American university annual tuition fees will be a five-figure sum.

The certification of quality of education can also be instrumental in doing away with some of the aberrations which occur when universities compete with one another

19 *The Economist*, 15 August 2009.

20 'Germany Probes University Professors over Corruption Charges', 22 August 2009, at: http://www.dw-world.de/dw/article/0,,4591787,00.html.

21 One Chinese student at University of Toulon admitted having paid that much, according to a report on A2 (the government's TV channel) on 19 October 2009.

for students. For several years, in Europe this has been the case with MBA degrees, but a late June 2009 advertisement in *The Economist* trumpeted the message that a Dutch university will now award PhDs through online courses. That's wrong, and it will degrade the doctoral degree for the following reasons:

- Doing advanced research by correspondence is equivalent to sending the concept of research to hell.
- A large part of the doctorate's acquired skill is provided by osmosis, learning from the experience of knowledgeable professors – which is not transmitted by correspondence.
- Higher education at doctoral level is 90 per cent *tacit knowledge* (see Chapter 1), which is never delivered by the Internet or the postman.

To make ends meet, given tight budgets, EU high schools, too, are cheating students through an unwelcome one-year reduction in the course of study. This has created a crisis at university entry level by debasing the young generation's knowledge, particularly in mathematics and the sciences, and obliging the universities to spend time and money to fill gaps in students' knowledge left by high schools.

The process of accreditation would sanction such twists, and would also blacklist universities which try to deliver diplomas on the cheap. By contrast, well-managed universities have nothing to fear from accreditation, but plenty to gain from it. Impartial evaluation will also help university chancellors who:

- do not suffer fools gladly and
- want to be ahead of the curve in keeping the curriculum dynamic.

Any faculty worth its salt is not afraid of accreditation, and neither is it in a hurry to retire. Under the title 'To Harvard instead of Retirement', an article published a few years ago makes the point that in line with the general regulations of the administrative law in Germany, in July 2001 the German immunologist Klaus Rajewsky (then 65) had to retire.[22] Instead:

- he emigrated to the United States with his wife and eight colleagues,
- led a research team at the Harvard Medical School and,
- because of his research results, was considered a potential Nobel Prize candidate.

At Harvard, Rajewsky built up a research team of 16 post-doctorates studying RNA-interference – a technology discovered only in 1998, which appears to subdue certain genetic illnesses in the body. This brings another theme into perspective: the faculty's quality can be raised by capitalizing on laws in other countries which tend to throw away knowledge, rather than make it grow.

In 2006 the University of California, at Santa Barbara, hired the internationally renowned environmental scientist Ernst Ulrich von Weizsäcker, then 67 years old, as dean – since in Germany there were no more any interesting employments for the former director of the Wuppertal Institute for Climate, Environment and Energy. Bert Hölldobler,

22 *Focus*, 30, 2006.

a German behavioural biologist and sociobiologist, moved to the US in 2004 at the age of 68. At Arizona State University, he led an international team which set milestones in its field of research.

'Only the effort counts [in the US]. If a senior scientist is capable of getting funding for research work, one can work as long as one likes,' explained von Weizsäcker in the aforementioned *Focus* article. He also stated that he appreciated the US model for research funding. Anyone who cannot survive in the competition for funding slowly loses influence and, in the end, his or her position.

Could accreditation have changed these throwaway policies? The answer is 'yes', because it would have pressed home the message that skill should not be separated from the university's body of knowledge because of stupid laws about age limits. For the increasing number of European scientists who don't want to retire, the EU has become an alien environment. Peter Gruss, the president of Max-Planck-Institute, says that this strict age regulation is absurd, because it hurts the country.[23]

The process of accreditation will work best if it is coordinated with the goals the economy sets for itself and the government wants to achieve. One of the best examples is provided by post-World War II Japan and the policy followed by Saburo Okita, one of the architects of the Japanese economic miracle, who has also been instrumental in creating a new university system.

Education has been a primary channel for Japan's post-World War II ambition. To rebuild their factories from the ashes of war, companies actively searched for new workers with good basic schooling, particularly in mathematics, on a level well above their counterparts in America and Europe – the markets they were targeting for their exports.

- They sought achievement in a country where achievement was honoured, and
- they realized that the best education was the key to their goals.

Working to their advantage was the fact that the demobilized generation was exceptionally well prepared for an industrial society which became increasingly meritocratic. In planning the revival of the university system, emphasis was placed on producing engineers which, as Saburo Okita and his men realized, was of the essence.

- The world in which Japan had to compete was increasingly technological, and
- only by capitalizing on the mathematical and scientific skills of the young generation would the country get ahead of the curve.

According to David Halberstam:

> *If the West produced scientists who were more original, the Japanese countered by producing more good competent engineers ... more than any industrialized country in the world. To encourage entry into engineering, incentives were offered to promising young students. In the ten years after the war, Okita practically doubled the number of engineer graduates.*[24]

---

23 The early retirement of men aged 60 to 64 is about 30 per cent in America and Japan, 32 per cent in Britain, 58 per cent in Germany, and a whopping 78 per cent in France.

24 David Halberstam, *The Reckoning*, William Morrow, New York, 1986.

Just as important was assuring the quality of the engineering schools and obviously of the faculty. This objective, too, was met, partly by learning from World War II. Supported by the government, Japanese universities had to take radical measures, and their action is a blueprint for *the rebirth of Europe's universities*.

## 7. Teaching Novel Areas Like Personal Finance

Personal finance, budgeting and accounting should be taught at high school. It is inconceivable that in a debt-ridden society, with many families having only one parent, that the parent does not know how to make a family budget, keep a balance sheet and update basic accounting records.

Based on personal experience, as well as that of peers, clients and suppliers, I am convinced that financial education is critical for carrying out meaningful, well-informed decisions. Personal knowledge of finance and accounting counts for a great deal. Financial advisors can help, but they should not be given free rein.

Every modern person should be trained in financial management, from budgeting to contracting debt and to the management of assets. Moreover, financial products are quite often complicated, and in many cases the quality of contractual information leaves much to be desired. Difficulties in understanding financial products are often the result of the instruments' sophistication, but may more basically be due to a lack of fundamental financial know-how.

It would be a tall order for the high-school system to teach these subjects, when its curricula are in regression and it cannot even teach mathematics properly, as we have already seen. But it is an absolute aberration that, no matter in which subject they specialize, university graduates don't know:

- how to distinguish assets from liabilities;
- what obligations and costs come with leveraging;
- the risks associated with indebtedness (including credit cards);
- how far a person and a company can depend on banks and the money market;
- how to calculate intrinsic value and cash flow';
- how to make and balance the personal, family and company budget;
- how to keep at least basic accounting records, and read the books;
- the fundamentals underpinning finance and investments (more on this later).

Take credit card debt as an example. In a short speech he gave on 22 May 2009 at the White House, on the occasion of signing a new bill to curtail credit card abuses, Barack Obama said that one out of five Americans pays interest of over 25 per cent for his or her credit card debts. That's worse than the worst usury, particularly at a time when the interest rate fixed by the Fed is zero-point-zero. It is also evidence that this one out of five people is plain illiterate in financial terms.

In the background of this highway robbery lies the fact that, according to a 2008 survey, 40 per cent of American credit card holders do not pay the full amount due every month on the credit card they use most often, despite the punitive interest rates charged by credit card companies. Responding to a survey, nearly one out of three said they had no idea what the interest rate on their credit card was.[25]

It makes absolutely no sense – in any walk of higher education – to be a university graduate and look at money as the great taboo. 'Buy what thou hast no need of, and ere long thou shalt sell thy necessities,' advised Benjamin Franklin; but people just don't know how much money they spend, and how they will pay back debt. This is part of the reasons for the subprime mortgage scandal and the huge economic crisis of 2007–2011.

Financial education is inseparable from the ability to live in a modern society – starting with personal finance and proceeding with banking, deposits, loans, interest rates, investments and the economy. Young people must learn about them in their higher education, because without such knowledge they put themselves at personal disadvantage.

Just as an example of where financial illiteracy may lead, in terms of percentage of US house loans, subprime borrowers on adjustable interest rates represented 7 per cent of the total but accounted for more than 40 per cent of the foreclosures. This is not surprising because:

- every politician talks about education,
- but nobody has bothered to ensure that schools are teaching children about money.

Not only children, of course; also grown-ups in evening courses. In Britain, a research project by the Financial Services Authority (FSA) established that 25 per cent of adults do not realize that their pensions are invested in the stock market. As this statistic suggests, financial illiteracy is not limited to the inability to make a family budget or to sign up mortgages, but is pervasive in all financial matters and in all age groups and income brackets.

'Subprime is a mere symptom,' says Niall Ferguson of Harvard University, noting that many of the students he has taught in the 'best universities in the world, including MBA programs, don't even know the difference between the nominal and real interest rate.'[26] Because money is the red blood cells of a modern economy, Ferguson suggests that financial literacy is more pressing than ever. In addition, governments have relegated more of the personal financial responsibility to individuals:

- by encouraging homeownership,
- by promoting personally-managed retirement accounts, and
- through other means which are leveraging society's status.

It is no less true, however, that the educational system deserves a great deal of the blame for the financial illiteracy of its graduates. Whether at high school or university, students learn nothing about personal financial instruments, the need for a nest egg in savings, let alone about finance and the economy at large.

If *personal finance* should be a required course at high school, what I call *more sophisticated finance* should be a required (not elective) course at university level – for all professions. University graduates must be knowledgeable people in derivative financial

25 *The Economist*, 5 April 2008.

26 Idem.

instruments; and most particularly in risk control. They should also be able to appreciate the evolving complexity of these instruments.

'The growth and complexity of off-balance sheet activities and the nature of credit, price and settlement risk they entail, should give us all cause of concern,' says Gerald Corrigan, former president of the New York Federal Reserve. 'Sophisticated trading strategies and complex instruments, by their nature, require robust risk management and controls,' adds C. Feldberg, also of the New York Federal Reserve; and W. Heyman of the Securities and Exchanges Commission was to say: 'I cannot believe that all these derivatives people are competent.'[27]

Since the 1990s it has become a fad that mathematics departments convert themselves into fountains of financial modelling. This is done by mathematics professors who don't know a dry fig about finance, and teach as much to their students.[28] The result is incomprehensible equations which have nothing to do with financial reality, embedded into weak and unstable models which don't serve marking to market;[29] they only mark to myth.

'We do not know the web of interconnections between banks established through derivatives,' suggested Alexandre Lamfalusssy, a former general manager of the Bank for International Settlements and of the European Monetary Institute (predecessor of the European Central Bank).[30] With the 2007 subprime crisis, this web of interconnections became the road to disaster as bank after bank revealed huge losses because of securitized instruments it bought from other institutions.

'26-year olds with computers are creating financial hydrogen bombs,' said Felix Rohatyn,[31] formerly senior executive of Lazard Brothers and US ambassador to Paris. There are competent people who could have taken care to diffuse that bomb, but in the George W. Bush 'go-go' years they were not given the authority they needed to be in charge, including information on causes and effects, as well as warnings about the level of exposure. University students should be taught all the facts about the 2007–2011 deep economic crisis.

## 8. Reversing the Trend of Functional Illiteracy in the Knowledge Society

In the early 1990s the Bank of Wachovia[32] carried out a study on the obsolescence of know-how in the banking industry. According to its findings, a banker who does not renew and update his or her skills over five years loses 50 per cent of his or her professional ability. This statistic dramatizes the fact that:

- in our society functional illiteracy moves by leaps and bounds, and

27 All quotes from notes taken by the author during business meetings.

28 Which is financial illiteracy of a different kind.

29 Which in practice means establishing the fair value of an asset by means of market pricing.

30 Personal communication.

31 *Institutional Investor*, July 1992.

32 A super-regional bank in the south-east of the United States, which in 2008 merged into Wells Fargo.

- even university graduates can become functional illiterates if they don't maintain their skills through lifelong learning.

This is one of a modern university's top-most responsibilities through evening courses (a university extension programme) as well as special offerings which – depending on what they aim to achieve – may last a week, a month, or a few months. There is a crying need for wiping out functional illiteracy which makes a mockery of the 'knowledge society' label.

Functional illiteracy is not limited to the professionals. It reaches all the way from board level to the production floor. According to some estimates, functional illiteracy in the United States runs as high as 20 per cent. In spite of its notoriously difficult language Japan has a much lower level; some say it is close to only 1 per cent. The Japanese outpace other nations for the following reasons:

- They have been trained to understand and apply the information they possess.
- They are skilful in cultivating and refining creative discoveries made by others.
- They are quick in taking advantage of the leading technologies of the day.

This rapid and profitable adaptation has become a 'must' because new developments accelerated the obsolescence of know-how during the last couple of decades. The life cycle of what we learn and what we know has shortened. To avoid losing contact with the state of the art, professionals must spend a good share of their time *learning*.

- The choice is *not* between investing and non-investing in new knowledge.
- The real choice is between investing or falling behind, and quite often falling out of one's job.

Universities have a great role to play in the *lifelong learning* of professionals, just as primary and secondary schools must be active in eradicating plain illiteracy – which has recently characterized some of their own graduates. Lifelong learning is what Yehudi Menuhin answered a young person who asked him how to get to Carnegie Hall: 'Practice, practice.'

As was emphasized in section 1, every member of society has the obligation not only to prepare himself or herself to become productive and contribute to the common good, but also to keep on doing so. This is not done by wishful thinking:

- It takes steady effort to be literate and numerate across a broad range of disciplines.
- It is important for people to be exposed not only to a variety of fields, but also to many cultures and civilizations, while at the same time keeping their knowledge base fully up-to-date.

Professionals tend to think that what they have learned years ago in a school or university will see them through their active life. That's definitely untrue. Some years ago a 13-year-old boy sued the State of Massachusetts because the labour laws did not allow him to work in a computer store, given his age. The owner employed the young high-school student on a part-time basis, and he partly financed his studies through this work.

The boy was a genius. The case went to court, and the judge asked for a test of the youngster's skill and know-how. The local business community arranged for the test, which involved computer professionals from about two dozen companies. The results proved that the boy knew more about PCs than 75 per cent of the computer experts employed by these firms.

Most skills and know-how decay. The companies which take care to provide their employees with lifelong learning are in the minority, particularly in Europe. A law enacted by Georges Pompidou when he was president of France (in the early 1970s) requires that companies either spend 2 per cent of their earnings on training or pay a tax into a common training fund. That law is, however, very poorly applied.

Having been a university professor, banker and prime minister prior to becoming president of the Republic, Pompidou had correctly assessed the effects of the greatly increased internationalization and technological complexity of business on the nation and its industries. The effort to survive in a globalized market places a very high premium on the work produced by the educated elite, but:

- supremacy in know-how wears out rapidly, and,
- like Alice in *Through the Looking Glass*, professionals must run ever faster to stay in the same place.

Moreover, increased global competition makes it difficult to adopt high-cost social welfare programmes and to levy the taxes to fund them. When Reagan and Thatcher ended controls on capital flows, they left high-cost welfare states and trade-union practices naked in the ensuing gale of international competition, with disastrous results on jobs which moved massively east – all the way to China.

Back in 1990 the US government set up a Commission on the Skills of the American Workforce, which came up with some interesting findings. Most companies were weary of creating jobs calling for workers with broad-based skills and the ability to adapt to fast-changing technology and markets.[33] In other words, business was by and large lowering its sights, and society was not delivering the large-scale improvements in education and training that American industry needed.

The commission conducted in-depth studies of workplaces as well as education and training systems in the US, Denmark, Germany, Sweden, Ireland, Japan, Singapore and Sweden. The conclusion was that (except for Ireland) foreign countries provided far better schooling and job training for non-college-bound youth than the US. American youth ranked near the bottom in comparisons of school performance. Twenty years down the line, in 2010, this has become more or less generalized in Western countries.

Another interesting finding by the aforementioned commission has been that high-performance workplaces call for multi-skilled workers and employees who have good maths, science and problem-solving skills. These can readily absorb new knowledge. Technology, however, along with its production and sales requirements, changes. With people who adapt quickly to new conditions, manufacturers can:

- introduce new products on short cycle times,
- frequently switch production runs to create greater flexibility, and

33 *Business Week*, 2 July 1990.

- manage change in a way that promotes both adaptation and greater performance

These findings are most interesting, particularly since the effort to stamp out functional illiteracy at the core of this whole process. Quite clearly, schools and universities have a great role to play by establishing a steady literacy effort (andragogy), instituting knowledge-updating programmes, elaborating formal human development procedures in collaboration with industry and also ensuring that there are visible goals in order to motivate professionals to engage in lifelong learning.

## 9. Making University Management Effective

It would be ludicrous to say that the university must teach its students how to plan, if cannot plan its own business and finds it difficult to manage its own future. Planning at university level (as with every enterprise) starts by stating objectives, working out how to get there, costing everything systematically, monitoring progress and judging effectiveness. Management has six basic functions:

- forecasting
- planning
- organizing
- staffing
- directing
- controlling.

The administration of an institute of higher education poses intriguing questions with regard to forecasts and plans, foremost among them being: 'What abilities, knowledge and skills must be available at faculty and administration level to carry out courses, programmes and other activities?'

Forecasting necessarily connects to the institution's educational philosophy, by reason of its specific and fundamental nature. In any school of higher learning, this philosophy will probably change very slowly, but some of the elements associated to it will doubtless evolve over time. This should be properly reflected in the mid-range plan.

The execution of plans requires a sound organization and structure. Examples of organizational queries are:

- What functions, responsibility and authority should be associated with each position?
- What interrelationships should exist among the different positions in order to best achieve the institution's objectives?

The staffing challenge can best be confronted through able answers to the questions:

- How can the current and projected abilities, knowledge and skills used in an effective way?

- How can the products and services the university offers be translated into requirements for specific faculty, research, administrative and non-academic positions?

Behind staffing decisions stand ordinary human beings – the contributions they can make as well as their unpredictability.

Directing must account for the fact that no two universities are alike. Diversity is welcome. The requirement it poses is to study and define the pattern tailored to the institution, from its objectives to its evolution towards the desired direction.

Equally important is to study changes taking place in market demand for the educational services that universities are expected to provide. It's a fair bet that not only classroom teaching but also auxiliary services may (and often do) need restructuring. These include, but are not limited to:

- professional, social and personal guidance for students,
- adult education opportunities and faculty recycling,
- research for corporations and government units, and more.

Directing requires assigning priorities; deciding on facilities and translating these into action plans for predicting future registration by faculty, as well as deciding on courses and programmes. Forecasts on human resources by faculty, programme and course must be critically evaluated, and proposals for new projects, as well as for laboratory extensions and renewals, reviewed and approved or changed.

Part of ordinary administration is the establishment of time schedules, decisions on grants to undergraduate and graduate students based on performance criteria, the hiring of supporting personnel and plenty of other issues. Campus(es), real estate, buildings and other assets have to be managed, and this requires funds, though some of these facilities may also produce an income.

Without doubt, a most important activity in university management, which should carefully match the evolution of operational objectives, is financing. The budget is a financial plan. Typically included in income sources are:

- student fees,
- research funding,
- state support,
- income from real estate and investments,
- endowments to be used for both capital reserves and operating funds.

An integral part of financial planning is assessing courses, programmes, projects, structural issues, staff and the upkeep of facilities. All these inputs are important in determining the total funds required. Costs must be scrutinized and operating funds, as well as forecasts of obtainable operating funds, critically evaluated by source. Another basic mission is:

- establishing priorities of financing requirements and
- adjusting these to projected attainable funds.

Quarterly, annual, medium-term and longer-range financial plans are a 'must'. Operational plans not backed by appropriate financial resources are mere daydreams.

An annual budget is not enough. There should be also a rolling year financial plan and a five-year plan – as a minimum.

Quite often, planning is conceived as simply a mater of future projections. This should not be the case. Planning and implementation are highly interrelated. Effective planning should be detailed in matching goals and resources, leading to implementation and making possible the exercise of timely and focused management control.

Planning and implementation activities are interrelated and interactive. Therefore good coordination can be achieved only through advance consideration of the problems that will be encountered. By involving all interested parties through appropriate participation in the planning processes, control becomes so much more effective. The reader should, however, note that while planning, implementation and control are closely interconnected,

- planning proceeds from objectives to financing, but
- implementation progresses precisely in the opposite direction, from financing to objectives, and
- control is exercised on deliverables, their quality and adherence to plans.

In management jargon the relation between planning and implementation is known as means–end inversion. Planning must follow choices made, and directives given, by the board of trustees, the university president and members of the top administration – and, in return, all of them should stand behind and support the plan's implementation. Quite often plans are not implemented because those responsible do not have the interest or support of the aforementioned people and bodies. Successful implementation requires that:

- each party knows what the goals are;
- everyone identifies himself with the goals; and
- the board, administration, faculty, alumni, students and the community provide positive support.

This in turn requires that the administration carefully defines duties and responsibilities; foresees the required action roles and prepares the various stakeholders for their tasks; anticipates major problems and prepares early for solutions; resolves controversial issues; provides effective controls to channel the effort in the desired directions; and drives towards achievement – without wasting time or resources.

All this is so much easier to implement if those responsible for the university's fortunes have clear conceptions of their own purpose and utilize the best means for accomplishment. Clarity of educational purposes and programmes, as well as a factual outline of the steps required to facilitate institutional growth and improvement, are an integral part of good administration.

To facilitate acceptance and achievement, the planning process itself must be planned, which means well thought-out in advance with a proper relationship established between planning steps and action, always keeping in mind that implementation activities affect the plans. Each institution of higher education should explore this interplay within its own environment because it marks out the nature of progress towards purpose, revealing:

- opportunities,

- limitations and
- the basic character of ongoing operations.

For instance, challenges may arise from the numbers of types of students the institution seeks; their educational background and application; how far and how fast they learn; how well they respond to intellectual, social, vocational, personal and moral developments the institution provides; as well as how well the skill they acquire match the business community's requirements for professionals.

Other questions affecting sound governance are much broader. What obligations, if any, does the institution have to the community in which it is located? To the state or nation? To basic research and applied research? To its faculty, non-academic staff, alumni, those who contribute to its financial support? Answers to all these queries make the formulation and adoption of objectives a fairly complex task.

The nature of other queries may vary by jurisdiction. Does the university have an obligation to provide education for all applicants? If not, where should it draw the line? What are its obligations with regard to the quality of educational offerings? Do quality obligations change as the number of applicants increases? In these and other issues, choices have to be made because, inevitably, no university can be all things to all people.

Another 'must' in terms of sound governance is promoting staff morale and performance, capitalizing on the fact that there is always satisfaction and pride in being part of a dynamic institution with clear objectives and plans for achieving them. It should always be remembered that the distance society can travel is critically influenced by the performance of its educational institutions.

# CHAPTER 4 The Devil's Advocate in University Business

## 1. Quantity or Quality in Graduate Studies?

Along with other segments of the social structure, including those of primary and secondary education (see Chapter 1), the university system faces challenges of a fundamental nature. These have been described unambiguously by Mark C. Taylor, of Columbia University, in an article published by *The New York Times*. In his opinion, graduate education is the Detroit of higher learning, and he adds that most graduate programmes in American universities:

- produce a product for which there is no market,
- develop skills for which there is diminishing demand, and
- do so at a rapidly rising cost, sometimes well over $100,000 in student loans[1] (see section 4).

Taylor is right in his critique. The first three chapters of this book have delivered the same message extended over all levels of education, starting with the primary level. This is particularly true with regard to producing an unmarketable product and developing unwanted skills (the affordability of costs is discussed later in this chapter). Several reasons for this can be found at the core of the problem. The most important are as follows:

- Pushed and pulled by the mass society, universities are bent on producing quantity rather than quality, while paying lip service to costs.
- Because university education has become a status symbol, scant attention is paid to qualifications (of students and faculty alike).
- Courses, programmes and faculties have divorced themselves from the knowledge and skills necessary to an advanced society, delivering an on the basis of 'can do' rather than society's evolving requirements.

In addition, while it is only normal that parents want their children to get higher education, this cannot be said of the students themselves when they go on almost permanent strikes and demonstrate on the streets, and a good number of them never finish their studies. It is also regrettable that the university system is following rather than leading the whims of the mass society on:

- which way to go and

1 Mark C. Taylor, 'End the University as We Know It', *The New York Times*, 27 April 2009.

- how to shape up the educational challenge.

As Taylor aptly points out, the university model of mass production has led to separation between the goals to be attained and the effort invested in doing so. The academics have essentially become trustees 'not of a branch of the sciences, but of limited knowledge that all too often is irrelevant for genuinely important problems'. And while the returns decrease (see section 2), the costs soar (see sections 3 and 4).

Where I disagree with Taylor is in his reference to cause and effect related to graduate students. He says that without underpaid graduate students to help with teaching and in laboratories, universities could not sustain the current model. True enough, without this low-cost and relatively good-quality labour the institutes of higher education would not be able to instruct their exploding undergraduate populations. But, speaking from personal experience:

- what the graduate students don't make in wages, they do get in learning, and
- what is called 'slave labour' in academia provides a large amount of *tacit knowledge*, if the graduate student is lucky enough to work with a highly qualified professor.

At the same time, however, Taylor is right when he states that too much emphasis on specialization is not producing the crop of graduates that the twenty-first-century society needs. Hence his call for restructuring the curriculum, beginning with graduate programmes and proceeding with undergraduate programmes. I would rather start immediately with primary and secondary education – doing precisely the opposite of what Rose proposed (see Chapter 1).

Mark Taylor's solution is that of abandoning the so-called division-of-labour model of separate departments because it is obsolete, and replacing it with a web of courses that are cross-disciplinary. Nevertheless, one has to graduate in something. One cannot get a degree in generalities.

In the early 1950s Llewelyn M.K. Boelter, my dean at UCLA Engineering who had set up engineering education from scratch at the University of California in Los Angeles, adopted precisely the structure Taylor suggests – but within the engineering curriculum. The College of Engineering was not divided into departments, and its students were advised to diversify their skills by taking a number of courses on campus. Through this diversification in student knowledge:

- Boelter aimed to make engineering education focused on problem solutions, and
- aimed to ensure that the graduates were able problem-solvers, rather than just degree-holders.

Mark Taylor proposed 'sunset clauses' which would either bring up every course in the curriculum for re-evaluation or eliminate it automatically. Under Llewelyn Boelter's leadership each course was evaluated on a regular basis, thus avoiding curriculum obsolescence. Depending on the results of this evaluation, courses were continued, significantly changed depending on their utility and appeal, or abolished.

In addition, although Mark Taylor's article in *The New York Times* is excellent there are two important issues in university education that I feel are missing and should be addressed. This is essential if current trends towards quantity at the expense of quality in university education, both in America and Europe, are to be reversed. These trends are:

- the ever increasing size of institutes of higher education and
- the regrettable movement away from a policy of small (under ten graduates) seminars towards big classes.

Today's tendency to increase universities' production capacity is a response to the growing size of the student population; and higher education institutions themselves are also multiplying in number. This quantitative explosion reflects not only Detroit's wrong policies, but also the (equally wrong) policies of European, Japanese, Korean, Indian, Chinese and other automobile manufacturers.[2] We all know where this has led.

Worldwide, automobile production capacity stands at about 90 million vehicles per year. However, in normal times the global market demand stands at 55 to 60 million vehicles, or less than two-thirds of available production. Worse still, the current slump in demand for automobiles has created more than 50 per cent overcapacity. (In 2009 Americans are expected to buy less than 10 million cars versus the 14 million or so purchased in 'normal' years. In Europe and Asia overcapacity is higher.)

Practically the same pattern of overcapacity exists in universities, as governments race ahead of themselves and of demand, increasing the institutes' size. Institutes of higher education have multiplied like mushrooms after rain. Even schools tuned to provide education at 'skills level', teaching foremen, became universities. In one stroke:

- this eliminated the teaching of urgently needed skills at middle-professional level and
- created unemployable people, because there is simply no huge increase in demand for university graduates able to match their rapidly increasing annual production.

Statistics document the thesis that universities are expanding too fast to accommodate a swelling student population, particularly in currently fashionable 'soft' subjects. Based on numbers published by *Business Week*, Table 4.1 shows a double-figure rise year-on-year in student applicants for business administration PhDs – a wave that has followed on the heels of the MBA tsunami.

**Table 4.1 The rapid rise in applications to business PhD programmes, 2009 versus 2008**

| | |
|---|---|
| University of Chicago, Booth School of Business | +40% |
| University of Pennsylvania, Wharton School | +34% |
| Columbia Business School | +27% |
| Stanford University, Graduate School of Business | +25% |
| INSEAD (Paris and Singapore) | +20% |

*Source: Business Week*, 1 June 2009.

2 Year-on-year 2008–2009 car sales rose 48 per cent in China, according to a Merrill Lynch study.

The accompanying article in *Business Week* notes that completing such a programme takes five years on average, and strains the universities' resources. The economic crisis brought along tight budgets, and universities cannot absorb many more doctoral candidates than those already enrolled. In addition, many of these students get tuition waivers and stipends which:

- deprive the institute of higher education from the income it needs and
- have a negative after-effect on the quality of education, whether there is a rapid increase in faculty, a substantial increase in class size or both at the same time.

It also puts to rest the urgently necessary redirection of policy away from quantity and towards higher quality. The challenge is formidable because this issue is more than 90 per cent political, and whether we talk of the European Union or of the United States, political leadership is (at best) wanting. Instead, plenty of attention is paid to the wrong issues – which are handled in the worst possible way, as the following section documents.

## 2. Much Ado About Nothing: The Bologna Initiative

The careful reader will recall from Chapter 1 that European education ministers met in Bologna to rethink and harmonize university programmes. This took place in 1999, when they also promised to forge a new era for universities within a decade. Ten years down the line, this 'new era' is not yet in sight.

Superficially, but only superficially, some things have been done. For instance, certain obstacles that stopped students studying abroad for a term, or getting degrees recognized, have been tackled. Under the Erasmus Programme, many students have been travelling to other EU countries for between a term and a year, but they have often found their universities reluctant to give them credit for it. This issue has been partly addressed, but:

- is it enough and
- what have been the negatives of the Bologna Initiative?

Critics say that, without a system of accreditation of universities, programmes, courses and faculties, the aforementioned freedom of movement to study abroad – which is good on paper – can become quite counterproductive. Today, the quality of higher education varies so widely from one university to the next, let alone from country to country, that:

- it is simply not possible to know what worth the course taken abroad, despite the 'diploma supplement', and
- even the labels of programmes and courses can be misleading, because there are no standards against which to gauge their content.

In my judgement, the worst after-effect on educational quality is that many EU universities have tried to cram bachelors degrees into just six terms (three years). Combined with chopping off one year from high-school studies, this makes the bachelor's degree a poor shadow of the formerly prestigious European university diploma. However, as explained in section 1, the university system is crying out for precisely the opposite: a thorough restructuring and strengthening of degrees, not a weakening of them while putting some cherries on top of the cake. Yet there was no sign of any awareness of ten years of negative incentives and lamentable results in education on 28 April 2009 when 46 EU and other education ministers from neighbouring countries gathered in Leuven, Belgium, to declare the Bologna Initiative a triumph. A triumph of what?

One of the cherries on the Bolognese cake has been the announcement of a standardized diploma supplement, giving details of what students have learnt. Another cherry is that three-year bachelor's degrees will be followed by a two-year master's degree (which is becoming a sort of EU academic rule). But nothing has been set regarding the quality and depth of learning at:

- bachelor's
- master's or
- doctoral levels.

It is a great disappointment that uniform EU quality standards are nowhere to be seen on the radar screen, having been substituted by labels. In fact, to my knowledge, educational standards are being lowered, not raised, and they are heavily manipulated

(In one of the better known EU technical universities a professor told me of a plan for a new 'master's degree on spreadsheets', in which the student will be taught how to use a spreadsheet – not necessarily understanding its structure and philosophy. In response, I couldn't stop myself asking whether the master's was intended to be at kindergarten level.)

One of the key issues that should have been addressed by the Bologna Initiative is the basic qualifications for admission to undergraduate and graduate programmes. Another is how long the bachelor's and master's degrees should take in each branch of science or art. There is no EU rule or even roadmap on these issues. For instance, the Bologna Initiative specifies two years for a master's, but an advertisement in *The Economist* (6 March 2010) promises to produce 'world class economic analysts' in one year. This miracle is (supposedly) performed by Barcelona GSE.

Another key question is how fast a university can grow and still maintain high educational standards. An example is provided by another advertisement in the same issue of *The Economist*, posted by a known university searching for faculty staff because it has doubled its turnover over the last six years. That means an increase of over 16 per cent per year. Is quality of education sustainable under these conditions? I doubt it.

Still another challenge comes from the fact that most of the tools, models and theories put into practice by different curricula – be they economic, finance, engineering or physics – are never more than just parts of a gigantic bow. An investment letter sent to subscribers points out that faculties '[a]re not looking beyond conventional methods because of their ego and pride'. The writer of this investment letter presses the point that he feels sorry:

> *... for all these MBA graduates and high-paid fund managers that, after studying all the theories and models, still don't have anything unique to offer, at least nothing that comes close to the fees they charge the clients and the risks they take. They always compare their performances with S&P, and if they beat the index, they feel like they have won the world war!*

The root of all this lies in the fact that students spend too much time in theory while practical experience takes a back seat. I have learnt from my professional practice that:

- countless so-called financial professionals have never come up with any advantageous model that can guide investors over the longer term, and
- there are cases of Doctors of Philosophy with over ten years of university studies, who don't even know how to cash a cheque. (A real-life case can be found in the Appendix to this chapter.)

A crucial issue that the Bologna Initiative failed to address is who is going to pay the costs associated with a rapidly growing body of European students? (See also sections 3 and 4.) That's a major headache for rectors, deans and administrators of institutions of higher education, as the formula used since the end of World War II that 'the taxpayer pays all' is broken.

- Experience shows that when universities depend on taxpayers, their independence and standards suffer, and,
- with government budgets deeply in the red, it's a fair bet that taxpayer financing will become increasingly unsatisfactory, with detrimental effects on the quality of education.

The European universities that have joined the Bologna Initiative (in other words, practically all of them) should have moved as a big lobby to push through parliaments a significant increase in student fees. Only those who study the hard sciences and who finish the year with high grades – rather than spending their time loafing, and extending a four-year course of study into ten – should qualify for tuition waivers. The top 5 per cent of the class is a good target.

Another headache comes from the fact that during the last 30 years, throughout Europe and America, children growing up to become pupils and students are pampered and indulged. They don't learn to accept discipline and hard work as the way to achieve success in life. In addition, the degree of this pampering and indulgence varies considerably from country to country, and the educational system has adapted to it by looking the other way. Most unfortunately, this has led many students to become lazy, defiant of authority and with little respect for learning – which is contagious. The evidence lies in statistics which show that a large number of students who start university studies never complete them – almost 60 per cent according to OECD statistics (see Chapter 3). The people who gathered in Bologna in 1999 failed to recognize that:

- the reality associated with successful completion of studies is seldom a simple story, and
- the unstoppable explosion of the university system makes it hard to find truly first-rate minds for the faculties.

Had the Bologna Initiative provided EU-wide rules and regulations, including regulations on entry, annual examinations and a thesis at end of studies, it would have helped universities trim this 60 per cent failure rate by half (as a first step), and it would also have supplied evidence of serious work on restructuring. However, these would have had to have been:

- firm rules signed up by all participating 46 education ministers and their governments,
- validated by statistics of, and telling examples on, successful completion of studies in terms of results.

In addition, an initiative aimed at improving university education (Bolognese or otherwise) has to be accompanied by ways and means aimed at making higher learning more agile, adaptive and imaginative than it is today, as well as assuring the quality of faculty, laboratories and libraries. This can never be achieved through words, labels and a ten-year celebratory gathering. Only a rigorous pan-European accreditation system, whose essence has been presented in Chapter 3, can give the message that something significant is happening.

The pros say that some governments embraced the Bologna Initiative to give some momentum to reforms they wanted anyway. For instance, shorter, more work-related degrees appealed to the German government which (like other EU authorities) is faced with 'professional students' hanging on for years at taxpayers' expense.[3] But the German and other governments are wrong if they think they can kill two birds with one well-placed stone.

(It is also interesting to note that the relatively mild – and inconsistent – changes in higher education did not please those students who look at free education as an opportunity for plundering. The proof is that they have taken to the streets in France, Italy, Spain and Greece in protest. Neither is it bringing unanimity in faculties, as many professors think their aim is to privatize universities.)

The message that all this commotion provides is that, whether or not the Bologna Initiative is regarded as a sort of 'free-market fix', it will not solve a chronic problem with the higher education system – starting with the students, quality of knowledge and preparation for further studies. Students raised in primary and secondary schools without appropriate parental guidance and within a rather substandard learning environment as well as high drop-out rates (see Chapter 3), cannot do well in universities.

- Only an extraordinary personal effort could stop and turn around this drift, and
- this is something the majority of students are unable or unwilling to provide.

One of the positives of the Bolognese gatherings has been the mild endorsement of more autonomy for universities. This is welcome because it can lead to greater freedom in hiring, promotion and pay, but most governments find this difficult to deliver because of political opposition. Moreover, the vision of self-governing institutes of higher education cannot subtract from one big reason for European universities' decline: money[4] – as well as the fact that although 'more money' may well be needed,

- no two parties agree among themselves from where it should come, and

---

3 This practice of 'professional students' should be ended by reforming admission and readmission criteria, not by reducing the years of schooling, which penalizes those who want to learn.

4 More on this in sections 3, 4 and 5.

- money alone is not going to solve the quality issue, because no problem has ever been solved by throwing money at it.

In conclusion, whether or not the participants to the *Bologna Initiative* appreciate it, the quality of higher education will never be raised without a most significant increase in merit, pay, accountability and transparency – a statement just as valid for the faculty as for the students (in terms of scholarships and prizes). Without any doubt, the biggest problems in education today – at all levels – is how to attract and use talent.

This is written in full appreciation of the fact that our mass society has an astonishing record of neutralizing reform-minded academics and politicians. Entrenched vested interests and inertia combine to squash most promises of improvement. For the sake of the young generation, this awful policy must end. But is anybody listening?

## 3. Financing University Research and Education

Derek Bok, president emeritus of Harvard University, once said: 'If you think education is expensive, try ignorance.' This is a dramatic statement, and there is truth in it, but costs also matter. University education is expensive, at least to those who provide the funds, and it's a fair bet is that it will become increasingly expensive over time.

Costs matter, but not everybody appreciates that. America's Goldwater Institute draws attention to the new enemy of university education: administrative bloat. In the short timeframe of 1993 to 2007 spending on university bureaucrats at the leading 198 US universities rose much faster than spending on faculty teaching staff. As the Goldwater Institute points out:

- 'Harvard increased its administrative spending per student by 300 percent' and
- '[at] Arizona State University, almost half the full-time employees are administrators'.[5]

This is clearly a trend that must be reversed because it works to the detriment of higher education – its goals, its tradition, its teaching faculties and its students. Breaking trust can be done quickly, but re-establishing it can take time. On its own, however, cutting administrative staff costs will not solve the financial problems confronting university education – particularly for those institutions which have to go cap-in-hand to the state.

Therefore, let's start with the premise that budgets are always short, with the result that schools and universities will need more money 'tomorrow' than they are getting 'today'. This is true throughout Europe, in America and everywhere else. But the South Koreans are much more effective[6] than the Argentinians and other Latin Americans. Better management makes the difference.

Let's first look at the source of funds. In America, at least up to a point, the gap between what state governments pay and what universities need is made up privately, mainly by tuition fees and through endowments (see section 4). By contrast, practically

5 *The Economist*, 4 September 2010.

6 In terms of funds provided to primary and secondary education.

everywhere in Europe students pay almost nothing. Even in Britain the rather recently introduced tuition fees are currently (2010) capped by the government at £3,290 (€4,100, $5,300) per year.

Since 2005 Germany has allowed states to charge tuition fees of up to €1,000 ($1,400) per year. This caused an uproar. Critics said that the government was trying to foster elite universities by encouraging them to compete for money. Those who welcomed the fees as a way of diversifying funding, responded that the German government had the courage to do what the majority of governments in the EU would like to do, but didn't dare.

In the US, support by state governments to universities stands at about 1 per cent of GDP, and another 1.9 per cent of GDP is contributed through private sources. Over and above that comes federal aid in the form of sponsored research projects. These are average figures. Some states have been much more forthcoming than others, but in this century the glut of money has been turned off. The University of California System (UC) provides an example:

- In 1990 the state's General Fund support per student stood at $15,860.
- In 2009 university authorities estimated that it would drop to $7,680. The decline has been gradual but steady.[7]

Don't think that this 51.6 per cent reduction in financial support by the state is unheard of in Europe. In the European Union, over three decades, universities have seen the state's funding per student fall behind wage inflation by 1 to 2 per cent per year. At 2 per cent, compounded over 20 years, this amounts to over 46 per cent. Taking into account California's severe economic crisis of 2009, we speak of approximately the same budgetary woes.

At the same time, however, although the 2009 budgetary cuts reflect the financial problems faced by the state government in Sacramento, the trend in budgetary contributions for higher education is unmistakeably heading south. UCLA alone faced a cut of $132 million – approximately 17 per cent – from the General Fund budget.[8] The UC system as a whole is estimated to have absorbed $800 million in cuts in 2009.

To its credit, the University of California did not send delegations picketing at Sacramento, and the students did not take to the streets. To the contrary, as the letter by the chancellor of UCLA underlines, it looked at the facts and made the right decisions. The chancellor wrote: '... the financial crisis in California will, most likely, be long-lasting and require fundamental restructuring in the way UCLA operates.'[9]

This is true of practically all other universities in America, Europe and (probably) Asia. Restructuring will be painful. In 2009 it was estimated that the University of California would face cuts among its ten campuses which have been judged to be roughly equivalent to:

- 50,000 fewer students and
- perhaps 5,000 fewer faculty staff.[10]

7 Most recently available figures.

8 Quotation from the open letter by the Chancellor sent to alumni of the university.

9 Idem.

10 *The Economist*, 23 May 2009.

Downsizing takes lots of courage. Only first-class management can make such a radical decision. But, given today's realities, this is in the right direction, and those in charge must be congratulated because they did not allow things to drift or make the 'easy' decision of lowering quality of education – as second-raters would have done. The regents appreciated the fact that:

- it takes 40 years to build up a great university,
- but four or five years of indecision and drifting are enough to tear it down.

Apart the downsizing, one of the painful decisions UC had to make was to increase student fees. These provided an income of $210 million in 2009, roughly one-quarter of the system-wide deficit. In 2008–2009 other income came from research projects.

- At UCLA alone, the faculty *won* $966 million in research funding through competitive contracts and grants.
- This has been a record which kept the university ranked among America's top institutes of higher education in research.

Allow me to further amplify this last point. For American universities, research is not just a source of funds to sustain and grow a body of knowledge; it is a mark of distinction. For 15 years in a row the University of California has developed more patents than any other university in the country. There is *nothing* comparable in the European Union. Moreover, of the more than 4,000 higher education institutions in the US, only 60 research universities, public and private, have been judged worthy of membership in the prestigious Association of American Universities. Six of the UC campuses are members. No other state system has more than one.

This combination of research and higher education is an incredibly powerful process, particularly at the level of postgraduate studies. It not only helps the student body participate in the critical mass of innovators, but it also contributes a great deal of financial independence to the university. The leaders in research and education have a fairly steady channel of funds.

This brings us back to the issue of how and by whom higher education is financed. As we have already seen, together with student fees and endowments, research income represents more than two-thirds of American universities' cash flow. Here are some depressing statistics from the EU that came under discussion during professional meetings that I attended. They compare state funds to other income sources in a selected number of countries.

- In Sweden, government support is 1.5 per cent of GDP, while private contribution stands at a meagre 0.2 per cent.
- In Poland, it is 1.1 per cent of GDP for the government and 0.4 per cent for private sources.
- In France, these statistics are, respectively, 1.1 per cent and a 0.2 per cent.[11]
- In Britain, the figures are 0.9 per cent and 0.5 per cent.
- In Germany, they are 0.9 per cent and 0.2 per cent.

11 To appreciate the shortfall the reader should note that France has 1.4 million students enrolled in 82 universities.

- In Italy, they are 0.6 per cent and 0.3 per cent.

This is not intended to be a critique of what the state contributes per se. The budget for higher education put up by governments is all the taxpayer can afford, given so many other entitlements. The real shortfall in the EU is in private contributions which includes fees, research projects and endowments – in short, whatever is conspicuously absent in Europe.

The fact that the Bologna Initiative has failed not only to concentrate on student fees associated with the necessary increase in the quality of education, but also to provide valid suggestions is bad enough. But politicians, too, shy away from what it takes to restructure the universities' finances – which is, after all, their duty.[12] It is *as if* governments and politicians:

- don't understand that some of the world's oldest universities risk a future that is a lot less glorious than their past, and
- only autonomous institutions, mainly dependent on private income (such as fees, donations and investments) rather than taxpayer financing, can become flourishing universities.

This fear of touching the sacred cow of 'university education free for all' has a long legacy. Critics have a point when they say that education funding formulas in Europe are awfully outdated. They rely massively on the government because they date back to the immediate post-World War II years when household finances were in shambles. Today a large part of the population can afford vacations abroad; it should also be able – on a priority basis – to afford its children's educational expenses.[13]

## 4. Is it Possible to Right-price Higher Education?

The evidence the post-World War II years have provided – particularly with the free-of-charge higher education system, overflowing student bodies, reduced quality standards and high attrition rates because of drop-outs and unfinished studies – is that this 'free lunch' policy is a sham. Something that pretends to be 'social' and incurs no cost to the takers can be:

- neither appreciated
- nor efficient in the results it produces.

What then? *Right-pricing* is the answer, closely knit with quality of results. Right-pricing higher education is not going to be easy, let alone painless. The options have to be weighed, at the same time as making every effort to stop the ongoing downward drift

12 No doubt America's universities have their problems. Inflated tuition fees is one of them. But there are tuition waivers for the best students and, overall, America's approach looks sustainable in a way that the Old World's does not.

13 During the week-long strike of early 2009 at Thailand's airports (for reasons of internal political upheaval), it was astonishing to learn that 350,000 tourists were stranded and could not leave. People have money for far-away holidays, but not for education.

in educational standards which, from primary school to university, find themselves at the edge of a precipice of unprecedented proportions.

Pulling away from the precipice will evidently require hard, painful decisions. However, we can no more rely on business-as-usual to see us through, because it is this sort of spirit that brought us to the mess we are in. Numbers talk. Some years ago *The Economist* published an article which put the British universities' financial numbers into the right perspective.

According to these statistics, Oxford and Cambridge Universities, combined, had investments of £4 billion ($6.2 billion) and the rest of the British university system had £1.7 billion ($2.6 billion) to play with. In America, Harvard alone had twice Britain's total.[14] One does not need to be a genius to appreciate the consequences of such a huge funding gap.

Closely associated to university budgets is the question of what it costs to educate an undergraduate. Take again Oxford or Cambridge. The answer is not £3,290 ($5,000) per year – the maximum fee the government will allow the British universities to charge. A private study (carried out at the time that this issue was raised) showed that the average figure was £18,600 per student per year, excluding accommodation and catering.[15]

No governments can afford to pay that money but if they don't pay, then university studies will become exclusively an elitist affair. Since the severe economic crisis of 2007–2011, cash-strapped states in the US and countries in the EU have been more likely to slash, rather than grow, public universities' budgets. The counterpart of the steady increase in the student population is necessarily cutting posts, salaries and aid to students, which is evidently counterproductive.

It must also be appreciated that there is also another side to the coin. The swarm of graduates, whose performance has been uncertain as exams were watered down, creates an unprecedented unemployment problem. University degrees mean less and less, as there are more and more of them. Indeed, the returns of a degree have fallen significantly in recent years.

New departures are necessary and they have to do with both *financing* and *downsizing*, along the lines the University of California is establishing (see section 3). This is by no means elitism. The guiding principle should be Napoleon's 1789 principle: careers open to talent. Both pay-as-you-go schemes for sharing the financing burden and selection by using examinations as a criterion to right-size classrooms and cut costs are important ingredients of a well-rounded restructuring policy.

As with every other case in governance, somebody must assume the responsibility for new departures, and this 'somebody' is first and foremost the country's CEO (head of state or prime minister) seconded by the minister of education. The problem is that:

- few politicians have the guts for bold decisions, and
- not all governments have the authority and staying power necessary to see through major reforms.

Britain provides an example of this instability. In mid-June 2009 the so-called Department for Innovation, Universities and Skills, created in 2007 by the then newly-

14 *The Economist*, 24 January 2004.

15 It ranged from £17,000 for an arts degree to £21,000 for science.

enthroned prime minister, Gordon Brown merged with the Department for Business, Enterprise and Regulatory Reform (created that same busy summer from part of the old Department for Trade and Industry) to form a new superministry, the Department for Business, Innovation and Skills – and the kitchen sink, too.

Many critics said that if a change was due at the level of higher education and associated ministerial responsibilities, this should have been a return to the Department for Education and Skills structure (which prevailed prior to Brown's organizational acrobatics) by joining together its two halves: 'Innovation, Universities' with its alter ego, the Department for Children, Schools and Families. The prime minister's new initiatives led plenty of knowledgeable people in Britain to fear a further shift towards naked utilitarianism, with fundamental research in science sidelined in favour of commercial ventures.[16] Indeed,

- *if* the government authority itself is in a state of flux,
- *then* there is nothing to be expected in terms of right-pricing, upgrading and restructuring university education.

An analysis made by the General Accountability Office (GAO) in the US, relating to spiralling college costs, serves to document the need for greater operational efficiency. What this study found is that tuition costs can get out of control: increased tuition costs had outpaced household income gains by a 3-to-1 margin over the past 15 years, even as:

- government subsidies more or less increased and
- the volume of federal student loans rose over the same period.

Runaway expenses in education mirror the trajectory of another major expense both in America and in Europe: healthcare. Particularly in the US, healthcare costs have been growing at double-figure annual rates. Federal healthcare-related outlays have risen more than fifteenfold over the past quarter-century, with the result that they have come to represent nearly 17 per cent of GDP. A causal link between government subsidization and commodity inflation is plausible in the case of both healthcare and education because of the way in which the systems work. University fees in the US are usually adjusted to cover costs, and runaway costs in higher education present future performers with the challenge of financing their studies – as the fees become more and more substantial.

In 2009 fees stood, on average, at roughly $25,000 per year at an American private university, and nearly $7,000 at a state one for in-state tuition (that is, for residents of the state). That's not easily matched by students and their parents, but only a few universities are in a position to help as cash-strapped legislatures are no more generous as they used to be.

Moreover, the old spirit of pay-as-you-go is fading away. In the immediate post-World War II years, many young men and women of college age had taken an active hand in financing their education through part-time jobs. Graduate students could find part-time employment as teaching assistants and research assistants on campus. These were the underpaid jobs to which Professor Taylor made reference, (section 1).

16 *The Economist*, 13 June 2009.

Although the pay was not high, students could still go through knowing that a good deal of the compensation was the opportunity for hands-on experience and a higher degree. There is intrinsic value in study-and-employment. That changed with a Democrat initiative in the 1960s when the Johnson administration tried 'to make things better' through student loans promoted by the federal government. This state supermarket practice:

- turned many students into leveraged junkies, and
- easy money on credit contaminated a working population at an early age, teaching it how to load itself with debt.

Unlike their elders who worked to finance their studies, in today's America the popular 'solution' is student loans. Students can borrow money for tuition and other expenses, but this incurs problems, the most significant being that if they don't use that monetary facility most carefully, they will end up saddled with debts of up to, or more than, $100,000 at graduation.[17]

What was supposed to be the state supermarket's helping hand ended as red-ink statistics. Nearly two-thirds of US students who graduate from a four-year programme are in debt. This poses yet another problem. Most student loans come from the government, with complex eligibility criteria and a lot of paperwork, because, like credit card receivables and mortgages, student loans get securitized.

What all this suggests (indeed, the reason for bringing it to the reader's attention) is that while tuition fees at reasonable level are inevitable, there should be no copycat of the American model applied in Europe. Efficiency in the management of educational institutions calls for:

- fees supplement by an active policy of endowments and
- a great deal of attention paid to costs in conjunction with downsizing through entrance examinations and tough year-on-year exams.

As it cannot be repeated too often, *costs matter*. Like quality, reliability and availability, expenses should not be allowed to run away. In their enterprises, businesspeople worth their salt see to it that day-in, day-out a sharp knife is being used to cut costs. To paraphrase, Sam Walton, the founder of Wal-Mart, 'Never buy somebody else's inefficiency' (by paying for his high-cost goodies).

One of Walton's benchmarks was that administrative costs, taken together, should never exceed 2 per cent of business, and expenses associated with business trips should never exceed 1 per cent of purchases done. Converted to a university setting, these principles should be etched on a plate which finds itself on the desk of every president, vice president, dean and department head of every educational institution. It should also be on the desk of every prime minister, education minister and minister of finance.

---

17 Statistics from a meeting on education. According to the College Board, as an increasing number of students are borrowing to finance their education, student debt has ballooned – more than doubling in a decade to $87 billion.

## 4. The Complex Case of University Endowments

In at least one respect, college and university education is a rather safe business. Parents will always want their children to be educated, and therefore future demand is relatively easy to predict. But, as with any other business domain, there are risks. When most or all of the financing comes from the state, the biggest risk is political (as we saw in sections 3 and 4).

One of the alternatives to state support available in America is that of *private universities* which, to a very substantial extent, are independent. As such, they neither have to hang their fortunes on the state budget nor are they obliged to match the methods and curricula of state universities. They choose:

- educational criteria and
- quality standards of their own.

Private universities, particularly those best known, stake their future on *endowments*, which mainly, but not exclusively, come from their alumni. Income is also generated from existing endowments (and from research funds and student fees).

Taken together, ongoing endowments and past endowments which have been reinvested are one of the basic pillars of American higher education. Taken individually, the contributions by alumni as well as other gifts may be major or minor, but they add up to plenty. The tax laws help, as in the US:

- educational gifts are tax-deductible, and
- the state's tax indulgence makes the normal obligation to help one's *alma mater* so much easier to honour.

Until quite recently there has been nothing like it in Europe. This is now slowly changing, but tax law changes made so far for gifts to universities, like the one recently introduced in France by Nicolas Sarkozy, are still timid. Though welcome, tax deductions are capped at a relatively low level, while in some European countries the law is even counterproductive in regard to endowments; donations are taxed at 10 or 15 per cent.[18] This, too, is changing, but slowly.

Plenty of people are now aware that all that must change, but this means revamping the law of the land which depends on the government and on parliament, not on the universities' faculties. It would not happen overnight – even if some initiatives, like Germany's projected nine top universities, brought a 'big change in mentality', according to Werner Müller-Esterl, president of Frankfurt's Goethe University. Goethe hopes to build its puny €125 million endowment up to €5–6 billion ($8.4 billion) – but we shall see.[19]

An endowments initiative in the EU must definitely go beyond tax indulgences. Human nature being what it is, vanity helps the endowments culture – or, at least, it does so in America. The name of the game is *name-plating* which may apply to a building, a

---

18 For example, donations to the Swiss Philanthropic Foundation of over CHF10,000 pay 15 per cent which comes off the donation. In Canton Lucerne there is a tax deduction ceiling of CHF 5,000 for gifts to recognized institutes of education, and it is only applicable if the beneficiary institute resides in the Canton.

19 *The Economist*, 27 June 2009.

chair, a school or the whole (private) university. Harvard and Stanford are the best-known examples.

Name-plating of course, has its risks. Chairs may be restructured, with the result that the donor's name-plate disappears. But schools tend to have permanence and, having been named after a donor (for an amount which tends to vary but is usually upward of \$10 million),[20] the name-plate stays. It is protected by the law of the land.

- There is nothing like that in Europe, particularly in regard to permanence.
- Where name-plating is possible, it is usually protected through a law for commercial labels which, after a few years, no longer obliges the university to keep the label despite the privilege which had been granted.

Lack of a donation culture, the absence of tax incentives and the lack of appeal to human vanity see to it that donations, particularly major ones, are a very rare bird in the European Union's university system. Consequently there is no income from endowments worth talking about, let alone king-size endowments like those of Harvard, the largest of them all, Yale and Princeton. (The high-water mark of Harvard's endowments was \$36.9 billion.)

A minor exception to this statement is found in Britain – more precisely, at Cambridge and Oxford. In 2008 Oxford University launched a campaign to raise £1.25 billion (\$2 billion), the biggest fund-raising drive of any European academic institution standing a chance of being at least half-fulfilled.[21]

All this should not be interpreted to mean that US universities with endowments are not struggling to make ends meet. However, they are better off than their peers because they not only have a steady source of income, but also a good cushion of capital to lean on, if need be.

But are endowments well run? Generally managed as *institutional investments*, until recently US endowments have traditionally been rather conservative in their choice of securities. This, however, changed in the 1990s when they hired professional asset managers and gave them the mission to grow the capital, even by assuming significant risks.

- That policy was initially applied to the big endowments,
- but, in a relatively short time, it spread like a bushfire through the university landscape to include the small ones.

There has been plenty of 'me too' in increasing the appetite for risk, as the rapid growth of the big universities became the envy of the smaller. The latter, however, were not diversified and sophisticated enough to understand the risks embedded in complex investments.[22] It has been *as if* no one really appreciated the exposure being assumed with the so-called '*Yale strategy*' – namely:

- investing in the 'best' hedge funds[23] and private-equity firms, and

20 A few years ago Columbia University had put up its Business School for name-plating for \$50 million.

21 John Bingham, 'Oxford University Launches "Historic" Fundraising Drive', *Daily Telegraph*, 28 May 2008, at: http://www.telegraph.co.uk/education/2040948/Oxford-University-launches-historic-1.25-billion-fundraising-drive.html.

22 Which does not mean that the big universities understood it either.

23 Whatever this means ....

- taking on an inordinate amount of risk exposure, in a race to be a star performer in terms of return on investment.

With the economic crisis, banking crisis and credit crunch of 2007–2011, the result has been an unmitigated disaster. Particularly bleak were the 2008 results. Worst hit of all was Yale University's endowment, second largest to the tune of $22 billion. Its 'winner takes all' strategy (imitated by many other universities, charitable foundations and other parties) has been blamed for the torrent of red ink.[24]

Results were stellar in the good times. For some years, Yale University's endowment posted double-figure returns. In fiscal year 2000 it gained 41 per cent. Institutional investors marvelled. The fund's manager wrote a book about it. But in December 2008 Yale's president announced that the value of the endowment had fallen 25 per cent since June that same year[25] – and it hit –33 per cent by the time the blood–letting stopped. Bad news, but not unusual. A study of 235 American universities found that:

- donors' money flowed under the bridge while the guards were asleep by the switch, and
- their endowments dropped, on average, by 24 per cent in the last six months of 2008.

Between end of June 2008 and end of December of that year, Harvard lost 22 per cent of its huge endowment, eventually shrinking by 30 per cent until it turned around.[26] At Stanford University, which featured the third largest losses (after Yale and Harvard), the president, provost and other senior executives took a 10 per cent pay cut. Williams College saw its endowment plunge 27 per cent in 2008; at Wesleyan University it tumbled by 24 per cent.

Underlying these hefty losses was the fact that most of the Ivy League endowments significantly increased the allocation to illiquid assets during the good years – according to some estimates, to over 37 per cent of their funds.[27] With hindsight, many experts, like Bill Gross of Pimco, criticized the 'Yale strategy' and its policy of heavily investing in illiquid assets. Other critics pointed out that little attention was paid to the fact that the value of risky investments, particularly in private equity and hedge funds, can be

---

24 Another negative for universities has been the fact that paying investment managers too much in salary and bonuses creates stress on the faculty side, leading to friction between those benefiting from the windfall (the endowment managers) and the less well-paid faculty staff.

After two Harvard endowment managers each earned $34 million in 2003, the university capped future compensation to $25 million per year – still a hefty sum. But see Steven Syre, '6 Harvard Investment Managers Earn $26.9m', *Boston Globe*, 20 December 2008, at: http://www.boston.com/business/articles/2008/12/20/6_harvard_endowment_managers_earn_269m/.

25 'Web Update: Yale Announces 25 Percent Drop in Endowment', 16 December 2008, at: http://www.dailyprincetonian.com/2008/12/12/22446/.

26 Ibid. By December 2008 Harvard was rumoured to be trying to raise $1.5 billion by selling some of its limited partnerships in private equity funds, fuelling speculation that as the market dived it was facing a tight cash-flow situation.

27 Just for the record, by 2006 Yale was aiming to invest a staggering 69 per cent of its endowment in illiquid 'alternative assets' like hedge funds, 'strategic' private equity, real estate property, forests and more. *The Economist*, 13 December 2008.

clobbered. In addition, the belief that 'alternative investments' could prevent investors from losing money in bear markets is very false.[28]

## 6. Promoting Not-for-Profit Foundations as Partners of Higher Education

Endowments under the wings of universities are not the only way in which a private citizen can assist the quality of higher education. It is always wrong to limit one's imagination in designing ways and means that will help in raising educational standards. A good alternative to endowments is independent not-for-profit foundations working as partners to universities. Allow me to offer a personal example.

The Dimitris N. Chorafas Foundation was established in March 1992 (it will soon be 20 years old), in collaboration with the Swiss Academy of Engineering Sciences, Swiss Academy of Humanities and Social Sciences, Swiss Academy of Medical Sciences and the Swiss Academy of (Natural) Sciences. In its first years of operation the Foundation awarded two annual prizes, each amounting to CHF100,000 (roughly $95,000 per prize), for outstanding applied research.

- The focus of the prizes has been on nature, man and his responsibilities.
- The awards have been given in collaboration with the four Swiss Academies of Sciences, in an equal number of scientific fields, without regard to gender, religious beliefs or nationality.

The Foundation's awards targeted extraordinary scientific achievements in computers and communications technology, knowledge engineering, free-market financial products, risk management, the promotion of understanding between different cultures and societies, control of population explosion, prevention of mental and physical disabilities, long-term preservation of natural resources, and environmental protection.

This emphasis was chosen in appreciation of the fact that family planning and safeguarding nature have become key areas of scientific research, even more than developing and using high technology. At the same time, attention has been paid to the crucial concept that researchers must continually confront the consequences of their work on man and nature. Prize winners had to prove the following:

- They are aware of the consequences of their work for man and his environment.
- They are ready to assume personal responsibility for what they are doing.

The willingness to accept the moral obligations of being a scientist has been a feature that made the Foundation's prizes unique. For this reason, as a rule, the prizes were primarily awarded to individuals, not to organizations.

To guarantee the global perspective of these prizes, and their multi-disciplinary character, the Foundation worked in partnership with the Conference of the Swiss Scientific Academies which undertook a strict selection process. The Conference of the

28 D.N. Chorafas, *Alternative Investments and the Mismanagement of Risk*, Macmillan/Palgrave, London, 2003.

four Academies administered the prize competition throughout the world, and run the secretariat of the Foundation.

Selection committees nominated by the Swiss Academies of Sciences examined candidates and their work in each prize category. Prize winners were selected by the board of the Foundation based on the proposition made by the Conference of the Swiss Scientific Academies. Examples are:

- Fischer Black (finance prize) of Alfred P. Sloan School of Management, MIT, for his 'Black-Scholes algorithm for options pricing'.
- Tibor Vamos (engineering prize) of the Computer and Automation Institute, Hungarian Academy of Sciences, for 'Implementation of knowledge engineering in edge detection algorithms applied to the human nervous system'.
- Sheldon J. Segal (medicine prize) of the Population Council, New York, for 'Development of the implantable contraceptive Norplant, as aid to birth control'.
- Jakob Jakobsson (environmental prize) of the Marine Research Institute, Reykjavik, for 'Preservation and sustainable management of fish populations in northeast Atlantic'.
- Hans-Peter Grünenfelder (environmental prize) of the Swiss Foundation for Maintenance of Genetic Resources, for 'Rescuing, safe-guarding and preserving in situ genetic resources selected and used in agricultural development'.

Since 1996 the Foundation's awards have been granted directly to prize winners selected by partner universities. These awards target the best doctoral students selected by each partner university and are confirmed by the board of the Foundation. Each award is of $4,000, unless the partner university chooses to split the prize between two students. Selection is made among a statistically valid sample of candidates.

There have been 25 to 33 prizes per year, the exact number depending on the candidates retained for the prizes by partner universities in Europe, America and Asia – namely (in alphabetical order):

- City University London
- Ecole Normale Supérieure
- Erasmus University Rotterdam
- Hebrew University of Jerusalem
- Hiroshima University
- Karolinska Institute
- London Business School
- Massachusetts Institute of Technology (MIT)
- National Technical University of Athens
- Politechnico di Milano
- Purdue University
- Swiss Federal Institute of Technology Lausanne (EPFL)
- Swiss Federal Institute of Technology Zürich (ETHZ)
- Technical University of Berlin
- Technical University of Budapest
- Technical University of Munich
- Technical University of Vienna
- Tokyo Institute of Technology

- University of California, Los Angeles (UCLA)
- University of Fribourg
- University of Ottawa
- University of Toronto
- Weizmann Institute of Science.

Initially, in 1996, in continuation of the fields of scientific work to which the Foundation devoted itself in 1992–1995 in association with the Swiss Academies of Sciences, the annual prizes were divided into four groups of equal weight: systems engineering and information technology; finance, risk management and rocket science; environmental protection and birth control; and the physical sciences. Over the years, however, there has been a great deal of evolution in prize themes, as evidenced by research projects which cover a wide area of scientific disciplines (more on this later).

- The number one goal of the prizes is to reward exceptional performance.
- The Number two goal is to encourage future contributions to science and technology.
- The number three goal is to help in completing a higher degree and/or significant research project.

Typically, a faculty committee at each partner university selects the prize winner from a statistically valid sample of candidates, which helps to introduce an element of competition. In all cases, along with the complete file of the chosen prize winners, the Foundation needs a shortlist with names of the other candidates who were considered but not retained, and their field(s) of research and study.

Another statutory requirement for awarding prizes is that the candidates must be of good moral standing and should give evidence that they have considered the further-out aftermath of the work they have been doing. Further details regarding the choice of the prize winner are the partner universities' own. This permits a greater degree of flexibility. The Foundation, however, reserves the right to examine the qualifications of each proposed prize winner since there are rules to be observed, such as age (younger than 30 years) and area of specialization.

The candidate should be a student in the partner university, but he or she could also be junior faculty staff member, such as a teaching or research assistant. Full-time faculty members do not qualify for the prizes.

The competition for the prizes is repeated annually. Most partner universities announce it to all of their students, then screen the applicants on the basis of their accomplishments. To announce next year's prize(s), partner universities use the classic information boards, electronic mail, the campus newspaper or several media.

The best results are obtained when the call for candidates is done in September of the year preceding the final selection. The variety of subjects eligible for the competition documents their broad appeal. These include (in alphabetical order):

- Applied science
- Biology
- Biotechnology
- Civil engineering

- Environmental protection
- Financial engineering
- Information science
- Life sciences
- Mathematics
- Medical sciences
- Nanotechnology
- Physics
- Risk control
- Telecommunications.

The partnership with selected universities is a long-term proposition. The Foundation is appropriately endowed and, looking into the future, there is no limit to the prizes as long as there are graduate doctoral degree candidates to be awarded for distinction in their field of activity.

A different approach, also based on an independent foundation, has been chosen by Mike Lazarides of Research in Motion. He has endowed the Perimeter Institute for Theoretical Physics in Waterloo, Ontario, with Can$150 million (€90 million, $130 million) and, with a separate fund, the Institute for Quantum Computing at the University of Waterloo.

The goal of the Perimeter Institute is to promote research in theoretical physics including cosmology, particle physics and quantum theory – and to enlarge the public's understanding of these fields. The institute has 60 resident scientists and hosts many international visiting researchers.

The Institute for Quantum Computing aims to use principles of quantum physics to develop novel techniques for information processing, using, as human capital, resident researchers, postdoctoral fellows and graduate students. 'Philanthropy can be seen as a kind of venture capital for really long-term investment,' says Lazarides who feels that theoretical physics is not being funded to the level it should be.[29]

As these examples show, there exists no single model of private initiative aimed at promoting research and education. Diversity is welcome, as it is preferable that private support addresses a range of scientific fields by using different models. But there should be good governance (including very small overheads),[30] quality control of deliverables and accountability for results.

## 7. Trustees and the Management of University Assets

The Center for Excellence in Higher Education (CEHE)[31] was established by a small group of donors who contributed millions of dollars to US institutes of higher education and have been concerned about the continuing decline of colleges and universities. At the centre of its preoccupation lies the fact that even if America's top universities are among

29 *Financial Times*, 14 July 2009.

30 At my foundation, overheads constitute a single-figure percentage of the annual budget.

31 An Indianapolis-based organization.

the best in the world, the majority of them (which amount to nearly 2,500) are struggling to keep up. The same is true in Europe.

There are reasons for this preoccupation, as the reader is already aware. Competitiveness can drop rapidly because of problems which have to do as much with the literacy of the population coming out of primary and secondary education and into universities (Chapter 1) as with the quality of teaching and management of the universities themselves. Indeed, a study by the American Research Institute found that:

- only 38 per cent of all students at four-year colleges and universities were proficient in reading and understanding such things as newspaper editorials,
- just 40 per cent were really good at completing documents such as job applications, and
- no more than 35 per cent were able to perform quantitative tasks, such as balancing a chequebook or understanding the terms of a car loan.[32]

These are heart-breaking statistics. Based on these and similar findings, the CEHE asked itself whether American taxpayers, parents and philanthropists are getting value for the money they are spending on higher education – and it came to the conclusion that this is not the case.

Proper governance, a good faculty, due diligence and administrative accountability help, but these are not the only ingredients of excellence in higher education. The CEHE points out various other symptoms of the problem. Examples include the trivialization and politicization of courses and curricula, high school graduates who are ill-prepared for rigorous college work, ever rising costs and more emphasis on athletics than on academic issues,[33] as well as the failure to confront the salient problems of decline such as:

- poor curricula decisions, spending policies and, in some cases, curtailing the president's authority;
- the fact that most college administrators are responsible principally for revenue and physical plant, while paying little or no attention on productivity and on deliverables;
- having financial matters relegated rather than managed in an astute way; and
- the growing number of college and university trustees who cannot or simply do not provide serious oversight of the institution under their watch.

There is no better example regarding the curtailment of the president's authority than that of Larry Summers – a former secretary of the US Treasury and currently economics advisor to Barack Obama – who was president of Harvard in the early years of this century. While participating in a panel, Summers was asked why, in his opinion, there women were underrepresented in the sciences and engineering, and he answered that maybe they have less 'intrinsic aptitude'.

This raised hell not among the Harvard's sciences faculty, but among the social-science professors who are producing bureaucrats; and not so much among the women in the faculty as among the males. Eventually, following a vote of no confidence, Summers

32 Cited by the Center for Excellence in Higher Education at: http://www.cehe.org/.

33 Remember the reference in Chapter 1 to Ross Perot, and how he was castigated for speaking his mind.

was forced to resign.[34] In other words, in an what is otherwise one of the best universities, a president is not allowed to express his opinion. He is only permitted to say what is acceptable to the wider society. Socrates' must have turned in his grave the day Summers was pushed into quitting.

Regarding the second bullet, it is beyond question that university administrators have a responsibility to see that the institution they manage not only focuses on its mission – research and education – but also provides consistent and commendable results. This includes using resources wisely and efficiently in pursuit of that mission as well as:

- challenging the faculty and students to aim high and
- ensuring that, as a recipient of financial support, the university accomplishes something significant and responds by contributing to society in a meaningful way.

The third bullet has been dealt with in sections 3, 4 and 5. However, to bring this very important subject of managing endowments into perspective let me add that there is no excuse for saying: 'We always tried to do what Yale does.' Like pension funds, institutes of higher education must be very conservative in managing their financial resources, making decisions not in imitation of others, but based on their own:

- concerns,
- financial situation,
- problems they confront and
- academic programme requirements.

These decisions must be thoroughly considered and taken by the board of trustees, with the administrators being the executors. However, as the CEHE points out, a study by the Association of Governing Boards of Universities and Colleges has found that; nine out of ten college trustees have no say in academic programme requirements or faculty workloads; 53 per cent are not involved in establishing faculty compensation policies; 34 per cent do not evaluate the president's performance; and 22 per cent are not even responsible for appointing the university's president.[35]

This essentially amounts to abdication of trustee responsibilities. It needs no explaining that trustees and the university's administrators are morally and fiducially accountable for the proper governance of the institutions they serve. Therefore, not only must they have appropriate authority, but they should also understand and exercise that authority. A trustee's abdication from his or her responsibilities has a profoundly negative impact on the quality of higher education.

Specifically in regard to endowments, the board of trustees should carefully monitor the use of donations and its conformity to the donor's stated wishes. An all-too-common practice is for colleges and universities to solicit donations for one purpose and use the money for something else, says the CEHE.[36] This is an inappropriate practice that

34 'Beleaguered Harvard Head to Quit', *BBC News*, 21 February 2006, at: http://news.bbc.co.uk/1/hi/world/americas/4738030.stm.

35 Cited by the CEHE at: http://www.cehe.org/about.html.

36 Idem.

is condemned by the Council for Advancement and Support of Education and other reputable organizations.

Princeton University provides an example. In early December 2008 Princeton settled a lawsuit over an endowment valued at more than $900 million, ending a six-year dispute about how the money had been spent.[37]

The case was brought to court by members of the Robertson family, heirs to the A&P supermarket fortune, and it cost each side tens of millions of dollars in legal fees. The suit hinged on whether Princeton was meeting the donor's requirements of using the gift to educate students for government careers. Members of the Robertson family contended that the school did not honour the donor's vision.[38]

'We were being ignored, we were being abused and they were abusing the foundation,' William Robertson said. The settlement should give caution to donors of more than $1 million who want to have a say in how their gifts are spent, commented Fredric Fransen, executive director of the CEHE, 'The lesson for donors is they need to be very careful how they structure the control over the gift.'[39]

## 8. It Takes More Than Good Words to Restructure Higher Education and Careers in Europe

'EU members want to be competitive, but the EU is not ready to accept competition.' said Esko Aho, a former Finnish prime minister, as quoted by the news media. This is true all the way to higher education. Recently, after three months of protests by faculties and students, the Greek government abandoned plans to legalize private universities. In France, selective entrance exams for public universities remain a taboo, contrary to the policy followed with the *grandes écoles*.

Karl-Erik Michelsen of Finland's Lappeenranta University complains of a 'big social-democratic project to create a massive number of people with master's degrees'. The result, he says is that 'quantity overrides quality'.[40] This was covered in section 1 of this chapter as well as in connection to the Bologna Initiative (section 2).

- The European Commission works hard at busting cartels and tries to stop governments bailing out no-hopers with taxpayers' money.
- But the EU has no powers to establish, let alone regulate, education policy in a way that will give the old continent's universities the leadership they once had.

It needs no explaining that the lack of an imaginative and audacious strategy on education and on career development talks badly of the EU's stated goal about unleashing the universities' full potential, mobilizing the brainpower of Europe and creating a knowledge-based economy. Just as futile is financing research with taxpayers' money without demanding deliverables (see Chapter 6), because the same governments that do

37 *Robertson* v. *Princeton University*, C-99-02, Superior Court of New Jersey, Mercer County, 2002.

38 Princeton responded that from 1973 to 2006, 14 per cent of students took jobs in the federal government in connection to international relations, but this answer did not satisfy the donor's family's claim.

39 Oliver Staley and Janet F. Lorin, 'Princeton Settles Lawsuit Over Endowment (Update 3)', 10 December 2008, at: http://www.bloomberg.com/apps/news?pid=newsarchive&sid=aMXdCghYl7Gw&refer=home.

40 *The Economist*, 5 May 2007.

the financing are shielding the national research labs from public criticism of the results they obtain.

At root, the European universities' problem is social and political. Emile Durkheim, who discovered early enough the laws and mechanisms governing the development and behaviour of human societies, has illustrated the complexities of social change by comparing it to the composition of water which, formed from oxygen and hydrogen, exhibits different properties from those of its individual components.

- In the same way, societies exhibit properties which are unlike the individual parts from which they are composed.
- This is important because progressive society is a team which, although competing in many different ways, has to coordinate its activities in order to get results.

When it started with the Treaty of Rome as the Common Market,[41] the community of European member nations began to take shape as an economic and business team. Slowly, it was discovered that a team playing exclusively in the commercial area has limitations, so the member states extended their sights to other domains, but without the political will to do so in earnest. Research and education have been the weakest areas. As a result,, to a surprisingly large extent higher education in the EU is largely stuck with a mindset that is characteristic of the Industrial Revolution. The necessary change in mental models, referred to previously on several occasions, has not taken root. Therefore, with a few exceptions like the two Swiss technical universities (which are not part of the EU anyway), the system has not adapted to the post-industrial world whose criteria are as follows:

- What one learns is a perishable commodity.
- Innovation must come from and go to everywhere.
- Hierarchies must be flat and companies lean.
- Everybody should not only be well educated, but also appreciate the need for many careers in their lives because jobs, too, are perishable.

The younger generation must be taught the wisdom of *taking risks* rather than rent-seeking as a way of survival. We all have to take risks in life in order to succeed, but to do so we must be self-confident. This type of culture is one of the most important intangible benefits in combining research and education (see Chapter 5). Robert Kahn was working on packet networks when he decided to take this idea further and designed the ARPANET (now known as the Internet). As Vinton Cerf, the Internet's co-designer, put it in a lecture he gave to UCLA graduates:

- he and his colleagues deliberately did not try to tailor the network to an application;
- instead, they decided to have a very general packet switching capability.

Kahn, Cerf and plenty of others did not take the beaten path. They took a risk and they succeeded. One may feel pain in dropping past practices because this means abandoning their safety clauses which used to characterize a steady work contract. But educators should teach that jobs are no longer available to young graduates the way they used to

---

41 D.N. Chorafas, *The Business of Europe is Politics*, Gower, Aldershot, 2010.

be, and that the 'old way' is counterproductive as rigid labour laws deter employers from creating those jobs.[42]

Rarely, if ever, do continental European universities teach their students this basic fact of present-day life. The most clear-eyed students, however, should be able to read the writing on the wall. Nietzsche said: 'Since I grew tired of the chase and search, I learned to find; and since the wind blows in my face, I sail with every wind.' So did Jules C. Stein[43] who paid for his college tuition at the University of Chicago Medical School by leading an orchestra. One night he found himself double-booked. Someone else would have been confused and unable to fulfil one of the two commitments. Stein hired another band and made a 20 per cent commission.

- From there, he founded the Music Corporation of America (MCA) and,
- after he had made a fortune, he financed UCLA's Jules Stein Eye Institute, one of the finest in the world.

In conclusion, the education system in the European Union is drifting, and politicians cannot continue looking the other way as it goes downhill. It's enough that two generations have paid the price of this failure with their professional future. To turn the situation around, governments must both institute far-reaching changes in labour laws *and* restructure the educational system, including the universities. Here is a summary of the key points made in this chapter:

- Entry exams should become a pan-European practice, as they were prior to World War II.
- Endowments to universities should be promoted with name-plating to attract donors.
- Costs must be controlled *as if* the not-for-profit university were a profit-making private company.
- Free-of-charge education at university level should be abolished, because it makes the whole system dependent on the meagre means of the state and its patronage.
- Because universities must have the best of faculty skills, salaries should be commensurate with those in industry provided that they are justified by personal background and experience.

In regard to the first bullet, the European university system can no longer process a rapidly increasing number of students who are loafing. The implication of having entry examinations is that talent and hard work, not entitlement or political patronage, decide who enters university life.

Endowments and student fees should be promoted, because an important ingredient in restoring European universities to their former leadership is minimizing the role of the state. This is easier done when universities get their funding from a variety of different sources, such as

- philanthropists,
- businesses and

---

42 A reason which led to the choice to combine, under one cover, education, research and employment.

43 After whom has been named the Jules Stein Eye Institute at UCLA.

- the students themselves,

not just the government.

If students pay for their university education, they will also be more careful about their learning, because they would want to have a return on their investment. The student's performance brings us to the subject of career opportunities – therefore to brains and borders.

A 2006 study by the French Senate (just prior to the economic crisis), provides some interesting figures. From the mid-1990s to 2005, the number of French expatriates increased by 40 per cent, and a whopping 70 per cent of this increase went to the United States. About 66 per cent of scientists and executives who left have been what the French consider *hyperqualified*

- businessmen
- researchers and
- senior managers.[44]

When he was minister of finance, Laurent Fabius, a former prime minister under François Mitterrand and one of the Socialist Party leaders, said to his friends: 'Every morning I ask myself what I would answer to my boys if they come to tell me: "Father we are leaving for America".'[45] Nearly every father in the EU is faced with Fabius's dilemma.

Laurent Fabius knew very well why he was worried. A few years down the line, on 24 February 2006, *Le Figaro* quoted a forecast by the National Institute of Demographic Studies that new departures of researchers who are also teachers would amputate a massive 46 per cent of their number – nearly one in two. That is the price being paid for featherbedding those who do not want to work and learn, while those who do suffer under the yoke of the unable, unwilling and unnecessary sail abroad. 'Brains, like hearts,' Robert McNamara once said, 'go where they are appreciated'.

## Appendix: Cashing a Cheque

I chair a Swiss not-for-profit foundation which each year gives prizes to the best graduating PhD students of partner universities. The choice is made by each university, according to the criteria set by the foundation.

In connection to 2009 prizes (the cheques were mailed at the end of August that year), after an inexcusable five months' delay (bankers guaranteed cheques expire at end of the sixth month), the secretary of the foundation received the following e-mail:

> *Dear Ms …,*
>
> *I'm writing to tell you that I have problems cashing the prize money of the Chorafas Foundation.*

---

44 *Le Figaro Magazine*, 11 March 2006.

45 As reported in the French media.

*I've tried to cash it at my bank (PostFinance) but unfortunately it was impossible since they don't accept cheques at all. Then I went to Credit Suisse (the issuing bank), but they didn't want to cash it either, since I'm not a customer and the amount was too large.*

*So could you please help me in receiving the money. Thank you very much in advance.*

*Kind regards,*

The answer has been of exemplary simplicity:

*Dear Dr. ...,*

*Thank you for your email.*

*As a resident of Switzerland you must know that the law does not permit the Postbank to accept cheques from other banks.*

*You should also appreciate that the best solution for you is to open an account at Credit Suisse and deposit the cheque.*

*After you receive the money you could keep or close the account.*

*Note that 5 months have already gone by, and the certified cheque expires at the end of February.*

*All the best,*

That man had a doctorate in science and was employed by a well-known firm. But he could not search out and find how to cash a cheque.

PART II

# *Innovation: The Synergy of Education and Employment*

# CHAPTER 5 Research, Development and Innovation

## 1. Research and Development Defined

*Research* is the process of investigating, exploring and inquiring into the domain in which one is active. Neither the term nor the process is limited to the physical sciences. Research on issues underpinning a legal case is known as *discovery*; historical, literary and financial research are other examples. What all research projects share is the culture of investigating, fact-finding, scrutinizing, examining, probing, analysing and experimenting. In science,[1] research divides into:

- *basic*, which aims at uncovering physical laws, principles, facts, materials; and
- *applied*, which targets the practical application of basic research findings and leads to product development.

Prior to the relatively recent wholesale switch of emphasis on to applied research, basic research aimed at scientific discovery was characterized by an allocation of funds amounting to about 10–15 per cent of the total R&D budget. Today, that ratio is much lower.[2] The way to bet in terms of deliverables from basic research projects, between 1 cent and 5 per cent are tops;[3] 5 to 10 per cent are interesting and the remainder leads nowhere, some of the projects being killed early on in their life.

- These ratios are typical.
- Therefore they are more or less expected.

Research activity must be properly financed. Lavish budgets, however, are no guarantee of obtaining commendable results. The two most exciting recent findings – the discovery of dark matter (which pushes space itself apart) and of planets beyond the solar system – were made using relatively modest equipment, but great brains.

One of the weaknesses of the US, Britain and the EU is that they do not produce enough scientists, particularly engineers, to satisfy high technology's requirements for know-how and skills. Germany's engineering companies have warned the government that the country's competitiveness could be put into jeopardy by a shortage of engineers and skilled labour. There are simply not enough young people in Germany (or anywhere else in the EU) who are willing to work hard to gain an engineering degree.

1 The term 'science' is defined a few paragraphs later on.

2 By contrast, work done in government laboratories and sponsored research is often of the basic type.

3 This statistic pertains to the number of projects, not their share of the basic research budget.

*Thinking* is what counts the most in R&D, which is evidently true in any business. As Chapter 3 highlighted, thinking means challenging the obvious, and this is one of the qualities characteristic of leadership – the greatest R&D asset. Both vision and difficult decisions are part of leadership.

- High-risk, high-reward projects require hard decisions, and
- these decisions are best made by individuals, not by committees or communities of nations.

Research is based on vision, imagination, hypotheses made about unknown elements or factors, and experimentation. That's why directors of research should be young. Older people know too many things that cannot be done. The ability to motivate people is very important. While a single thinker may see far and wide, the deliverables of modern R&D have much to do with synergy.

Universities play a key role in R&D. This is less appreciated in Europe, but it is a rule in the United States where there exists a culture of collaboration between industry and academia. A good deal of basic research is performed in university laboratories, sponsored by companies and by the government.

Government-sponsored projects tend to focus either on weapon systems or on pre-competitive research (see Chapter 6) which will eventually benefit all industry[4] (with every company making its own products). Industry-sponsored projects largely concentrate on applied research. An excellent example is the initiative taken by universities to assemble, say, 60 companies to sponsor a pre-competitive advanced research project – as MIT does so successfully.

Applied research and development correlate. The term 'development' means evolution, advancement, evolvement. Its aim is to bring forth marketable and usable products, processes and systems. Its deliverables are at the origin of novelty in concepts and solutions. They advance or broaden existing devices, products and processes, improving their potential. Development is a fundamental ingredient of progress in industry and in society at large, consistent with the fact that:

- the goal of applied research and development is a technological leap through innovation, and
- presently this line of activity consumes more than 90 per cent of total R&D, resulting in 60–90 per cent technical success.

When properly managed, the money a company spends on R&D, as well as in manufacturing engineering, marketing and sales (sections 3 and 7), positively impacts on revenues and earnings per share. R&D projects, however, have to be planned, managed and regularly controlled as Chapter 6 will document with examples from the European Union.

R&D entities organize themselves and plan their activities along the aforementioned general lines, The chosen structure may be based on subject areas or on a functional concept. An example is provided by Britain's National Physical Laboratory whose

4 At least within the jurisdiction doing the sponsorship.

Electricity, Metrology and Physics Divisions, as well as the Test House, were regrouped some years ago on a functional rather than on a subject basis in three divisions:

- *basic physics*, aimed at pioneering developments in certain branches of modern non-nuclear physics, which have potential applications in industry;
- *applied physics*, whose remit is secondary standards, test work, electrotechnics, acoustics and radiology; and
- *standards*, addressing fundamental norms of mass, length, time, electrical units, magnetic units and temperature.

In this and the following chapter we will be concerned with research and development of a scientific nature, including concepts, rules and theories underpinning the application of knowledge. The word *science* is a relatively recent term. In 1660 when the Royal Society, the world's first academy of scientific discipline, was founded in London, the subject to which it addressed itself was referred to as 'natural philosophy'. A quarter of a century later, in 1686, Isaac Newton titled his famous book: *The Principia: Mathematical Principles of Natural Philosophy*. It is also interesting to note that the *humanism* of the Renaissance was originally a technical term applied to studies centred on grammar and rhetoric – in contrast to the logic and natural philosophy of the *scholastics*, who were the early scientists.

In a modern society, the need for scientific research and development is present in practically all industries, from manufacturing to banking and insurance. Even when times are hard and there is a profit squeeze, no industry sector (or company) can allow itself to fall behind in R&D, because eventually this leads to oblivion. Studies show that since the late 1960s there has been a correlation between R&D spending and growth in gross domestic product (GDP).

An example is provided by the American economy, where, in the four decades from 1969 to 2008, R&D spending from all sources – government, business and universities – is only slightly ahead of or behind the rise in GDP. The wave of competition which followed on the heels of globalization[5] sees to it that no country and no company can allow itself to grow complacent about its:

- technological prowess, in regard to product innovation,
- productivity increases attained by a better infrastructure and improved solutions,
- return on R&D investment, which requires first-class projects, a rapid development timetable and no delays from lab to marketing

In the globalized market, both companies and nations must not only become, but also remain, internationally competitive; and *innovation* is the means for doing so. Therefore, well-managed companies are refocusing their R&D efforts, placing more emphasis on the reduction of product cycle times, quality improvements, a steady squeeze on costs and greater marketing effectiveness (see also sections 3 and 8).

As the opening paragraphs of this chapter made clear, the downside of current trends is that less emphasis (and smaller budgets) are dedicated to basic research, largely because the results are longer-range. This means that a prime source of innovation and

5 D.N. Chorafas, *Globalization's Limits: Conflicting National Interests in Trade and Finance*, Gower, Aldershot, 2009.

launch-pads for future products has been put on the backburner – with the result that the system coupling basic research findings to development, engineering and commercial applications is in danger of disintegration.

'Industry is not doing the required basic research job; universities or national laboratories have not been doing it either because they are no longer funded to do it,' said one of the experts who participated to the research leading to this book. The irony is that each Western government, and the Group of Eight (G-8) as a whole, runs on a platform that theoretically puts strong emphasis on technology as:

- a driver of the economy and
- a key factor in the economic and social future

Particularly in Europe, dramatic cuts made across domestic discretionary accounts typically include all of the agencies that fund research. This emerged as a policy in connection with the so-called 'peace dividend', after the fall of the Soviet Union, which led to a sharp reduction in weapons systems projects and to an overcapacity in scientific R&D. The after-effect prompted downsizing and the elimination of many industry-built research efforts such as:

- strategic partnering,
- virtual laboratories and
- aggressive technology acquisition and transfer.

The 1990s and first decade of this century have witnessed resource-shifting from invention to deployment, as well as a move from expert-driven to consumer-driven technology. Both signalled that industry investments have shifted from science to the marketplace. It can be described as a shift from R&D to R,D&I – where R,D&I stands for research, development and implementation.

## 2. Making Knowledge Work Productive

One of the unexpected positive consequences of the shift from R&D to R,D&I is that it strengthened the link between education and development on the applications side. The urge for practical results leading to funding ensured that more emphasis was placed on a policy of change, innovation, and renewal. But, at the same time, global competition moved into high gear and Western education, research and development now face a permanent risk of falling behind:

- *if* universities, labs and companies are unable to manage change, and
- they don't reinvent themselves and their strengths not just once, but every day, every month, and every year.

Those that are ahead of the curve make profits. As the late 1990s showed, it is always possible to create significant wealth with high-tech companies – though the leveraging associated with an industry's rapid rise eventually leads to a bubble which bursts, as happened in 2000 with the dot-coms and in 2007–2009 with banking.

Knowledge creates wealth, but the late Peter Drucker was definitely right when he said that we don't really fully understand the economics of knowledge because we have not yet had enough experience to formulate an appropriate theory about it, let alone test that theory. What we do understand, however, is that today, in order to gain competitive advantage,

- we have to put knowledge at the centre of wealth production, and
- this is precisely why education, research and development should be seen in unison.

The reader should, however, be cautioned that as far as innovation and new product development is concerned, research money is only a small (even if vital) part of the total budget. Based on 50 years of experience in high-tech industry, I have developed a rule on budgetary requirements which is presented in Table 5.1: as can be seen, R&D proper represents a relatively small part of the total budget for new products.

**Table 5.1 Relative costs in launching a new technology product**

| | **Cost units** |
|---|---|
| *If* R&D is<br>*Then* manufacturing engineering require | 1<br>1½ |
| The making of total hardware (HW) technology requires | 2½ |
| Software (SW) developments, including some applications, requires | 2½ |
| The making of HW and SW technology requires | 5 |
| Marketing (sales, training, systems support, maintenance*) requires | 5 |
| Grand total | 10 |

* Roughly half of the *cost units* occur in tuning up marketing, sales and field operations. Sections 3 and 7 explain why marketing activities are more capital-intense than R&D.

Neither is it enough to start a company (or a major new product line) in order to succeed. The effort must be relentless. The way an article in *The Economist* had it, start-ups that went bust were 32 per cent less productive than mature incumbents, while mature companies that survived were 27 per cent more productive than their peers. Start-ups that survived were more productive than mature companies and they continued to be so several years down the line.[6]

At the level of R&D proper, a great deal can be achieved through interdisciplinary solutions which, apart other benefits, help to expand the innovation horizon. An example is provided by a General Electric (GE) research project for jet fighters which ended up with an invention that revolutionized the way in which doctors diagnose their patients' illnesses.

Scientists at GE's global research centre in Niskayuna (upstate New York) were investigating how LCD displays could improve the instrumentation of aircraft cockpits.

6 *The Economist*, 30 May 2009,

One of them, who had worked on a related medical programme, suggested applying the technology to X-rays. By the mid-1990s, GE was studying *digital X-rays*, which:

- require no film,
- do not need to be placed on light boxes, and
- give a more accurate view of organs and bones than was previously possible.[7]

The discovery of digital X-rays and other similar projects which have benefited from interdisciplinary know-how underline the merits of having several fields of research under one roof, so that cross-fertilization is possible. (An interesting hindsight on how the aforementioned research effort at GE channelled itself in an unpredictable way is that the original programme for cockpit LCD displays was dropped.)

At the same time, it is wise to appreciate that many inventions don't come from a big lab, but out of one man's brain. Ralph Waldo Emerson was famous for being a one-man interdisciplinary laboratory. He was a master in making knowledge work productive because he used his fertile imagination in a way that was appreciative of the importance of innovation and cultural change. This enabled him to find, by himself, what he needed for to make his research practical.

It is, however, no less true that not all practical research results make society a better place. In 1895 Hiram Maxim (1840–1916), an American engineer working in London, harnessed the recoil energy released by the firing gun to load and fire again in a repeating cycle. As sometimes happens with other developments, military officers initially regarded the advent of the machine gun as a curiosity rather than as an obvious start of a new era in warfare. Its wide acceptance as a weapon of defence and offence came nearly two decades later.

- Maxim's machine guns accounted for 80 per cent of killings in World War I, and,
- time and again, the machine gun has shown that in three minutes it can decimate a battalion of 600.[8]

What is true about innovation in weapons is equally valid for all products where a new ingenious idea, and an engineering design based on it, can turn the tables on long-established competitors. But technological leadership does not last forever. Improvements can also be produced by copycats. Throughout the 1960s Japan played a sustained role as an adapter of Western technology. Swiss watch companies and German camera-makers were the first to pay the bill; others followed.

What Japanese companies understood is that costs matter. Innovation can also be based on quality improvements and lower costs compared to those of an existing product. In addition, the solutions obtained from R,D&I must have global appeal. And because of rapid changes in technology, all markets and all companies have to keep up the pace or they will lose their:

- competitiveness and
- global market share.

7 In 2000, GE began marketing the first digital X-ray machine, which supplanted traditional equipment.

8 Reference from the Royal Armouries Museum at the Tower of London.

Cost and quality improvements require a deal of laboratory work. Taiwan, which depends on exports for its living, provides an example. Statistics from the OECD show that it now has more high-tech researchers than Britain. In addition, as demonstrated by a list of the world's 250 biggest technology firms, Taiwanese companies spend more on R&D than the British.[9]

South Korean companies, too, have embraced R&D in a big way. In 2007 Samsung spent more on R&D than IBM, and it has moved into second place in terms of the number of patents granted by the US Patent and Trademark Office. This contrasts sharply with the fact that in the late 1990s Samsung was not even in the top ten in terms of R&D spending.

- Today, South Korean firms spend more on R&D as a percentage of sales than European and Japanese firms (6.5 per cent versus 5 per cent), and
- South Korea has more high-tech researchers than Britain and Germany, even if its firms prefer to concentrate on hardware rather than the more development-intensive software.

The strategy able to fulfil the requirements for competitiveness in global market can be expressed in few words: in the twenty-first century making knowledge work productive is a 'must'. Products must be highly competitive, lagging projects must be killed off, and companies must be reinvented. Research by Nasdaq carried out in Silicon Valley in the mid-1990s came to the conclusion that a technology company has to reinvent itself every two-and-a-half years in order to survive. This requires a great deal of internal discipline.

## 3. In a Service Economy Internal Discipline is as Important as R&D

*If* we plan for market leadership, *then* our efforts to produce ingenious product designs must be amplified through internal discipline in all domains ranging from research to marketing. 'To build an airplane and fly an airliner is no problem. The challenge is to fill it up with passengers,' Harold D. Koontz, my professor of business strategy at UCLA, taught his students. He then explained from his experience at TWA that filling the airplane calls for:

- a master plan against competitors,
- using technology to cut down costs, and
- ingenuity in marketing (see also section 7).

I call this the *Koontz principle*, and it is equally valid for companies and for nations. Taken together, the notions embedded in these three bullets make up *innovation*. Today, the global leader in innovation is the United States. Using a top score of 6, the World

9 *The Economist*, 3 January 2009.

Forum's *Global Competitiveness Index: Innovation and Sophistication Factors*[10] scores the countries below as follows:

- United States – 5.77
- Finland – 5.53
- Germany – 5.11
- Republic of Korea – 4.84
- Britain – 4.60
- France – 4.50
- China – 3.93.

One way of judging the productivity of R&D budgets, and therefore of researchers, is through patents. In 2007, 2008 and 2009 there were about 460,000 patent applications per year in the US,[11] while in Europe they numbered fewer than 150,000 annually.[12] Interestingly, with nearly 320,000 patents in 2009, China finds itself on the way to overtaking Japan which in 2009 featured 350,000 patents – down from almost 4000,000 in 2007 (see also the discussion on patents in section 6).

In terms of private companies' R&D budgets, the latest available statistics have been provided by the European Commission and these are shown in Table 5.2. The amount of money and deliverables, however, don't always correlate. (In Chapter 6, Table 6.1 presents statistics on R&D financing as a percentage of GDP in major industrial countries.)

**Table 5.2 R&D budgets of ten leading firms, 2009**

| | US$ (billions) |
|---|---|
| Toyota | 10.4 |
| Microsoft | 8.9 |
| Volkswagen | 8.1 |
| Roche | 8.0 |
| General Motors | 7.7 |
| Johnson & Johnson | 7.3 |
| Nokia | 7.1 |
| Sanofi-Aventis | 6.4 |
| Panasonic | 5.8 |
| IBM | 5.6 |

*Source:* Statistics by the European Commission in euros, converted into US dollars.

10 Table 8 in World Economic Forum, *The Global Competitive Report 2009–2010*, p. 20, at: http://www.weforum.org/pdf/GCR09/GCR20092010fullreport.pdf.

11 The bad news is that, according to the Kauffmann Foundation, which studies entrepreneurship, the productivity of US federal funding for R&D in terms of patents and licences has been falling while funding is spread too thinly.

12 *The Economist*, 2 October 2010.

In 2008 Toyota, the car-maker, increased its annual R&D budget spending by 7.6 per cent to $10.4 billion. This is not surprising since three of the five biggest spenders are motor vehicle firms.[13] This increase knocked Microsoft off the top, but did not help Toyota which went straight into an engineering, marketing and public relations earthquake with severe quality problems and millions of cars being recalled.

To a large extent, the amounts of R&D financing in Table 5.2 reflect the spirit of industry in each of the aforementioned countries – from manufacturing to services. The reader should, however, be aware that R&D spending by companies is only one of the inputs. Some obtained results are disproportionately bigger or smaller than the research money, because of:

- the effectiveness with which it is spent and
- the value of tangible deliverables from the R&D effort.

Innovation resulting from the synergy of strategic planning and R&D may focuses on one key issue, not two or three at the same time – for instance, higher quality or lower cost, greater functionality or simpler maintainability.

In the 1950s when the Koontz principle came to life, a highly competitive price was one of the principal strategic weapons used by air carriers to gain and hold market share. Strict observance of timetables was another index of performance appealing to air travellers. Moreover, Koontz advised, investment in facilities must exceed the projected growth of the market regardless of its short-term impact on profits; and new services must be constantly introduced to continue the cycle of:

- market appeal,
- cost control and price target(s),
- market share gain and
- control of business risk.

All four bullets have, as a prerequisite, a high degree of internal discipline, together with great sensitivity to market drives and switches in preferences, promoted by close market contact. In the twentieth century, global companies tried to keep close to their markets by hiring and training local staff and also by sending highly-paid domestic executives to live abroad, but not all company headquarters made good use of market information provided by those staff.

Slowly but steadily, staff on foreign assignments have gone from being special and unique, with plenty of fringe benefits, to being an everyday part of a company, as companies became conscious of their cost base. The strategy of product development has also changed. New products now grow in a global network of labs, capturing brainpower where it exists and at the same time reflecting local drives and tastes; at the same time, cost-consciousness has become a basic ingredient of project planning.

Figure 5.1 shows the complete cycle of the evolved procedures. It starts with analysis, preliminary design and modelling, to be tested through market research in order to benefit from customer input. It's a fair bet that the original idea will be changed as prototyping and simulation help in making such changes:

---

13 Other big R&D budgets are found in biotechnology companies and pharmaceuticals.

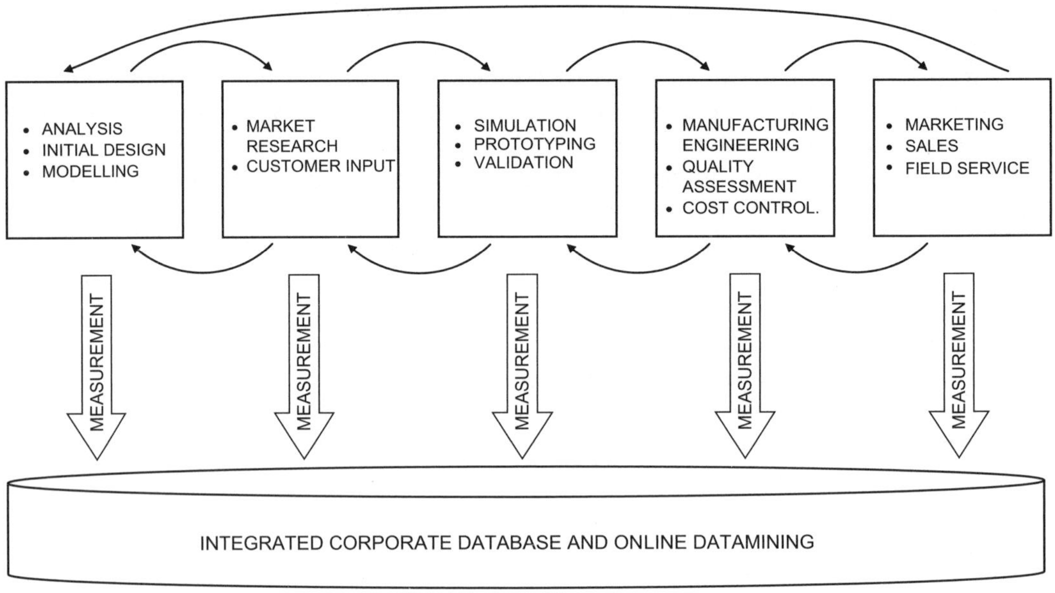


**Figure 5.1 Winners take a holistic approach to research, development, production and marketing**

- rapid,
- effective and
- rewarding.

Once the prototype stabilizes, the chores of manufacturing engineering begin, including the setting of quality standards and precise cost targets (cost guidelines should have been established at market research level). Set in parallel to this are marketing plans, including the training of sales engineers as well as projections regarding their quotas. The skills of field service personnel also need upgrading. It should also be noted that, throughout the outlined procedure, everything has to be monitored and measured.

Technologists are taught early on in their training that research and engineering are the two pillars of innovation. That's true, but it is only half the story. Cost control and marketing are the other two pillars, and handling them effectively requires as much self-discipline and concentration as R&D does.

If we look back at the beginning of marketing, as contrasted to sales, we see that it evolved as a result of applying management concepts to the tasks of linking technical development to market whims and vice versa. In the mid-1920s and early 1930s, marketing pioneers like Thomas Roebuck began to question the way in which manufacturing was organized, particularly the lack of anticipating:

- how the market behaves and
- what one should expect in two, three or five years' time.

Roebuck and others also concluded that the assembly line was a short-term compromise. They thought that, despite its great productivity, Henry Ford's method represented poor economics because of its planning inflexibility, difficulties in engineering changes and less than optimal use of human resources.

One of the business leaders who revolutionized marketing was Thomas Watson Sr of IBM. But Watson did not particularly address the manufacturing side. It was left to the Japanese to restructure the manufacturing process along flexible lines, promoting teamwork through quality circles and creating the information-based organization as the way to impact on human nature. The net result has been a holistic concept which integrated:

- Roebuck's attention to prognostication,
- Watson's sales quotas which embody a premium for hard work,
- the Japanese contribution on quality and timeliness of deliverables, and
- budgeting based on variable costs, whose entries provide benchmarks for management control.

'What sort of guidelines could we follow in establishing quotas?' asked the CEO of an engineering company of which I was consultant to the board. In response to this query, raised during a project centring on the performance of the firm's sales engineers, together with the CEO and his immediate assistants we established that, as well as objectives, there are other basic considerations that should be taken into account in elaborating product sales targets:

- training of sales engineers, which must be steady;
- product-mix of the equipment they are given to sell;
- orientation of the sales effort towards more effective client hand-holding;
- expert systems support provided to the salespeople in fulfilling their duties; and
- compliance of the sales effort with the company's overall product and market strategy.

It is a fundamental principle of management, and a sign of a sound policy, that the know-how and efficiency of salespeople must be steadily upgraded and that they should be informed without delay on new products and design changes. They must also believe in the company's product effectiveness and in their own. In addition, at least two-thirds of the salespeople's salaries must be quota-based, and these quotas regularly reviewed. This makes people run faster to get results.

- They work in a more disciplined manner and
- they gaining greater confidence in their territory and the work they are doing.

In its heyday, IBM was a master in training, in terms of both quality and quantity, with the result that it had a first-class salesforce. In the years I was with IBM (during the late 1950s) about 24 per cent of the computer salespeople's and system engineers' time was spent on training and information sessions. This ratio continued till the mid-1960s, as documented by a research project I did with the American Management Association (AMA). By the 1970s, however, it ebbed, and IBM's fortunes slid.

A different way of expressing all this is that while research, development and innovation are most crucial to survival, they are not everything. A company can continue being a player in the market *if* it offers a superior service, characterized by high quality and competitive prices, and *if* it keeps on providing added value to its clients. Increasingly, this added value is revolving around solutions to specific problems faced by the company's clients.

In conclusion, along with steady innovation at an affordable cost, provided by well-directed R&D, marketing policies must be instrumental in increasing *our* company's appeal. Top-of–the-range manufacturing and merchandising companies don't need to be told that they must solve the marketing and sales problems they face with abundant energy and singleness of purpose. But, in the majority of firms, the board does not always appreciate that nothing should be left to chance.

## 4. Lessons on Innovation from Silicon Valley

Contrary to a rather widespread belief, Silicon Valley companies do not have generally better concepts on the innovation of products and processes, and their people are not smarter than people in the rest of the world working for other outfits. Where Silicon Valley firms have the edge is in:

- relentlessly developing new product ideas and
- executing them faster than their competitors.

The speed of action and reaction has a high premium. Delays result in competitors creaming the market. Americans excel in 'R&D time to market', and they are followed by the Asians. Europeans tend to take it easy. Many R&D projects are left to rot in laboratories as if the passage of time increases the appeal of their deliverables. It does not.

We owe great scientific developments to antiquity, but slow motion is not an asset. According to the history books, the Egyptians were the first to work with glass. The evidence found in one of the palaces of the pharaohs, near today's town of Tell el Amarna, dates back to 1350BC. The furnace was essentially a hole in the earth and the product, a round ball of glass, was broken into pieces to be used as

- weapons,
- ornaments and
- cutting-edge instruments.

Centuries later, the Greeks and Romans improved on the Egyptian glass-making technology, but the new epoch really started only in the eleventh century AD with the glass-making furnace, described by Theophilus. Developed in the lower Rhine valley, and using wood for energy, this highly improved glass-making process could melt up to 40 kilos of glass per day.

Then the pace of significant process improvements quickened. A better version of the glass-making furnace was developed in the seventeenth century, but still used wood for energy. In the mid-nineteenth century Henning Boetius, of Hannover, came up with a furnace whose energy was derived from burning coal. Then, sometime between 1856 and 1867, Friedrich Siemens developed the glass furnace of the industrial age, using gasified coal.

However, research and development in Silicon Valley does not take centuries, or even years. Time-wise, the unit of measurement is weeks or, at maximum, months. The overriding drive is for deliverables *now*, and practically every one of Silicon Valley's firms, entrepreneurs and people subscribes to a cradle-to-grave culture.

As section 3 highlighted, an orderly rapid pace requires a great deal of purpose and self-discipline. Another 'plus' is Silicon Valley's culture which celebrates the achievement of individuals, including their ability not only to innovate, but also to turn on a dime in managing change to remain ahead of competition. The algorithm which expresses these concepts is very simple:

$$\text{Success} = \text{Talent} \times \text{Drive} \times \text{Opportunity}$$

Less appreciated is the fact that successful start-ups in technology are also characterized by public relations wizardry. Microsoft provides an interesting example. In 1983 Bill Gates's then relatively small company was one of many software upstarts barely noticeable in the sea of other firms competing in the same market. That year's COMDEX,[14] however, was an inflection point in the firm's fortunes.

- The technical trigger was the prelaunch of Windows.
- But the real event was created by two marketing masterminds, Rowland Hanson and Bob Lorsch, through a public relations blitz.

'There wasn't a taxi on the Strip not promoting Windows. Stickers were all over the backseats of cabs; the drivers wore Windows buttons,' say Jennifer Edstrom and Marlin Eller. '... people couldn't go to bed without Windows.' There was a marketing *Blitzkrieg* around a technical product in the making: 'Microsoft's competitors were crazed, but Gates and his marketing crew were ecstatic.'[15]

While the PC operating system called Windows looked *as if* it were the focal point, its release was still a couple of years away. Microsoft's strategy had borrowed a leaf out of IBM's book. Despite that delay which the technical people knew about but potential customers didn't, the marketing blitz was ingenious. In a matter of a few days (and at an affordable cost of $450,000):

- Microsoft went from being one of many software players
- to being *the player* in operating systems for personal computers.

Hanson and Lorsch reinvented and redefined the concept of consumer product promotion, recasting it around a piece of software which became a licence to riches.[16] Microsoft would manage to keep a near-monopoly on that licence for over a quarter of a century, despite the swarm of challengers that emerged on the way. It was not until 2009 that Google mounted an assault that might succeed in the realm of cloud computing.

---

14 The computer distributors' exhibition whose annual gatherings in Las Vegas started in 1979.

15 Jennifer Edstrom and Marlin Eller, *Barbarians Led by Bill Gates*, Henry Holt, New York, 1998.

16 They also reinvented and recast Bill Gates.

There is nothing similar to this in Europe. EU start-ups have a great deal to learn from American start-ups and their strategies – collectively known as *Silicon Valley*. Negative lessons can also be learned from Detroit and the zombie banks.[17]

Without success stories in innovation, a common market, a country or a company is something of an also-ran. That does not mean that the EU has no innovative firms, for it certainly has them in some areas, but these tend to be exceptions and furthermore lack the ingredients necessary for a public relations blitz. It is no exaggeration to state that, apart from mobile telephony, Europe has not come up with an innovation having a global impact for more than a decade.

Some countries, like Finland and Ireland, do better than others. Cambridge in the UK can claim to have created Europe's best innovation cluster, but it falls far short of Silicon Valley. The main things holding back continental Europe are as follows:

- The overall political climate is not conducive to new ventures.[18]
- Bureaucracy and taxes discourage initiative.
- There is scarcity of venture capital even though General George Doriot, who invented venture capital during his time teaching at Harvard, was a Frenchman.[19]

This is regrettable because there is plenty of evidence that the link between venture capital and innovation is strong. According to some studies, a Euro, pound or dollar of venture capital could be up to ten times more effective in stimulating new patents than a dollar of traditional corporate R&D. This is not in the least surprising because:

- a knowledge economy is driven by brilliant service ideas, and
- out-of-the-box concepts are the motor of steady innovation that creates value for a company, its stakeholders and society at large.

The challenge is to motivate the innovators so that they produce a fast-growing share of GDP. This was the theme of the 2006 World Economic Forum in Davos, Switzerland, which included an unprecedented 22 sessions on innovation. The highlight was *thinking-for-a-living* by:

- building a culture of innovation,
- making innovation real, and
- appreciating what can be achieved by creativity

The emphasis on thinking-for-a-living reflects the fact that companies can no longer generate value by competing only on cost. They have to become customer-centric which implies changing mental models as part of a strategy of business transformation, characterized by an ability to turn on a dime – the way successful Silicon Valley companies do.

---

17 A poll after the GM salvage has shown that 58 per cent of Americans would have liked to see GM disappear rather than be saved by taxpayers' dollars.

18 When, some years ago, Siemens put together a venture fund, 75 per cent of the money was allocated in the US.

19 Doriot's first and foremost investment as a venture capitalist was in Digital Equipment Corp.

It comes as no surprise that this readiness to change mental models is best demonstrated by start-ups which have to run fast in order to survive. The exact opposite is the now-defunct Detroit model. As Figure 5.2 shows, no two countries have the same pattern of start-ups. Many of them fall by the wayside, but a good number become established new firms.

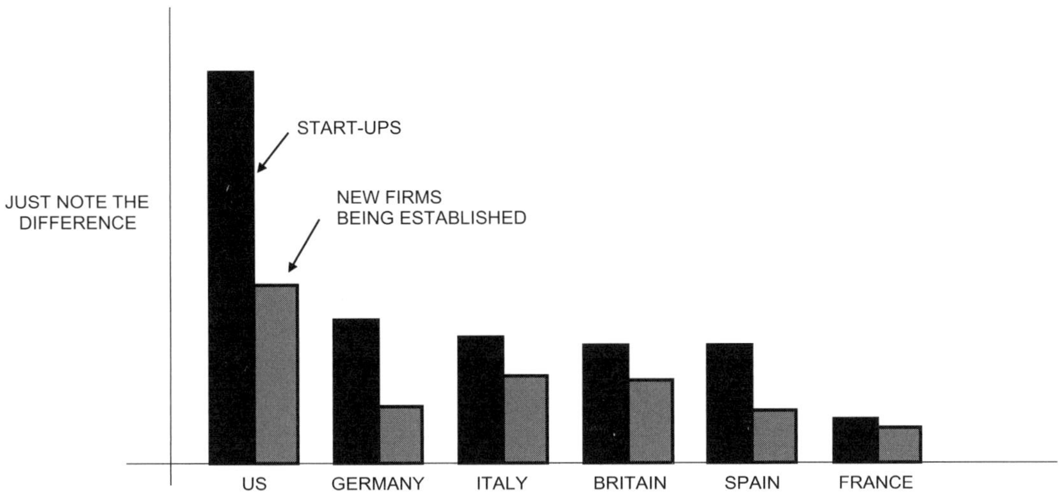


**Figure 5.2 Patterns of start-ups and new firm activity by country**

Indeed, new firm activity principally comes from two sources: start-ups which have survived the market test and have begun to mature and existing firms which have been able to reinvent themselves, or have developed their own brand of new products and services.

McDonald's, the fast-food chain, is an example of a non-high-tech start-up. Its innovation was to run a restaurant in a way quite different from the traditional one, with fast service and low cost as guidelines. By contrast, the idea underpinning Silicon Valley is that new products and services are an important part of personal and business success. They are almost the essence of it, but they don't need to come out of huge laboratories. In fact, they rarely do.

- The giant Bell Labs and General Motors Research Laboratories are gone.
- The ideas which propelled Amazon.com, E-bay, Google and plenty of others came out of the brains of one, two or three people – not of 10,000.

This has a tremendous implication for the future because it suggests that higher R&D spending does not assure better performance in terms of new products, company growth, profitability or shareholder returns. Instead, fresh thinking that creates value and real breakthroughs require risk-taking and the ability to absorb failure. Large organizations are incapable of doing so.

The idea that 'big size' is important is a weak hypothesis characterizing the minds of lesser marbles. The spirit of successful innovation is swamped by 'big size' which has a negative effect on free rein, willingness to take individual risks[20] and ability to absorb failure – which are basic ingredients of *steady innovation*. This has to be matched by:

- *operational excellence*, including marketing and public relations, as Microsoft's blitz pointed out, and
- *first-class governance*, characterized by intent and therefore by strategic planning.

Among the basic characteristics of operational excellence is steady watch. Whatever moves and does not in terms of the company itself, its products and the market must be monitored, measured and controlled. As illustrated Figure 5.3, steady innovation, operational excellence and (most evidently) good governance must be promoted by the organization's culture – which should be kept dynamic the *Silicon Valley* way.

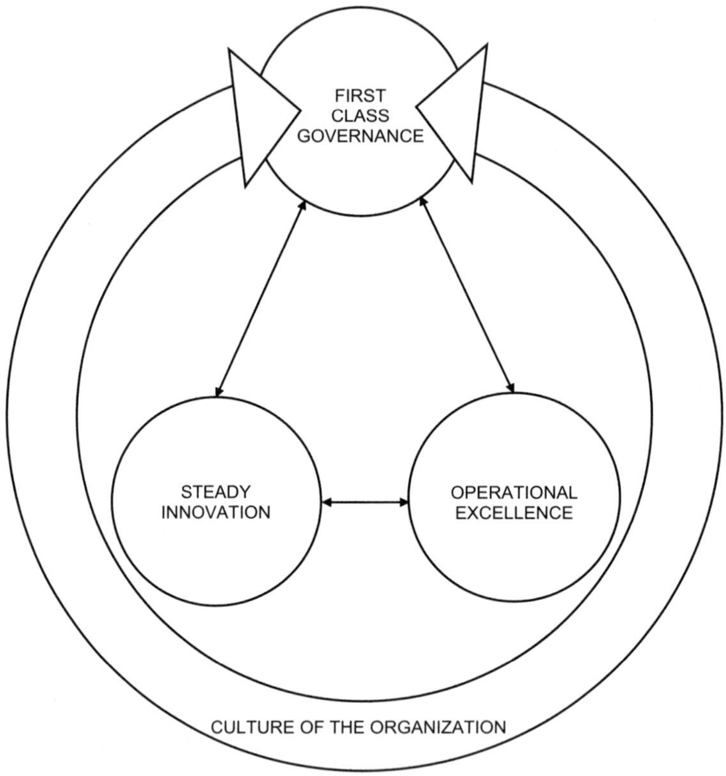


**Figure 5.3 A change in organizational culture may not assure success, but lack of it will lead to failure**

## 5. Patents as a Measure of Creative Activity

The term 'patent' derives from the Latin *litterae patentes*, or open letters, which implies accessibility. Early patents were documents issued by a ruler who conferred certain rights,

20 As contrasted to mammoth exposure like the big banks took in 2005–2007, bringing the global economy to the edge of the abyss. D.N. Chorafas, *Capitalism Without Capital*, Palgrave/Macmillan, London, 2009.

such as rank, title, nobility, official appointments, or monopoly. Today the term is used for patents granted for innovation in process, products and devices.

A major Western country's patent office can receive hundreds of applications per week. In the nearly 180 years of its existence, the US Patent and Trademark Office has issued more than 3 million patents. At the same time, patenting work has been:

- praised for stimulating invention and
- condemned for sustaining unholy monopolies.

At the end of the nineteenth century an economy-minded US Congressman suggested that the government closed the Patent Office as a needless expense, because 'everything worthwhile has already been invented and there is nothing left to incite the imagination of man'. In fact there is never a lapse in the curiosity of the creative mind, nor a day when something better is not needed. The sequence is continuous between:

- the one dimension of an idea,
- the two dimensions of a blueprint and
- the three dimensions of the manufactured product.

Patent protection is much stronger for two- and three-dimensional innovations, like those characterized by engineering designs, than for other intellectual property, such as ideas and software. On 1 June 2009 it was announced that the US Supreme Court was going to grapple with what might be called 'the method uncertainty'. The Justices would take up a key issue in intellectual property law whose bearing had not been so far tested in high court – namely:

- What kind of *business methods* are entitled to patent protection?

Plenty of cases have made a court decision imperative. One of most important is that over the past decade many e-commerce, financial and consulting firms have massively patented business methods as a way of gaining an upper hand in a highly competitive market and stepping ahead of their competitors. (At the centre of the case heard by the Supreme Court[21] is a method for hedging risk in commodities trading.)

- Because intellectual property can be so varied in nature, even after a court decision it may be difficult to protect it through patents.

In February 2010 Sergey Aleynikov, a former Goldman Sachs computer programmer, was charged with having stolen proprietary computer codes used by the investment bank to make lucrative, high-frequency trades (HFTs) in the financial markets.[22] The case is still pending and, ironically, a court decision in favour of Goldman may have unexpected consequences.

In an article he published in *The New York Times*, after Aleynikov's initial arrest, Tobin Harshaw made the point that 'if a computer code is valuable enough for someone to steal,

21 *Bilski v. Kappos*, 35 USC 101 (2009).

22 Ryan McCarthy, 'Sergey Aleynikov: "Goldman Sachs Spy" Indicted, Allegedly Stole Data on Bank's Trading Secrets', 11 February 2010, at: http://www.huffingtonpost.com/2010/02/11/sergey-aleynikov-goldman_n_458931.html.

and critical enough for a Wall Street firm to go to federal authorities to protect it, one would think that regulators would want to know why it is so important.'[23] Harshaw is right: it is time for regulators to investigate the impact of high-frequency trading on the markets, and Aleynikov's case may serve as the trigger.

- Patent protection should come at reasonable cost, so that it is affordable to individuals and to small firms.

This is a subject which so far has received scant attention. Costs vary widely among countries, as we will see in Chapter 7 in connection with the 'do nothing' policies of the European Commission. Patent protection in the EU is very poorly planned, and it is executed in the most inefficient way. This puts European researchers at disadvantage.

While there exist (and have been used) several proxies to measuring the creative activity of a university, a lab, a company or a person, the intensity of patenting is a popular one. A comparison between industrialized economies indicates that, since the mid-1990s, Euroland has been lagging behind its competitors in number of patents. A study by the European Central Bank points out that although the link between patenting activity and export performance is difficult to estimate,

- the lag in patents may have notable negative repercussions on Euroland's exports in the long run, and
- catching up requires enhanced significant effort, innovation and ability to keep up with international competition.[24]

Even if the correlation between number of patents and export business is not perfect, together with the number of new marketable products, patents are an indicator of research results. In a way, a patent is a government grant of monopoly rights to manufacture the invention for which such patent is sought.

The life cycle of a patent varies by jurisdiction. In the US, the rights run for 17 years, after which time it is assumed that, profitable or not, the idea should move freely into the public domain. Hence, although to the inventor or the company for which the researcher works patents are permissions to make a fortune, this opportunity is not unlimited in duration. (It is also true that some people abuse the patent mechanism by trying to block others from obtaining a patent.)

The European Central Bank also says that there is substantial heterogeneity across Euroland countries in terms of their technological competitiveness. R&D spending on high technology is relatively low in Germany, Spain and Italy – but within this spectrum exist graduations. For instance, R&D intensity for Italy is one-third that of Germany.

An interesting characteristic of patents is that they are discrete whereas in a great number of cases the underlying process is continuous. One invention feeds another: missile technology and space travel owe their existence to a long sequence of discoveries and improvements since the advent of the first simple, crude, man-made tools, Sperry's aerial torpedo being a milestone. Discrete patents can be seen as stepping stones to this

23 Tobin Harshaw, 'Is Wall Street Picking Our Pockets?, *The New York Times*, 24 July 2009, at: http://opinionator.blogs.nytimes.com/2009/07/24/weekend-opinionator-is-wall-street-picking-our-pockets/.

24 European Central Bank, *Monthly Bulletin*, July 2006.

continuous process, and at the same time a mark of excellence for the researcher and the lab.

All sorts of inventions from basic science to products, processes and more can qualify for a patent. Originality rather than practicality is the criterion. Although there is no rule characterizing the advancement reflected in a product pattern, it will probably tend to concern innovation. By contrast, the chances are that in the bottom line of a process patent the dominant issue with regard to its adoption is cost.

Patents are evidence of innovation, and, as the reader is well aware, innovation is the culture of discovery and novelty. It prompts firms and individuals to take risks by turning products and services inside out and by inventing new ones. Many big firms find difficult to implant that culture of questioning the 'obvious' and proceeding with creative destruction, so, to fill the gap they look outside for radical ideas by buying start-ups in their home country and in foreign markets. Maintaining a culture of innovation poses challenges to small and medium-size enterprises (SMEs). Several EU SMEs, particularly in Italy, Germany and Scandinavia have come to appreciate that in this century the very nature of their business has changed because of innovation.

For instance, most of the innovation in pharmaceuticals these days comes from small new firms, while R&D activity in big pharmaceutical firms concentrates largely on identifying and doing deals with innovative firms. The latter are much smaller in size, but a good deal more creative.[25]

Companies ahead of the curve who want to keep on improving their competitiveness are now using patents and patent information as benchmarks. Apart from the market appeal of novelty in product design which, up to a point, can be documented through patents, another reason for holding patents is to have legal evidence of in-house technical breakthroughs permitting:

- enforcement invention ownership and
- more negotiating power in licence negotiations with bigger firms.

There is little doubt that larger companies are more likely to hold patents, but this does not mean that smaller firms should be negligent at a time when novelty and innovation count for so much. Moreover, SMEs using the patent system are better able to carry out searches for checking on existing patents or patent infringement, as well as obtain technical and commercial information which can lead to better-focused pricing. (See also, in section 6, the race for patents among big companies).

Small and medium-size enterprises (and most evidently the larger ones) should also appreciate that nowadays many of the best students and academics at America's universities, as well as a good deal of entrepreneurs are foreign-born. During the last five decades, starting with Europe's brain drain of the 1960s, America's success in turning ideas into dollars has been based on the brain gain – whose source, more recently, is in Asia.

For most of the 65 years after the end of World War II America benefited from huge inflows of human capital, as many young people from the educated elite of other countries flocked to the US to make a career. Globalization has broken down the obsolete country

25 It is a curious fact that in recent years many of the big firms' laboratories have proved sterile. By contrast, marketing departments became a hive of creative activity by forging alliances.

barriers. Brains develop in many countries around the globe, but events seem to favour the countries which are 'on the go'.

- The better scientists go where they are appreciated, and
- plenty of those left behind are those who are unwilling or unable to provide creative work.

Scientific immigrants (and I consider myself as an example) are motivated to move ahead because they can only depend on their know-how. This pushes forward the frontiers of knowledge. It also motivates people to run faster because they know that rewards come with hard work.

## 6. The Changing Influence of R&D on Corporate Performance

The careful reader will recall, from Chapter 1, that in 2005 Booz Allen Hamilton (BAH), the consultancy, made a comprehensive study assessing the influence of R&D on corporate performance. The study concluded that there is no one-to-one relationship between R&D spending and the primary measures of economic or corporate success. What matters most is not how much money is spent on R&D, but how it is spent – as the BAH study pointed out. Judging by the number of patents obtained in 2005, the top ten winners in the global patents rally have been:

1. IBM – 2,941
2. Cannon – 1,828
3. Hewlett-Packard – 1,797
4. Matsushita – 1,688
5. Samsung – 1,641
6. Micron Technology – 1,561
7. Intel – 1,549
8. Hitachi – 1,271
9. Toshiba – 1,258
10. Fujitsu – 1,154.[26]

This list comprises five Japanese, four American, one Korean and no European firms. It should be appreciated that all ten are global firms, and their R&D budgets are directly linked to projects that address the international market. Note, however, that the large majority of these patents concern applied research projects – not the products of basic research (section 1).

The whole model of corporate R&D has changed in a fairly radical way. Immediately after World War II major basic research breakthroughs came from the huge corporate laboratories, particularly in America. We owe to them a great deal of the technology we are using today.

Researchers at AT&T's Bell Labs earned six Nobel prizes for inventions, such as the laser and the transistor. More recently, however, what is left of a hugely downsized Bell

26 *The Economist*, 14 January 2006.

Labs (now part of France's Alcatel-Lucent), is turning its attention almost entirely towards development – and it is doing so with a very average performance.

- Bell Labs reached a low point in 2003 when it had only some 1,000 researchers and a $115 million budget.
- By contrast, half a century earlier it boasted 25,000 researchers and its own physics department.

Xerox's Palo Alto Research Center (PARC) devised the personal computer's distinctive elements, including the mouse, graphical user interface and the Ethernet protocol for computer networking. In 2002 Xerox PARC became an independent subsidiary able to provide research services and intellectual property to outside clients and not just its parent company, but it failed to commercialize its products and then fainted.

Other times, other markets, other priorities and different criteria of success in R&D ... The old AT&T ran the world's biggest telephone network, and Xerox was a synonym for photocopying. The companies themselves saw the cost of basic research as a small price to pay for maintaining their corporate appeal and power. Modern technology firms don't think that way.

New policies have led to splintering of research divisions. Even though big American and European firms still spend billions on R&D, none has shown any intention of filling the shoes left empty by Bell Labs, GM Labs or Xerox PARC. In addition:

- It looks like the big labs' method of bringing together thousands of smart people no longer works.
- Labs have become much smaller, and the mission given to product teams is to solve the immediate needs of the firm paying for them.

The strategic vision, structure and objectives of companies' R&D efforts have changed. In terms of objectives, most of the big spenders in R&D today follow diverse strategies but at their core is a single aim: to assure significant returns. The better-managed companies have five main sources from which they draw *new ideas*:

- universities, where they fund research in areas of interest to them;
- government bodies, which sponsor weapons projects that leave footprints on the civilian market;
- small and medium-size enterprises, from which they license or buy new ideas;
- their in-house venture capital funds, which search the market for worthy start-ups; and
- their own in-house laboratory which is relatively small in size compared to the post-World War II giant R&D labs.

There is a rationale behind this diversity, but also a great need for planning, organizing and controlling sprawling R&D interests. The reasons for the shift in policies on how to spend research money are best explained by the prevailing opinion that R&D has become a profit centre.[27]

27 Like the company's treasury, with its intensive hedging.

In addition, the highly competitive global market penalizes delays in renovating the product line; and big labs are not known for timely results. Delays see to it that someone else creams the market and the new products will not be big hits – if they find a place at all. Acquiring start-ups also contributes to the product line's *breadth* of range by including more alternatives and to its *depth* by providing a greater number of options. The bottom line is how well this policy:

- fits the overall strategic plan,
- contributes to the company's future cash flow and
- promotes its medium- to longer-term profitability.

Quite often, marketing will make the difference between the success and failure of an acquired product or product line (see section 7). The same is nevertheless true for products developed in-house. Inevitably, not all R&D projects can succeed, but, in many cases, poor management at both corporate and lab level make the statistics worse than they might have been. Among the factors behind new product failures are:

- poor timing of product launch,
- substandard project management,
- responding to competitors rather than serving the company's own strategic plan',
- little attention paid to the steady training of engineers, scientists, product planners and marketing people,
- Meagre marketing budgets and failure to make a sustained sales effort.

In an attempt to avoid poor timing, sloppy project management and the competitors creaming the market, companies invented new approaches to lab control. A great deal of Motorola's Razr mobile phone, a big market success, was developed in a new laboratory that the company set up in downtown Chicago, 50 miles from its main R&D facility. The building and its workspace were very different from Motorola's classical offices, with:

- lots of bright colours,
- movable dividing walls and
- very rigorous schedules.

This emerging new R&D organization pays more attention than its predecessors to the environment in which people work, as well as to the quality of communications. In a way, it is a descendent of Lockheed's Skunk Works®, whose people worked on a project outside the company's classical R&D culture.

To improve performance and deliverables, in the new R&D culture researchers are not just left to make pure intellectual contributions. They are constantly brought into contact with designers, as well as experts in marketing, production, finance and accounting. This way, they ultimately emerge with products that:

- make their competitors jealous, and
- make customers want to buy them.

Another critical factor behind the change in R&D policy and organization is that in the twenty-first century innovation comes more from software than hardware. In addition, computing costs are low and continue to drop, so it makes sense to use simulation – as development times must be very fast for the product to succeed. Siemens claims that software has been a basic ingredient in its business revolution. Today:

- Siemens has more software developers than Oracle or SAP, and
- the software it makes or buys is embedded in its trains, machine tools and factory automation.

The company's CEO calculates that as much as 60 per cent of his firm's sales now involve software, while about 90 per cent of the development in machine tools is in electronics and related hardware – a far cry from Siemens' origins.[28] Much the same is true for cars. Today a BMW or an Audi is a network of computers and uses fuzzy engineering chips which learn the driver's habits in order to optimize fuel consumption.

## 7. Planning for Market Leadership

'Clothes and automobiles change every year,' said Paul M. Mazur, of Lehman Brothers. 'But because the currency remains the same in appearance, though its value steadily declines, most people believe that finance does not change. Actually, debt financing changes like everything else. We have to find new models in financing, just as in clothes and automobiles, if we want to stay on top. We must remain inventive architects of the money business.'[29]

Mazur's statement applies hand-in-glove to practically all industries. New products are not made for the fun of it. They have to be sold in a competitive market, gain market share and produce an income. *If* they fail to do that, *then* the CEO is no inventive architect of innovation; instead, he or she becomes the person responsible for the slow (or sometimes rapid) disappearance of his or her firm.[30] I underline the importance of the marketing angle because it is by no means certain that new products will be given the attention they deserve to become leaders.

- One of the reasons is that senior management is not sensitive to the changing product promotion perspective.
- Another reason is that they are too often evaluated outside the context of their environment.

Either market research did not do its job properly, or the sales organization has been deficient. Quite often, after having spent a small fortune on R&D, management wrongly decides to make economies in the marketing budget. Or the new product calls for lots of customer training to increase its appeal, but senior management does not allocate

---

28 Personal communcication.

29 Joseph Wechsberg, *The Merchant Bankers*, Pocket Books/Simon & Schuster, New York, 1966.

30 A study by Kodak has shown that, after six years of poor management, a company runs out of luck and of business. Look at Chrysler and General Motors.

the appropriate funds to that mission. Many companies take too long to come to this strategic decision.

- IBM was a master in customer training – an activity with high return on investment.
- Univac decided to move to that policy only after it had lost ground to its number one competitor.

Cost-effectiveness, too, is at a premium. In the 1960s and 1970s respectively, with the 360 and 370 mainframes, IBM thrived. But in the late 1970s VAXes demolished the mainframes' hold on the market for business computers, and supercomputers creamed the upper end of the 370 line. By the early 1980s personal computers spread like a bushfire, and by the late 1980s IBM and its mainframes were in deep trouble.

As far as the IBM PC was concerned, inside the company there was a battle between those who wanted to stay with commodity chips (made by Intel) and commodity software and the pure-blooded for whom everything had to be made by Big Blue. Even IBM's sales networks, which used to be the best in the industry, bend to a culture that proclaimed that:

- the company was *über alles*, and
- therefore everybody, including its clients, had to click their heels.

This monumental failure teaches a profound marketing lesson. The mission of the salesforce is not limited to pushing the products. It also includes the responsibility of acting as ambassadors at clients' premises, and the firm's top management has the responsibility to listen to what salespeople report about market drivers. The source from which salespeople derive their knowledge is customer satisfaction and dissatisfaction:

- What is wrong with the product?
- What sort of improvements do customers want to see?
- How do our company's products hold up against those of our competitors?
- What has to be done to come up from under?
- How fast this should be done to avoid alienating the market?

These are qualitative factors and, evidently, they are less easy to measure quantitative factors, but they are nevertheless very important. Consequently, the CEO and the board should be eager to hear about them – and, after having heard, prepared to act. Although price counts, it is not always the principal competitive weapon to gain and hold. After all, the second component of cost-effectiveness is 'effectiveness'.

A sound marketing plan also pays significant attention to *time-to-market*. Few CEOs appreciate the fact that when new products stay too long in the lab, the result is disaster. Superficially, this may seem to be an R&D problem. In reality, it is a fault of top management in balancing the impact of R&D and marketing on the company's future.

Even big companies which should know better don't understand that right timing is a key factor of success in their business. An example that sticks in my mind dates back to the mid-1990s. The stated goal of the August 1995 (unsuccessful) reorganization at General Motors had been to:

- speed development of new models by 25 per cent, to 36 months;

- slash engineering costs by 30 per cent; and
- restore pizzazz to GM's bland brands to revive the market's interest.

But, on Wall Street, financial analysts were quick to point out that, in hallmark fashion, GM's efforts to both renew and simplify itself have created an ever-more complex structure. Neither did the way in which these changes (and their goals) were presented please them – and for good reason. GM's targeted 36-month time-to-market compared poorly with the 30-month timescale that Toyota had already achieved.

There is yet another issue to bring to the reader's attention. Dead cats don't bounce. Six decades of intensive work in industry have convinced me that no matter how great may be the engineering behind a product,

- *if* it takes years to lift its sales curve,
- *then* it will never lift it, no matter how much money is spent to resurrect it.

The electric car presents an example. Invented a century ago, it never lifted off the ground in a marketing sense. It is therefore most curious that big motor vehicle companies – some of them, like GM, badly wounded from their other mistakes – continue pouring hundreds of millions of dollars into electric cars whose return on investments continues to be dismal.

Shai Agassi might have an answer to one of the electric car's problems with his start-up, Better Place. Its goal is to build a global network of charging points and battery-exchange stations to create mass market for electric cars by overcoming customer resistance due to the lack of facilities for charging the batteries and servicing. (Lack of a servicing network is a king-size hurdle for any type of motor vehicle.)

Better Place will not make cars. Agassi's approach is to look at electric transport as a system in which cars, batteries, recharging points, electrical utilities and billing systems must all work together. To attain that goal, he plans to use a business model borrowed from mobile telephony: charging not by the minute, but by the kilometre. This is a large investment, and it is uncertain whether investors will be forthcoming. If they do, we will have plenty of time to judge whether the electric car's dynamics can be changed.

With these and many more real-life examples in mind, it can be surely said that an able management will be keen to excel not only in R&D, but also in marketing. This means right-budgeting both research requirements and sales spending (see Table 5.1). In addition, marketing people and salespeople must be running fast, which can best be promoted through quantitative targets (quotas). When it comes to investments associated with the innovation of products, slippages kill the product – whether their origin is in R&D or in marketing. Quantitative targets should cover:

- sales,
- cash flow,
- profits.

Note, however, that even when laboratories are nearly sterile, marketing departments can bridge the gap by becoming a hive of creative activity through forging alliances. Not everyone appreciates that marketing can be creative, but top salespeople are conceptual beings like great architects and engineers.

The right pay helps in motivation, and salespeople's pay must be commensurate to the effort being made. A sound policy is to make at least two-thirds of the salesperson's earnings quota-based, and to regularly review these quotas. In addition, salespeople must be steadily trained, informed about new products and design changes, and believe in the company's effectiveness, as well as their own.

In conclusion, research, ingenuity and technical innovation have become the hallmarks of business organizations whose success is measured by their acceptance in a burgeoning global marketplace. But, as competition continually intensifies, the need for marketing-oriented leadership grows. Without it, companies cannot provide industrial and professional competence even of they are way ahead in R&D. It seems to me that the European Union paid scant attention to this principle when it started financing research projects.

CHAPTER

# 6 The EU Research and Development Challenge

## 1. Managing and Financing R&D in the European Union

Beginning in 1951 with the establishment of the European Coal and Steel Community, a forerunner of Common Market and European Union, some research and development (R&D) projects have been financed at transnational level (see section 4). The Treaty of Rome in 1957 and, more so, the Single European Act of 1986,

- empowered the EU to promote research,
- but little attention was paid to research management.

Research and development was a domain of private initiative rather than of government attention and support well before World War II. But neither before nor after World War II did the academic and industrial communities, which together could get research funds from European governments, strengthen their ties.

With each country practically following its own policies, investment in R&D has become one of key criteria which have divided EU members. For instance, companies in Germany have been very successful in financing R&D in-house from reinvested profits, without seeing the contribution of state finance as crucial. The more successful companies:

- have developed an in-house venture-capital activity and
- have cross-subsidized innovation with surpluses from mature cash-cow divisions.

Several SMEs moved production facilities abroad, to benefit from lower costs, but only the best paid due attention to innovation, mainly owing to entrepreneurial risk aversion which made them feel comfortable in their existing businesses. There has also been a relative scarcity of emerging innovative firms declaring high-growth ambitions. Altogether, this served to downplay R&D-funded growth, particularly in the absence of support from individual EU governments.

Brussels then became a little more active. Beginning in 1994, the First Framework Program for Research and Development was put in motion with the objective of coordinating national policies concerning research carried out in the EU, as well as promoting certain common projects (more on that later). By financing and helping to define the direction of research, the EU Executive hoped to assist member states and their firms. However, while countries and companies were happy to get EU money,

- the idea of having someone set the direction (like Japan's Ministry of International Trade and Industry (MITI) did after World War II) was a non-starter, and

- the EU policy on common multilateral projects was a non-starter,with the exception of projects kept at the level of pre-competitive research. However, the ESPRIT project, which *was* pre-competitive research, led practically nowhere (see section 4).

So much for co-financing R&D on an EU-wide basis. Research projects that are 100 per cent EU-financed are supported by the Joint Research Centre (JRC), which directly depends on Brussels and covers different scientific and technological areas. Its sites are in Belgium, the Netherlands, Italy, Germany and Spain; but its management leaves much to be desired.

Critics say that nothing really has come out of all these efforts, including those under JRC and other only partly financed projects. Promoting the technology of EU member states and European companies has not been successful. Some experts give as a reason economic nationalism;[1] others think that the ingredients for successful research have not been in place.

- Sound management and EU-wide collaboration in R&D have been conspicuously absent, and,
- although money is important, 'more funds' change nothing in terms of end results if business continues as usual.

This runs contrary to an undocumented political opinion expressed by a former Finnish prime minister who headed an EU Commission on the sorry state of the European industry. His 'conclusion' was that all is needed is more research money, and this is patently wrong. Even if a lot more money were available for European R&D, without a holistic view of the economy and strategic choices on where it should be invested,

- R&D money will represent only a fraction of the effort necessary to come up from under, because, as we saw in Chapter 5, research must be focused, and
- in terms of priorities, the definition of expected deliverables, quality results and fast timetables to conquer targeted markets should precede financing.

The second-raters who run the (mis)fortunes of the European Union probably fail to appreciate that unless its companies (and member countries) lose no time in immediately implementing research results, developing countries catch up and cream off the global market. The BRICS[2] and other emerging countries are rapidly expanding beyond the niches they had originally found for themselves. Among the world's top 250 technology firms, which used to be exclusive domain of the US, EU and Japan,

- Taiwan features in 12th place, up from 3rd place in 2000,
- while many are now from South Korea, Hong Kong, China and India.

The rise of Asian companies in high technology is characterized by the welding of the region into a global supply chain. In terms of research, development and implementation, India has focused on software and services which, unlike physical goods, can be delivered

1 D.N. Chorafas, *The Business of Europe is Politics*, Gower, Aldershot, 2009.

2 Brazil, Russia, India and China.

through networks. Both Chinese and Indian firms are now setting up shop in central and eastern Europe as a low-cost stepping-stone towards high-tech exports to the Western EU countries.

Seen from a different perspective, while large R&D budgets provide no guarantee that return on investment will be high, lack of money results in downsizing and soft-pedalling the research effort. This impacts on deliverables. Relatively small research budgets, compared to GDP, have led to bleak outcomes with the result that that European countries lost their technological supremacy after World War II.

Plenty of harm has been caused by the fact that Europe's technological supremacy during the pre-World War II years instilled a sense of arrogance with regard to the R&D capabilities of European companies, which persisted without justification after the war. This arrogance bred complacency with the result that the technological prowess of European companies has been repeatedly challenged:

- first by American and Japanese companies and
- more recently by the rising Asian challengers and, to a lesser extent, by Brazil.

Let's face it. Despite all the various dime-a-dozen 'summits' and the various egocentric pronouncements emanating from them, the EU has no master plan on how to come up from under in R&D. An integral part of this plan should be a higher educational standard (as discussed in the first chapters of this book), because education, research and development work in tandem.

- The best scientists flock to renowned centres of education and research,
- while many of those left behind are less able, or less willing, to do creative work.

Another reason why research, development and innovation don't flourish in the EU is the state supermarket and its culture. In well-funded national laboratories, this culture makes bureaucrats out of researchers and lulls them into believing that once they have a job, it will be for life. Hence, they see no reason why they should produce research results, particularly as these are not necessarily connected to advancement in their careers.

In addition, the various EU member states do everything to discourage companies from taking risks in R&D. Profits, if they make them, will be taxed to death; the exposure they assume is not recognized; and, by and large, EU society does not reward individual effort in the way it should be rewarded in order to motivate people to make the best of themselves.

## 2. The Lag in Funding Basic Research

Since the end of the Cold War, Western governments have progressively reduced (and, in some cases, altogether abandoned) their commitment to basic scientific research. Curiously, this has been seen as part of the 'peace dividend', and statements have been made that taxpayers will only support science that produces tangible, commercial results.

- It looks *as if* the pursuit of knowledge for knowledge's sake has fallen from grace, and

- the consequence is that almost everywhere new policies are marked by the outrage of pure scientists, coupled with a fallback in exploring science's frontiers.

As we have seen in Chapter 5, the disappearance of huge basic research centres, like Bell Labs, clipped off contributions to science. This has not been compensated by an equivalent increase in basic research spending. In the early 1950s there was a rule of thumb in Europe that basic research funding should stand at about 10 per cent of the R&D budget. Nowadays that share has significantly shrunk and, with few exceptions, we are scraping the bottom of the barrel in terms of knowledge connected to the physical sciences.

Let's look at some practical examples of attitudes towards basic research. In America, support for science has always been more diverse in origin and therefore more robust. Many scientists, however, consider 1994 as being the first year, for over 30 years, in which funding priorities switched to research problems relating to practical solutions and away from basic science.

Still, because the links between academic research and industry are close and the government provides plenty of funding, America has many sources of R&D spending. Half-way through the first decade of this century, when industry was in high gear, federal money accounted for $86 billion of the $288 billion spent on R&D. Spending on the life sciences increased particularly rapidly, and a reasonable bet for the future is that it will continue to do so, even if:

- federal support for basic research in the physical sciences and engineering at universities has withered, and
- some of the domains of research most directly coupled to technological innovation are now short of funds.

The increase in financing life sciences and biomedical research is most welcome, but does not compensate for neglecting basic research in physics. The latter leads several experts to the conclusion that America may be losing its future competitiveness in sciences where it was the leader for several decades.

The other two examples come from the European Union. Since the 1980s British governments have produced policy documents embodying seemingly radical proposals for the reorganization of research in the sciences, although at the same time they have cut the budget allocated to university research. Critics say, moreover, that:

- after nearly three decades in which government support for basic research, and the discovery of new knowledge was a stated objective of public policy,
- most of the British government's spending on R&D is now benefiting development projects.

New knowledge is given the back seat, in a way emulating what has already taken place in British industry.

Germany's public spending in R&D is somewhat different, allegedly for political reasons. Since 1993 federal research funds have been diverted eastwards to build up new research institutes in the former East German Länder (states). But federal governments in western Germany are not able to make up the shortfall, and basic research falters.

Ironically, research funds were further reduced to finance the project of moving the capital from Bonn to Berlin.

This change of funding priorities has been counterproductive because Germany's *Mittelstand* (the SMEs) are the backbone of its industry, and they depend heavily on the technical universities for research results. (This unwarranted switch also hurt the higher education budget.)

Neither Germany nor Britain are in the forefront of financing R&D. Statistics dating back to the mid-2000s indicate that, worldwide, the first position belonged to Sweden with R&D funding standing at nearly 4 per cent of GDP, followed by Finland with 3.5 per cent. Germany has been spending 2.5 per cent and Britain a meagre 1.8 per cent of GDP. The US was slightly above Germany in percentage terms – easily surpassed by the aforementioned two frontrunners, as well as by Japan, South Korea and Switzerland (in that order).

Published in March 2010, the most recent data on R&D spending as a percentage of GDP per year pertain to 2008 (the most recent available). As the reader can see in Table 6.1, Japan continues to be above the US which leads Germany by a meagre 0.2 per cent – but spends more than France and Britain. (In the elapsed three years – 2005 to 2008 – Britain improved its R&D spending by a tiny 0.1 per cent.)

Industrial countries are in competition with each other in terms of the share of GDP they spend on R&D. In Austria, for example, this share has steadily grown from 1.2 per cent in 1990 to nearly 2.8 per cent in 2010, with a large amount of money going to biotechnology. The good news is that this increase is propelling the country to the top ranks of the EU in R&D terms; the bad news is that the EU is not a top performer in R&D.

**Table 6.1 R&D spending as a percentage of GDP per year***

| Country | Percentage of GDP per Year |
|---|---|
| Japan | 3.4 |
| US | 2.8 |
| Germany | 2.6 |
| France | 2.0 |
| Britain | 1.9 |

* 2008 data, which are the latest available.

*Source: The Economist*, 13 March 2010.

As for the EU Executive, its preoccupation with basic research has been anything but brilliant. The projects which it sponsored and financed, such as BRITE (industrial technologies), ESPRIT (information technology), RACE (telecommunications), EUREKA (a broader European programme of advanced technology) – which were jointly funded by industry and government – are worlds away from embracing scientific idealism. Euratom has been a somewhat better story and owes its improved fortune as much to its people as to political drive.[3] (ESPRIT, EUREKA and RACE are discussed in section 4.)

3 Euratom is a European atomic energy agency which emerged in the late 1950s. Atomic energy research is an appropriate vehicle for enhancing EU ties.

There is also the European Science Foundation which dates from the early 1970s; this is a pale shadow of the National Science Foundation in the United States, and there is therefore no reason to spend time talking about it. There are, however, two important exceptions to the statements made in the preceding paragraphs:

- CERN, financed by public European money, and
- basic research in biosciences and pharma, financed by private companies.

The provisional agreement establishing CERN, the European high-energy physics facility, near Geneva, was signed in February 1952. Since then, basic research has continued to figure prominently in its objectives. CERN and its scientific research is the European success story, with the financial burden being shouldered by the European governments.

Throughout the years of its existence, CERN has featured top-quality scientists and research groups, and its deliverables have assured it a steady flow of money as well as raised expectations for the future. The supercollider[4] might eventually prove to be an important strategic field of research, overtaking similar projects in the US.

European successes also exist in basic research projects in drugs, bioengineering, biochemistry and the broader area of life sciences. These are well financed by private money. Work is progressing nicely, which is important because this is one of the areas at the frontiers of knowledge deserving the greatest attention. But all by itself it is no compensation for the absence of Bell Labs-type investigative work and scientific exploration in the physical sciences.

Governments lack the political will to fund basic research, even through universities. This has been true in Europe and is becoming so in America, as well. The latest US figures show that federal support in constant dollars for research is about half what it was in 1985 – just a quarter-century earlier. In the EU, too, funding reductions imposed on already low levels are worrisome, and the toothless European parliament (which itself costs a huge – plainly unwarranted – sum of money) has done nothing to correct the balance in favour of scientific discovery.

## 3. Benefits From Bringing Together Industry and Academia

In the early 1940s Vannevar Bush, professor at MIT and science advisor to Franklin D. Roosevelt, wrote, at the request of the president, a report that served as blueprint for America's enormously successful university–industry collaboration in the post-World War II years. Under the title *Science: The Endless Frontier*,[5] Bush:

- laid out a vision for government-funded science and engineering, and
- set the state up for a superb process that would unite academia, industry and the defence establishment.

---

4 The world's largest and highest-energy particle accelerator which is expected to answer the most fundamental questions of physics.

5 *Science: The Endless Frontier. A Report to the President by Vannevar Bush, Director of the Office of Scientific Research and Development, July 1945*, US Government Printing Office, Washington, 1945.

The blueprint called for university projects in basic science, with industry capitalizing on the findings to develop products it could market. Companies soon organized themselves to embrace this concept and benefit from it – an effort which, for several decades, achieved stunning success.

According to the Vannevar Bush model, apart the basic research done in half a dozen giant labs of US corporations, universities had to maintain and possibly create the infrastructure across all fields of science. The plan was far-sighted and among its many deliverables was that of stimulating the emergence of new interdisciplinary fields.

This brought a double benefit. To excel in basic research, universities needed to train a future generation of scientists, at graduate and postgraduate level, laying the foundation for future innovation as well as for strategic research. With government funding in the background, the orientation was at least partly based on public policy, but it did foster individual, communal and national scientific awareness.

However complex this mission seemed to be, the economic contours which emerged over the years have been both clear and beneficial. They also cut new ground. On the surface, the challenge facing universities and research scientists was not so different from that facing other R&D organizations. They were being asked to:

- improve their investigative performance,
- use their skills more effectively and
- work towards goals which appealed to the research community, with little or no worry about research project financing.

There has been nothing comparable to it in Europe, which is not surprising since European universities are not forthcoming in implementing joint projects with industry, while, by carrying almost 100 per cent of the cost of higher education, governments are left with very little money (or even incentives) to finance basic research. What *is* surprising is that the Americans decided to abandon a successful system.

Already by the late 1980s when the signs of a switch in policy became visible, some voices were raising doubts whether America's supremacy in research and technology would continue into the twenty-first century. Funding for the process which had produced more and better US physicists, chemists, mathematicians, aeronautical engineers and medical researchers was drying up at a time when the big corporate laboratories had started to melt away.

In retrospect, turning off the tab of federal funding was not the only reason for the reversal in research fortunes. Primary and secondary education, too, was failing, and the brain gain which immensely benefited American in the 1960s was drying up.[6] By the late 1980s in the US fewer than 1 per cent of college freshmen said they intended to major in maths, compared with 4 per cent two decades earlier, while:

- physics and chemistry students fell from 3 per cent to 1.5 per cent of the intake, and
- one in three PhDs awarded in the natural sciences and engineering went to foreigners, compared with one in four just a decade earlier.

6 D.N. Chorafas, *The Knowledge Revolution*, Allen & Unwin, London; McGraw-Hill, New York, 1968.

Although, unlike Europe, the US attracted lots of scientists and engineers from Asia, the overall result was not comparable to that which followed the brain gain of the 1960s. New scientific immigrants may be compensating for the retirement of aging scientists, but the shortage of new students because of their aversion towards the sciences is painfully felt (a deficit that also prevails in Europe).

This science deficit is clearly reflected in university research and threatens Europe's and America's prosperity. Capable science professors and teachers are becoming difficult to find, particularly in the EU, partly because university salaries are no match for the incomes to be made in private companies. As a result, the men and women who do choose the classroom over the corporate lab are not always the best role models for potential young scientists.

Yet another problem faced by many EU universities, which might have been partially corrected had there been close academic–industry cooperation, is their rapidly aging laboratories. Without new facilities, it is increasingly difficult for many schools to continue doing leading-edge research. One has to have modern facilities for research at the frontiers of knowledge. In fact, it is no exaggeration that cash-strapped universities are having trouble just keeping up with their crumbling bricks and mortar. Many European academics say that their research facilities are in need of a great deal of renovation or new construction, but there are no funds for this because of budget constraints.

In 2007, after he was elected president of France, Nicolas Sarkozy authorized the sale of part of the government's equity in EDF, the energy company, to make money available for the renovation of some university buildings. These days, things are not that much better in America. Even back in 1989 Stanford University, which had helped spawn California's Silicon Valley, turned to its alumni to find the money for renovating its labs for materials science and applied materials research (housed together in the advanced materials research building).

As the careful reader will recall from the preceding chapters, another benefit from close collaboration between academia and universities, particularly in applied R&D projects, is that students working on them can get a good idea of what it takes to turn laboratory results into exciting products. This is not an issue that is given top priority in theoretical studies.

To be able to perform in the new R&D culture and expand the reach of their intellectual contributions, researchers must be constantly brought into contact with designers, marketing experts, production engineers, finance executives and accountants – and also, selectively, with important clients. This provides a background that is most valuable in professional life.

In conclusion, from partly government-sponsored basic research through joint university–industry projects in research and applied science, there exists a whole range of opportunities and challenges for faculty and for graduate students. Joint academia–industry projects in European universities can shake off past lethargy, revamp their rigid structures and begin to get them fit for the increasingly more globalized twenty-first century. Why? Because while globalization may be constrained here or there as it reaches its limits, it will not be reversed.[7]

7 D.N. Chorafas, *Globalization's Limits: Conflicting National Interests in Trade and Finance*, Gower, Aldershot, 2009.

## 4. Are Common EU Research Projects Worth Their Salt?

The alter ego of innovation is *performance*. Today's customers are demanding because they know better than their predecessors what they want. Besides this, many products and services must comply with a growing body of governmental regulations, and companies also face shareholder pressures for increased income.

What has the European Union done to promote a better performance from R&D in member states? As briefly discussed in section 2, starting in the 1980s the EU Commission established and financed cooperative projects limited to *pre-competitive research*. This was done on a cost-sharing basis:

- Brussels provided 50 per cent of these joint projects costs, and
- the remainder was borne by the partners in the sponsored research projects.

Participation has been open to all industrial firms, research institutes and universities within the EU. The caveat was that each member country *should* get back all of the money it contributed to the budget of the EU pre-competitive research effort – which made an EU-wide optimization of funds poured into, and results expected from, this initiative practically impossible.

Proposals for cooperative projects were submitted by the interested parties to a central authority in Brussels, in response to periodic *calls for proposals* initiated by the EU Commission according to its agenda. Each project had to include at least two industrial partners from different member nations. Submitted proposals were evaluated mainly on their pre-competitive merits, with three areas attracting the most attention:

- Basic Research in Industrial Technologies for Europe (BRITE). This was a misnomer since the project sponsored mainly applications-oriented R&D in traditional industrial sectors. Its budget was ECU600 million.[8]
- The European Strategic Programme for Research and Development in Information Technology (ESPRIT)., This programme, which lasted from 1985 to 1992, promoted cooperative projects in pre-competitive information technology, with a budget of ECU3.2 billion.
- Research and Advanced Communications in Europe (RACE). This was a project that promoted selected efforts with the goal of establishing an advanced integrated broadband communications network. Its budget was ECU1.1 billion – this was the most applications-oriented of the three projects.

Altogether, because they span several years, the financial resources of slightly over ECU5 billion were not impressive, representing a very small portion of total R&D spending by European industries, over the aforementioned timeframe. And, with a couple of minor exceptions, the primary impact of all these projects was not one of obtaining specific results that could be commercialized, but, rather,

- to bring together scientists, engineers and developers from different countries, and

8 The ECU (European Currency Unit) was the EC's unit of internal accounting before the establishment of the euro as a common EU currency in 1999,

- have them get to know one another by working together.

Bringing people of diverse cultures into one team and making them communicate with each other was an important objective. The EU Commission was right to undertake such an initiative. This, however, was not research, and each of the different projects ran itself in its own way and at its own pace without cross-project coordination. The experts Brussels used as advisors had no power to take action if something went wrong; they had even to watch their words to avoid ruffling the national economic feathers of the different project members.

In addition, while the pre-competitive nature of the EU-funded research had a rationale, the nature of the required deliverables was, by necessity, a watered-down compromise. This was admissible as long as the stated projects mainly targeted bringing together R&D people from different EU countries, but the results ranged:

- from being rather inconsistent
- to being some sort of an unproven prototype.

Seen from a cultural perspective, ESPRIT, BRITE and RACE made sense even if they were confronted by the aforementioned problems. Still other problems were linguistic in nature. English became the *lingua franca* of these projects, but some of the participants' knowledge of English left much to be desired. Also serious was the lack of a policy on what to do with results if and when they were obtained.

Correctly, every funded project had a finite life cycle. The question which soon arose with ESPRIT was whether the use of its deliverables – for instance, a new software shell for prototyping – should become mandatory for subsequent IT projects. Or should each project be free to choose its own shell and programming language? This type of question

- repeated itself several times and
- was never answered.

Another common research programme which ran along fairly similar lines was EUREKA. It was not sponsored by Brussels, but by 19 European governments – both within and outside the EU – to promote international cooperation in advanced technological research. Since this was not a purely EU initiative, its funding was provided independently of ESPRIT, BRITE and RACE by the governments of each participating nation. It was stipulated that EUREKA projects must:

- include partners from more than one member country (fair enough);
- be able to demonstrate a significant expected benefit from such cross-border cooperation (a vague notion); and
- provide 'just return' to country sponsors, which meant every country should get its money back (a bad policy).

EUREKA was founded in 1985, and sponsored projects had a ground-up structure. The projects were conceived directly by industrial firms according to their needs and prospects and were then presented to the member nations for consideration. As a result, EUREKA projects – which were financed to the tune of ECU3.8 billion – were closer to producing tangible results than RACE, BRITE and ESPRIT. Nevertheless, there have been no success stories associated with EUREKA-sponsored research.

Quite different in terms of nature and structure has been the case of Galileo, an EU project intended to provide global positioning and navigation services. This was initially expected to cost in the region of €916 million, but subsequent delays, revisions and add-ons put the figure at around €3.4 billion – a 371 per cent increase in outlay. In addition:

- these delays put Galileo behind updated versions of GPS and
- made it more or less uncompetitive with similar satellite navigation projects planned by Russia and China.

Critics say that the common EU project should have been killed early on, because the news about progress in the common effort was never exciting and became really bad in October 2007 when Galileo reached an impasse. The reasons why the initial budget of EU public money fell short by over €2.4 billion were not just the overrun, but also, and mainly, because the industrial companies participating in the project did not put up their part of the research budget.

Although Galileo's partners were originally due to fund two-thirds of the project, they simply expected the taxpayer to pay the full bill. Eight companies – EADS, Astrium, Inmarsat, Thales, TeleOp, Finmeccanica, Alenia, Hispasat and Alcatel Space – participated in this game of vested interests. (A particular characteristic of that group of contractors was the absence of major German firms.)

To close the gaping hole, Brussels offered to give the money, by raiding other EU budgets. But, on 2 October 2007, Germany vetoed this plan in favour of a direct contribution by each EU member that had companies participating in Galileo's R&D. Since from the outset the EU principle on budgets for research projects has been that each country in practice gets for its firms the amount it contributes to the common goal, 'this' explains 'that'.

Among the contributors, Britain and Spain have been particularly strident in their criticism of Galileo's mismanagement. In October 2007 the House of Commons transport committee released a report on Galileo that found not only that just the cost of defining and planning the flagship EU satellite project was $53 million – 66 per cent more than anticipated – but also that development and validation so far had cost €402 million, or 37 per cent more than planned. The committee's report stated:

> *We have no reason to believe that even the very substantial costs now estimated for the total programme bear any significant relationship to the likely out-turn.*[9]

Many people in the EU expressed the opinion that this immense amount of money could be better spent by the EU on roads, power links and other infrastructure. They also supported the House of Commons committee's call to scrap Galileo, and the option of reducing its scope or dropping the project altogether cannot and should not be ruled out. But Galileo was a political, rather than a technological, undertaking – and killing a political project is an unheard-of feat.

---

9 *Total Telecom Magazine*, January 2008.

## 5. Common Weapons Research in the EU has Fared Worse Than Galileo

In the 1950s President Eisenhower spoke about the industrial–military complex and its effect on the US budget, as well as on the country's economy, by acting as promoter and consumer (at the taxpayer's expense). It is no secret that an industrial–military complex exists in every major country. The so-called *Iron Mountain Report*, published anonymously during the Johnson administration,[10] had put that issue squarely under perspective: the armaments industry is the flywheel of the economy.

Analysts tend to look at the weapons industry as a dual entity – economic and political – and they appreciate that it is protected by all governments, whether of the Right or of the Left. This gives it a sort of extra-commercial (even almost extraterrestrial) nature. Several facts suggest that its importance goes well beyond defence policy. Altogether, in the EU, the weapons industry is estimated at €80 billion ($112 billion) per year and its products are:

- making a major contribution to the exports of Britain, France, Germany, Italy, Sweden and other states;
- employing, about 1 million people, including suppliers; and
- representing an estimated 2 per cent, or more, of industrial production of the aforementioned countries.

If five EU countries are in the forefront of weapons development and production, other EU member states, too, participate in armaments-connected exports. Each country, however, develops weapons of its own for home use and for exports – in competition with other EU countries. There are no joint development initiatives, despite labels that have been used. As Martin Bangemann, a former EU commissioner, once remarked, this fragmented nature of the European defence industry clearly gives it a competitive disadvantage.

Could weapons systems research be the next successful EU common project? In early 2006 the French national armaments agency called for a €200 million ($280 million) programme in which EU countries would collaborate on basic research and technology in defence. Part of this proposal has been that such a programme should be run by the European Defence Agency (EDA), which is a successful offshoot of the EU's bureaucracy. There were no takers.

More recently, others have suggested that the better entity to act as coordinator for more or less similar initiatives is the new European Research Council (ERC). Designed to boost investments in pioneering scientific research, it was originally scheduled to inject some €335 million ($470 million) in grants to individual research projects. But bypassing national governments is a perilous exercise.

The ERC planned to award grants to some 430 of the 9,137 researchers who put in bids for them, on the basis of peer review. Then the question was asked: why not entrust it also with the administration of financing for weapons R&D, which requires a

10 *Report from the Iron Mountain: On the Possibility and Desirability of Peace*, 1967. Authorship was later claimed by Leonard C. Lewin.

supranational body to make decisions? So far, however, nothing worth talking about has been done along these lines.

But if results are not on hand, there is no lack of ideas. One opinion has been that since the theme of weapons research is indeed sensitive, the European Parliament may be the best decider on financing – as well as the arbiter when problems crop up. The MEPs (members of the European Parliament) are not particularly busy with projects which make a democracy tick,[11] so such an assignment would be a welcome change.

There is scepticism about whether or not this is doable, partly because the work of the European Parliament is carried out in committees whose debates are time-limited (from what one hears, many speeches are limited to 60 seconds and practically consist of monologues which allow MEPs to let off steam). In addition, trivial issues take an inordinate length of time and the impartiality of MEPs is questionable (MEPs grumble that the press is obsessed with scandals over parliamentary expenses on perks). That's scarcely an environment able to control weapons systems research, including its:

- timetables,
- costs and
- deliverables.

If it were not for all these negatives, it might have been a brilliant idea to give the European Parliament the responsibility of authorizing the budget of the EU's weapons systems R&D paid by the common purse and also of controlling the execution of these projects along the framework defined through project planning. This can be effectively done by means of *design reviews* (see section 7) in which the MEPs are assisted by the best independent experts available in each project's realm.

The pros say that when it comes to the EU's weapons systems projects and their financing, it matters little that the European Parliament is a corporatist assembly in which big parties rule by consensus and horse-trading. In fact, corporatism may be a distinct advantage in resolving disputes.

*If* parliamentary oversight of weapons systems R&D proves to be successful, it will correct the public opinion that the European Parliament is worse than dull. Today it spends an inordinate amount of time on subjects outside its mandate. Tomorrow its mandate could be R&D, including weapons. Curiously enough, Eurosceptics and federalists might even find a common ground of *entente*, while the opposition will be the Franco-German Greens.

On the other hand, while (as often discussed in this book) money alone never guarantees success, bickering over small sums leads to failure. It needs little explanation that the €200 million mentioned earlier in this section is peanuts as a weapons systems budget. The US Defense Advanced Research Project Agency (DARPA) is just one (and the better known) of the Pentagon's several agencies that finance weapons research. DARPA spends almost $3 billion a year in grants, and a great deal of that money is invested in advanced research done in American universities.

- The EU's proposed defence spending, at 8 per cent DARPA's budget, is not going to reach anywhere.

11 D.N. Chorafas, *The Business of Europe is Politics*, Gower, Aldershot, 2010.

- That budget's impact will be much smaller than 8 per cent, if one considers the fractured nature of the EU's weapons R&D.

Not only has this proposal for €200 million financing brought in evidence that the money allocated to common EU weapons systems R&D is too little, but its goals have also been unclear. With reason, the British thought that an EU programme on weapons research was not the right way to proceed. They favour bilateral projects. For example, Britain and France have been working on a small, portable radar system to be mounted on unmanned drone aircraft.

Anything more than a project-by-project approach, said the British government, would be unworkable. Defence projects are totally different from those of civilian aircraft. The downside has been evident in EADS' military transport plane which has fallen way behind its schedule, with the governments sponsoring it now demanding compensation.

In conclusion, mini-budgets for an EU-wide approach to weapons research are counterproductive, and the results are sure to be deceiving. A little bit of money does not permit more than one small project at a time, which is totally inadequate for an EU defence policy (*if* there is one) – particularly for a policy that aims to be independent of the US by developing leadership through its own weapons systems R&D.

Failures in common projects strengthen the policy established by practically all EU countries that they will not commit themselves to weapons systems R&D they do not control – and the EU has 27 different countries with no sign of political integration. Beyond this comes the fact that the organization of common R&D projects is far from being ideal, and the need to use rigorous methods like design reviews (section 7) is not properly appreciated.

## 6. Planning and Organizing R&D

Science as motor of economic advancement has only existed for some 150 years. Bertrand Russell once observed that when we consider how recently science has become a power, we find ourselves forced to believe that we are at the very beginning of its work in transforming human life.[12] Furthermore, in the past 60 years there have been enormous changes in the scope of scientific inquiry and inventive activity.

- For all practical purposes, research and development became a primary agent of industrial growth.
- But, as the examples in the previous five sections have demonstrated, research in industry must be properly organized for economic growth expectations to materialize.

As pointed out in Chapter 5, in the early 1950s the most advanced and best organized research was conducted in large laboratories. By contrast, today the most effective research effort is done in smaller labs; gigantism has had its day. In addition, while in the 1950s only a few famous companies developed out of research done in a garage – an example

12 Bertrand Russell, *The Impact of Science on Society*, George Allen & Unwin, London, 1952.

being Hewlett-Packard – these days, from biotechnology to information technology, the most advanced products of research come from start-ups, and it is largely from applied research.

Speaking from personal experience – from having worked for nearly five decades as consultant to the boards of major European companies – there are three reasons for losing competitiveness in terms of research, development and implementation of R&D results, and, by consequence, missing the opportunity to conquer the world's markets in a globalized economy. The *first* reason is that:

- R&D deliverables are not coming in rapid succession,
- new products lose time in the lab, which is inexcusable, and
- European companies keep too many secrets close to their chest, which prevents them from capitalizing on insourcing and outsourcing research effort.

The point made in the last bullet contrasts to the policy of US firms which are increasingly looking outside their own R&D to build new products and services. With regard to the first two bullets, again speaking from personal experience, in a surprisingly large number of cases the companies' R&D laboratories are in no hurry to deliver their dues. Worse still, the board and senior management condone this attitude:

- which is awfully wrong in terms of business strategy[13] and
- puts European companies at a disadvantage in the global market.

The *second* reason for falling behind in competition is lack of close collaboration with marketing, which should be strong from the very outset (Chapter 5). Input from marketing helps to enlarge product appeal and irons out rough edges that may impede marketability by influencing choices made at the drawing board. In technology neither the designer of a new product nor those who market it should decide its future impact on their own. They must work in unison.

The *third* reason is slow motion in turning a vision into practice. A brilliant new idea for a product or service is a vision. But 'vision is nothing without execution,' says Mark Hurd, CEO of Hewlett-Packard.[14] Unfortunately in the EU we are awfully short of both rapid execution and personal accountability – the EU Commission itself providing an example. Good governance does not work that way; it:

- announces clear objectives,
- documents its plans,
- scrutinizes operational data,
- measures performance,
- uncovers inefficiencies, and
- punishes poor deliverables while rewarding good results.

---

13 D.N. Chorafas, *Strategic Business Planning for Accountants: Methods, Tools, and Case Studies*, Butterworth-Heinemann, London and Boston, 2007.

14 In an interview in *The Economist*, Vol. 378, 2006.

Governments and companies should not pay for other people's inefficiencies, even if these people happen to be sacred cows. Merits and demerits, which become publicly known, are a good policy for increasing the transparency of obtained results. We should never forget that the goal of an organized R&D process is that of making knowledge work productive.

Planning for applied R&D projects is essentially *product planning* which must follow guidelines established by strategic planning and be executed in close collaboration with marketing – a domain in which the EU is not ahead of the curve. Applying Mies van der Rohe's dictum, 'God is in the details', the product planner's golden rule is to start with answers to strategic questions such as:

- Which direction the market takes in products and services?
- Which are the strengths and weaknesses of *our* product line?
- How can the new product under investigation promote *our* strengths? Kill *our* weaknesses?
- What are the special characteristics of this product that will put our company ahead of its competitors?
- Which way might the market shift? Will our product continue to be appealing *after* that shift?

Another crucial question to which product planning must respond is:

- From which product will come *our* firm's income in the next 10 years? 20 years?

The answer to this query should not only be factual and documented, but also account for what is demanded by the market as it is projected to evolve. This requires a holistic approach characterized by a *product life management* methodology.

When the microprocessor was invented in the early 1970s, General Electric's Far-Out Planning unit in Santa Barbara, California, asked itself, and answered, the following questions:

- How many GE products can benefit from the microprocessor?
- When will microprocessors be integral parts of the majority of GE products?

Projections made at that time looked 10 to 15 years down the line, and they proved to be quite correct.

Some of the answers in product life management must be elaborated in collaboration with engineering; others with marketing; still others with finance; still others with customers; and the majority with all these stakeholders. The best responses are not given in the abstract, but in a pragmatic way that:

- reflects different viewpoints and
- is elaborated within the current and projected competitive environment.

Contrarian responses to the product planner's questions are most valuable. Contrarians will often challenge whether a new product's price can compete favourably with similar products made by competitors, and whether the company has pricing freedom. In the early 1950s, at one of the graduate seminars at UCLA, colleagues asked Dr Ralph Barnes, our professor of production management and former senior executive at Ford, how Ford was establishing its price list. Barnes answered that:

- Ford is not really establishing an independent price list, because as No. 2 it lacks pricing power.
- It reads GM's price list and tries to do better in terms of cost-effectiveness by 5–10 per cent. Otherwise it does not sell cars.

If one takes an industry-wide view; substitutes China Inc. for 'GM' and companies in the EU and US for 'Ford', Barnes's statement is perfectly valid in 2010 – and full of wisdom. In two sentences it encapsulates the direction American and European firms should take in terms of nuts-and-bolts product planning and shows how careful they should be in pricing their products, so that they:

- cover all costs and
- leave a good profit margin.

When different advisors with zero experience in industry, including former prime ministers, suggest that the EU Executive put plenty of money into research (provided money can be found), and say nothing about production, marketing and after-sales service, they are not serious in their advice. The latter shows lack of depth and experience.

In conclusion, there is an urgent need in present-day industrial operations for coordination between product policies, R&D and sales. Strategic planning and business policy should not be buried somewhere because of lack of skills. Neither should the planning and organization of the R&D effort be left to the bureaucrats. If it is, no matter where you put them, they will be in the way.

## 7. Design Reviews for Control of R&D Projects

In pre-industrial economies, product risks were mostly physical due to the unpredictability of nature. Now, as well as physical risks (many of which are under control), the industrial system is subject to economic risks conditioned not only by financial factors and leveraging, but also by technical characteristics, the marketability of the product and the behaviour of the economy. Product risk stems from unforeseeable shifts in demand, such as:

- changes in fashion,
- a significant innovation, or
- ingeniously improved products introduced by competitors.

Management tools like marketing research, product analysis and product planning (section 6) can, to a certain extent, help in controlling product risk. However, they cannot correct the sloppiness of the work we may be doing in our lab, of quality problems on the manufacturing floor, of failures in the sales network, or of less than adequate after-sales service. All these issues are important and each must be addressed with great care.

All things being equal, the more the R&D effort produces *fast* deliverables, the more successful it is in promoting the survival and growth of the firm. This often means cultural change, and top management should apply itself to removing the obstacles to change. One of the battles requiring great endurance is getting a new idea into the factory.

When Charles F. Kettering was developing electrical ignition for the automobile, one of his great problems was overcoming resistance set up by the expressed opinion of some outstanding electrical engineers that to crank an automobile engine with a storage battery would be a physical impossibility. There are hundreds of Ketterings coming up with new concepts and thousands of reactionaries who 'know better' that they will not work. To promote research deliverables, the CEO must:

- create the *incentive environment* able to ensure the growth of ideas and their evolution into new marketable products;
- keep the lines of communication between R&D, sales, engineering and production open at all times; and
- establish an R&D control procedure which is focused, clear, fast, direct and effective.

This is precisely the role of *design reviews*, which are a basic tool of good governance, but are not popular in European industry. According to some, it is not nice to criticize people if they do something wrong; experience, however, shows that it is necessary. Design reviews mean technical and financial control action which, to be effective, presupposes the existence of performance standards and yardsticks against which to measure interim R&D. Other prerequisites are:

- the authority to kill a project, if it goes badly;
- a common language, generally understood in all corners of the organization, not only in R&D; and
- well-timed evaluation procedures, with rewards and disciplinary action according to the design review's outcome.

In a nutshell, the mission of a design review is to control the project schedule, cost, functionality and, obviously, the quality of deliverables during the development cycle. The schedule is all-important because time-to-market is crucial factor in product design, as companies must bring their products to market faster than their competitors; but the other factors mentioned in this paragraph are also important.

Regarding quality criteria, some companies turn their wheels in a vacuum when they verify quality because they have not made it an explicit target through tolerances established at the drawing board. The alter ego of quality is cost – a major theme in design reviews whether the project is made in-house or outsourced.

Few research, design and engineering projects are able to control timetables, quality and cost at the same time, which is pity because the tools are available. One such tool is Six Sigma, a methodology that quantifies quality goals and makes them measurable.[15] Figure 6.1 presents an example of a design review methodology which I learned in the early 1960s at General Electric and have been using very successfully ever since. The process is done at two levels.

15 D.N. Chorafas, *Integrating ERP, CRM, Supply Chain Management and Smart Materials*, Auerbach, New York, 2001.

- Major design reviews take place at 25 per cent, 50 per cent, 80 per cent and 90 per cent of a project's timetable.
- These milestones roughly correspond to 10 per cent, 25 per cent, 50 per cent and 75 per cent of the project's cost.

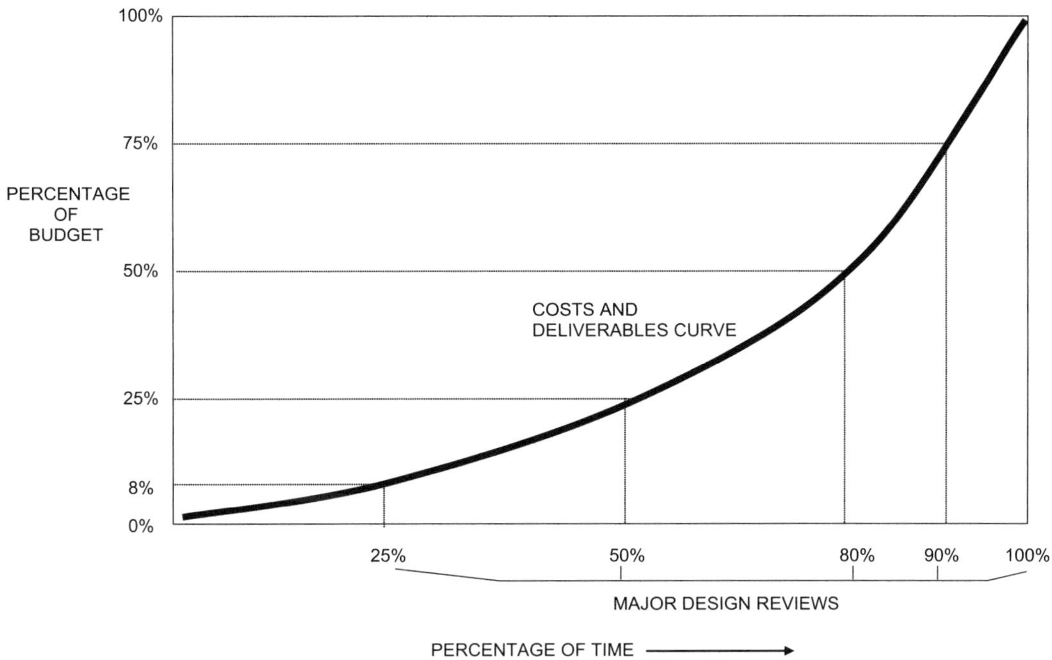


**Figure 6.1 The need for design reviews is present in any project. It is better to stop a non-performing project at an early date**

In between the major design reviews should be verifications, which are minor design reviews. Preferably, they should take place weekly and be oriented to rapid problem-solving. The major design review can kill a project, if need be. The object of the minor design review is to remove the roadblocks, focus the effort and resolve conflicts – but they can also lead to an extraordinary major design review.

Provided that the principles outlined in the foregoing paragraphs are observed, there are good reasons to believe that product development projects will be well managed. The value of verification lies as much in assuring the quality of engineering and other skills, as in being on-time and on-cost. Not every firm appreciates that hiring inexperienced designers with little domain expertise may:

- cause more problems and
- cost more money than looks likely at first sight.

Readers with experience in information technology will appreciate the impact of these two bullets on software development projects. Fred Brooks, who managed the design and development of IBM's operating system for the 369 Series has written an excellent book

– the *Mythical Man-Month*[16] – on his experience. Adding more people to a software project does not advance it; it brings it backwards. In IT the saying is: 'Nine women will not make a baby in one month.'

Dr Harold D. Koontz, my professor of business policy at UCLA, from whom I learned a great deal, taught his students that no other crucial function of management is more closely associated to corporate effectiveness than control. Research projects may fail for many reasons; these are among the most frequent:

- The scope has been ill-defined.
- Chosen technology is not state-of-the-art.
- The product's cost structure is uncompetitive.
- Work progress is managed poorly or not at all.
- The research team lacks people with appropriate know-how.
- The project manager ignores best practices and lessons learned from past failures.

Each one of these bullets documents the fact that project planning and control are inseparable, and they have to be fully integrated into daily practice. Planning is very important, but planning without control is daydreaming, and control cannot be exercised without having a solid plan against which to gauge progress. This is perfectly true of design reviews.

Yet, a challenge I often encountered in my professional work is that many companies lack the *progress review* culture, and they don't appreciate what it takes to maintain a state-of-the-art verification environment which is independent of pressures due to company politics. As R&D endeavours translated into engineering projects continue to increase in complexity, design reviews, walkthroughs, post-mortems and general independent evaluationd are 'a must'.

Verification requires engineering, marketing, cost accountancy, financial and other skills. Policies, ways and means must be provided within this frame of corporate governance, and facing the challenges associated to R&D by means of design reviews is the best possible way to assure transparency.

---

16 F.P. Brooks, *The Mythical Man-Month: Essays on Software Engineering*, Addison-Wesley, New York, 1975.

PART III

# *Employment is an Opportunity, Not a Right*

# CHAPTER 7 Employment Means Different Things to Different People

## 1. Is There a 'Right' to Employment?

Since early organized human societies, men have created their own employment. They have been hunters, farmers, artisans, traders and providers of services. Employment by the state was more or less limited to two sectors: the military and bureaucracy. In fact, in many cases (up to and including the Middle Ages) armies were raised by landowners and warlords, rather than by central government.

The fact that in old times the state's role in employment was subdued practically meant that, to a large extent, the labour market was free. People could enter and exit the labour market without the government's intervention, and this was interpreted, by several experts, as being synonymous with the 'right to work'. Opportunities for work might not have been abundant, but as long as *people themselves created them*, the labour market remained relatively

- flexible,
- expandable and
- appreciative of skills.

One of the characteristics of labour markets since the epoch of man the hunter, and more so when communities settled and developed agriculture, has been the *division of labour*. There is nothing surprising in a trend towards specialization, because a division of labour exists, even between polyps.

In species of coral, certain polyps specialize in prey-catching while others provide digestive functions. This specialization of labour is particularly impressive given the primitive nature of these organisms. The body of a coral polyp consists of a hollow tube, through whose centre runs the blind gut: food is taken in and waste expelled. A similar concept of division of labour characterizes the members of the human body.

By contrast, an interesting evolution in human societies is that, without any direction 'from above', labour market flexibility has been associated with finding a better job to improve one's condition. This has created stimuli to employment. Several things, however, really changed with the Industrial Revolution of the early to mid-nineteenth century and the introduction of machines which:

- interfaced between and replaced different types of job, restructuring the nature and rhythm of labour, and

- introduced a new political dimension – the labour union – which invented the 'right to work' and endowed itself with growing power to interrupt any type of production (see Chapter 9).

In the long run, machines created work by significantly lowering the cost of man-made goods. By so doing, they helped in improving the people's standard of living and, at the same time, created a larger market for manufactured goods. In the short run, however, and most particularly from a near-sighted viewpoint, machines damaged the job opportunities of those unable to work with them – producing *structural unemployment.*

Reactions to the advent of machinery have been mixed. A glaring example of a near-sighted response comes from the British Luddites' mid–nineteenth-century attempt to protect their jobs by destroying new textile manufacturing gear. This action disregarded the fact that, overall, many workers found employment in industries created by what was then new technologies, such as textile manufacturing and, later, steel, automobiles and aircraft production.

About a century later, in the post-World War II years, computers, automation and robotics met with a similar reception from many European politicians, labour unions and some intellectuals, who suggested that the number of possible jobs in a market economy was shrinking due to computers and other technological advances. Supposedly, these reduced the need for workers, but in reality they:

- created the service economy wave, and
- at the same time upgraded the requirements for skilled workers.

Trend charts support the statement in the second bullet. During the last two decades unemployment levels for men and women without particular skills rocketed, while people with qualifications found it easier to get employment, depending on the degree of their qualifications and their thrust in searching for a job.

Based partly on statistics and partly (where statistics were missing) on an estimate, men fared better than women. This is shown in Figure 7.1. As these graph lines suggest, a college degree offers no guarantee of finding a job – not only because there is a surplus of degree-holders, but also because many of these degrees are in *soft* subjects which are not in demand by industry (as already discussed in Part One). Nevertheless, the level of unemployment for people with higher education is lower than for those who lack skills.

Many sociologists today argue that all people have the 'right to work', and that this should be guaranteed by the state. The fact that many people don't have what it takes to find a job in the society in which they live and from which they profit makes no difference according to that school of thought.[1] But it does make a difference in the labour market.

- The right to search and find work should be guaranteed.
- But it is not the state's business to find a job for everyone, and even less so a job that the individual 'likes'.

*If* finding jobs for everyone were the state's responsibility, *then* the state would have the right to tell everyone what kind of job he or she should do for the rest of his or her

1 In some countries, such as Germany, the 'right to work' has curiously become a 'constitutional right', without the corresponding obligation by the citizen to get a specialization that society needs.

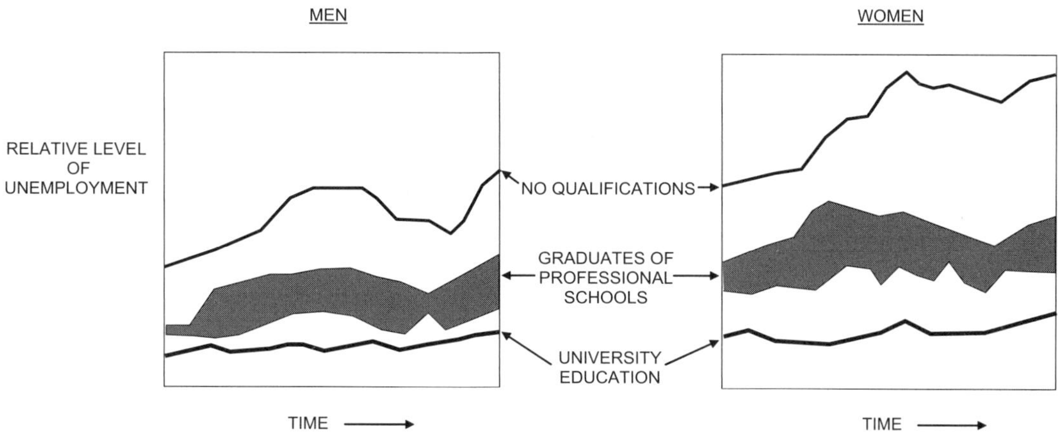


**Figure 7.1 A 20-year trend in level of unemployment by level of schooling, for men and women in the European Union prior to the 'go-go' 2005–2007 years**

life. Let me be clear about that. If many graduates have been having a tough time getting jobs, this is largely due to the subjects they chose in their studies. Hence, it is only normal that they carry the risk of a bad choice.

For instance, with birth rates way down in the European Union (though in some countries slightly higher than in others), the need for language graduates to be employed as teachers is very substantially reduced. By contrast, an aging society requires many more medical doctors, who are in short supply.

Indeed, the need for more doctors is just as critical in America as it is in Europe, and it comes up at almost every Congressional hearing on healthcare, writes Robert Pear.[2] 'We're not producing enough primary care physicians,' President Obama said at one forum. 'The costs of medical education are so high that people feel that they've got to specialize.' General statements like that are in no way the solution.

The cost of education has something to do with young people not going into the medical profession, but it is not the whole story. Medical studies, like physics and engineering, are much tougher than those characteristic of the pseudo-social sciences. Careers are open in the hard sciences where there is great demand, while in soft pseudosciences supply far exceeds the number of jobs on offer.

Evidently, the shortage of healthcare professionals is having serious consequences. There are simply not enough doctors in primary care and other specialities. In the US, the Association of American Medical Colleges is advocating a 30 per cent increase in medical school enrolment, which would produce 5,000 additional doctors each year (and will take eight to ten years to change the dynamics of supply and demand). But in both America and Europe few kids care to become medical doctors.

- This is no fault of the state, and
- the state does not have to pay for damages by bending over backwards to find a job for 'everyone' who has misdirected his or her life.

2 R. Pear, 'Shortage of Doctors and Obstacle to Obama Goals', *The New York Times*, 27 April 2009.

In her book *My Life* Golda Meir expresses this concept beautifully. As she relates it, she told the Israeli citizen repeatedly that:

> *The government cannot do everything all at once. It can't wave a magic wand and meet everyone's demands simultaneously: eradicate poverty without imposing taxes, win wars, go on absorbing immigration, develop the economy and still give everyone his due. No government can do all this at one and the same time.*[3]

Meir also gives some excellent advice to those who have made *rent-seeking*[4] *their policy:*

> *In the first place ... those among us who are poor must not permit themselves to be turned into the passive objects of other people's concern. They must be active on their own behalf.*

And she also perfectly described a major problem in modern society:

> *The gap between those who have education and training and those who don't is at least as great and as tragic as the gap between those who can cope economically and those who can't.*[5]

Franklin D. Roosevelt, too, had given a similar warning. At the depth of the Depression the president pointed out to the American public that continuing dependence on relief induces a spiritual and moral disintegration fundamentally destructive to the individual and to the national fibre. To dole out relief in this way is to administer a narcotic, Roosevelt said, adding that continuing subsidies are a subtle destroyer of the human spirit.[6]

## 2. The Evolution of the Labour Market

The OECD has estimated that over the next three decades the projected decline in the labour force could cut growth in its member countries by a third, compared with the previous three decades. In other words, rather than an improvement in job opportunities there will be deterioration, which always accompanies slower growth.

During the most recent 'good times' (2004 to mid-2007), countries like Britain, Denmark and Ireland experienced marked improvement in employment, but in other countries – notably France, Germany, southern and central Europe – few people profited from the upturn. As is to be expected, less qualified men and women have done far less well than the average (see also Figure 7.1). There have been two groups of special concern:

- the young entering the labour force and
- people aged 55 or over.

Regarding the latter, differences between EU countries are enormous. Statistics show that 70 per cent of Swedes aged 55 to 64 work. By contrast, a mere 32 per cent of Austrians

3 Golda Meir, *My Life*, G.P. Putnam's Sons, New York, 1975.

4 The demand for financial support by the state because of a number of reasons, some of which fall under the social net.

5 Meir, *My Life*.

6 State of the Union Address, 1935.

and Belgians in that age range do so. Too many countries have encouraged older workers to drop out early, though this is beginning to be reversed.

For their part, young people often find it hard to get established in the labour market because of their lack of experience, but even more so because of government policies on minimum wages (see also the discussion on the effect of minimum wages in Chapter 8). For instance, in Britain, between 1998 and 2004 the jobless rate for 10 to 24-year-olds was lower than the average for the OECD. Then, between 2004 and 2007 it increased.

According to experts, the minimum wage was pushed up (by the Labour government) too much in a few years. When it was introduced in April 1999, the main rate was set at £3.60 an hour with a lower floor of £3 for 18 to 21-year-olds. By 2009 both rates had risen by nearly 60 per cent, outstripping average earnings, which have gone up by 45 per cent over the same period. This hit hard the younger people who are:

- less skilled and
- more likely to be made redundant.

Economists list many issues that distort labour markets. High and rising minimum wages is one of them. Generous unemployment benefits (particularly those that last a long time) is another. Such benefits are essentially wage substitutes presented as social transfers, and they have become part of labour market policy on a more or less indiscriminate basis.

Critics say that this policy has been wrong, the proof being that over the past ten years it has led to the increase in long-term unemployment and also distorted proactive labour market measures. Therefore, it should be considered unsuccessful, with governments taking the initiative to:

- either discontinue it, or
- radically revamp it.

Longer-term unemployment (usually, though not always, defined as being out of a job for 12 months or more) is another major preoccupation, both because of its negative social impact and because when people are unemployed for a long time their skills wane. As a result:

- over time they find it even harder to get a job, and
- they also become less keen to search for work in the first place.

Searching for solutions for longer-term unemployment is a challenging job, particularly given its persistence. Some countries are better at it than others, one of the criteria of success being the ratio of longer-term unemployed over the total number of unemployed. In the mid-1990s Italy topped the list of Western nations with a 60 per cent ratio. This was reduced to a little over 50 per cent by 2006. In other EU countries, the corresponding figures have been as follows:

- Spain: 55 per cent and 50 per cent
- Netherlands: 50 per cent and 45 per cent
- Britain: 46 per cent and 22 per cent.

Britain did much better than other EU countries, but not as well as America which stood at 12 per cent (for the mid-1990s) and 10 per cent for 2006. It is also necessary to count *underemployment*, which occurs beneath the surface as not everybody gets fired and many people are pushed into part-time work involuntarily because they have no other choice. In the 2007–2011 economic crisis, for example, the number of people working part-time for 'economic reasons'[7] surged.

This is most relevant for those who like to draw comparisons of the unemployment rate from one country to the next. Underemployment is one of the factors reminding experts, statisticians and the general public how much the definition of the labour force has changed over time.

Current statistics on unemployment rates are not inclusive in terms of accounting for all forms of underemployment – a deliberate tactic by governments which tend to downsize unemployment figures. Another strategy is to keep out of official statistics those people undergoing some sort of training sponsored by the state supermarket, even though this has minimum impact on people's ability to find a new job.

Nevertheless, the right government policies can help in eliminating longer-term unemployment. Experts suggest that Britain, which managed to reduce its longer-term unemployment, has a better-performing labour market than other EU countries like Germany and France, where the share has risen between the mid-1990s and 2006.

Labour market restructuring is a sizeable part of the answer. An example of restructuring has been Germany's Hartz reform of the labour market, enacted in the early years of this century and implemented in four phases.[8] Enacted by the Social Democratic government of Gerhard Schröder, Hartz IV has made the social transfer system more transparent and more consistent. The adopted measures:

- restricted unemployment benefits and
- curbed an interventionist labour market policy, easing pressure on the government's budget.

According to several economists, a better-studied, more conservative and consistent implementation of social policy instruments, coupled with increased labour market flexibility is far more promising in labour terms, than experimenting with new subsidies to the unemployed and minimum wage models. The 2007–2011 crisis has also demonstrated that Hartz IV has been able to cope with the economic downturn.

By contrast, high unemployment benefits have proved to be a disincentive to seek work, while the hypothesis that 'sufficient diligence' by a well-funded employment service (of the state supermarket) can offset efforts to play the system has proved to be a myth. It is most important to maintain the incentive to look for work. Countries which pay high benefits:

- discourage job-seeking, and
- deprive themselves of means for pushing the jobless into seeking work.[9]

7 As opposed to other reasons, like personal choice.

8 Its effect does not show up in the aforementioned statistics because it takes some time to seep down the social structure.

9 Another negative is that their product markets are much more regulated and sclerotic.

An equally bad policy by governments has been the overstuffing of bureaucracies and state-run enterprises in order to falsify the unemployment statistics and avoid social unrest. An example from the end of the twentieth century is provided by published statistics, released in late 1994. These indicated that 30 million of the 100 million people employed by China's state-run industry were in excess of the numbers needed for sustained production. As a result, 50,000 companies owned by the state were writing their books with red ink.

While, for obvious reasons, reducing long-term unemployment, as well as structural unemployment, is the goal of practically every economic policy, legalized fake employment is by no means the solution. Job creation requires investments but in the end it substantially reinforces public finances, easing the pressure on both the revenue and expenditure side of governments' budgets.

In parallel to this, there are two other important contributors to this objective. One of them, at government level, involves reforms to the tax system to induce people to increase their take-home pay by working more. The other must be implemented at company level by means of lifelong learning. Its success requires consistent policies and inputs by both employees and employers.

## 3. Lifelong Learning: A Powerful Employment Weapon

In May 1968, at the time of the famous student uprising against the status quo, I was invited to a meeting by Dr Ponte, the chief executive of CSF (at that time, the foremost French radio communications company). Down in the street the firm's engineers were burning the CEO's effigy.

My problem, said Ponte, is that I hire the engineers out of school (roughly 25 years old), spend five years training them, see them peak in terms of their return on investment by age 35, and then their professional efficiency wanes. After 40 they contribute little or nothing to the firm. This pattern is illustrated in Figure 7.2.

The answer is *lifelong learning*, of which we spoke a great deal in Chapter 3 but in connection with education. By contrast, in this chapter we will look at continuing education from the perspective of an individual's career, as well as in terms of employment opportunities as years pass by and the individual ages.

Upgrading one's skills and know-how from cradle to grave is by no means a guarantee of finding employment. It's a fair bet, however, that failing to do so greatly increases the likelihood of becoming unemployed later on in life. In modern society, returning to school (so to speak) throughout one's lifespan is not an option; it has become an obligation for both:

- *employees*, who must convince themselves of the need of steadily upgrading their skills, and
- *employers*, who should provide their employees with incentives and facilities for doing so.

As cannot be repeated too often, everybody's know-how is perishable. In antiquity Socrates knew that when he said: 'I learn as long as I live.' In addition, a major change

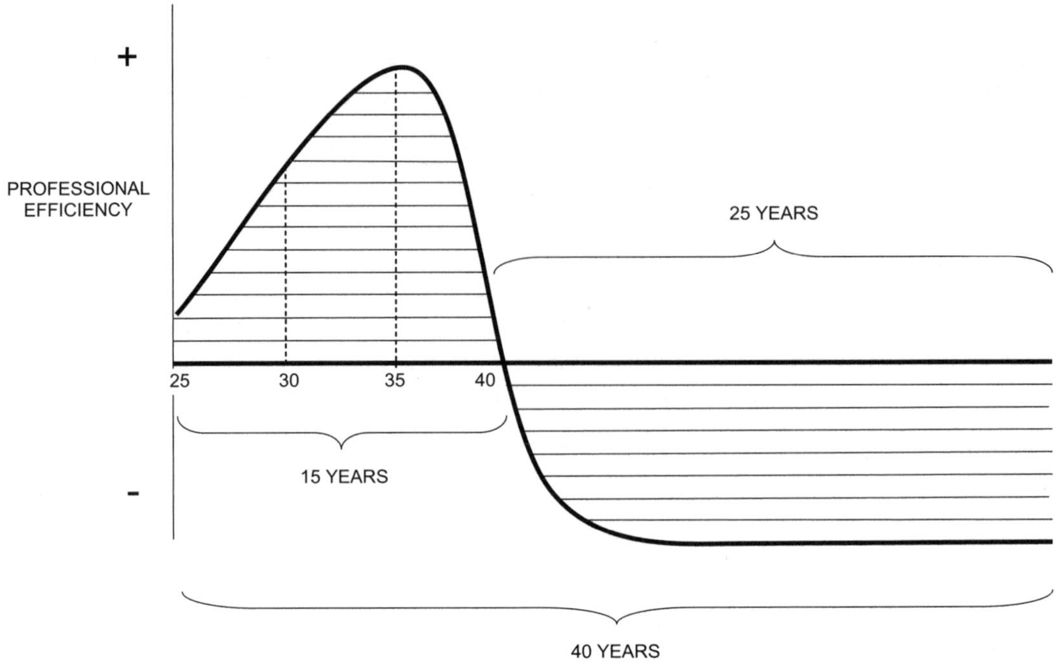


**Figure 7.2 The disastrous effects of obsolescence on human capital**

characterizing modern economies during the last three decades is rapid scientific and technological development. This should be inciting people not to fall behind in their knowledge.

The service industry, which has largely overtaken manufacturing as the number one employer (see sections 5 and 6), has a different set of criteria in labour relations. Unlike the paternalist manufacturing companies of the late nineteenth and early twentieth centuries, modern-day service companies can hardly afford to offer lifelong employment. This means that a young man or woman entering the labour market should expect to have three or four different careers in his or her active life:

- In a service economy, men and women can no longer count on sitting in the shade of their first job, *as if* they have been planted there like a tree.
- Today's employment opportunities disappear tomorrow and new ones develop, changing the established order of skills in demand and profoundly affecting careers.

This is not taught in school, as should be the case. Neither do parents explain to their sons and daughters that they should be keen to enlarge the breadth of their know-how because this deeply affects their career opportunities. To the contrary, young people today should not be comfortable with narrow or stagnant learning.

- *If* they are,
- *then* they will encounter major problems because they did not learn how to learn.

In developing their careers, young graduates should not be afraid of failure. An integral part of their schooling must be the notion that of two roads – an easy one and another which is challenging and risky – the latter will also prove to be the most:

- satisfactory,
- productive and
- rewarding.

Some sociologists are worried that switching careers may be associated with lower income, at least over a period of time. Indeed, it is possible for skilled workers to find new jobs after retraining, but not ones that pay as much as the work they were previously doing, but lost. Transition will be easier if something could act as temporary safety net.

The 'something' is known as *wage insurance*, an idea that has been kicking around Washington for a while. It would supply displaced workers and other professionals starting on a new job with a year or so of income supplement, to allow them to adjust to a new and lower wage structure.

There may be problems associated with a transition, but they can be solved – and nothing is worse than remaining unemployed. One becomes stronger by meeting challenges, and this is very important to every person's psyche because only the strong can be productive, and only the productive can be free.

Statistics document the need for finding solutions which will correct four decades of the younger generation's misdirection. In several Western countries almost half of all welfare recipients are young people.[10] The young generation cannot afford to wait for a *Deus ex machina* to pull things up from under. In the service economy's fluid environment, anyone tries to look like 'Mr or Mrs Status Quo' disappears from the professionals' radar screen. This has not yet entered the consciousness of young people, their families and their teachers. Governments, too, are to blame for this failure whose consequences are easy to see and count.

- The more one shifts through economic data, the more one realizes that one is confronted by a whole new paradigm.
- Being tempted to believe that the 'easier years' of the past will make a comeback is due to an illusion, as well as to failing to pay attention to the *negative* feedback of technological progress.

The absence of lifelong learning increases the structural unemployment figures and even makes them look like a sort of *natural rate*[11] – which it definitely is not. Indeed, the absence of continuing education caused structural unemployment to become omnipresent, and the likelihood is that it will get worse rather than better without a rigorous programme for recycling human resources into domains needing help, such as hospitals and other social services. Such a switch would serve to:

- beef up missing personnel to improve an aging society's services infrastructure, and

10 On 28 August 28, 2007, a news item on Bloomberg Television made this reference to Switzerland, but similar statistics can be found all over the European Union.

11 As a term, *natural rate of unemployment* is a rather fuzzy notion, generally thought to be the rate at which labour markets are so tight that further declines are likely to spark inflation.

- avoid falling into the trap of more and more structural unemployment created by the status quo.

While work for everybody cannot be guaranteed by any stretch of the imagination (see section 1), reforms do help. Labour market reforms in Britain are a good example. Under Tony Blair (who followed Thatcher's roadmap, without admitting he did so) Britain lowered labour taxes and introduced regulations which greatly weakened the economic and political power of labour unions. With this came:

- a rapid expansion in private employment and
- a reduction, over time, of unemployment to under 5 per cent (prior to the 2007–2011 severe economic and banking crisis).

Similarly, in the US (prior to 2007–2011) the relatively flexible labour markets have created jobs at an impressive rate since the early 1980s, as we saw through longer-term unemployment statistics in section 2. Note, however, that almost 70 per cent of men and women of working age have been employed in the private sector, and this has been instrumental in reducing unemployment.

By contrast, countries in continental Europe with rigid labour markets have experienced no net increase in private employment since the mid-1970s. Two questions are at stake here, and it is important not to muddle them up:

- Are Europe's labour rules are sensible?
- Who should assume responsibility for lifelong learning?

The answer to the first is straightforward: EU labour rules are too rigid and inflexible, and therefore counterproductive. It cannot have escaped the notice of governments, politicians and labour unions that continental Europe is afraid to tackle its unemployment problems – which are due, at least partly if not largely, to assorted impediments to the hiring and firing of labour.

Regarding the second bullet, not only governments and employees, but also schools and employers, must recognize that labour markets have changed – even if the laws and rules governing them have not. Lifelong learning and multiple careers are at the inflection point of this change, and they have to be given the attention they deserve.

In conclusion, the evolution of the economy and the labour market has provided lots of evidence that there is no more dangerous illusion than that the *status quo* should be preserved and that, no matter what happens, the government owes the citizen a living. The people themselves must appreciate that they cannot rely on the state to bail them out whenever they run into trouble. The time has come for everyone to write an inventory of all his and her strengths and weaknesses, and to seek to correct the latter through lifelong learning.

## 4. Trying to Come Up from Under in Employment

In macroeconomics, unemployment is a lagging indicator of economic health. By contrast, in politics it is a leading factor of public dissatisfaction with government policies. Rising unemployment is hated even when the economy is in deep recession – when there is good reason why, short of costly and unaffordable redundancies, the loss of jobs is unavoidable.

An additional problem is that Western countries are losing their competitiveness. Examples are Britain, France, Spain and the US. In Euroland, for the first decade of this century, Germany has kept unit labour costs flat; but in France they have risen by 17 per cent and in Spain by 27 per cent. In the aftermath, unemployment has reached double figures: 10 per cent in France and, about 20 per cent in Spain.

As if this was not enough, on both sides of the Atlantic manufacturing industry has been devastated by cheap Chinese imports. This is less true in Germany, and much more so in Britain and the US. Table 7.1 shows some scary statistics.

**Table 7.1 Percentage of employment and total gross value added in the manufacturing industry**

| | Employment (%) | Value added (%) |
|---|---|---|
| Germany | 17.5 | 19.0 |
| Japan | 14.0 | 21.0 |
| France | 12.5 | 12.0 |
| US | 11.5 | 13.5 |
| Britain | 10.0 | 12.0 |

*Source: The Economist*, 13 March 2010.

As if this was not enough, work is being degraded by various left-wing theorists who fail to account both for the pride that work fosters and the income necessary to people and families. In March 2010 the *Guardian* published an article by researchers from the New Economic Foundation promoting a working week of 21 hours as the solution to major crises of the twenty-first century.[12] The 'researchers' fail to note:

- how families will live on half their current income *if* present labour costs are maintained, and
- how British and other Western companies will be able to compete in the global markets *if* salaries and wages are doubled to make up for the shortfall in hours.

It was low – very low – wages that allowed China to conquer the world market for manufactured goods, with well-known disastrous effects on Western employment. This is now spreading into the service industry, wiping out jobs that would have been normally filled by Western workers.

The huge cruise ships of prosperous Italian companies capitalizing on the wave of Europe's tourism are now employing a crashing majority of Chinese, Filipino and Asian service workers, evidently because of lower wages. After having taken care of the manufacturing jobs, low-cost labour from China is devastating the service industry – but

12 As quoted in *Courier International*, 11 March 2010.

this is, of course, of no importance to the 'researchers' of the New Economics Foundation, who call for still higher labour costs in the EU.

One of the features of unemployment which depresses public opinion is the interpretation that it is due to the government's lack of interest in social solutions coupled with a lack of vigour and daring in the conception of economic remedies. Generally, the public pays scant attention to the fact that, because market rigidities lead to lack of self-confidence and innovators are distrusted,

- too little can be expected in the way of new job opportunities and
- employment outlets are stagnant because they are too confined to conventional paths.

Lack of self-confidence, daring, imagination and aspiration on the part of the labour force in coming up from under is partly due to old-style thinking and partly the result of backward training and tradition – that of expecting the welfare nanny state to provide all. Several generations have been brought up with repressed job-seeking attitudes and a lack of imagination that limits individual initiative.

- Many people are too passively waiting for the job to come forward, rather than running to catch it, and
- this widespread passive attitude has also failed to produce first violins in the labour market orchestra.

Nor is it surprising that the passive attitudes towards employment that have grown over the years are equal to the torrent of money spent in concealing the after-effects rather than really combating unemployment. The proof is the lack of active guidance offered as to the type of skills an individual should obtain to enter a profession, the lack of wider awareness on the projected demand for skills and the provision of little or no training to improve the individual's ability to get ahead of the curve by adapting to changes in demand.

In Germany an imaginative idea used by people to come up from the depressive state of unemployment is *self-employment* through setting up a small service-oriented enterprise. This is known as *Ich AG* ('I Inc.'). Several cases have been successful, and the reason why it has not been widely followed up is because people are not trained for being self-employed and standing on their own two feet. However, the significance of *Ich AG* has been heralded by the media.

Less commendable are the 'one-euro-per-hour' jobs, which also originated in Germany. The good news is that such jobs allow people who want to work to get out of unemployment's depression. The bad news is that in very many cases they practically amount to overexploiting labour on the cheap – for instance, various communes using one-euro-per-hour workers to demolish an old house or do some public service work. But

- €8 per day does not even pay for the worker's transportation costs and a fast-food lunch, and
- at the same time, this practice may be taking away fully paid jobs.

It is not difficult to appreciate that the number of people in these one-euro-per–hour, low-paid, part-time mini-jobs has never been too high, even if some economists consider them as subsidized employment opportunities. Statistics show that they increased sharply in the third quarter of 2005, some time after they were launched, but their attraction fell shortly thereafter.

True enough, in order to regain their competitiveness in the global market where the *China price* and its effect on wages is ever-present,[13] EU countries and the US find themselves obliged to instigate a wage-cutting cure. Only then can local employment (let alone exports) get back on its feet, but this should not be done at a level that devastates part of the workforce, even if some wage adaptation is inevitable.

A better example of coming up from under originates from France, and it speaks volumes about what can be achieved by people who use their imagination and also have the will to succeed. Here is, briefly, the story of Malamine Koné and his company, Airness.

Koné's family arrived in France from Mali in 1982, when he was ten years old, and he was brought up in a rough *banlieue* of Paris. But, unlike other immigrant kids, Koné decided to come up from under. Taking his cue from Nike, Adidas and other sportswear firms, he began hawking his sweatshirts around the *banlieue*. In a few years Airness was off the ground and in 2008 it had an annual turnover of some €120 million ($168 million), co-sponsoring three first-division French football clubs and a Russian tennis player.

An out-of-the-box idea would be for governments to sponsor a venture fund for poor kids with a good idea and drive. In the background lies the fact that the economy needs start-ups and unemployment is associated with social and economic costs. The fiscal costs of unemployment are reflected in both sides of national budgets:

- that of expenditures, because of unemployment benefit payments, and
- that of revenue, due to losses from taxes and social insurance contributions.

This balance-sheet effect outweighs the macroeconomic effect of unemployment which causes reduced economic output owing to unused potential factors of production. It is not always appreciated that only part of unemployment's total costs are macroeconomic costs.

Taxes and social insurance contributions are paid from labour income, and their reduction, as an effect of unemployment, does not have a one-to-one correspondence with lower production factors, because transfers to the unemployed represent a redistribution of income. This may involve not only direct costs, but also indirect ones, such as housing allowance payments, health costs, food vouchers and more.

These challenges, which confront all EU member states, also raise the question of whether national governments or the EU as a whole should make policy on matters concerning unemployment. Despite various 'summits', the EU still lacks a worked-out idea of how governments should coordinate their employment and labour market policies.

A fruitful way of thinking about the issue, even if it is insufficient to settle it, is to ask to what degree any particular measure of harmonization in employment policies and labour laws promotes or retards competition in the EU, *both*:

- among companies and

13 D.N. Chorafas, *Globalization's Limits: Conflicting National Interests in Trade and Finance*', Gower, Aldershot, 2009.

- among governments.

Instead of spending lots of time enjoying lunches and dinners at the various useless EU 'summits', it would have been much better to do some basic research on employment and unemployment policies, not from yesterday's perspective but from tomorrow's – that is, what we really wish to attain and what are the pluses and minuses of each alternative.

The goal should be that of establishing for the EU a common denominator of strategic directions that will enable governments to decide how far they need to go to get out of the status quo.

## 5. Part-time Employment and Structural Shifts

Two structural shifts will particularly interest us in this section: part-time work and the absence of cradle-to-grave guarantees in employment. The two correlate and they significantly influence the existing concepts and policies regarding pensions. (The theme of pensions is the subject of Part Three.)

*Part-time work* is considered to be employment in which, by contractual agreement, a person works on a regular basis for part of what are 'normally' standard or negotiated working hours. There is not one, but several, reasons underlying part-time employment, although official statistics, so far, do not consistently differentiate between them. For example:

- Students may choose part-time work to finance their studies, and working mothers may choose it so they can look after their children.
- The service economy (which now represents well over 60 per cent of employment in Western countries) has made part-time its basic model.
- There are economic reasons leading towards part-time employment, as section 2 pointed out.

It would be utterly superficial to consider part-time work as being 'good' or 'bad' just to attach a label to it. It is a fact that will not fade away, and, as already mentioned, statistics don't differentiate between its background reasons. German statistics indicate that by the middle of the first decade of this century, well before the 2007–2011 economic crisis,

- over one-quarter of all employed individuals belonged to this category, and
- their number has almost doubled since the early 1990s.

In rough percentages, German statistics on people at work are as follows: a little over 60 per cent are in full-time employment (the 'good old way' which is in the process of severe structural change); about 12 per cent are self-employed; 15 per cent have well-paid part-time employment; and 13 per cent work part-time in low-paid jobs. (Beyond this distribution are the unemployed.)

The public attitude towards part-time employment is not monolithic. Traditionally, this has been a female domain. In the Federal Republic, women still account for a share of around 85 per cent. However, over a 15-year period (1991–2006) the number of men working limited hours has more than doubled.

Moreover, in Germany there is an interesting correlation between part-time work and self-employment. Over the stated period self-employment has become more important, and includes members of families who assist in family-run businesses. These people are increasingly working part-time; according to figures from a 2004 census, the proportion of self-employed individuals working part-time was 14 per cent.

Another characteristic of part-time work is its prevalence among employees who are receiving some kind of welfare payment. In a way, this has created the popular impression that part-time work is precarious, which does not need to be the general case.

Statistics from other EU countries are not too different than those of Germany. On 27 May 2009 Rome's *La Repubblica* published an article under the title 'Italy of the Precarious: 1 out of 5 Without Security for 10 Years'. That article maintained that one out of five Italian families was 'in crisis'.

- Such findings are ambiguous at best because Italian standards, as well as EU ones, on what it means to be 'in crisis' are missing.
- On the other hand, *if* (for the aforementioned reasons) part-time work is taken as evidence of being 'in crisis', *then* the claim is only intended to make newspaper headlines.

When evaluating the structural change of labour markets towards part-time work, one should not forget that over the last two decades the work environment has changed, and globalization is one of the basic reasons.[14] The lowering of commercial and financial barriers on a worldwide scale brought many benefits, but it also had unwarranted consequences, the outsourcing of jobs being one of them.

Neither is this process affecting western Europe and America exclusively. Asian countries, too, are subject to job displacement. South Korea provides an example of exporting work from Asia to Europe – of all places. The way a May 2009 *Financial Times* article had it, Hyundai Motor India was planning to shift production of one of its premium models to Europe after a strike over unionization at its south India plant.[15]

This move by South Korea's biggest car-maker has been the first time such a step has been taken because of labour unrest since the country opened up to foreign investors in 1991. And it is not the only case of a shift in production facilities. Rather, it is a sign of outsourcing shifting into reverse gear.

In June 2009 General Electric (GE) announced that it would create 400 jobs at its plant in Louisville, Kentucky, making a low-energy water heater. This equipment was previously manufactured by GE in China. GE also said that it would hire 1,100 people to staff a software research centre. Both investments were helped by US government incentives.[16]

True enough, these are partial measures as both the EU and America find it difficult to establish what they really want to do about employment as a whole in terms of outsourcing and insourcing – let alone with part-time employment. For instance, the EU

14 D.N. Chorafas, *Globalization's Limits. Conflicting National Interests in Trade and Finance*, Gower, Aldershot, 2009.

15 *Financial Times*, 8 May, 2009.

16 *The Economist*, 25 July 2009.

has failed to reach an agreement in its five-year effort to tighten working-hours rights. Correctly, Britain has objected to a policy that could end the culture of longer working hours.[17] In the background lies the fact that:

- EU national governments, law-makers and stakeholders have been unable to agree on common labour market and work issues; and
- the collapse of EU talks on maximum working hours means that the European Commission must draft new legislative proposals, potentially opening the way for years of further interminable negotiations.[18]

Not to be left out of the grand design *against* work, a number of trade unions have said that letting people work more than 48 hours pressures them to do so and 'raises the risk of accidents'. If that is the prevailing logic, *then* it is better that people don't work at all (according to some people's irrational minds) while the 'negotiators' could look at part-time work as the best possible compromise.

The way things stand, the EU 'negotiators', and the governments behind them, don't seem to have clear in their minds what it means to be ridiculous. It is not the risk of accidents that should be addressed with regard to longer hours, but rather so-called 'work sharing',[19] as well as the rising inequality in pay which threatens many families' sense of security and leads them into an unaffordable and unsustainable accumulation of debt.

In conclusion, I don't consider part-time work as something that should be reversed, because it is an outlet which, in its way, compensates for a marked reduction in employment opportunities – a *substitution* created by one of society's inflection points. Looking at this issue in terms of sectors of the economy, the changes in employment in hotels, restaurants and the retail trade – in short, *the service industry* – support this substitution:

- The sharp expansion of lower-paid part-time employment is accompanied by reductions in what was considered to be 'normal' employment where government intervention would hurt the service industry.
- Expanding sectors of the economy, like that of service providers in healthcare, require a very flexible labour market to be able to deliver – and part-time employment embodies that market.

Healthcare is by no means the exception. Commercial service providers, including all sorts of business outlets and real-estate activities, are heavily staffed with part-time labour. The same is true of the food and drink industries and construction, as well as various types of subcontracted work. Part-time work is here to stay, and, rather than tilting at windmills, it is better to prepare for its after-effects on society.

Closely associated with part-time working is the case of *silver workers* (see also Chapter 11, section 6,). This is particularly important in regard to those with valuable science and engineering skills, who like to continue being productive even if governments do not

---

17 This has been the case of an early 2009 proposal which sought to reduce exemptions to the EU's 48-hour maximum working week. Such exemptions are used by Britain and 14 other member countries out of 27.

18 These are also senseless 'negotiations' since their aim is to discourage people from working.

19 Which essentially means part-time work.

raise the retirement age. Companies are coming round to this solution as the percentage of young people versatile in technology – from engineering to special craftsmanship – shrinks.

An example of reversing past trends is provided by BMW. The German motor vehicle manufacturer decided to staff one of its production lines with older workers and called it *the pensioners' line*. To do so, it brought the line up to the level of its users by introducing a number of relatively small changes, such as new chairs, adjustable tables and magnifying lenses. The goal is to spread this practice throughout the global organization.[20]

Not only must careful attention be paid to the wisdom of part-time work and workplace redesign, but other issues also have to be rethought and re-established to save the skills that are being thrown away with retirement. A major issue is that of breaking the time-honoured link between age and pay so that employees and workers enter retirement as a phased process rather than as a sudden event. Concomitant to this is paying people *for value* – not for age or because of pressure from bad labour habits such as wildcat strikes and sequestrations.

## 6. Service Jobs and Productivity in the Service Economy

One of the major structural changes characterizing the last 30 years in Europe (as well as nearly 40 years in America) is the rapid increase in the size of the services industry. The share of the workforce employed in services in the EU crossed the 70 per cent level of total employment in 2004. That same year in America it was somewhat over 82 per cent. It is appropriate to point out, however, that this domain is by no means uniform; it is composed of:

- finance and insurance
- education, from kindergarten to universities
- real estate and business services
- transport, storage and communication
- wholesale and retail trade
- restaurants and hotels
- community, social and personal services.

Of these seven classes, community, social and personal services is by far the larger, accounting for over one-third of the total.[21] However, during the last two decades the rise in the services' share in employment has been mainly driven by increases in finance, insurance, real estate and business services – with finance having provided some of the more lucrative jobs.

A number of explanations for the increasing trend in services employment have been put forward by economists, including: a rise in the demand for services per capita as income levels increase; the fact that the structure of expenditures is switching away from

20 C.H. Loch, F.J. Sting, N. Bauer and H. Mauaerman, 'The Globe: How BMW is Defusing the Demographic Time Bomb', *Harvard Business Review*, March 2010, at: http://hbr.org/2010/03/the-globe-how-bmw-is-defusing-the-demographic-time-bomb/ar/1.

21 In Europe, the share among the other classes exhibits a large heterogeneity across countries.

materials-based industries; a rise in female participation in the labour force; the upward push in the proportion of labour channelled into new businesses that are largely service-oriented; and the slower labour productivity growth in the services sector relative to manufacturing.

Other frequently discussed reasons are the rising demand for services because of demographic shifts and the process of urbanization. Education and labour market policies implemented in Western countries have also contributed to increasing employment in the services industry, but in the EU the trend has not been matched by appropriate structural reforms to address those issues which are the services industry's own – for instance, challenges associated with part-time jobs (section 5), self-employment (section 4), lifelong learning (section 3) and labour productivity in services. A factor that could lead to higher prices of services is the relative lack of competition in this sector because many jobs are part-time or temporary (and therefore not particularly wanted) as well as the fact that:

- at the higher end of the services jobs spectrum, it is not always easy to find the needed skills,[22] and
- at the lower end there is limited supply because many people prefer to live on unemployment benefits rather than work in hospitals or care for the elderly – with market demand often filled by immigrants (section 7).

The result has been inflation in labour costs connected to services, as per capita income rises and the population ages. This shows up in terms of unit labour costs. Ireland, which experienced an explosion in demand for services and in labour costs between 1999 and 2007, provides an example. An early 2009 study by the European Central Bank found that Irish unit labour costs had risen by a third over this eight-year period.

Critics say that labour costs escaped the Irish government's watch and the country became too pricey.[23] Ireland's 33 per cent wage inflation rate contrasts very badly with only 2 per cent in Germany over the same period, as well as with an average of 14 per cent in Euroland. But Ireland has not been alone. Other EU countries in which wages ran wild in the 1999 to 2007 timeframe include:

- Greece – 28 per cent
- Portugal – 27 per cent
- Spain – 26 per cent
- Luxembourg – 25 per cent
- Italy – 24 per cent.[24]

Economists point to supply-side factors that exist behind the sustained gap between services inflation and price inflation in other goods. This is further accentuated by the service industry's lag in productivity growth, despite large investments in information

22 Another factor is that at the high end of the services industry (banking, insurance, consulting), people overexploit their position by inflating their pay and bonuses.

23 One contributory factor was a big rise in public-sector wages after a 2002 review. But the banking sector, too, contributed a great deal to wage inflation.

24 *The Economist*, 3 January 2009.

technology. The corresponding gap between manufacturing and services is 1.3 per cent for increase in labour productivity, according to the study by the European Central Bank.

It is also true that the case of productivity in the services industry has not attracted the attention which it deserves. In manufacturing, *factor productivity* is attributable to increasingly sophisticated machines, computers, more experienced workers and improved work processes. The aftermath of the wave in IT capital expenditures suggests that technological progress has been an important cause of productivity growth – even if this may be overstated for two reasons that are particularly valid in the US:

- The American economy was lifted by two financial bubbles in a row – stock market and credit – leading to excessive growth in finance and real estate.
- There have been problems with the measurement of consumer durables prices: although import prices have risen, the price paid by consumers fell, and this has been hailed as a consequence of greater US productivity.[25]

Exogenous factors distort the productivity and growth statistics, making them look a lot better than they really are. An added problem is that the service industry has failed to clearly define what is achieved by a more productive person.

Table 7.2 presents some interesting statistics from a productivity study I did some years ago in an office environment. The tool used was *work sampling* – which is a standard in industrial engineering. As these statistics document, the individuals participating to the study (a group of department managers) had thought that the pattern of their work was quite different to that quantitatively assessed, particularly in regard to:

- coordination and supervision,
- report preparation, and
- information–gathering.

**Table 7.2 Comparative study of results from work sampling and self-rating**

| | Work sampling observations | Self-rating questionnaire |
|---|---|---|
| Meetings | 34% | 28% |
| Coordination and supervision* | 24% | 7% |
| Report preparation | 8% | 18% |
| Phone | 7% | 5% |
| Information-gathering* | 6% | 21% |
| Travelling | 4% | 4% |
| Miscellaneous | 17% | 17% |

* Managers think of themselves as planners, with their supervisory role being minor. In reality, the opposite is true.

25 *Business Week*, 15 June 2009.

There are also other approaches to the measurement of service productivity, but none achieves unanimity. To make sense of the work accomplished by its army of consultants IBM tracks individual performance in mental productivity through *stochastic analysis*, mapping the behaviour of humans onto mathematical models which estimate productivity through deliverables.

IBM and other companies using analytical models to measure person-by-person deliverables (in terms of productivity and other contributions) would not say so publicly, but metrics do help the service industry when it is downsizing because the demand in its sector has ebbed.

- Knowing who are the best performers assists in smoothing the volatility of turnover when business takes a downturn and costs rise.

This is not always associated with firing. In mid-2009 BBVA, the Spanish bank, encouraged employees to take sabbaticals of between three and five years on 30 per cent of their salary with a guaranteed job on return. The measure forms part of BBVA's cost-cutting. (Citing this example does not mean that the proposal is great, but it is at least off the beaten path.)

In other cases, personal productivity and similar measurements provide a basis for deciding which people to keep or let go. This has classically been a matter of the supervisor's personal opinion,[26] but the increasing sophistication of services prevents supervisors from having a clear opinion about individual performance.

- Measurements also make feasible better scheduling of human resources as the service industry has more complex planning requirements than manufacturing.

The changing pattern of work leads to a corresponding change in planning means and standards. The way it is currently practised, part-time work is not an effective way of cost-effectively providing the odd hours the service industry requires. It is much better at placing people in work for concentrated stints, such as the first and third weeks of each month – but this is not what service firms need.

Therefore, it comes as no surprise that service companies are adopting analytical approaches which are rapidly integrating into the industry's current policies. For example, Wal-Mart has implemented a new computer-based scheduling system to move its more than 1 million workers to new types of shifts. Its goal is to man shifts according to the number of shoppers in its stores. Workers come and go in groups during busy and slack times during the day,[27] and this is, in its way, becoming a kind of new standard for our service society.

## 7. Labour Mobility in the European Union: The Bolkestein Directive

To appreciate the forces against labour mobility in the European Union the reader needs to remember 20 May 2005, when the French rejected the draft EU constitution. This was largely a vote both against an unpopular president, Jacques Chirac, and against the forces of globalization, including those within the ever-expanding EU borders.

26 And quite often of nepotism.

27 *The Economist*, 6 January 2007.

A case in point in public reaction against transborder labour mobility in the EU is the European Commission's Services Directive, known as the *Bolkestein Directive* after the former EU commissioner Frits Bolkestein who initiated it. Its object was the full deregulation of all services by 2010, but the roadblocks it encountered on its way have been innumerable.

At the foundation of the Bolkestein Directive is the 'country of origin' principle. It says that services can be offered in any EU country, under the wage, social, and regulatory conditions existing in the 'country of origin', rather than those of the country where the services are being performed.

- Many governments criticized the directive's labour mobility clauses, even if they generally conform to the common market for goods and labour.
- Western Europe's labour unions launched a mobilization against it, claiming that it would drive down wages and erode social and health standards.[28]
- Eastern Europe's labour unions, too, were concerned with stemming the migration of workers to better-paying western Europe.[29]

Frits Bolkestein, however, did not invent the liberalization of the EU's labour market. He did his duty by following the EU's statutes, but the reaction was negative from nearly all sides.

In mid-February 2006 the members of the European Parliament (MEPs) adopted, by a large majority, a watered-down version, particularly in what its critics regarded as a controversial 'social dimension'. The weakened text was voted for by 391 MEPs, including the German social democrats, Spanish socialists and populists and British conservatives. Among the 215 who voted against the diminished version were the French socialists and communists, as well as the greens and liberals.[30]

This has been a show of protectionism within EU's borders, but the mistake rests with the second-raters who opened up the EU to a wild increase in membership, prior to having established a federal constitution and economic structure which could withstand the stress of larger membership. Since Jacques Delors retired as the EU's CEO, the Commission cannot afford to walk into the line of fire as it used to, because:

- economic nationalism is on the rise and
- the balance of power has turned towards national governments.

Pure and simple nationalism, too, has flourished. In 2004 Jacques Chirac, then president of France, blocked the election of Chris Patten as the EU's new CEO. Moreover, there are no EU commissioners who are considered as political heavyweights.

In addition, because the EU Commission is weak, it failed to argue effectively for freeing transborder trade in services. It has also been tempted into curious trade arrangements, like the deal on textiles with China, while at the same time failing to take a stand on the French and Spanish governments'

- 'statism' and

28 By confirming the low-wage, low-standard status of eastern Europe.

29 For instance, in Poland there is an acute shortage of some 20,000 nurses. Many Polish nurses are working in the West, because they cannot make a living on the low pay they receive in their own country's hospitals.

30 33 MEPs abstained.

- anti-EU protectionism.

In violation of the Treaty of Rome, France has persistently attempted to water down a draft law to open up the market in services, which represents 70 per cent of the EU's economy. Instead, it has been gripped by fear that the Bolkestein Directive will open the floodgates to a wave of 'Polish plumbers' and other low-wage workers.

Trade unions joined the protests of EU member governments in being largely hostile to the free movement of labour. Examples have been the rally of 40,000 German trade unionists in Berlin and Europe-wide rallies in Strasbourg. Other grievances, too, were added to the cocktail. In France, the labour unions staged protests in about 100 cities against a government plan to give firms 'greater flexibility' in hiring and firing.[31]

In Britain, too, the biggest trade unions lined up against Tony Blair over plans to dismantle barriers to cross-border trade in services. Unison, Amicus, TGWU and GMB combined their political and financial muscle to try to stop parts of the Bolkestein Directive that they believed were threatening 'workers' rights' and damaging public services. What the four unions particularly opposed was the 'country of origin' principle – which was also the *bête noir* of the French labour unions.

At the time of the aforementioned February 2006 MEPs' vote on a highly diluted directive, many EU members imposed 'transitional arrangements', which is Brussels-speak for restrictions on labour coming from the east to the west of Europe. Theoretically, Britain and Ireland stood alone in opening their markets to all, but in practice even they adopted rules to stop benefit-seekers, and Britain created a registration scheme. Sweden was more or less alone in keeping its labour market open, after its parliament rejected restrictions. At the end of the day,

- only three of the 15 pre-enlargement member states applied the principle of free movement of people to the ten states that joined the EU on 1 May 2004.
- The other 12, France and Germany included, chose the so-called 'transitional arrangements' aimed at protecting their labour markets for up to seven years.

Short-sightedness, populism and economic nationalism carried the day. As Jacques Chirac said, 'liberalism is as dangerous an ideology as communism, and like communism it will not prevail'.[32] No wonder that, with that sort of political philosophy, 'statism' is carrying more weight than cross-border integration in the EU.

Some people remarked that all this fervour against labour mobility did not really make sense, if for no other reason than workers from the new members made up less than 1 per cent of the total of the labour force of the 15 EU countries. Only in Ireland was the percentage higher – at 3.8 per cent. In addition, far from stealing jobs from locals, most incomers were taking jobs that locals shunned.

In terms of the economy, much worse than the movement of labour from eastern to western Europe has been the heavy national debt. There has in fact been some awakening to the fact that western Europe's national economies are weighed down by the heavy burden of government debt, but very little progress has been made in dealing with this

31 The government's policy originated with the EU Commission's pressure for labour market deregulation.

32 *The Economist*, 15 October 2005.

problem.[33] Yet, as an American saying goes, 'If the federal government is allowed to spend money only on functions of some importance, the budget could be balanced in seven hours.'

Much of the political rhetoric about government protecting the labour market and the poor came into question as well. The best protection for all is a vigorous economy that can yield new jobs and advancement to higher levels of income. The irony with the movement of labour from eastern Europe has been that as soon as the local economies improved, migrant workers went back.

- By 2008 many Poles working in Britain returned home, as work in Poland improved and the zloty sharply rose against the British pound (although it fell flat in 2009).
- Germany's Gerhard Schröder laughed at the argument about the loss of local jobs to Poles, saying that the best proof of benefits from labour mobility is that a German pope picked up the job of a Polish one.

By early 2009, however, the deepening economic crisis restoked the fire against labour mobility in the EU, as the Lindsey incident documents. On 28 January 2009 800 local contractors went on strike, leading to hundreds of British workers outside the Lindsey oil refinery, brandishing placards protesting against the presence of foreign labour hired to expand the plant. Though the wildcat strike was technically illegal since legislation passed after the 1984 miners' strike, other workers staged sympathy strikes, and eventually[34] more than 20 other British sites were affected, with an estimated 6,000 workers walking out. Emotions ran high because of fear of job losses, concern about foreign workers, unease over a 'powerful' European Union, disillusionment with the prime minister, Gordon Brown, and a Labour Party in full disarray.

Yet, no Polish plumbers were involved! Total, the French oil firm that owns the refinery, had hired a Californian engineering outfit to extend the plant. After tenders from British and foreign firms, the US company subcontracted the work to an Italian enterprise which shipped several hundred European (mainly Italian and Portuguese) staff to Britain. More were to come.

Given EU rules and the (watered-down) version of the Bolkestein Directive voted for in February 2005 by the European parliament, legally the protesters were on shaky ground. The Italian and Portuguese workers were in Britain under the 'posted workers' clause designed to let firms use their own staff on temporary projects elsewhere in the EU without distorting competition. In addition, workers in Britain have few legal protections compared with their counterparts in continental Europe – but they do have the right to strike.

Gordon Brown talked up the benefits of open labour markets and Peter Mandelson, his business secretary, warned that a surge in protectionism would turn recession into depression. But, as reported in the TV news, in the end, the government gave in through a face-saving sort of compromise that (at the aforementioned hot site) half the workers would be British and half foreigners. This is the EU.

---

33 Which became much worse with the 2007–2011 economic and banking crisis.

34 The strike temporarily ended on 4 February, but it resumed on 11 June that same year with more support.

# 8. Young People Should Not Make Themselves Unemployable

Elaborated in Portugal in 1999, in one of the many interminable EU 'summit' meetings, the *Lisbon Strategy* for Social Policy proclaimed that the EU should aim to become the world's 'most competitive and dynamic knowledge-based economy by 2010'. Judging from results obtained in the 11 years that followed that Lisbon summit, these three keywords – 'competitive', 'dynamic' and 'knowledge-based' – have proven to be hilarious overstatements.

One of the highlights of this social policy agenda of 1999, was an agreed on – but nebulous – 'modernization and improvement of social protection', which was supposed to also combat discrimination. This abstract, highly imprecise notion was expected to create employment, wealth and widespread opportunity. But, as usual, there have been no precise plans, let alone the will to implement them, and therefore no progress. Nothing has been achieved by the Lisbon Strategy.

The EU is not alone in specializing in grandiose empty pronouncements. In April 2006, for instance, the UN launched its *Principles for Responsible Investment* (PRI), with the then secretary–general, Kofi Annan, ringing the opening bell at the New York Stock Exchange. Six 'principles' were supposed to commit signatories to integrating environmental, social and governance (ESG) issues into conventional investment analysis and other 'do good' unspecified acts – but immediately after the communiqué was issued, it was put into a time capsule.

Whether it is the Lisbon Strategy, the UN's ESG principles for responsible investing or any other exercise in futility, their authors should know that the failure of the enterprise which they project and promote reflects on them.

- They are losing face with its failure and
- they cannot be taken seriously in the future.

Honed by experience, a general rule states that the more vague and imprecise 'good principles' are, the shorter are their legs – which is, after all, the very reason for their vagueness. Here are a couple of examples on what happens when one tries to change the status quo; they come from France in early 2006 when the students massively rejected, through noisy rallies in the streets, the government's (rather sensible) plan of integrating unemployed young people into the labour force.

- Even if they did not yet have a job, the students were already on strike, and
- even if they were confronted with solid unemployment, they did want to be see measures that would provide them with at least temporary work.

Job-seekers took to the streets to defend the unrealistic notion that in modern society, which is in perpetual motion, one's first job should come with a lifetime guarantee and that the government should pay for it. Yet the *Contrat Première Embauche* (discussed in Chapter 9, section 3) had its merits and it was worth giving it a try.

The European Union has a deeply ingrained problem: its young generation is frightened stiff of uncertainty and therefore of the future. Traditions relating to an overgenerous social safety net, which has become perfectly *unaffordable* and *unsustainable*, partly explain this attitude (see also Chapter 9). In much of the EU there's still a hatred of hire-and-fire.

- Having a well-paid job is seen as being one's right, which it definitely is not (section 1), and
- the likelihood of multiple careers in a person's life (sections 2 and 3) is not seen as an opportunity and a personal responsibility, but as hell.

It is surprising that young people don't take notice of the fact that a growing number of companies market themselves differently to job candidates. They no longer mention a glamorous career. Instead, their new selling points are getting to know the boss better, opportunities for advancement, flexible working hours and deferred start dates to new hires, giving them a few months to round up current business.[35]

These are symptoms of the evolving labour market which is no richer in possibilities than that which preceded it. Because it is characterized by a certain distress, it is not logical to revolt against future conditions in the employment arena, but this is what happens.

'The university is going up in smoke,' read a handwritten banner strung from a tree at the entrance to the University of Nanterre, near Paris. In the social-science tower block, where many of the *future unemployable* tend to study, desks and chairs were stacked in the entrance hall in a bid to make teaching impossible. On and off, that curious battle of students against themselves and their future has been disrupting about a quarter of France's 82 universities, with many campuses blocked by strikes.

All over France, students from colleges and universities – the very people who should appreciate that arteriosclerosis of the labour markets is their greatest enemy – took to the streets and stayed there for nearly three months. Nobody in their homes, in the government or in the political opposition explained to them that:

- a knowledge economy never forgives the loss of three months of learning,[36] and,
- nepotism aside, which is a disgrace, today superior learning is the young generation's only ammunition in finding employment.

Among researchers there has been mistrust of Nicolas Sarkozy, the French president, who correctly mocked the output of many of them. The policy of a wide gap between academia and private industry has been misfiring for years. This is not just a French phenomenon, even if in France it happens in a big way. The whole of Europe is confronted with the problem that large numbers of students in higher education have turned themselves into 'future unemployables' as politicians fail to explain to the public that in present-day society the choice is between:

- oblivion and
- job flexibility.

---

35 New hires are often reluctant to accept that offer, in case the economy sinks further and new lay-offs put paid to a promised job.

36 Even if the government bent over and passed them through their 2006 *baccalauréat* at hugely discounted criteria and degrees.

But politicians are not the only ones to blame. Parents, too, spoil their children who grow up to become lazy adults, disobedient to the rules, and with little respect for social values. Few fathers exercise discipline in teaching, correcting and guiding their sons and daughters.

This does not only happen in Europe; it is also prevalent in America, and it characterizes both families and the government itself. In an interview with the *Financial Times*, David Walker, former US Comptroller General, stated that the administration 'is on a "burning platform" of unsustainable policies and practices with fiscal deficits, chronic healthcare underfunding, immigration and overseas military commitments threatening a crisis if action is not taken soon...' Walker also warned of declining moral values and fiscal irresponsibility – just like in the EU.

Let me add this in conclusion. Inadequate political leadership has led young people into the bad habit of *making themselves unemployable*. There is little doubt that young men and women entering the labour force typically find it hard to get established because of their lack of proper training and experience. This makes them vulnerable.

There are various theories regarding the deeper reasons. One of them says that, at least in western Europe, they get displaced by the influx of youthful migrants from eastern Europe. The other maintains that they make themselves especially vulnerable by their attitude that society at large owes them a not-too-difficult job with good pay. I personally believe that they lack the drive to come up from under, and wait for a *Deus ex machina*.

It is foolish to believe the empty-of-substance promises made by politicians. The young generation's prospects are not going to change because of hollow pronouncements about a 'competitive', 'dynamic' and 'knowledge-based' EU economy, promised by the Lisbon Strategy. The era of easy jobs at good pay is gone. The young in any and every EU country no longer compete only with their countrymen, but also with young Indians and Chinese who:

- learn well and
- do not go on strike.

Science has a very good rule: First find the facts. The fact is that globalization has tremendously changed the nature and frame of reference of competition;[37] the 'good old days' (if there were any) will never come back, no matter how much one protests. There is no reason, therefore, for the students to worsen their lot by letting it be known down the street that they are unemployable. They had better get busy finding their way up the social ladder.

37 D.N. Chorafas, *Globalization's Limits: Conflicting National Interests in Trade and Finance*, Gower, Aldershot, 2009.

CHAPTER **8**

# Wages, Salaries and the Destruction of the EU'S Middle Class

## 1. Income, Entitlements and Social Change

In post-industrial countries, wages account for approximately 65–70 per cent of final product prices. It is therefore quite important to consider the effect of higher wages and, most particularly, of the weight of entitlements such as healthcare for retirees whose lifespan has greatly increased over the post-World War II years.

While people should get good salaries and wages, costs associated with the social safety net have run out of control. This is visibly contributing to western Europe's and America's problems of competitiveness in the globalized economy.[1]

- The more open the global market becomes with the deferent 'trade rounds', the more competition is coming from emerging markets and their underpaid, but hardworking, human resources.
- Western governments have failed to properly notice that modern telecommunications and transportation facilities have made international arbitrage on salaries and wages much easier, as firms and service providers can scan the globe for lower costs.

Emerging countries have also taken serious towards becoming more investor-friendly, and these steps have made international firms (as well as major investors) comfortable with capitalizing on these emerging markets' lower costs – while they simultaneously expand their sales activities. Emerging markets in eastern Europe, Asia and other parts of the world are now doing work previously done in North America and western Europe. Another major change associated with the twenty-first-century economy is that:

- labour and
- capital became unstuck.

Repudiating, in a way, the thinking of both Adam Smith and Karl Marx, labour and capital have split their fortunes. This is true both in a *global* framework and *at home* in practically every country – industrial or emerging. For their part, companies have been able to boost productivity by using a combination of:

- restructuring,

---

1 D.N. Chorafas, *Globalization's Limits: Conflicting National Interests in Trade and Finance*, Gower, Aldershot, 2009.

- downsizing and
- investing in new technology.

Particularly in the manufacturing sector, this triple solution has produced competition for labour *at home*, over and above that characterized by the quantitative effect of cheaper manpower in Asia and elsewhere. Even in Western countries where, prior to the 2007–2009 economic crisis, the unemployment rate had fallen, wage growth was held down by new technology that needs much less labour – which is, for all practical purposes, the productivity argument.

At the same time, technology and international competition have compounded the impotence of labour unions (see Chapter 10). In the 1960s real compensation per hour in non-financial companies rose at an average annual rate of 2.1 per cent. By contrast, *real* compensation per hour fell in the 1990s and the first decade of this century. The inflection point can be found in the early 1990s.

- General Motors spent 26 per cent of its revenues on wages, salaries and benefits in 1989.
- By 1994, the percentage of revenues going to labour was only 21 per cent while, by contrast, fringe benefits like healthcare increased significantly.

As a result of the redistribution of earning power, the dynamics of labour negotiations changed, leading towards impotence of the labour movement. By the mid- to late 1990s wages became much less important than they used to be as a source of income. For example, Americans were getting only 57 per cent of their personal income from wages and salaries, which was a post-World War II low in the (then) elapsed half-century. Instead, investments, dividends and self-employment income became progressively more important, even dethroning one's house in the list of priorities.[2] Wage income will shrink even further (in size and importance) as the labour market becomes deregulated. Leon Brittan, Margaret Thatcher's former chancellor of the exchequer, predicted this at the 1995 World Economic Forum in Davos, Switzerland.

Statistics from 2009 show that there is little or no link between prices and wage changes in the services industry in an impressive 60 per cent of cases, while in manufacturing this goes up to 50 per cent. Moreover, while is a link between prices and wages for a share varying between 22 per cent in services and nearly 30 per cent in manufacturing, this is not characterized by a single pattern.

By contrast, if the list of fringe benefits under the umbrella of *endowments* is added to wages, the picture changes, and labour costs again become the key determinant of overall production costs. In France, for instance, so-called social costs or *acquis sociaux*, nearly double take-home wages. It is therefore only reasonable that, in their studies of wage- and price-setting, economists tend to distinguish between:

- time-dependent and
- state-dependent costs.

2 As an American saying went in the 1950s, 'Your house is your castle.'

The former costs are the more classical. In time-dependent approaches wages and prices are linked more or less directly. In state-dependent models, prices and wages are linked indirectly as rule changes by the state bias their old linear relationship, and the weight of entitlements varies significantly for political reasons (and as a result of industry-sector negotiations).

In the one as in the other case, of course, developments in costs can be in no way discarded in deciding whether or not to raise prices, and a price increase becomes more likely if it is accompanied by a cumulative increase in materials and wage costs since the previous price change. On the other hand, the globalized market ensures that costs can no more be seen as 'the one and only' determining factor in price adjustments because global competitors can siphon the company's market.

The result is that time-dependency between wages and price adjustments, at firm level, is not as pronounced as it used to be, or could be assumed, but it is still there. Both global competition and other cost factors seem to play a greater role than wages alone: a 2009 survey indicated that only 20 per cent of German manufacturing firms reported a clear link between the timing of wage and price changes – and this specifically came from companies with higher labour costs.[3]

The reader should nevertheless appreciate that the results of this survey reflect, to a significant extent, a much better level of organization in Germany than in the other countries. As a feature article in *The Economist* had it, 'Germany has not just looked after its public finances more prudently than others; its export-driven model has forced its companies to hold down costs, making them competitive not only in Europe but also globally.'[4]

This result has been reached despite the fact that the mid- to late 1990s market misalignments in the global monetary system adversely affected the international competitiveness of German enterprises. In addition, in the late 1990s and early years of this century, the German economic situation was overshadowed by intractable employment problems, which increased in severity despite the improvement in the overall economic environment. There have been various reasons for these occurrences, including:

- structural problems and inflexibility in the labour market and
- stronger competitive pressure to which the German economy was exposed because of increased globalization.

To overcome these disadvantages it was necessary for the government and the companies' top management to review the factors that put pressure on labour costs and provided too little incentive for searching for new employment. Correctly, the Schröder government gave priority to the elimination of structural causes of employment problems and other issues whose correction reinforced the basis of Germany's economic prosperity in the ensuing years.

The lesson from this reference is that Western countries don't necessarily need to match the wages prevailing in developing countries, even if this is feasible. To avoid doing so, however, they have to thoroughly restructure their labour market, past endowments and the social system itself. The time has come to accept that it is better

---

3 Deutsche Bundesbank, *Monthly Report*, April 2009.

4 *The Economist*, 9 May 2008.

to have people in work than impressive endowments accompanied by a wave of strikes aimed at safeguarding them.

- Personal discipline and hard work are at a premium, and
- the effect of discipline in work rules and wages can be dramatic.

The proof is provided by Germany's competitiveness which by 2009 had improved by around 13 per cent since the euro was introduced in 2002, despite the 2007–2009 severe economic crisis. There are similar hopeful signs in other EU countries as well. In 2009 Confindustria, Italy's biggest employers' body, signed an accord with two of the country's three largest trade unions to overhaul the national wage system. CGIL, the largest of the three, did not sign up to the deal, but the Italian government said it would go ahead anyway. It must.

## 2. The Work Ethic and Social Cohesion

Neither economic growth nor social cohesion is ever created by strikes. Economic growth is generally achieved through fiscal and monetary prudence, a decent legal system and entrepreneurial dynamism. None of this can be brought into social life by going wild in the streets – whether the strikers are students (Chapter 7), teachers, workers, government employees, pensioners or whoever. Nor is the work ethic promoted by:

- attending heads of state conferences and 'summits' or
- theoretical pronouncements which are good for the summit's *communiqué*, but are out of touch with reality.

Pragmatic approaches, work ethic and social cohesion correlate. The latter's definition varies not only from country to country, but also from village to village, depending on family ties, religion, the work ethic itself and national traditions. No gathering of people – whether yelling their brains out in the street or talking in parliament – could agree on what social cohesion is, let alone how to encourage it, but this does not change the fact that a society:

- either *is* or *is not* characterized a cohesion, and
- the one that is prospers, while the other that is not disintegrates.

Social cohesion is important because it contributes one of the basic characteristics of stable societies, allowing them to work together towards common goals, foster competition, welcome innovation and create economic dynamism. In the mid-1990s, the years when the American economy was still in high gear, an MIT study showed that 80 per cent of net new jobs created in the US came from only 4 per cent of the companies. These were typically small, rapidly growing high-tech firms.[5]

Such companies are usually characterized by a work ethic. The people working for them do not look at their watch when it is time to go home, neither do they consider

5 *The MIT Report*, January 1996.

the weekend as reserved exclusively for relaxing. Small, rapidly growing firms have a top management team that is close to the employees – with both the decision-makers and employees dedicated to rapid development. The managers are large shareholders of the company, creating an environment in which the firm can move quickly to commercialize an innovative technology. The lesson to retain is twofold:

- People lacking passion for the job they do use the first barrier they encounter as an excuse for failure.
- By contrast, people with a high passion for accomplishment do everything possible to overcome the barriers, positioning themselves against the adverse forces.

Unfortunately for Western society and its citizens, the work ethic is not taught in school – and it is rarely promoted in the family. Both families and schools, and therefore the government, are to be blamed for not infusing to the young generation with a work ethic – something similar to the *Protestant work ethic* which made America strong.

In addition, pupils and students are never taught the golden rule reflected in the American saying 'Your company, love it or leave it', and they are not instructed that, in a tough labour market, only those who are productive are employable. Entrepreneurs choose people for their:

- intelligence and learning,
- attitude to work and
- enthusiasm in delivering results.

These are important ingredients of education, because they help young people understand what they need to do to develop their career. Neither is job flexibility part of the teaching schedule. Yet, the 2007–2009 downturn has highlighted the miserable result of lack of flexibility in the labour market. It put the burden of adjustment on groups with little or no tenure – such as women and the young – while it protected the bulk of the workforce with built-in seniority and other entitlement advantages.

What we have seen in 2008 and 2009, as unemployment rose, is precisely what happens in fossilized economies. Significant flexibility regarding jobs, wages, salaries and social costs – particularly those connected to less qualified working people – is the cornerstone to both better social cohesion and a more effective solution to unemployment problems (more on job flexibility in Chapter 10).

Because urgently required changes face resistance by voters, or at least by organized interest groups, governments decide to accept the status quo rather than offend important constituencies. This attitude, however, cannot continue unabatedly. Ultimately, the various benefits bestowed by the state supermarket are paid by the public at large through:

- higher taxes across the board and
- inflation, which erodes the value of money and most hurts those citizens who are financially weaker.

When at the beginning of this century Gerhard Schröder, the German chancellor, revamped the country's system of labour and social benefits, he did so to avert a major crisis, under the pressure of an empty public purse. A less appreciated but very important part of Schröder's overall change to the rules of the game was the 'promote and push' principle characterized by:

- the introduction of a means-tested basic allowance for people who are able to work and
- the strengthening of the risk-insurance nature of unemployment benefit,[6] which corrected some of the worst abuses.

In addition, improved working-hour arrangements allowed a higher utilization of fixed capital, while longer working hours alleviated the problem of nominal wage rigidity, thereby preserving the purchasing power of labour income. Such measures, as a whole, can increase people's willingness to take up a job and thereby reduce the length of time spent in unemployment.

The previous government of Helmut Kohl had paid no real attention to the fact that, after the fall of the Iron Curtain in 1989, the cost of producing cars in Germany was $31 per hour versus $3.50 in the Czech Republic – with Czech workers being as good as the Germans. In this sense, the low-cost well-educated work forces of eastern Europe offered the best chance for corporate western Europe to solve a chronic competitiveness problem.

While western Europeans struggled to cling to their standard of living, politicians were running scared from bringing up urgently necessary, if unpopular, changes – at the expense of both work ethic and social cohesion. Superficially, this avoided strikes, but in reality it hurt the economy and the common citizen.

Contrary to this policy of hiding one's head in the sand, a great deal can be gained by modernizing outdated labour-market structures. In the aftermath of Germany's aforementioned labour changes, manufacturing value added in 2006 compared to 1996, a decade earlier, grew to nearly 24 per cent from 23 per cent, while in other Western countries it retreated. For instance:

- In Britain, it shrunk to 13 per cent from 21 per cent,
- In France, to 13 per cent from 16 per cent, and
- in the United States, to 14 per cent from 18 per cent.[7]

Other measures, too, can help. An example is the revision of personal and corporate tax rates, as extravagant government expenditures are weeded out of the system. Indeed, corporate-tax rates have been falling during this century, and anecdotal evidence suggests that workers have gained jobs as corporate taxes have fallen.

Not everything, however, should come from the state. Companies, too, must contribute a large part of improvement to general well-being by reinventing themselves and sharpening up their competitiveness. Britain's Rolls-Royce presents an example. Over the last 20 years, Rolls-Royce has transformed itself from a loss-making company into the world's second-largest designer and manufacturer of large jet engines. This transformation:

- blurred the lines between producing things and offering services, and
- the company's experience indicates that sound governance is the key.

6 Implemented by economic policy-makers since 2003.

7 *The Economist*, 10 January 2009.

The Rolls-Royce rebirth has been a countertrend to developments in the British economy as a whole. Although the country is the world's eighth largest exporter of goods, its share of the global market has shrunk to a little more than 3 per cent, far behind America, China and Germany (though in services Britain ranks second).

Technology has played a crucial role in the ability of Rolls-Royce to reinvent itself. Its new departure in engine design proved to be the base for a whole family of winning products. These are more complex to build and maintain than those of rivals, but they:

- use fuel more efficiently and
- suffer less wear and tear.

Most importantly, the company's new engines can be scaled up or down to fit larger or smaller aircraft. Hence, Rolls-Royce does not have to design a new engine from scratch each time a different airframe design comes up; this also allows it to compete for sales across a wider range of aircraft than its rivals. The beneficiaries are all stakeholders – from the economy and the shareholders to the workers.

## 3. Wages and the Distribution of National Wealth

'The public is being asked to swallow that all manner of human troubles – from anxiety, interpersonal squabbles to misbehavior of many kinds – be viewed not as inevitable parts of the human comedy, but as psychopathology to be treated, usually with drugs ...' says Stuart Kirk, UCLA Professor of Social Welfare.[8] One of the drugs of our society is that of clinging to one's odd job (and to the minimum wage) for posterity, rather than reinventing oneself and one's skills.

'What we're now pretty sure of is that it's not labor versus capital but labor vs. labor – the low-skilled losing out to the higher skilled worker. Our concern is what kind of society we are turning into if we have huge inequalities. And does there come a point where people say "I'm mad as hell and I'm not going to take it anymore",' comments Paul Krugman, professor of economics and Nobel Prize winner.[9] In his opinion, to the extent that it might be a labour versus capital case there may come a point where government should intervene in an effort to determine:

- who is really being adversely affected by wage trends and
- what is causing this current huge divergence between high and low pay, as well as why.

Right in the middle of these two bullets lies the issue of entitlements and their negative aftermath, particularly that connected to relatively high unemployment benefits which discourage re-entry into the labour force. This issue is far from being academic. At the heart of it stands:

- the need to reward work, rather than state-supported idleness, and

8 *UCLA Magazine*, January 2006.

9 *The MIT Report*, March 1997.

- ways and means to discourage the exploitation of unemployment benefits, by living at the expense of others.

'Everyone worries about the beneficiaries while the people who pay for it all are ignored,' says Guido Westerwelle, German foreign minister and leader of the Free Democratic Party (FDP).[10] His argument follows a ruling of the German constitutional court that the government's method of determining the level of Hartz IV (entitlement to long-term unemployment benefit) is unconstitutional. This has revived a debate over whether welfare beneficiaries are:

- exploiters of state largesse or
- victims of an unjust social safety net.

The problem presented in Germany, and practically all over the EU, is that market wages are often lower than long-term unemployment benefits. The aftermath is that, according to some estimates, in Germany only 1.4 million of the 4.9 million beneficiaries considered able to work actually do so[11] – which means that roughly two-thirds are loafers.

This issue has a great deal to do with the distribution –or, if you prefer, redistribution – of national wealth. It is a real and present problem which cannot be solved through an expedient (and populistic) increase in market wages – because the global economy severely punishes such moves by wiping out jobs in high(er)-wage countries.[12]

Here we don't talk only of China (and other Asian countries) versus the US and the EU. The way a news item on 18 March 2010 had it, a small handworkers' shop in Egypt closed down because it could no longer compete with handwork imported from China. That is a step too far for the Chinese. After having swept clean jobs and companies in America and Europe, they are now doing the same with the workforces of less developed countries.

Anecdotal evidence suggests that Joseph Kennedy, who made a good part of his large fortune by selling at the stock market high in 1929 (just before the crash), got his tip from a shoeshine boy in Chicago. As the boy was polishing Kennedy's shoes, he said: 'Eh, Mister, you want a tip for the stock market?' Kennedy thought that if stock-market fever had reached shoeshine boys, who were going to be the next suckers?

- Beijing's communist/capitalist party bosses should think about that very carefully.
- If Egyptian handworkers are wiped out of jobs because of Chinese lowest-cost wares, who will be the next suckers?

The effect of globalization on jobs and labour costs necessarily underpins any serious discussion on salaries, wages and distribution of the national wealth. The better way to bring this issue into perspective is to begin well after the end of World War II, when its ravages had started to become a memory and a new social structure was taking the place of the old.

---

10 *The Economist*, 27 February 2010.

11 Ibid.

12 D.N. Chorafas, *Globalization's Limits. Conflicting National Interests in Trade and Finance*, Gower, Aldershot, 2009.

Statistics from 1995 upheld Pareto's law,[13] but they did so with a difference. After World War II (1945–1970) people worked hard to rebuild from the ruins and kept a good measure of social cohesion. The first signs that this was about to change, and that society was moving towards confrontation, came with the student revolt in Paris, in May 1968.

The revolt against the status quo subsided, as a new generation took up the reins. Curiously enough, in the 1970–1995 years people and governments did everything in their power to widen the gap between the 'haves' and the 'have-nots'. If we divide the Western population into five strata, from the richest to the poorest, then from 1970 to 1995:

- the income of families in the top 20 per cent increased by 40 per cent;
- that of families in the next 20 per cent richest layer increased by 27 per cent;
- In the middle 20 per cent *tranche* income increased by 17.5 per cent;
- the income of the fourth 20 per cent grew by less than 9 per cent; and
- the income increase in the bottom 20 per cent has been a mere 3.5 per cent.

These are average figures for Western countries (US and western Europe),and are not intended to be precise. The objective of the professional meeting which led to these figures was to show the trend – an unmistakable trend even by only comparing averages. Another aim was to document the fact that the gap between rich and poor has not only widened most significantly, but also continues to do so.[14]

If anything, the part of the third post-World War II generation which has already passed has amplified these inequalities (more on this later). The political *overcompromise* by the second-raters who have run the state supermarket since the mid-1960s have made things much worse – because, from the start, these policies were unaffordable and unsustainable in the longer term. Taking as an example the United States:

- In 1965 President Johnson established Medicare for the old and Medicaid for the poor.
- In early the 1970s President Nixon dramatically expanded food stamps for the poor.
- The 1972 Congress indexed social security benefits to inflation.

All these social handouts, introduced amidst buoyant economic growth, were aimed at reconciling Americans' historic dislike of big government with their post-war taste for 'more government', but it did not work out that way.[15] As a result, by making more promises than it could keep, particularly after the US economy went through a long stretch of 'stagflation' in the 1970s, the government shot itself in the foot by systematically generating distrust.

In Europe, in the decades following World War II, while post-war reconstruction to repair the ravages of war was being carried out, many job opportunities dried up. Manual jobs have been displaced to developing countries while, at the same time, universities

13 Vilfredo Pareto, a Swiis-Italian economist and mathematician, professor at the University of Lausanne, fostered his law at the beginning of the twentieth century by studying wealth distribution in Switzerland. He observed that a small part of one factor, such as people, controlled a large part of another factor – for instance national wealth. This was later developed into the 80:20 principle.

14 See also British statistics from 2007 in section 5.

15 *Newsweek*, 8 January 1996.

have increased their intake and output of graduates quite significantly. Fewer jobs and more job-seekers saw to it that unemployment, even among college graduates, rose. The Lisbon Strategy (Chapter 7) and other empty pronouncements did nothing to change that.

There is, moreover, a case of mismanagement of the working population at the national economic level – all the way from benefits to minimum wages. To keep the young off the streets, in the mid-1960s continental European governments instituted a hefty unemployment allowance (*rent*)[16] for people over 25 years old who could not, or did not want to, find a job. This meant easy money, and so-called *rent-seekers* multiplied. Little by little the benefit system created a generation of *unemployable* people who:

- no longer needed to look for a job because the state supermarket was taking care of them, and
- deliberately let their skills drift, making a mockery of the university education they had received.

The most intelligent among university graduates dreaded this degrading situation and tried to come up from under (see section 5). In the news recently was the case of a young lady of 25 who had studied foreign languages. But after a year's frustration, due to finding no takers for her language skills, she decided to change professions. She became a cook, worked hard and developed good professional prospects – albeit outside her 'major'.

The law of supply and demand being what it is, a massive demand for jobs and few jobs on offer, even for graduates, combine to depress salary levels. During the first seven years of this century many young French graduates who thought that having a job meant something to them, left to work in Britain, the US and Canada. The language barrier that kept them 'at home' was broken. They did not want to continue living on benefits and decay, along with the system, as the state supermarket and its bureaucrats:

- regarded the material instincts of the young generation as 'diminishing' ordinary people's morality, and
- could not understand that the status quo is the worst possible condition; though when they leave for abroad, people vote with their feet.

Equally bad for the future of the young generation, including graduates, and of French employees at large, has been the castration of the time-honoured curriculum vitae (CV). Attached to the coat-tails of de Villepin's *Contrat Première Embauche* (CPE) (see Chapter 9) was a decree of pure hallucination. Since then, French companies seeking to hire staff have to make do with *anonymous* applications by employees-to-be. Identification and photos are no longer permitted on a CV – the outcome of a crazy initiative supposed to tackle discrimination. This means job applicants do not have to give their:

- name,
- age,
- sex or

16 People living at the expense of society through any its eleemosynary activities, are *rent-seekers*. The word 'rent' should not be confused with the act of paying rent for a house.

- address on CVs for jobs.

The law applies to the 30,000 French companies employing 50 people or more. Experts say that this silly amendment has been instrumental in *increasing unemployment*, as companies get overconcerned on the sort of employees they might be getting: Is the applicant a *real professional* or is he or she a professional striker, *casseur* or suchlike? Socialists (who else?) pushed for that amendment, and the parliamentary majority, which was (supposedly) right-wing, accepted it.

It is bitingly ironic that shortly thereafter the CPE died at the hands of street demonstrators, but the 'invisible man' practice, which has a highly negative impact on French employment, stayed. A further irony has been that the '*No ID*' amendment worked *against* the government's efforts to solve the challenge of unemployed graduates and others.

## 4. Income Inequality, Wages to Buy Social Peace and Extravagant Bonuses

While time is being lost on trivia, a deep social problem has been left unattended. Nevertheless, EU countries and North America should be concerned about it. Paul Krugman phrases it beautifully: 'What worries me are the gathering social and political problems resulting from *income inequality* that could unravel the whole social and economic consensus on which this society is based. I think there's a high probability of that in the next 20 years.'[17]

The trend of rapidly increasing income for the top fifth of the Western population and corresponding stagnation for the lower two-fifths explain the reason for Krugman's worries. This growth in income inequality has been based on two legs:

- minimum wages and
- extravagant bonuses.

In most cases, the former don't quite make sense. As for the latter, during the last couple of decades they have already exceeded what anyone would have thought possible. That's bad because history and statistics provide a lot of evidence that societies highly polarized between two extremes – in this case, too rich and too poor – have trouble remaining democratic or simply maintaining a viable economy, let alone keeping growth on track.

Proponents of the minimum wage say that it helps reduce poverty and income inequality by raising the incomes of the lowest-paid employees and by narrowing the gap between their pay and that of those further up the pay scale (which is pure science fiction). Critics argue that, far from helping the poor, a minimum wage is more likely to leave them worse off.

German unions, for example, have been demanding a minimum wage of €7.50 per hour, about €1,250 per month. This is lower than in France where it stands at €8 per hour (*smic horaire brut*) and higher than in Austria. But, according to a study by two economists,

17 *MIT Report*, March 1997.

Joachim Ragnitz and Marcel Thum, such a wage imposed across the economy would wipe out 1.1 million low-wage jobs – corresponding to:

- 3 per cent of employment in western Germany and
- more than 6 per cent in the east, where productivity is lower.[18]

Raising unskilled wages means that employers take on fewer workers, pushing up unemployment and increasing poverty. Raising low pay through blanket statutory measures does little to reduce the gap in family budgets, critics suggest, since relatively few of the lowest-paid workers are from the poorest families – because the lower the wage, the less likely it is to be a household's only source of income. More scary is the correlation between:

- many European countries' relatively high minimum wages and
- rising unemployment, especially among young people.

There is little doubt that, at some level, minimum wages damage employment, partly because of the reasons stated above and partly because a rising minimum wage pushes up the wages of higher-paid employees. The irony is that this increases the gap while tending to reduce employment overall, even if the job losses are not immediately felt by the minimum-wage-earners. It is a fair bet that:

- the higher the minimum wage is set the greater the knock-on effects will be, and
- on the other side of the scale, a very low minimum wage does little to reduce family poverty.

Table 8.1 shows the minimum wages as a percentage of average blue-collar worker pay in a selected group of countries.

Precisely because the minimum wage is a political ploy, rather than a solution to the prevailing huge inequality in pay, the state supermarket tries to compensate (and attenuate) social unrest through other benefits. But people who get benefits:

- often find them inadequate and
- also fear that they will be cut.

By making more promises than it can keep, the state supermarket systematically generates distrust. Almost everyone fears the imposition of higher taxes to pay for these benefits and those who don't receive enough benefits resent those who do, while practically everyone is embittered by the harsh and growing inequality in pay – not without reason.

Companies, most particularly big banks and other financial entities, have gone completely overboard in terms of executive *overcompensation*.[19] Although it was issued nearly a decade ago, a Goldman Sachs' proxy statement for 2002 has stuck in my mind because it revealed an outrageous 'restricted partner compensation plan' intended to 'perpetuate the sense of partnership and teamwork that exists among our senior

---

18 *The Economist*, 8 December 2007.

19 D.N. Chorafas, *Financial Boom and Gloom: The Credit and Banking Crisis of 2007–2009 and Beyond*, Palgrave/Macmillan, London, 2009.

**Table 8.1 Minimum wage as a percentage of average blue-collar worker compensation**

| Country | Percentage |
|---|---|
| Austria | 37.7 |
| Belgium | 35.7 |
| Canada | 35.3 |
| France | 38.1 |
| Israel | 26.5 |
| Japan | 26.2 |
| Mexico | 27.4 |
| United States | 26.3 |

professionals'. In plain English, this meant swelling executive pay with a new scheme that offered top directors 1 per cent of annual profits up to $35 million.[20] This was a 'first' in its time, although it has since been dwarfed by more extravagant executive compensation 'plans'. Nearly 30 of the bank's top staff could have been eligible for this handout of shareholders' money, which was estimated to cost more than $1 billion in the event that they were all awarded near the maximum amount.

(Goldman converted from a partnership to a public company in 1999. The company said that the scheme was a result of laws that prevented pay above $1 million being 'tax-deductible' unless a precise formula is followed. Listen to that: not only were the bonuses were outrageous, but they also had to be tax-deductible!)

Though at less extravagant levels, Goldman Sachs' high-handedness was preceded by the fallen empires of Enron, Global Crossing, Adelphia, WorldCom and others. As their dust settled, Paul Volcker, the respected former chairman of the Federal Reserve, pointed out the basic reason for this huge distortion of pay values:

> *The dominance of the investment banking profession corrupted the legal profession and the accounting profession. They were so highly paid that it created pressure on the legal and auditing professions. People in those professions would ask: Why are investment bankers being paid so much and why are we being paid what, by comparison, is a pittance?*[21]

In Paul Volcker's opinion, such tensions led to catastrophic results. Accounting firms felt that auditing was a dead-end job and their rewards in the future would depend on diversification and the promotion of cross-selling among their divisions. For certified public accountants (CPAs) the discipline in the auditing side of the firm's attenuated, while for their clients the CPAs' greed provided a golden opportunity to rape the shareholders, the financial reporting standards – and the law.[22]

---

20 *Daily Telegraph*, 22 March 2003.

21 *Financial Times*, 25 September, 2002.

22 Arthur Andersen, one of the global Big Five CPA firms, crashed in the wake of its auditing scandals.

Instead of the so often trumpeted 'shareholder value', we are now at a state of 'shareholder rip-off'. In late July 2009 Morgan Stanley, the only surviving Wall Street investment bank at that time, besides Goldman Sachs, announced that it will retain 70 per cent of its 2009 earning for bonuses. Think of that:

- Shareholders assume 100 per cent of the bank's inordinate risks because of its super-exposure (which is also wrecking the American economy), and 70 per cent of the 'profits' will go to the risk-takers.

Workers, of course, are far worse off than Goldman Sachs and Morgan Stanley shareholders (some of whom are pension funds). As the recession created by the big banks Ponzi games has deepened, hard-pressed companies have not just laid off workers but have also cut wages and implemented 'furloughs' – unpaid, compulsory time off.[23] The only things that are untouchable are the fat cats' salaries, options and bonuses.

Extravagant pay practices have been exported to the European Union from the United States. The pay of Josef Ackermann, CEO of Deutsche Bank, reached €6.2 million in 2002, more than double the salary of John Bond, the chairman and chief executive of HSBC, Britain's biggest bank. That same year Deutsche Bank's chief executive received a cash bonus of more than €3 million on top of a basic salary. Share-based compensation further boosted his total pay for the year.

This has been an inflection point in what I consider to be a very, very bad practice. 2003 was the first year in which Deutsche Bank directors disclosed their salaries. It vindicated Rolf Breuer, Deutsche Bank's previous CEO, who had always insisted that the bank's directors 'were underpaid' (in global terms). But it had little to do with performance. The 2002 wage bill of the entire management board amounted to €27.2 million. Yet during 2002, Deutsche Bank made pre-tax profits of €1.9 billion, 15 per cent less than its pre-tax profits of €2.2 billion one year earlier.[24]

## 5. A Huge Inequality in Pay Destroys the Middle Class

In mid-2007 a report on wealth inequality in Britain found that the gap between rich and poor is now bigger than it has been for 40 years, with the proportion of middle-class households shrinking.[25] This is one of many examples of inequality in pay which can be found all over Europe and America. In that same year, 2007, which was a time of crisis,

- Wendelin Wiedeking, Porsche's chief executive, earned an estimated €70 million ($84 million) – small fry compared to what American bankers make.[26]

---

23 In late June 2009, a survey by YouGov for *The Economist* found that 5 per cent of respondents had taken a furlough that year and 13 per cent had taken a pay cut (*The Economist*, 27 June 2009).

24 For the totally unjustified, irrational and self-destructive American bonuses see D.N. Chorafas, *Financial Boom and Gloom: The Credit and Banking Crisis of 2007–2009 and Beyond*, Palgrave/Macmillan, London, 2009.

25 *The Economist*, 15 September 2007.

26 'Porsche Chief's €70 Million Pay Package fuels Anger over Germany's Fat Cats', *The Times*, 30 November 2007. Don't pity Wiedeking, however. When he got fired in late July 2009, he was also awarded €50 million ($70 million) for having gambled and failed in an attenuated takeover of Volkswagen.

- As an example, at exactly the opposite end of the pay scale, hairdressers in Germany made less than €3 per hour – that is, less than €7,200 per year.

At the end of World War II the difference between high and low pay was not much more than 1-to-20, and rose to 1-to-40 in the late 1980s. In 2007 it reached 1-to-11,666 – and it is an unheard-of scandal. Denunciations of the corporate high wage spiral get applause, but nothing is done to curb these unprecedented excesses. In America the bankers who ruined the economy and brought it to its knees:

- continue rewarding themselves with God-size salaries, options and bonuses, and
- they don't give a penny for the destruction of the social fabric, the annihilation of the middle class and its after-effects.

Many German, French, Italian, British, American and other economists find it scandalous that full-time workers can still be poor, but both the trade unions and their followers are divided among themselves on what needs to be done and how to go there. Some say minimum wages will save money on welfare spending. Others respond that this will reduce employment opportunities (section 4), but no-one comes up with:

- a holistic plan on how to save the middle class and
- how to right the balances of inequality in a way that is politically doable.

On the politicians' side there is no lack of big words and empty promises. One of the reasons for their confusion is that they are still living in the interwar years 1918–1938 and their entitlements. They have not thought out the consequences of the new reality that the labour force has changed and one-third or more of workers are now part-time or temporary, rather than 'regular', staff. On 7 November 2008, right after being elected, Barack Obama set for himself and for the US three top priorities:

1. establishing a rescue plan for the middle class, with the emphasis on employment; addressing the credit crunch impact on small business, from the perspective of a global challenge;
2. reviewing and restructuring the rotten Bush programme, in order to help the people who are not in the big banks.

By November 2009,[27] a full year after the new president's priorities were publicly announced and over nine months after he took residence in the White House, none of his goals has been reached, nor have any of his decisions given confidence that his political promises will be fulfilled. Could there be any further evidence needed that he, too, is a second-rater?.

The number one priority of a rescue plan for the American middle class has been put on the backburner in favour of several ill-studied rescue plans for the self-wounded global banks and their big-ego CEOs. That's precisely the opposite of what Barack Obama had promised with the third of his proclaimed priorities.

---

27 When these lines were written.

As for priority number two, small businesses have been left out in the cold with CIT, one of their main credit institutions, teetering at the edge of the precipice. From 21 January to 21 July 2009, over 40 small to medium-sized banks have failed in the US, while financial institutions which were 'too big to be saved'[28] and too arrogant have got billions of taxpayers' money in their coffers as well as the freedom to continue demolishing the American economy.

All this is forgetting the fact that both the US and Europe have prospered with the rise of the middle class because of the social stability and cohesion it provides, as well as its entrepreneurship which benefits the whole society. Another distinctive contribution is the way it uses its assets, thinking and acting quite differently from:

- the high net-worth individuals and
- The lower net-worth working-class community.

Nowadays, overburdened with taxes and with debt the middle class and its small to medium-sized businesses are going under. 'We perceive ourselves as a middle class society, with people in trailer parks and townhouses regarding themselves as essentially middle class without much separating them,' Paul Krugman, the economist, noted. 'That's always been a bit of a myth, but we were closer to that being the case in the 1970s than we are today.'[29]

Politicians who tend to refute Krugman's thesis are out of their minds. They are blind to the fact that the gap in incomes and lifestyles between the 20th percentile and the 80th percentile is much larger today than 20 years ago, and this has set a trend that deforms the nature of our society. The way in which the members of the EU and America are evolving in social terms is highly disturbing.

Practically every country in the EU is highly uncertain about what sort of society and of economy works best in the modern world. The question is very badly posed when politicians and the media talk of a choice between the so-called 'liberal Anglo-Saxon model' and the more classical continental European one which leaves much more power in the hands of the state and its nanny policies. The *real* choice is between:

- a democracy based on the middle class, which Pericles (?–429BC) invented in ancient Athens, with his populist policies, and
- an aristocratic oligarchy of birth, wealth,[30] military power or theocracy (the latter led to the Middle Ages), where a small minority keeps the rest of the population subservient.

To put this statement in the right perspective, the reader should recall that in Pericles' time the Athenian principle was 'one-man, one-vote', but only for those qualifying as a 'citizen'. Robert H. Bork, the jurist and unsuccessful nominee for the US Supreme Court,

28 The irony with these mammoth banks and other oversized financial institutions like AIG, Fannie Mae and Freddie Mac is that they are simultaneously 'too big to be saved' and 'too big to fail'.

29 *The MIT Report*, March 1997.

30 Which Barack Obama seems to have joined by espousing the case of the big banks' fat cats. None has been so far prosecuted for violations of the Sarbanes-Oxley Act (the law of the land) and for having destroyed the American economy.

wrote, in a scholarly article, that there is no constitutional basis for one-man, one-vote.[31] If it were not for the Athenian middle class, Bork would have been right.

Compared with the rich and the poor, the middle class contains a greater range of interests and covers a wide landscape of occupations. Emerging countries aspire to middle-class status. Anecdotal evidence suggests that 450 million Chinese have already joined it. But in Europe and America the middle class is *under siege* – an almost broken system.

In Brazil, Eduardo Giannetti da Fonseca, an economist, describes members of the middle class as people who are not resigned to a life of poverty, but are ready to make sacrifices to create a better life for themselves and their children. That's a little too idealistic. More pragmatically, *The Economist* suggests that there are two main ways to define a middle class:

- in *relative terms*, as the middle income range of each country, and
- in *absolute terms*, using a fixed band for all countries in the globalized economy.

For his part, Lester Thurow, of MIT's Sloan School of Management, defined the American middle class as the group with incomes lying between 75 per cent and 125 per cent of the median. Bill Easterly of New York University also focused on the mid-range, leaving out the poorest 20 per cent and the richest 20 per cent (the two top and bottom deciles).[32] The problem with these approaches is that they are too statistical.

*The Economist*'s 'relative terms' sounds better as a middle-class definition, suggesting that 'the middle' consists of people with about a third of their income left for discretionary spending after providing basic food and shelter. In other words, they are:

- neither rich, having saved or inherited enough to escape the struggle for existence,
- nor poor, living from hand to mouth, season to season, job to job, or on state supermarket bail-outs.

More to the point, however, 'middle class' does not describe just an income category, but also a set of attitudes. Ascension to the middle class requires consistent effort. Therefore, contrary to what many people think,

- the welfare state destroys the middle class because it erodes competitiveness and downgrades jobs, and
- clipping the wings of the welfare state sharpens the chances of ascension to the middle-class by promoting the competitive edge.

Inward-looking policies, too, work against the middle class. Europe has fallen into this trap as it tries to solve a surge of unemployment problems, social tension, mass migration (both legal and illegal) and other issues connected to the economic slowdown. Inordinately high taxes, short working hours, lack of labour mobility and luxurious social benefits also work against the middle class, as well as:

- being incompatible with a healthy economy and

31 *Business Week*, 18 December 1989,

32 *The Economist*, 14 February 2009.

- tending to create a hell of a lot of unemployment.[33]

Like inflation, runaway social costs hit those they are supposed to help – the poor and the underprivileged– harder, while simultaneously hitting the middle class by devastating personal initiative. That's an ill-advised strategy because, with its aspirations and capacity for hard work, the middle class is more likely to bring the economy forward, invest in education, promote human capital, develop new businesses and become a motor of economic growth.

## 6. Offshoring Distorts the Process of Social Change

German industrial jobs will fall by 25 per cent by 2015, predicted a 2004 study by the Boston Consulting Group (BCG). It also made the bold statement that of the then 8 million jobs in the manufacturing industry, 2 million would disappear in a decade. Half a dozen years down the line is a good time to look at reality versus projections.

In 2004 the BCG study forecasted that German imports from low-wage countries – mainly from eastern Europe – would increase from 6 per cent to 14 per cent. It also said that this would reinforce the growth curve of millions of unemployed in Germany which had lifted off in the early to mid-1990s (with the leveraged buy-out (LBO) for East Germany) and continued to grow, as shown in Figure 8.1.

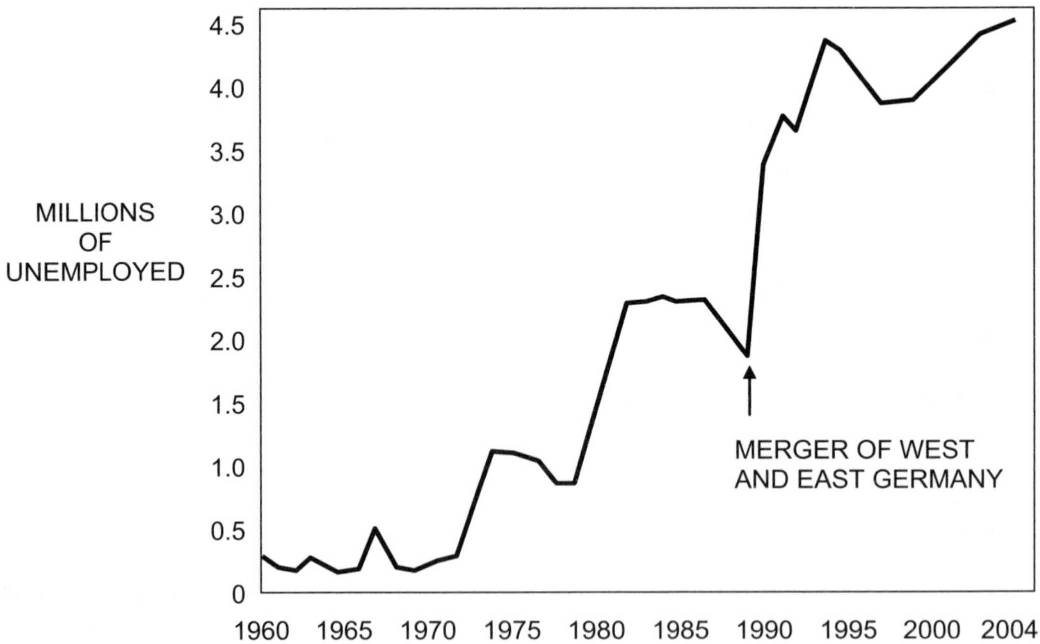


**Figure 8.1 Unemployment in the German Federal Republic, 1960–2004**

33 As an example, lax standards in the Netherlands have put 17 per cent of its workforce on permanent disability benefit. Even psychologically disabled workers can get 70 per cent of their salary for life.

As the careful reader will appreciate, this German unemployment curve has been a multi-modal distribution. After the devastation of World War II, through sound economic policies Germany was able to achieve, by the late 1950s and early 1960s, nearly full employment with a stable level of about 200,000 unemployed over a decade. In the late 1960s came a spike with 500,000 unemployed, but their numbers again dwindled until the early 1970s when, in the aftermath of two major oil crises, unemployment statistics started moving steadily north. This saw to it that by 2004 western Germany had 11 officially unemployed people for each job on offer, which is bad, while in eastern Germany there were 32 unemployed people for every job vacancy. As in practically all other EU countries there were just no jobs available. First, there was a relatively depressed economy due to stagflation, then, as things started looking better, massive outsourcing emptied the lot of jobs created by Germany's production machine. This led to two pieces of bad news:

- a reduction in overall national income and
- an increase in overall unemployment

In this environment, the loss of jobs because of outsourcing to low-labour-cost countries hit the hardest. A study made that same year, 2004, by McKinsey, the consultancy, said that, in Germany, the only 40 per cent of workers made idle because of displaced would be redeployed – with the result that both workers and the overall economy would suffer. (In retrospect, the predictions by both BCG and McKinsey have not been far off the mark.)

Fairly similar conditions prevailed in France and other western European countries, feeding the argument that jobs were being lost because of large-scale offshoring.[34] The pros said that offshoring benefited everybody. Critics denied that, predicting social strains as its after-effect, with unemployment being the tip of the iceberg. Economists who found find themselves poised between these two positions suggested that benefits to the offshoring country depended on two critical assumptions:

- *retraining* and *redeployment* for workers who lose jobs, to help them find new ones, and
- *recapture*, a vague notion meaning that the percentage of wages paid in lost jobs is recaptured by wages paid in new ones.

Neither of these two hypotheses has been clearly proven. Statistics from 1991 in the US documented that, of the 4.3 million people who over a four-year period lost permanent jobs, 72 per cent were re-employed, 14 per cent were still looking for work, and 14 per cent had left the labour force. Quite interestingly,43.2 per cent of full-timers back at work were earning less than their original pay, 27.5 per cent were earning up to 19 per cent more, and the balance were earning at least 20 per cent more.[35]

Other statistics contradicted these findings, pointing out that only 67 per cent of American workers who lost their jobs found another one within a year, while office workers with less education were even more vulnerable. Evidence from Japan further

34 D.N. Chorafas, *Outsourcing, Insourcing and IT for Enterprise Management*, Macmillan/Palgrave, London, 2003.

35 *BusinessWeek*, 16 September 1991.

sustained this argument. Between 2003 and 2008 Japan's big firms made record profits, but:

- they have not been sharing their good fortune with their workers, and
- take-home wages have remained stagnant in Japan and, in some cases, have declined.

As in America and western Europe, the Japanese middle and working classes have also suffered greatly from offshoring. By early 2008 the problem became so severe that Yasuo Fukuda, then prime minister, uncharacteristically urged companies to pay their workers more.[36]

On the other side of the fence, *Nikkei*, Japan's daily business newspaper, reminded its readers that wages in Japan are ten times higher than in China.[37] This is precisely the argument that exists on the old continent, between western and eastern EU member states. In addition, jobs disappear not only because of offshoring, but also because of the global jobs crisis whose contours are becoming clear and whose:

- severity,
- breadth and
- likely length

are causing major changes in the structure of labour and of society as a whole. Structural changes in western European labour markets suggest that jobs are disappearing faster than in previous downturns, with temporary employment contracts proliferating.

While recessions are known to bring huge, but temporary, swings in employment, the combination of recession and offshoring inflates the statistics. Measured by the share of the workforce filing for weekly jobless claims, the pace at which people are losing their jobs is much quicker than in the past – at least in some countries. Not without reason, some analysts comment that at least part of the solution is in *re-insourcing*. To appreciate this argument, the reader must remember that outsourcing is a two-way road:

- work that has been handed over to an insourcer is sometimes re-insourced, but
- this does not necessarily happen because it was being done badly, though quality is also a reason, as is security.

For instance, some banks are bringing the processing of payments back in-house because they have realized that the data that they have been handing over to insourcers[38] can be exploited in order to develop competing businesses. Software programs that mine data in novel ways can provide ideas for new products, new markets and customer-handling policies. At the same time, governments are bending over backwards to persuade companies to re-insource.

In early 2009 Renault, the French automobile manufacturer, arguably with state aid, brought back to its factories in France production work outsourced to its factory in

36 To its credit, Japan's conservative business lobby, the Keidanren, also pushed firms to improve wages and salaries.

37 *The Economist*, 22 March 2008.

38 Companies farming out work are outsourcers. Companies doing such work for other firms are insourcers.

Slovenia, foregoing the lower local labour costs. An issue on which pros and critics seem inclined to agree is that offshoring is a process of creative destruction with plenty of challenges for:

- labour,
- companies and
- governments.

Today, with unemployment spreading into the services industry, governments seem more interested than ever in re-insourcing. They must also concern themselves with the growth in inequality and introduce measures to reverse this trend. Lifetime employment and the seniority-wage system have gone, but social cohesion must be preserved and the middle class protected from its many enemies.

## 7. Tales of the Tax-and-Spend Bureaucracy

In several EU countries, as unemployment rose in the 1990s, one could hear this popular joke: 'What's the difference between a bureaucrat and someone who is unemployed?' Answer: 'The unemployed had worked sometime in the past.'[39] Another joke asked the question: 'What's the difference between a bureaucrat and a piece of wood?', the answer being 'Wood works'.

Whether in Brussels, Berlin, Rome, Paris, London, Washington or any other capital, well-paid bureaucrats imagine that throwing money at the unemployment problem solves it. This is patently not true. Yet, at regular intervals, EU bureaucrats come up with yet another 'plan' on how to reintegrate the unemployed and the excluded – double the currently available funds.

Similar quick-fix, but nonsense, 'solutions' are proposed to fight poverty and famine, although birth control would have been far more effective than fat foreign aid budgets. Everybody knows that the 'Just keep on spending and every ill will disappear' model is broken. It does not take a genius to appreciate that spending other people's money, as 'social scientists' suggest and the state supermarket is doing, is the worst of all solutions.

In the 1990s, for example, it was proposed that the EU budget of ECU55 million for the 'Poverty 3' programme be increased more than twofold to ECU121 million. Padraig Flynn, the commissioner who came up with that brilliant idea, justified this huge increase through his vague estimate that about 15 per cent of the European population was living below the poverty line. What the promoters of these silly policies of throwing money away forget is that:

- the capital to be spent must come from somewhere, essentially from taxation, and
- in the final analysis those working have to be taxed more and more so that the big spenders can throw money around.

It was André Tardieu, a French prime minister of the early 1930s, who first established that principle when he said: 'We must tax the poor. They are the more numerous.' In

39 Unless of course he or she spent their whole life on benefits, which is not unheard of.

modern times, the preferred way of raising taxation is through increasing value added tax (VAT) – and from this nobody really escapes, not even the estimated 3 million people in Europe of no fixed abode.

There is plenty of evidence that 'more taxation' and 'more spending' solve no social problems. Only private initiative does so. If anything, more taxes and more spending aggravate an already bad situation. By contrast, departures from the beaten path and imaginative moves could provide solutions, but the promotion of enterprise is nowhere to be seen in a world dominated by bureaucrats.

Underlying the social malaise created by bureaucracy and its love for sacred cows is a widespread sense of insecurity about doing something to justify one's job. The basic preoccupation of ordinary people is making ends meet at the end of the month; while that of bureaucrats is to prevent other people from showing initiative.

Vito Tanzi, formerly Italy's representative at the International Monetary Fund (IMF), tells the tale of a man who wanted to open a fish shop in a small town in Apulia, but was turned down by the council on the grounds that the town had one already.[40] Quite contrary to the sense of that silly 'decision', business grows through competition because it makes everyone:

- think faster,
- perform better and
- be more productive in what they do.

Thinking faster and performing better is not exactly what bureaucrats do. In the review of a book entitled *Politically Incorrect Tales of the EU Bureaucracy*, Michael D. Mosettig reminds us of a television show *Yes, Minister*, a British situation comedy series about the way in which government bureaucracies really work and plot among insiders. In this series, a high-ranking career civil servant would run circles around his minister,

- aware that he had a special power over him, which came from bureaucratic institutional memory and career longevity,
- whereas the minister, an elected member of parliament, might not last long in his job.

Even if they last longer on the job than originally expected, present-day politicians have demonstrated their unique ability to turn into disappointments. Jacques Chirac is one example. He came to the presidency of the French republic in 1995 vowing to heal the country's 'social fracture', cut youth unemployment and improve the lot of ethnic minorities in the *banlieue*. By the time he left the Elysée Palace, a dozen years later, he had fulfilled none of his promises. His tenure started badly.

- In his first term he half-heartedly backed the reforms of his first prime minister, but pulled back at the first sign of street protests.
- This set a pattern for the next years, culminating with Chirac's abandonment of a labour-market reform proposed by his last prime minister, which was also his last chance to leave some sort of legacy.

40 *The Economist*, 26 November 2005.

Matters are no different on the other side of the Atlantic, where politicians are at a loss on how to stem the high tide of unemployment and foreclosures,[41] while bureaucrats don't seem to be of any help. A comment made by analysts of Bank of America/Merrill Lynch is telling:

> *The (Obama) administration's plan to stem foreclosures is hitting a wall. Have a look at the front page of today's New York Times, 'A Plan to Stem Foreclosures, Buried in a Paper Avalanche'.*
>
> *In the four months since the Treasury announced the mortgage program, millions of new homeowners have fallen into foreclosure and delinquency, and progress remains limited by the capacities of mortgage servicers.*[42]

It looks *as if* the names 'Jacques Chirac' and 'Barack Obama' are interchangeable. Promises, promises, none of which is kept. The same story can be read about unemployment where, seconded by bureaucrats, politicians try to simultaneously attain two contradictory objectives: more jobs and more globalization (the Doha Round, plenty of 'summits' and other nonsense.)

In pursuing these incompatible (and contradictory) goals, the second-raters forget that because of 'globalization without limits', virtually all manufacturing in Western countries faces an unprecedented equalization factor towards the lowest global wages. Whether under the WTO or through bilateral past agreements different commitments[43] keep pushing American and western European wages well below the West's current middle-class levels.[44]

Workers cannot create jobs; entrepreneurs can. But even some entrepreneurs have been espousing the fallacy that doing away with the middle class, –indeed, with the Western nations' whole labour force[45] – may indeed be a solution. All this is ludicrous; it would be a comedy of errors, were it not for the fact that such mistakes have tragic consequences.

Carlo De Benedetti, an Italian entrepreneur, recounted how he tried to convince Enrico Berlinguer, the late Italian Communist Party secretary-general, that 'the working class does not exist any more'. 'Today, the worker is a consumer, a wage-earner, and a taxpayer. If you think to protect him only from the standpoint as a wage-earner, you cheat him on consumption and taxes,' De Benedetti said[46] – but he failed to explain where the 'consumers-but-no-longer-producers' will earn their money. Neither has he probably pondered on what will happen to society as a whole.

---

41 The two correlate.

42 Bank of America/Merrill Lynch, 'Morning Market Tickets', 29 June 2009.

43 Such commitments are predicated on the false assumptions of Western nations that they are 'rich'. In fact, they were rich, but today they are on their way to becoming poor.

44 On the ongoing annihilation of the middle class, see also section 5.

45 With the West's industries, too, because politicians on both sides of the Atlantic are so keen to penalize Western industry with a heavy burden of pollution-control costs – without getting a similar commitment from China, India, Russia, Brazil and other developing countries.

46 *Executive Intelligence Review*, 1 June 2007.

## 8. EU Bureaucrats Care Only About Themselves

One of the hilarious things about the EU's bureaucracy is that, with its huge (and unjustifiable) cost, it gives the worst possible example to member states regarding employment practices. In early January 2010 the EU's 50,000 employees threatened to go on strike because they wanted a salary increase of 6 per cent – despite the deep economic crisis, almost zero inflation and a double-figure percentage of unemployment. The EU top brass offered 1.8 per cent.

Salaries have to go up and up, but deliverables and management efficiency are at a very low point at European Commission headquarters. In his book *Life of a European Mandarin*, Derk-Jan Eppink, a Dutch journalist, writes from an insider's perspective during a decade (1995–2005) spent on the staffs of two European commissioners, Frits Bolkestein and Siim Kallas. The text is the product of a disillusioned individual who became cynical about what he encountered. Here is a snapshot of Eppink's thoughts:

> *The European administration is a world of open doors, closed doors, side doors, back doors, revolving doors and even trap doors… .*
>
> *The truth is never absolute … beneath the surface there is a desperate struggle taking place, a struggle for control of crucial economic and political interests.*[47]

'Too much is being decided by bureaucrats,' said Günter Verheugen, vice president of the European Commission in charge of enterprise and industry, in an interview he gave to Germany's *Süddeutsche Zeitung*.[48] In his opinion, commissioners sitting in Brussels have to be careful not to allow decisions in important questions fall under the control of bureaucrats with no democratic mandate; but this is not what happens.

Verheugen's particular targets were civil servants in the Directorates General (the big units into which the EU Executive is divided – something like ministries) in which thousands of functionaries work on everything in the EU – from taxes to agricultural policy. Verheugen took pesticides as an example of creeping bureaucratic mission.

- Laws regarding pesticides could have major consequences for European consumers and agricultural industry.
- Hence, decisions should be taken at Commission level, but commissioners only learn about them because there is sudden friction among civil servants.

This fight for one's turf is carried out among 27 commissioners, each with his cabinet, and 37,000 European civil servants.[49] Half of this army of bureaucrats are known as policy-makers or *mandarins*. But in reality, they are no policy-makers by any stretch of the imagination; their remit is to produce paper. Neither is the Commission the only bureaucratic bastion in the EU. There is also the Council of Ministers, representing the

47 D-J. Eppink, *Life of a European Mandarin: Inside the Commission*, Tielt, Lanoo, 2007.

48 'The Conservatives: Beyond "Banging on about Europe"', *Open Europe Bulletin*, 13 October 2006, at: http://www.openeurope.org.uk/media-centre/bulletin.aspx?bulletinid=42.

49 Also 15,000 lobbyists flooding the European Commission offices, corridors and stairways.

governments of member states, and the European Parliament – which every month trucks back and forth its files from Brussels to Strasbourg and vice versa.[50]

Don't forget either that each of these members of parliament (MEPs) makes up to €200,000 ($280,000) per year, more than the governor of the Banque de France. This gold-plated system might have been worth its wages if a gold-medal performance was the result of its diatribes. But the better-known output of commissioners, civil servants and MEPs – in short, of the system – is its obstruction of fast decision-making and its inefficient operations.

There are also 15,000 registered lobbyists in Brussels belonging to 500 'lobby groups', employed not only by companies, but also by trade unions and other interests. Their unique objective is to impact on and alter EU rules, regulations and legislation. By and large, though not exclusively, these lobbyists are former EU executives who, having left the government, stay around to:

- profit from their connections and
- damage the European public's interests, through their lobbying.

Part of the damage manifests itself through sky-high administrative costs at EU level. Chapter 5 discussed the importance of patents, the protection they provide (with some exceptions in intellectual property) and their use as a proxy for judging the output of research, development and innovation. Patents are not free of cost in any country, but, in most industrial nations, costs are rather contained. In the US, for instance, the cost of a patent is roughly $6,000 divided into 40 per cent for procedural fees and 60 per cent for renewable fees. In Japan, the equivalent in yen stands at just below $5,000, with nearly the same proportion fee-wise.

The exception is the European Union. When the EU had 13 member states, registration costs at the European Patent Office (EPO) stood at a wholesome $33,000 (at $1.4 to the euro) with translation costs running up to $9,000 because an EU patent must be in three languages: English, French and German[51] (which makes the Italians and Spanish furious). But the other costs, too, are very high. The total is roughly divided into:

- 27 per cent for procedural fees,
- 27 per cent for translation and
- 46 per cent for renewal fees.

An interesting hindsight is that in the EU's transition from six members to 13, registration fees at the EPO soared by 83 per cent, from $18,000 to $33,000, with translation costs having seen the largest increase, though renewable fees were not far behind. (Translation costs are also the source of huge expenditures at the European Parliament and everywhere else in the EU administration.)

'Language' is a huge, unsolved problem at the EU as most member countries insist that any patent must be translated into *their* language to apply on their soil. In 2008 the burden was reduced somewhat by the London Agreement, under which countries

---

50 D.N. Chorafas, *The Business of Europe is Politics*, Gower, Aldershot, 2010.

51 This is ineffectual. Unavoidably, translations tend to change the sense of a text, with the result that these three language versions are not necessarily compatible.

can waive the right to have patents translated into their national language. Only 14 EU countries, however – roughly one in two – have agreed to waive language rights.

Neither is patent litigation straightforward at EU level. It takes place country by country, and national courts can easily overturn patents granted by the EPO. In other cases, courts make the opposite decision to that of the court in another country. Therefore, to protect themselves, inventors and firms must file directly with national patent offices, which makes the EPO more or less superfluous.

Yet, even a blind man with black glasses could see that a single EU patent applying in all 27 countries is the thing to do, as it would simplify the process of obtaining protection. Companies would face less legal uncertainty, and costs, too, may be reduced. The obstacles to doing so are major because this means surrendering the veto over patents, which countries see as a substantial loss of sovereignty. Timid attempts to right the balance would not do, because politicians and bureaucrats quickly retreat when faced with:

- 'national prestige',
- vested interests,
- an onslaught by lobbyists or
- work stoppages by civil servants, truckers or students parading down the street.

'Bureaucrats must be ridiculed and removed,' says General Electric's 2000 *Annual Report*.[52] They have not been. Instead, they multiply in organizational layers and behind functional walls, which means that every day must be a battle to demolish this structure and keep the organization open, ventilated and free. This essentially means that citizens need to be vigilant because the allure of bureaucracy is part of human nature and hard to resist, and it can expand in the blink of an eye. Neither is bureaucracy lacking tools. Its preferred ones are:

- frustrating people,
- distorting the facts,
- limiting expectations and
- turning the face of the entire organization, state or enterprise inward.

Where is the EU standing with all that? Europe, said Daniel Cohen, a French economist and professor at *Ecole Normale Supérieure*, is like a bicycle which keeps rolling so as not to fall over. Very few voices are raised to ring the alarm bell – to say that, without radically changing our way of thinking and without reforming our institutions, we are going to become actors in a Greek tragedy. This voice is one of them.

52 'Letter to Share Owners', *GE 2000 Annual Report*, p. 3, at: http://www.ge.com/annual00/letter/index.html.

# CHAPTER 9 Ambitious Plans Run into Reality

## 1. The French Social Model Hits the Rocks

One hears quite a bit these days, at least in the European Union, about the French *social model* which, on-and-off, the French government wants to impose on the other EU members. Critics say that it is an ineffectual and highly costly approach to the solution of social problems. Its roots are found in the years immediately following the Great Depression.

On 3 May 1936, France voted for the Popular Front made up of socialists, communists and other leftists. Its weak and unstable government was headed by Léon Blum, an otherwise honourable and well-intended politician. The government itself was unstable because the Popular Front had carried the election by a relatively narrow margin, and, to gain a majority in parliament, Blum had put together a collection of diverse parties whose whims were unpredictable – particularly when confronted by even a small social problem.

A week after the Blum government was formed, a series of strikes paralysed France (and, in their way, set the stage for the country's military defeat in World War II). To appease the general unrest, the Popular Front rushed to offer the striking workers much more than the country and its economy could afford. This created the basis of the now tooted 'French social model', and it consisted of:

- the right of all employees to paid holidays – 12 days per year at the time, much more than a month today, everything counted;
- compulsory collective bargaining, with workers having the right to be represented in company management;[1]
- the elevation of labour unions to full social partners, to be consulted by the government and private industry;
- a limit of 40 hours to the working week – after World War II, other socialist governments brought it down to 39, then 35 hours per week (section 2); and
- a collection of other measures, such as nationalization of the armaments industry, assurance of an income to farmers and restructuring of Banque de France.

The end of World War II exported many of the labour–government agreements of 1936 to other European countries, at the same time broadening their extent and creating a policy of permanent contest. At first there was no sense of urgency, as most economies were on their knees, but as the economies of the old continent improved, the French

1 Hitler made a similar law in Germany, after he came to power.

model of labour relations served as reference. In fact, it was elevated in status by the labour unions and socialist learning programmes.[2]

Some of the aforementioned points of the 1936 settlement, like paid holidays, were a 'first' in modern society. They not only benefited workers, but also gave birth to the mass tourist industry. This was the beginning of the so-called 'leisure society' (*société des loisirs*) with paid holidays being its originating conquest. It was enriched in the following decades with what I call 'the right to laziness' (more on this in section 2).

Some welfare benefits were a positive outcome of the 1936 Léon Blum settlement. But these grew and grew until, in the post-World War II years, they become unsupportable. European Commission officials estimate that currently in swathes of western Europe between 80 and 90 per cent of the unemployed are entitled to some interminable social assistance, which is paid by the working population by way of high social costs – which themselves contribute to unemployment.

- In southern Europe, this coverage is patchier, and
- in parts of eastern Europe only about 30 per cent of jobless citizens receive significant welfare payments.

Vacations and *flexi-security* aside, part of the legacy of the mid-1930s is that strikes end by twisting the government's hand. The right to strike is sacrosanct but when it is abused, as so often happens, it turns against the strikers' own interests. Nowadays, strikes supposedly motivated by 'anger' have become a social ritual.

There is no better description of that side of the French social model, and of its after-effects, than an open letter written by a working government employee to other government employees (postal workers) who are on strike.[3] Addressed to 'ladies and gentlemen' in anger, the letter points out that 'you have been on strike for more than a month because no doubt you have some minor claims to make'. Then it asks:

- whether their daily well-being is in danger and
- whether they face an employment problem.

A government employee herself, the letter-writer answers these two queries with a resounding 'No!', pointing out that (like her) the strikers are as privileged as they can be at the end of the twentieth century, when employment is far from being certain. 'I am aware of this every day because my husband has to work like crazy to save his company from going bankrupt,' the letter's writer says, adding that, by contrast, because they are government employees,

- the strikers' workplace is guaranteed whether or not they work properly, and
- their salaries will be paid as nobody can do anything about that, or against them.

---

2 In the US, Frances Perkins, Roosevelt's Secretary of Labor, masterminded the introduction of unemployment insurance and public pensions, as well as a major overhaul of labour laws, minimum wages, a ban on child labour and the 40-hour week.

3 Published in *Nice Matin* on 20 May 1995.

The writer then points out that, as is well known, for the majority of the strikers the 39-hour week (the 35-hour week was not yet introduced) has been reduced to only 30 hours. Yet, they strike! That's the government's indulgence. If they were employed in a private business, this strike would have ended long ago because employment is not permanently guaranteed. The long strike, however, has consequences because, as the letter aptly states, it puts in peril:

- the freedom of every citizen to communicate and
- the freedom of private companies to do business.

Post-office employees, for example, are paid by the state – which means the taxpayers. But do they have the right to block a whole region and put not only commerce, but also elderly citizens in peril[4] because they want extra privileges? Do they know that the 'others' – from company owners and employees to pensioners – don't even know whether tomorrow they will have the means to assure their daily meal?

The writer then informs the strikers that they are behaving like spoilt children who are playing with a doll, but want another doll which is prettier. The government is being too tolerant by allowing them to damage – without saying a word against it – the freedom of other French citizens – those who do not have guaranteed employment – to work. And, as the letter points out,

- *if* the angry government employees find their job of postal workers unsatisfactory,
- *then* they can search for another job, immediately afterwards adding: 'But what do I say ... Nobody will offer you employment because in other jobs you must really work.'

In conclusion, the working government employee, who decided to make her feelings generally known through this open letter, tells the strikers that with their behaviour they will kill the goose which lays the golden egg, and will end up being privatized. She adds: 'That's all you deserve. As for me, I would rather stay as a professor of literature (a public employee) with all the inconveniences this may present.' The writer was prophetic for two reasons:

- in 2009, 14 years after this letter was published, the French postal service is indeed going to be privatized, and
- under the leadership of President Nicolas Sarkozy, in July 2007 Christine Lagarde, the finance minister, has unveiled a new 'law in favour of work' – which is another 'first'.

'France is a country that thinks,' Lagarde declared. 'But enough thinking for now! It's time to roll up our sleeves.'[5] Sarkozy campaigned on the slogan 'working more to earn more', praising 'the France that gets up early'. Lagarde has tried to put this into action. It

---

4 Not only do social security cheques and other payments transit through the post, but also in France (as in Germany and Switzerland) the post office operates a community bank.

5 G. Will, 'Reforming France's Welfare State', 30 August 2007, at: http://www.realclearpolitics.com/articles/2007/08/francess_problem_and_challenge.html.

was time, she said, to break with a French 'tradition of contempt' for work 'that reaches back to the *ancien régime*.'[6] Theoretically The French social model may be changing. In practice, the more it changes, the more it stays the same.

## 2. Taken for a Ride: The 35-hour Week

Plenty of economists have been suggesting that miracles-in-waiting solve no problems. To improve their competitive position, EU countries must significantly increase the productivity of their workforce rather than targeting a permanent decrease in working hours. For a variety of reasons which mediate against greater performance, this is far from happening. Lower productivity is promoted by:

- too many legacy-based approaches to work methods and practices,
- product-market tariffs and regulations, established to keep low-cost competitors out, and
- the overwhelming rigidity of most European labour markets, because labour unions oppose change (see sections 6 to 8).

Apart from the reasons usually given to explain the rather significant difference in productivity between the US and EU there exists a political factor. Often, though by no means always, the aim of the economic and social partners in the US – including the labour unions – is to boost growth in order to make the pie bigger before dividing it. In Europe, as a legacy of the nineteenth-century 'Socialist Manifesto', the various social partners fight over the economic redistribution of the existing smaller pie.

This leads to some funny results. There is no better example than the rotten concept of less work for the same pay: the French 35-hour week,[7] which has been a costly miscalculation. When it was introduced in the late 1990s, some egghead economists said that the '*35 heures*' could provide an extra 1.4 million jobs over five years. The result was quite the opposite. The 35-hour week:

- increased overall labour costs,
- cut individual wages,
- reduced productivity,
- put off foreign investors and
- added to French unemployment.

The hindsight provided by a whole decade of the 35-hour week documents that its promoters were wrong, while its critics were far-sighted – the facts proved them right. Even the French labour unions came round to criticizing the 35-hour week, because by providing compensation to companies for paying the same money for less work, the

6 Meaning the royals decapitated in the late eighteenth century during the French Revolution, but some habits persisted. The Popular Front may not have invented them after all.

7 Anecdotal evidence suggests that, in some professions, French people work only 22 hours per week – and teachers less than that.

French socialist government (with the agreement of the labour bosses) froze workers' wages – a move that workers and the unions came to regret.

Those who have really profited have been the managers who increased their holidays by capitalizing on compensation they received for overtime. Another irony of the 35-hour week has been that it was in itself a deviation from past socialist practices in France and elsewhere. Thanks to the seminal work of Professor Milton Friedman, who demolished the deficit-bound Keynesian economics, by the 1990s governments had come to understand that:

- they cannot buy permanent employment for everybody at the price of more inflation, and,
- this model being broken, they searched for some other way. The answer has been 'less work'.

Let's look back for a moment. The Latin root of the word *travail*, which means 'work', is *tripalium*. This was originally an instrument used for torture. Maybe the Latins influenced the evangelists. The Bible writes that that when (because of the apple, the serpent and all that) God threw Adam and Eve out of paradise where they were living in idleness, he told them that from then on 'they will earn their bread through their sweat' – in short, through torture.

Not everybody likes to work. As a saying goes, 'Work makes one tired' (though for some of us work is pleasure). In 1880 Paul Lafargue published *Le Droit à la Paresse* (*The Right to Laziness*), recommending that men should work no more than three hours a day and spend the rest of the time lazing and feasting. Lafargue's concept supplemented the aforementioned linguistic and religious precedent.

Now let's look at the results. One of the consequences of the 'hello laziness' 35-hour week is that it increased labour law inflexibility. An incident worth recording took place in 2001 when Groupe Danone, a global food company, announced plans to close two cookie factories in northern France – offering compensation for the closure.

- The news, however, was not met with praise for the firm's rather generous terms.
- Rather, it created a wave of country-wide horror, because Danone was laying off anyone at all.

The enraged argument of an indignant Jacques Chirac, his government and labour unions was that the $12.7 billion Danone company was, after all, profitable. A furore swept across France about *l'affaire Danone*, including organized movements to boycott company products like Kronenbourg beer and its popular yoghurt.

Rather than leading, Prime Minister Lionel Jospin's socialist government succumbed to the public outcry. It announced plans to make it much more expensive for companies to lay off workers – exactly the opposite of what is needed to effectively tackle the unemployment challenge. There had been enormous damage to people's well-being, argued (without any evidence) the then employment minister.

The expectation of social peace through 35-hour weeks did not materialize. The socialist government's drive to export the 35-hour week model also failed. Starting in 2000 the government tried to generalize this failed 'hello laziness' practice throughout the

EU. There have been no takers, but in the week of 23 October 2006, the EU Commission confronted a clash of wills:

- a French demand for 35-hour week applicable to *all* EU member states and
- fierce opposition from the British to that poisoned chalice. The British Labour government said that *its* 48 hour week was not on the table; the British carried the day.

Some sociologists suggested that rather than spinning their wheels in a vacuum in an effort to satisfy worn-out doctrines, EU governments would be well advised to attend to our society's real problems – such as *social exclusion*. Every big city in Europe (and in America) has homeless people on the streets, and the families they have left behind are in despair. Delinquency is another problem. Some estimate that in the US 2 million children have a parent in prison.

Though there exist benevolent people who man the soup kitchens and look after the prisoners' children, or rent a hostel to provide shelter in the winter to people who lack one, they cannot solve all of the problems of citizens ravaged by poverty and crime. The state supermarket should pay more attention to social exclusion through a programme of retraining and rehabilitation – and it does not need to impose new taxes to do so. It suffices to:

- stop spending money on trivia and legacy issues, which are the easy things to do, and
- close the horde of loopholes that permit people to milk the nation's budget by rent-seeking (Chapter 10).

Rent-seekers have learned from other rent-seekers how to earn money by doing nothing, and the more this practice spreads the greater are the abuses of the social safety net and the less effort is made to clean the house. An excellent article in the Deutsche Bundesbank's *Monthly Report* examines the roots of this problem. Among the fundamental reasons that it puts at top of the list are laws, wage agreements and other measures which set legal precedence. These are seen as partly responsible for the fact that there is insufficient demand for legitimate employment in the low-wage sector.

The second most important factor working against employment, the Deutsche Bundesbank says, is social security system guarantees, such as the government-supported socio-cultural minimum subsistence level which depresses the supply of labour. This factor is particularly important *if* claims for benefits are not consistently reduced for people who reject job opportunities that are offered to them.[8] (To its credit, Switzerland has passed legislation to close that loophole.)

## 3. Le Contrat Première Embauche and Lifelong Employment

The previous chapters have made a brief reference to the *Contrat Première Embauche* (CPE)[9] and the 2006 events associated to it, in the sense that these provided an example of

8 Deutsche Bundesbank, *Monthly Report*, September 2006.

9 In an inflexible labour market characterized by nineteenth-century concepts, employers forego hiring because firing is a nightmare. The CPE did away with that nightmare in connection to young people entering the labour force.

resistance to change. At the time, French unemployment stood at 9 per cent, but among the young it was 23 per cent – or two and a half times higher than the average – and it needs no explaining that when future employees run wild, they shake the employers' confidence, and this makes matters worse.

The young students who demonstrated in the streets were against the CPE, against the government and against globalization – all at the same time. But they kept on buying Chinese-made products, and they did take holidays in Thailand and elsewhere in Asia – which is globalization at its best. De Villepin, the then French prime minister, failed to explain to them and their parents that:

- on one hand, globalization, deregulation, technology and innovation have unleashed a tremendous amounts of wealth and raised our standard of living,
- but, on the other hand, they have radically altered the old order as the 'classical' jobs have gone to countries with low wages – eastern Europe, China, Tunisia and elsewhere – with little chance of bringing them back.

There is therefore no alternative to creating new jobs within the realm of the knowledge society. However, everybody must know and appreciate that these require a great deal of change and adaptation. The life cycle of a job – any job – has been shortened; that's why young people must be ready to face multiple careers, doing so with a plan but with no anxiety. This adaptation is everybody's business – parents, the young and labour unions included – not just government's.

- Everyone has the right to work, but not 'the right to a job', and
- everyone must be personally responsible for managing his or her own career. Having a job is a privilege, not a divine right.

These two bullets represent the credo of the knowledge society – a stark antithesis to the beliefs of the industrial age which is not coming back. However, the knowledge society's forward spirit cannot flourish in an environment characterized by stagnation, defensive attitudes, embedded interests, and intellectual suspicion of capitalism and the *free market*, which is capitalism's latest incarnation.

The Chinese understood this, and the Communist Party dynasty saw to it that China today is the most capitalist country in the world. By contrast, Western democracies, particularly the states in continental Europe, find themselves at exactly the opposite end of the spectrum, characterized by:

- unwillingness to accept uncertainty as a way of life,
- objection to novelty as *the* means to renew themselves and
- unpreparedness or inability to manage change, including career change.

That's why the French CPE is so significant an example of our society's *déclinisme*. In a vain effort to stop change from happening, the university students took to the streets instead of enriching their know-how. The fact that three out of four French university students interviewed in one of the Paris demonstrations said that 'their dream' was a

---

But it was rejected by those it aimed to benefit.

government job – being bureaucrats rather than innovators – says everything about our society's advanced stage of disintegration and abandon.

Throughout the February, March and April 2006 CPE events, the various expressions of French unrest followed practically the same pattern. The daytime student marches went on rather peacefully. But a small group of hoodlums, mostly suburban youths looking for excitement and for whatever they could loot or set on fire, caused troubles at the endpoints of demonstrations and in their periphery. Typical acts of vandalism were:

- smashing shop windows,
- overturning and burning cars,
- throwing paving stones at the police and
- even robbing some of the demonstrating students.

What surprised many observers was that, despite the aforementioned happenings, which were widely reported, public support for the student demonstrators remained rather strong. This was all the more surprising because the *casseurs* left a sour aftertaste. Post-mortem, cool heads suggested that part of the reason could be found in the authorities' attitude. Nobody in the government cared to explain to the French public that:

- there is no natural-born right to a permanent job upon graduating, and
- in the knowledge society in which we live, what the students were doing by taking to the streets was highly counterproductive for their own future, for France and for society at large.

What the first bullet means is that people must try hard to get a job, rather than wait for it to fall from heaven. Flexible job markets make the finding of a job even more difficult because those who have one have taken those who have not as hostages. Protecting insiders from the competition of fellow citizens willing to work harder for less is totally *unethical*. It is also a practice that belongs to the past. Students who take to the streets are ignoring the fact that such actions quickly turn against them. As for the second bullet, the best commentary has been made by Laurence Parisot, head of the French Federation of Employers (MEDEF).

After talks on 24 March 2006 with Dominique de Villepin, the prime minister, Parisot warned that the protests were 'endangering the economy of our country' as well as 'endangering the image and reputation' of France.[10] What the president of MEDEF did not say, but should be added, is that governments that give in to the temptation to take the easy route out of the mess don't really govern. Nor can they pretend to serve their country and its people because, as we all know,

- the primary mission of a government is to address the longer term;
- it is not to bend over under pressure, in order to please 'this' or 'that' fraction of the electorate – or the demonstrators.

Logic, however, is not a characteristic of politics. The CPE's death sentence was pronounced on 13 March 2006 when President Jacques Chirac simultaneously confirmed

10 *Financial Times*, 25–26 March 2006.

and killed his prime minister's initiative. Double-talk, the reader may say, is commonplace in politics. Yes, but as a political commentator suggested, this one beat them all.

What Chirac said about the CPE, is another case – as if one was needed – of ambiguity overriding intellectual consistency. The president of the Republic said that the law on the CPE, already voted for by the French parliament, was confirmed and would be applied. But, at the same time, he asked for two important clauses of the 'confirmed law' to be changed:

- the duration of employment contracts and
- justification of firing the employee by the employer.

These were the two pillars of the CPE, and Chirac wanted them renegotiated with the other political parties and social partners (see sections 5 to 7) who had been manifestly opposed to the new law. A law and its applicability is never negotiated with opposing parties, and it is highly risky for the future of a nation when its president gives ambiguous signals about what a law is and is not.

In the aftermath of 12 long weeks of street demonstrations and of Chirac's ambivalence, the French prime minister accepted defeat. Commentators pointed out that the president of the Republic was defeated along with his 'chief operating officer'. As *Le Canard Enchainé* put it in a feature article, in less than ten days:

- the president confirmed a law (the CPE), while asking not to apply it,
- then he let go the changes he himself had asked to be made, and
- announced a proposed new law, thereby launching a hitherto unseen level of institutional confusion.[11]

Under these conditions, the editor of *Le Canard Enchainé* added, governing a country is not just impossible; it actually serves nothing. And this is a great disservice to the students themselves, in terms of their future employment. The demonstrators defeated the country's leadership, as showmanship overcame long-established political rules.[12]

## 4. Rebels Without a Cause and Their Wrong Incentives

The revolt of university and high-school students against the *Contrat Première Embauche* started in February 2006 and gained momentum rather rapidly. Incorrectly, the president of the Republic and the government put themselves on the defensive. The prime minister stayed aloof rather than explaining to the students, and their parents, why he used Napoleon's method in passing the CPE legislation through parliament.[13]

In a show of lack of responsibility in connection with the employment of young people, labour unions joined the student demonstrators (albeit with some delay and little

---

11 *Le Canard Enchainé*, 12 April 2006.

12 After three months of demonstrations, only one-fifth of French enterprises said in a poll that they would hire in 2006. So much for the pipedream of lifelong secure employment.

13 Napoleon's method consisted of giving the flat order and immediately thereafter checking that it had been implemented.

enthusiasm). A 36-hour support strike began on Monday night 27–28 March 2006, and lasted all day, bringing more than a million people onto the streets according to the police (and many more, according to demonstrators). Workers, opposition politicians and labour union bosses joined forces with university and high-school students (as well as with some professors) in more than 250 French towns and cities.

In the end, it was a half-baked strike, ironically emulating the half-measure that was the government's CPE. In Paris, 70 per cent of the subways and buses ran normally. So did two-thirds of the high-speed TGV trains and half of the other train services nationwide. But a third of the flights from French airports were cancelled, causing great inconvenience to passengers who were not party to the dispute.

As might clearly be expected, all these events had both side-effects and after-effects. On one single day, 23 March 2006, police arrested 630 people in the demonstrations and riots across France, about a third of them in Paris. Many, belonged to the same *banlieue* as the professional rebels whose high-water mark up until then had been the October–November 2005 Paris riots (which had continued for several days and nights, spread to the provinces and burned thousands of other people's cars).

It is interesting to note that the 2005 riots were triggered by the death by electrocution of two teenagers who had run away from the police and hidden in an electricity substation. How exactly that happened is unclear, but rioters were on the rampage at no time. Over two nights of violence, they torched:

- scores of cars,
- plenty of rubbish bins,
- a library and other public property.

This is the typical pattern, although the trigger varied from one incident to the next. In March 2006 the excuse for rebelling was the CPE, and on 25 November 2007 the riots started after two teenagers from the *banlieue* riding on a motorcycle (without crash helmets) were killed in a collision with a police car. The riots flared out in next to no time *as if* the *casseurs* were just waiting for the signal. On that occasion, apart from public buildings and cars, two schools and several shops were torched.[14]

Many *banlieue*, particularly north of Paris and in Toulouse, saw car-burnings. Some 182 policemen were wounded, several seriously. Correctly, on return from his visit to China, Nicolas Sarkozy set a hard-line tone. After visiting in hospital a police chief, wounded during the first night of violence, and calling it 'attempted murder', he vowed that anybody who fired at the police would end up in a criminal court. Some political commentators noted a change in the rioters' arsenal:

- In 2005 they wielded only petrol bombs and stones.
- In 2007 many policemen were hit by gunshots.

This arming up by city rebels provided one more piece of evidence that it makes no sense to throw money at the problem. In the first night alone of the November 2007 riots, 730 private cars were burned. Yet, in the two years between 2005 and 2007 the *banlieue*

14 'Paris Rioters "Criminal" says PM', *BBC News*, 27 November 2007, at: http://news.bbc.co.uk/1/hi/7115267.stm.

had had a huge injection of public cash, primarily for the renovation of the housing blocks that ring the big cities.

- Old tower blocks were demolished,
- streets were relaid and
- various 'allowances' were revisited and increased.

But the two biggest problems in these neighbourhoods remained. The first is the lack of skills among the young Maghrebians (many of whom are school drop-outs), as well as an unwillingness to do something for a living – even if the French economy had created enough stagehand jobs.

For instance, a TV commentary right after the March 2006 strikes and demonstrations pointed out that while the students were parading down the streets for jobs, 50,000 hotels and 30,000 restaurants were looking for people to hire and could not get them. While millions of people were being paid unemployment benefits, 500,000 jobs remained unfilled because the whole social system is distorted.

- The weeping boys who don't work are overpampered by social benefits.
- By contrast, those who work are overtaxed to pay for the other people's benefits and pleasures.

Another study's findings reported in *Nice Matin*, stated that there were 51,626 job vacancies in Côte d'Azur alone, many of them in construction and in the hotel business. 'In the construction of buildings it is not training that puts the brakes, but the lack of takers,' said Daniel Alberti, CEO of a construction firm. 'Over long years we had foreign workers. But today the kids of the Maghrebians don't come to work.'[15]

With manna from heaven in the form of steady, flowing unemployment benefits and extra incentives for producing children, young people have been unwilling to fill these jobs. Fighting with police and burning cars is their pleasure – while their parents have constantly failed to remind them that they are benefiting from public money to which they have contributed nothing.

At least according to sociologists, the second big problem in the *banlieue* is the tense relationship between the police and local youths. However, others say that this is a pseudo-problem, because these youths have been emboldened by socialist methods that were too lax, treating police officers as though they were social workers – not as law-enforcement officers – which did nothing to clamp down on criminality.

- In the 1960s de Gaulle passed a law (*la loi des casseurs*) whereby hooligans could be severely punished.
- But in the early 1980s the first socialist Mitterrand government did away with it, because '*la loi des casseurs*' was not to its liking.

As if street riots, burnt-out cars and broken shop windows were not enough, violence also became common currency in secondary schools. 'During the last five years the

15 *Nice Matin*, 29 April 2006.

number of so-called "difficult cases" has increased,'[16] said the provost of a college in Nice, 'These are very disturbed young people who should be followed by psychologists ... there is a banalization of violence.'[17] Another phenomenon is happy slapping – committing an act of violence and recording it on cellphone cameras.

During the same interview with the provost, one of the teachers made reference to a 13-year-old pupil who was hit by a young cyclist riding on the pavement. She lost her balance and fell down breaking her arm, but he disappeared. She registered a complaint, but nothing happened in bringing the youngster to justice.

Another teacher criticized the fact the education system wants to keep all pupils and students in school, no matter what their behaviour. Even those who don't want to, or simply can't, follow,the courses stay in the classroom, inhibiting the learning of the rest of the pupils. Many of these pupils virtually drop out of school at the age of 13 (see Part One), but the law says they have to stay in school until they are 16; so they stay and they don't let the others work.

The teachers are not the only victims. In mid-March 2007 in Nice a college student was beaten up by a gang at the perimeter of the school and was left there in a coma. The point is that many of the aggressors don't want to integrate into French society. They typically come from large immigrant families where there is often no father present and mothers have absolutely no control over their children. It's a state of total family chaos, which spreads like cancer in society.

## 5. The Culture of Anger and Violence is Spreading

The culture of violence eats up social values for breakfast. Government inspectors can no longer carry out their duties without fear of vengeful consequences. A veterinarian diagnosed peritonitis in a cow. In the evening, the farmer called: 'It won't be without consequences [if you report it]. You'll see, I will take care of you and your girlfriend [another inspector]. I will come to your place, and will break everything. I don't care if I go to prison.'[18]

There is plenty there to worry society, and for all its members to be on alert. Excesses have become common currency. A young woman was beaten severely by a small group of young *casseurs*. A journalist who was nearby was also beaten by other hooligans and had to be rescued by police officers. In many demonstrations the plate-glass windows of stores are smashed, particularly those whose displays can be looted. Before the police have time to intervene, bands of youths steal cameras and cellphones from other marchers in a demonstration.

'If it were only that,' said one of the cognizant people who contributed to the insights of this text. In the course of a mid-July 2009 discussion, he pointed to the news that workers, angry at the failure of French car parts manufacturer, New Fabris,[19] which had gone into receivership in mid-June, had threatened to blow up the factory unless the company's two biggest clients, Renault and Peugeot Citroën, stumped up extra

16 Read: student insubordination and 14-year-olds and members of their families beating up members of staff.

17 *Nice Matin*, 29 March, 2007.

18 *Le Canard Enchainé*, 11 January 2006.

19 In Châtellerault, western France.

compensation to the tune of €30,000 to each of the 366 workers facing unemployment The workers had occupied the factory and had rigged up gas canisters inside, and said that they would be detonated on 31 July if the two car-makers failed to pay the money in return for the company's remaining stock, ordered by the car-makers and valued at some €2 million ($2.4 million), as well as a machine belonging to Renault valued at another €2 million.[20] The government doubted that the canisters could set the factory on fire. Rather, the threat was symbolic and it could become a double-edged sword.

- If workers' violence brought them extortion money, this could set a bad precedent that might be imitated by many others.
- If the companies resisted, and the workers carried out their threat and the explosion was broadcast, it might find imitators in France and elsewhere as the economic crisis had brought many workers to the edge.

This protest marked a significant increase in labour tensions. The fire brigade was put on standby and emergency service reinforcements were sent to the area near the factory. In early 2009, the country was hit by a wave of *bossnappings*, in which to force better redundancy pay-offs or object to factory closures workers held the manager hostage, sometimes for several days.

In the background of these cases of anger and violence has been widespread resentment at bail-outs for big banks and car-makers. The CGT labour union (see section 6) that appeared to be leading the New Fabris protest, insisted that the battle would not be abandoned – while Renault and Peugeot stated that they would not give in to threats, but the protesters were not giving in. 'Renault and Peugeot have killed us,' said the local CGT boss, 'We want a share of the cake. They have been helped by the state.' The local CGT boss added that labour wanted a share of the cake because the companies were helped by the state.

'A share of the cake' encapsulates the concept behind the anger and violence. Among the students and workers nobody seems to be asking how long the cake will last. The sharp increase in the number of claims is eating it up while strikes, demonstrations or veiled threats are interlocking with serious risks of exploitation by people whose deepest aim is to create mayhem and mischief. The 2006 CPE protests have provided evidence of this.

Police said that the late March 2006 riots at Les Invalides, in the centre of Paris, were caused by 2,000 youths from the suburbs. This represented less than 10 per cent of 23,000 demonstrators who gathered there – but 2,000 hooligans still did a lot of damage. As the street parades by students continued, the problem of the *casseurs* who infiltrated them at the start of the protests, got worse.

- It needs no explaining such acts are bringing no credit to the student movement.
- The student organizers, and those who were behind them, should have thought of that before starting their street parades.

Being seen as in permanent revolt and involved in widespread public disobedience does not endear the Maghrebians to the French public. As for the angry students, they

20 J. Percival, 'French Workers Threaten to Blow up New Fabris Car Parts factory', *Guardian*, 13 July 2009, at: http://www.guardian.co.uk/world/2009/jul/13/france-workers-car-factory.

have been largely misguided and poorly informed by those who should have taught them ethics. Critics have said that some of their professors were party to this misinformation, because they were themselves rioters in May 1968 against de Gaulle's government.

One of the many billboard-size banners carried by student demonstrators stated: '*Sauvons Nos Droits!*' ('Let's save our rights!'). Nobody seems to have explained to the billboard-bearers that it is not the right of students, or of their accomplices, to paralyse the country. Neither are there an automatic 'rights'. Rights are the result of responsibilities, which must be served first.

'No to Globalization' read another banner. 'No to Outsourcing' was written on still another. 'No to Privatization and the Dictatorship of the Market!' was a claim that was frequently flourished on banners carried by demonstrators. This had become a '*non-non*' generation. Even Andrei Gromyko who used to say '*Niet!*' at the UN assembly, in Soviet Union times, had not said so many 'Nos' in his whole career.

Equally bad for the prospect of future employment, in France, Germany, Italy and continental Europe at large, is the fact that *student* labour unions have spread like wildfire. Among demonstrators and protesters arrested by police was Karl Stoeckel, head of France's main *union of high-school students*, the UNL. What employer would be happy to hire people who were strikers while still at school?

The background of these successive student revolts has been captured in an article by John Tierney who wrote: 'Someone needs to rescue France from its self-proclaimed malaise. Close to a quarter of its young people are unemployed, but they are too busy burning cars to look for jobs.' And Tierney added: '... [the] future is a generation of students whose idea of a good career, chosen by 75 per cent of them in one poll, is a government job.'[21] Being a bureaucrat is a career:

- without any future and
- with no intellectual excitement.

As scenes of violence in Paris and other French cities licked across television screens at home and abroad, and foreign newspapers as well as TV stations spoke of anarchy, some French people grumbled that the media coverage, especially in the English-speaking press, unjustly distorted the country's image.

- Yet, what the media gave were snapshots of street violence, and
- it is too bad that these were real-life scenes reflecting what was going on in city avenues and squares.

Plenty of parents whose kids had taken the streets, many of them members of a generation that grew up with full employment and lifetime jobs, said they wanted a *secure future* for their children. That was also in the younger people's minds. 'We are not revolutionaries, we just want our rights,' said one university student, identifying in one short sentence the nature of the young generation's problem. Nobody seems to have explained to him and his pals that, by rioting for their non-existent rights in the twenty-first-century environment, they miss the opportunities they might have had by joining the knowledge revolution.

21 *International Herald Tribune*, 29 March 2006.

## 6. Are Labour Unions a Relevant Social Partners or Anachronisms?

In the aftermath to the CPE events (section 3), it was said that one of the reasons why the 'labour unions' of high-school and university students roamed in Paris and other French cities is because they were not considered by the government as its *social partners*. This argument lacks weight because only in a decaying society would the government ask high-school students and their 'unions', whether it is allowed to take 'this' or 'that' measure. *If* it does so, *then* it falls under Charles-Maurice de Talleyrand's (1754–1838) dictum which suggests that ministers are not the right stuff: 'They [the authorities] were led by mediocre men who played a role in events because they found themselves in that place.'[22]

Created in Britain during the years following the Industrial Revolution, labour unions originally acted as a counterweight to worker exploitation. As such, they are a nineteenth-century development which was reshaped in the interwar years and gained in weight by becoming a quasi-political party[23] – but failed to adapt to the new economy over the last four decades.[24]

Sometime after the first trade unions were created in England, French labour unions got off the ground at about the same time (the late nineteenth century) as the union movement began in the United States. France's first syndicate, Confédération Générale du Travail (CGT), was formed in 1895 not long after Samuel Gompers organized the American Federation of Labor (AFL). However, in the following decades the pattern of labour movements in Britain, the US and France diverged:

- Whereas American labour politics veered to the right,
- French and British labour union moved further left.

Moreover, a foray of British and French trade unions into politics in the 1920s and 1930s took place without the benefit of a democratic electoral process. In 1936 French labour was instrumental in bringing Léon Blum's Popular Front to power, while British trade unions had their day of political power with the election of Ramsay MacDonald's Labour government in 1924 (more on British unions in section 7).

For its part, the American labour movement really took shape in the 1930s and 1940s when millions of industrial workers joined together into powerful unions under the aegis of the New Deal. In its heyday, organized labour bargained for:

- higher wages,
- better benefits and
- restrictive work rules.

'Better benefits' did help the workers get rising living standards (including generous health insurance), while their employers reaped the benefits of a stable workforce.[25]

22 Jean Orieux, *Talleyrand*, Flammarion, Paris, 1970.

23 In fact, in the 1920s and the post-World War II years they 'owned' the British Labour Party. Thatcher cut the knot.

24 An exception to this statement is the miners union in the US, which contributed funds to the development of open-pit technology. When reporters remarked to John L. Lewis, its boss, that this would halve the union's membership, he answered that he preferred to have half the members healthy rather than all of them sick.

25 Though health insurance is the individual's responsibility in the US, many companies have also been offering health insurance plans. General Motors have become known as 'the health insurance outfit with car production on the

However, the fact that, in the US, labour conceded to management the right to run the pensions business had an unexpected consequence: it created a division of responsibilities with the result that pensions are frequently underfunded.

One of today's problems with labour unions is that, with globalization, old-style management–worker bargaining has become tragically outdated in a service economy where, to survive, companies must react with lightning speed to changes in consumer tastes and technology – in other words, to the whims of the marketplace. This is incompatible with old labour practices.

Note that the old practice of putting a spoke in the wheels of the economy is no longer *en vogue* – not only in Western countries, but also in the developing world. In India, for example, labour unions vehemently objected to the introduction of personal computers in banking. It took nearly ten years to reach an agreement between banks and trade unions, which stipulated that banks can use PCs 'provided they can have only 256 Kbytes of memory' – a misery by any standard.

Hence the question: who are the *social partners* able to bring greater pluralism into governance? Militant student unions? Anachronistic labour unions? Paramilitary organizations? Community action groups? Maverick city councils? Who else? Moreover, in a democracy should this 'pluralism' be created with little regard for law and parliament?

Sometimes even labour union members can see that by sticking to early twentieth-century policies they have become anachronistic. To my knowledge, in the EU the first incidence of workers moving against their unions took place three decades ago, on 14 October 1980. On that day 40,000 Fiat foremen and workers marched in Turin, silently but massively against the long strike decided by their trade union.

- This was the nearest thing to a grassroots revolt, and
- it has had a long-lasting impact on management–labour relations.

Just as significant is that it took place in Italy where labour union *density* (union membership as a percentage of the total workforce) is higher than in other industrial countries. Union density stands at about 33 per cent in Italy, 28 per cent in Britain, slightly over 20 per cent in Germany, 12 per cent in the United States, and under 9 per cent in France.

In the case of France, labour unions derive their importance by being accepted as a *bon enfant*, rather than from their strength. They benefit from historical public sympathy for those who oppose the government. Post-CPE (section 3) polls have shown strong support for the protesters and their allies, the unions, as families with pushchairs turned out to show solidarity.

But for how long? An interesting sign of the times is that today in America more people own the company they work for (15 per cent) than belong to labour unions.[26] This is one of the few available statistics supporting the hypothesis that ultimately the middle class may survive the onslaught mounted by different governments against its existence (see Chapter 8).

Labour unions have very little to do with labour anyway. Slowly, they have turned themselves into a cross between political parties, lobbyists and instruments to promote

side'. Lavish health insurance benefits, and corporate mismanagement, eventually brought GM to bankruptcy.

26 *The Economist*, 26 July 2008.

the careers of their officials. Where is the labour union, including a college one, that has demonstrated concern and activism about curricula, quality of education (including examinations), laboratories and the teachers' ability to teach? Or has promoted the subjects society needs to improve the employment prospects of the young generation?[27]

Here is an example on what enlightened guidance might provide. In September 1995 Lincoln Electric in Euclid, Ohio, had 200 jobs available but could not fill them despite some 20,000 applicants. Only a few of these applicants could perform the high-school maths needed in a modern high-tech factory. One of the rejected applicants expressed his regret about his high-school years in these terms: 'If I knew then what I know now, I would have acted differently.'[28] *If* – but nobody told him in time, and the labour unions were too focused on the past to look into the future.

Something else that worries me is that the labour unions have managed to work outside (and sometimes against) democratic principles. This lack of a democratic process has its consequences. As the EU governments and labour compete for popular support, parliamentary legitimacy is locked in mortal combat with trade union solidarity. Normally, the parliament is *the* social partner of the government because, at least theoretically, it represents the people. This, however, is contested by:

- street rallies and
- wild demonstrations.

Critics say that through the power of traditional privileges – but no longer because of their numerical strength – unionism has become a serious threat to democracy. The fact labour unions and student unions are telling the government what to do is a negation of republican principles. Even if it is presented under the guise of so-called *social partnership*, it is a 'partnership' which:

- comes from special interests and
- represents no national consensus.

In fact, the danger to democracy is real even if many labour union leaders are constitutionalists. By expanding beyond its original role in labour relations, in recent years the union movement has moved into partial conflict with the democratic state. This was true in Britain prior to Margaret Thatcher, and it is true today in France, Germany, Italy, Greece and other EU countries.

## 7. Thatcher Engaged with the Labour Unions and Won

Most politicians in the EU steer clear from contesting labour union claims, because challenging them can diminish their chances of re-election, particularly when the public shows unusual patience over disruption caused by protests. As a popular saying has

27 'I would suggest that the British teachers' unions (which almost uniquely nowadays act as social partners to the (Labour) government) do this', commented a reviewer of this book.

28 *Asian Wall Street Journal*, 15 September 1995.

it, 'Under labour union pressure, politicians become of variable geometry'. There are, however, exceptions, and Margaret Thatcher is an example.

Based on her appreciation of the maturity and understanding of the British electorate, Thatcher engaged the labour unions in a fight and won. The way the former British prime minister relates it:

> *Unlike some of my colleagues, I never ceased to believe that, other things being equal, the level of unemployment was related to the extent of trade union power. The unions had priced many of their members out of jobs by demanding excessive wages for insufficient output, so making British goods uncompetitive.*[29]

During the years when she was in charge of British fortunes, Thatcher did not look at labour unions as social partners. Instead, with the Employment Act of 1982, she raised substantially the levels of compensation for those unfairly dismissed in a closed shop. She also put through legislation that, in existing closed shops, there would be periodic ballots to test support among employees for their continuation; and made unlawful what were then called 'union labour only' practices.

With this and other measures, Thatcher siphoned the strength out of arrogant British trade unions. This policy of cleansing the labour environment contrasted sharply to policies followed by previous governments, which had got into the habit of bending under labour union pressure. An example of unwanted consequences has been the high wages and benefits demanded, and obtained, by labour. For instance, in three continental European countries, these demands:

- obliged many German companies to move manufacturing operations abroad,
- turned some Italian industry sectors into the hole in the doughnut and
- pressured French industry in a way that substantially reduced the country's competitiveness.

There have also been other negative deliverables from a cost structure that became unaffordable and brought Europe with its featherbedded labour force to a crisis. On one side there have been strikes and street demonstrations and, on the other, inefficient labour practices coupled with wages that are unaffordable in a globalized economy. All this made many European regions and industries highly uncompetitive for manufacturing industry. Unemployment problems followed.

In just four years, from 1992 to 1996 – right after West Germany's leveraged buy-out of East Germany – a unified Federal Republic lost 1 million jobs, mostly in manufacturing. At the time, both in Germany and elsewhere in the EU, employers' organizations warned that an additional million jobs were at risk throughout the federal states, unless:

- wage costs were reduced and
- welfare taxes fell significantly.

Little wonder that within a matter of a few years the risk of losing their jobs became the biggest worry of most EU citizens. Nevertheless, labour unions did not reduce their

29 Margaret Thatcher, *The Downing Street Years*, HarperCollins, London, 1993.

activism, and governments did not cut the exorbitant and punishing welfare costs. The resulting unemployment testified that both governments and labour unions had erred by not joining together to agree a policy of cost-cutting which became the alter ego of globalization. Whether one likes it or not, to survive:

- both European and American companies find themselves obliged to reduce labour costs,[30] and
- *if* this cannot be achieved at home, *then* their solution is to shift work across borders.

In France, the first CEO of the French Republic to decide to get the country moving again was Nicolas Sarkozy. In his 2007 presidential campaign he pledged to get the country back to work, scrap exorbitant public-sector privileges and set free a strangled labour market. He also promised to end 'special regimes' that paid generous pensions to certain parts of the public sector, including the rail, electricity and gas industries.

Sarkozy's plans for reform were much more detailed than those Thatcher set out in her first election manifesto in 1979. They also represented a clear break with 'do nothing' Jacques Chirac who never really believed that radical change was necessary to improve the French economy and cut unemployment.

As Thatcher had correctly seen back in the 1980s, both discipline in the workplace and cost-consciousness are terms practically synonymous to survival. How far cost control can go is shown by many US companies that have photocopies made at minimum wage-paying shops across the street, rather than in-house at unionized wage levels. Labour unions should appreciate that the huge and growing advances in transportation, communication and information technology:

- made the process of levelling cost structures inevitable and
- created a *one-cost* world labour market which is way beyond their scrutiny.

A different way of making this statement is that *if* labour unions want to be the government's social partners, *then* they should understand that there is no more room for a protectionist welfare state – one that shelters workers and wages from market pressures. After all, the same people are producers and consumers, and, as consumers, they are buying the lowest-priced goods they can find. The keywords today are:

- better education,
- greater competition and
- a higher rate of investment.

In none of the above bullets can be found the word 'strikes', because the concept is antiquated. Experts say that the union leadership has managed to find itself in a self-made squeeze. It needs to sound militant in order to gain recruits, but it can also see that the result of labour activism is greater unemployment.

Thatcher understood this and she also appreciated the fact that, because of manufacturing globalization, companies had lost their pricing power. They could

30 Which is happening in 2008–2010 under cover of the severe economic crisis.

not pass on wage hikes and welfare costs as they used to do. Moreover, increases in productivity were not enough to compensate for increasing labour costs. For a couple of decades Britain had been at a huge competitive disadvantage, under both Conservative and Labour governments, to the point that it was rapidly losing its markets.

In conclusion, the political gift Margaret Thatcher gave to Britain is that it fought the labour unions and *won*. Skipping John Major's time as one of incompetence, Thatcher's successor, New Labour, was (at least in its first years) even-handed between management and workers – and wise enough not to revive the trade unions' past power. But under Gordon Brown Old Labour made a comeback, this time in a great love affair with the bankrupt big banks rather than with the trade unions.

## 8. Social Partners Which a Country Needs to Prosper

The question about whether or not labour unions are social partners of entrepreneurs, manufacturers and other productive elements of the economy was posed in section 6. A similar query is valid regarding governments and their policies towards the private sector.

There are plenty of examples documenting that policies which are not even-handed can tear apart the social fabric, and this has many unexpected consequences. During the last two decades, examples of repeated government failures have come from Japan – starting with an unwillingness to face the facts.

Here are some highlights. In mid-1995, some five years after the country's major economic downturn, the Japanese government admitted that there was a danger of losing all of its better companies to other countries. The two top reasons were:

- the high cost of doing business in Japan and
- an enormous web of stifling bureaucratic rules that frustrate business activities.

The rise of the yen against other currencies prompted many manufacturing companies to move their production bases overseas – a decision the Japanese themselves termed the *hollowing out* of industry. But, by the time the government became conscious of the shift's after-effects, the country was a less attractive location to do business relative to other countries in east Asia.

A White Paper by Japan's Ministry of International Trade and Industry (MITI) said that the country should lose no time in rectifying the situation. Its tone reflected the increasing concern among MITI officials that 'hollowing out' could cripple the Japanese economy unless something was done quickly to arrest and reverse the trend.

With only 6 per cent of Japanese manufacturing done overseas, compared with 25 per cent for the US and 20 per cent for Germany (statistics prevailing at that time – that is, the mid-1990s), the Japanese should not, in theory, have had misgivings about their country's de-industrialization. But the fact that official concern was high indicated how badly the economy needed a major overhaul.

- The problem with the economy, the MITI paper stated, was that not all sectors were subject to market mechanisms – and those protected remained subdued.

- This was the first time that the annual White Paper linked 'hollowing out' to the need to reform the Japanese economy with the aim of making it cheaper to manufacture in Japan.

It is quite interesting to note that in terms of identifying the country's problems and of suggesting corrective action, MITI's 1995 White Paper was on the mark. Manufacturing, which competed with cheaper foreign imports, was an efficient sector. By contrast, in Japan's energy sector and some of its service industries,

- heavy regulation kept prices high since market forces could not work to dampen them, and
- the result was that these sectors were, on aggregate, about 30 per cent less productive than manufacturing.

This cast the government's role in a new light. What entrepreneurs wanted to see from the political authorities as social partners were measures which would help to avoid industry being hollowed out through uncompetitiveness because of high taxation, the awarding from above of too many (unsustainable) social benefits, or the squandering of talent because rigid labour laws kept the young generation out of work.

In addition, as far as business managers were concerned, a major factor of being and staying competitive in the global market, was the demolition of old structures as companies reinvented themselves. This is a concept that continental European governments and labour unions don't fully accept. Yet, as practically every economist knows (but several political leaders and government bureaucrats don't), there are two sources of growth:

- increased capital per worker and
- increased productivity, also per worker.

Increased capital per worker may come from bought money[31] (which has to be repaid) or from savings – by far the better solution. The problem with the second option is that someone has to do the savings. Successful entrepreneurs appreciate this, but the majority of consumers don't; while by keeping interest rates too low and taxing the income from savings, the authorities push the citizen towards consumption.

By contrast, internal capital resources, which get a country ahead, have to be accumulated by postponing consumption, and this is something governments are afraid to talk about because it reduces spending. In the aftermath, the EU, the US and, recently, Japan live on credit; therefore, they super-leverage themselves at state, corporate and family level.

Increased productivity has the advantage of getting a country ahead without sacrificing consumption, provided the rise in productivity is sufficient to keep an economy growing in a respectable manner. As social partners, the federations of employers frequently tell governments that implementing state-of-the-art technology helps in boosting worker productivity, but machines have to be depreciated and therefore workers cannot collect all the resulting profits in higher wages, healthcare and other welfare. Additionally,

31 Including foreign direct investments (FDIs) which these days move in and out through any country's financial swinging doors.

- while over the longer term machines create employment, in the short term they tend to eliminate jobs and require structural changes, and
- both after-effects call for collaboration by labour unions rather than strike action.

Take Cisco, the US telecommunications equipment manufacturer, as an example of what technology provided in productivity terms. In the mid-1990s Cisco aggressively applied state-of-the-art technology to make its 80 per cent annual growth rate feasible. In less than two years, the company was able to handle over 80 per cent of support calls without human intervention, via the Web. The pay-off has been rapid. 'Going to the Web saved us 1,000 staff positions', said CEO John T. Chambers, 'and this resulted in $125 million a year in savings.'[32] Using high technology, however, calls for:

- steady improvement in skills,
- significant investments and
- rapid depreciation of such investments, because technology moves on.

Steady improvement in skills is the responsibility of schools, colleges and universities. But to fulfil this responsibility they also need an intake that is literate as well as able and willing to learn. This is hardly the case with pupils and students who don't have jobs yet and are already on strike.

A fact frequently discussed in Part One, of which both governments and labour unions have to be aware, is that one of the effects of increasing automation is to expand the gap between *knowledge workers* and the *unskilled*. As a result of research, innovation and rapid technological development,

- the job opportunities for the unskilled diminish,
- while knowledge workers with up-to-date skills are always in demand.

For employers and of knowledge workers, this awareness began in the late 1980s. A study done in the early 1990s by the US Congressional Budget Office compared the income and compensation pattern of the so-called 'baby-boomers' with that of their parents in the early 1960s. The study found that the younger group had:

- accumulated more wealth than its parents at same age, and
- its per-capita income was standing higher by a full 55 per cent.

Not bad for a generation who worked harder, learned better and has been motivated by the wealth effect. What that study did not say is that in the final analysis compensation is measured at the take-home pay level and those who are better compensated live and work in countries where social costs are kept low. The US (prior to the God-size government leverage of 2008–2009 which has wrecked its economy) and Britain (from Thatcher to Blair, but not to Brown) are examples.

Knowledge workers choose to reside in countries where the tax structure is not crushing and where they can get richer and more comfortable in their lives *if* they work hard. They don't depend on the state supermarket to feed them, because they know that if they do, they will regret it.

---

32 *Business Week*, 19 May 1997.

# CHAPTER 10 The Continuing Search for Miracle Solutions

## 1. The Brains Go Where They are Appreciated

Let's start this chapter, the last in Part Three, with a note that is both sweet and sour. The former is the theme of the first section. Young people who find good employment, rather than wait for the state supermarket to pay them a miserable subsistence, are not afraid to use both:

- their brain and
- their feet.

They become world citizens because they appreciate that staying in one place can only make a man grow poor. That was the concept that inspired the Spanish *conquistadores* and soldiers of fortune. More recently, it is driving the minds and hands of *global professionals*, particularly when the country in which they were born offers no enticing career opportunities.

In the West, this lack of opportunities finds its origin in the love of the status quo and near-sightedness of politicians. Political leadership is not exercised by following the crowd and by avoiding telling the voters that they are wrong when they resist change because of fears about the permanence of jobs and about 'tomorrow'.

The student body itself is divided into two asymmetric parts. On the smaller, but agitated, side are those who take over their school and bar the entrance to their colleagues who are there to learn, not to loaf or destroy property.[1] Meddled with by *agents provocateurs* (the troublemakers), this minority is labouring hard against its own future by:

- learning nothing,
- fighting with the police,
- breaking shop windows,
- burning cars and whatever else catches their fancy.

'It is anarchy. The law of the street. There is no security. There is no government,' said a Frenchman whose newsstand kiosk had been burned to the ground by demonstrators gone wild.[2] Is this the European Union in which one wishes to live? I doubt it.

1 When, in 2006, they took over the University of Sorbonne, students destroyed, in their 'rage', some ancient books and covered the walls with graffiti: 'Nous n'aurons que ce que nous saurons prendre.' (Roughly translated: 'We will have only what we know how to take.')

2 On the TV news, on the evening of 16 March 2006.

The other asymmetric part is the silent majority which, unclear about what it wishes to do for the future sits on the sidelines. Only small part of this population of French and other EU graduates thinks that the answer is 'We will find our way'. Once these young people complete their studies, they take their future in their own hands.

This population is composed of young graduates who, like the *conquistadores*, have decided that there are no career opportunities in their country of origin, and after graduation pack up and leave for abroad. Brains have no borders, and countries who welcome them gain a great deal. Foreign-born university *graduates* who find good employment (in their host country) make up:

- 10 per cent in Australia,
- a little over 7 per cent in Canada,
- more than 5 per cent in Switzerland,
- About 3.5 per cent in the US,
- 3 per cent in Britain and
- a trivial share in France, Germany and Italy.

In absolute numbers most foreign-born graduates flock to America where they are welcome as *knowledge workers*. The high-tech industry in the US has been powered to a remarkable degree by people born outside the country. According to some estimates:

- 3,000 of the technology firms created in Silicon Valley since the 1980s, which means about a third of the total, were started up by foreign scientists, and
- the science and engineering departments of America's leading universities have drawn the brightest graduate students from all over the world, many of them staying over as faculty members.

Lately, France and Germany have also been trying to participate in the brain gain through a variation on America's green cards. This is an interesting and welcome change because until the mid-1970s most immigrants to both countries came to do manual work. Nevertheless, France is attracting a lower proportion of skilled immigrants than Germany, which is way behind the US in brain gain.

A modern high-tech society does not need an inflow of stagehands, and it has much to lose when they become troublemakers. Hence, France tightened the immigration law.[3] In 2006 Nicolas Sarkozy, then interior minister, decided to change that through dual action. First, in reference to the Maghrebian and other African youths of the suburbs, he publicly stated that 'If certain people don't like France, they shouldn't hesitate to leave' (see also section 6). Then he introduced a new law favouring highly educated immigrants.

- Skilled migrants are encouraged through a new three-year *talent* work permit, and
- efforts are now made to retain in France the best foreign graduates.

But are French citizens who graduate abroad coming back to live in their 'old country', where taxation is high and employment less than certain? And, moreover, will those

3 Today, only 7,000 permanent workers arrive in a year, down from over 170,000 in the late 1960s. The large majority of legal entrants to France are family-related: spouses, children and sometimes extended families.

who graduate in France stay when they have better employment opportunities in the US, Britain or other countries in which their former colleagues have built up interesting careers.

Neither should it be forgotten that this law, which has been in the right direction, met with unanimity among politicians. There has been opposition to it from socialists and other fellow travellers to *déclinisme* – and, sometimes, a fierce opposition. The socialists accused Sarkozy of trying to seduce the far-right vote, thereby putting principles of 'generosity' and 'tolerance' in peril.

This repulse towards personal success is more or less an EU-wide illness. Australians and Canadians have been successful in attracting foreign talent by adopting a points-based immigration system which favours the highly skilled. By contrast, EU countries have been less successful – and of the three that are trying to catch up – Britain, Germany and France – only Britain has made headway.

Proponents of the French bill correctly argued that, under the pretext of protecting jobs at home, France has created a system that lets in only those who have neither a job nor any useful skills. It is only reasonable that France should try to benefit from international talent – and it is good news that, as of recently, the brain drain has become a *bête noire*.

Enlightened spirits rang the alarm bells more than a decade ago, but the socialist party, which was then in power, did not take heed. 'The best people are leaving at an incredible rate,' said economist Christian Saint Etienne, a professor at the University of Paris back in January 1998,[4] but neither Chirac (the then French president) nor Jospin (the prime minister) would listen.

Attracting brains is a question of synergy, not of pronouncements. Without a flourishing twenty-first-century industry to kick-start job creation, like Silicon Valley and other technology hot-spots in the US, European governments have been left praying for cyclical economic upturns to whittle down the unemployment figures (more on this in section 2). But the economic crisis of 2007–2011 trimmed projections for growth in gross domestic product (GDP), crushing government expectations for a drop in unemployment.

French politicians, particularly from the left, both accuse the EU of paternalistic interference and try to profit from it. The more clear-sighted planned to use the European monetary union to carry out unpopular public-sector reforms, including overhauls of the tax and social security systems. But as Jacques Chirac was president at the time, this did not happen. Instead:

- taxation moved higher, and
- job opportunities for higher skills went south.

According to Maurice Levy, CEO of Publicis, the French media company, the brain drain and high personal taxes correlate. The steady loss of brains, Levy says, is a loss to both the French economy and the government's budget. Hence his suggestion to lower French corporate taxes to the European average and do away with the special wealth tax

4 *Business Week*, 26 January 1998.

which costs the taxpayer an inordinate amount of money and induces him or her to move abroad.[5]

The Internet, Levy suggests, has radically changed the way we think, work and buy. What does the 35-hour week mean when everybody can be on the Internet any time during the day? Why forbid shops to open on Sundays when any consumer can buy on Sundays through the Internet? How can shopkeepers keep up when their clients have access to products at any time during the day, while shops can only open during permitted hours?

During the 2007 French presidential election, it was often heard that if Ségolène Royal were elected president, this would trigger an exodus of people from the financial and biotechnology sectors to London and other foreign cities – because of fears that her socialist mind would raise taxes for the highest earners and for companies. Even without *La Royal*, France was losing qualified people.[6]

The damage created by the brain drain amounts to much more than money. Reading the biographies of leading scientists, one is struck by the fact that great discoveries usually came from unconventional ways of thinking. And it is precisely the unconventionals who cannot live under the steamroller of the socialist mind. The embrace of the state supermarket is asphyxiating.

## 2. Ill-fated Summits Which Failed to Bend Unemployment

The EU's *Zeitgeist* is best described by what has happened in the years that have elapsed since the much-ballyhooed *Jobs Summit* on 20–21 November 1997. Tony Blair had hailed it as a new direction for the EU; Helmut Kohl welcomed its 'conclusions'; and the then cohabiting French duo of Jacques Chirac and Lionel Jospin proclaimed that this was the building of a 'social Europe'.

As is to be expected, nothing came out of these great pronouncements in the years after they were made. It is difficult to find more shallow opinions coming out of what was supposed to be a 'summit'. A social fabric torn apart by neglect, big handouts and contradictions needs leaders with guts to put it together again.

- It has no use for empty pronouncements in useless 'summits', and
- it matters little if these are embellished with contradictory interpretations of what the summit's 'agreement' is all about.

A similar statement is valid about the fate of the March 2005 European Council meeting which relaunched the Lisbon Strategy, supposedly by focusing on growth and employment. Changes made to the governance framework of the 1997 'summit', supposedly to improve the implementation of structural reforms, were so trivial that they led nowhere. The new hallowed promises were embedded in the European Commission's

5 As an example, a person with a wealth of €15 million must pay a special wealth tax of €200,000 per year over and above all other taxes, including an income tax which may go up to 68 per cent.

6 Mitterrand was quite pragmatic, able to shift his position after a couple of years when he saw it was not working. But Royal was ideologically fixed on her position, some people commented.

*Integrated Guidelines* package, consisting of a set of Broad Economic Policy Guidelines (BEPGs) and Employment Guidelines.

The soup of names has been further enriched by the EU member states' National Reform Programmes (NRPs), which set out a three-year strategy to implement the Integrated Guidelines at the national level, with zero results. The torrent of bureaucratic plans and papers continued, but the deliverables have been remarkable for their absence; hence it is a pure waste of time to talk about them.

There is, however, one reference which worth making. Jacques Santer, a former president of the European Commission, had good advice for his colleagues when he said 'If we are going to be serious about tackling the jobless problem, we have to start looking at all sorts of sacred cows.'[7] There are plenty of sacred cows in the EU, and many find themselves at the core of problems associated with high rates of unemployment in Spain, Germany, France, Italy, Greece and elsewhere.

The reader is right if he thinks that unemployment is nothing new in these countries. The challenge is that year-in, year-out we are not an inch nearer to abandoning old habits which have proved to be counterproductive. One action that has been considered and abandoned without even being tested is a drive to persuade member governments to make a firm pledge to implement every clause in EU legislation – even if it is not evident that this will indeed help.

There are two reasons for the doubt expressed in the preceding paragraph. The first is that EU legislation does not particularly promote a free labour market. Although it is generally better than the current mosaic of labour laws, it does not go to the heart of the problem. The second reason is administrative. As figures show, on average across the EU:

- no more than 90 per cent or so of existing EU rules and regulations have been written into national statute books, and
- there exists only anecdotal evidence as to how much has been *implemented* by 'this' or 'that' member country, the consensus being that it is 'not much'.

In addition, the various EU 'summits', supposedly organized to confront and solve the challenge of unemployment, fail to account for two most important issues. Yet, the continuing existence of each one of them risks turning the tables on any solution to unemployment, supposing that such a solution is found.

One issue is wage inflation which is not being attended to in most EU countries, particularly in those where higher unit labour costs are poison to the economy. The trend lines in Figure 10.1 are based on statistics published at the end of 2007, and they illustrate the following:

- In 1997, at the time of the famous EU *jobs summit*, unit labour costs in Germany and Italy were roughly equal, while they were about 13 per cent lower in Spain.
- But seven years after the euro's introduction, and the abuses suffered by the common currency, German labour costs shrank while those in Italy and Spain soared by an average of roughly 4 per cent per year.

---

7 *Financial Times*, 25–27 May 1995.

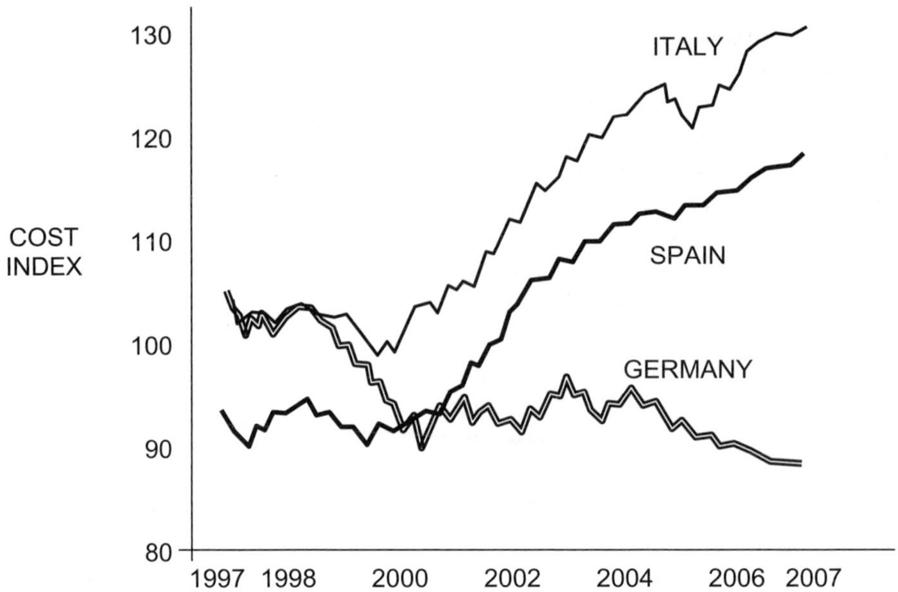


**Figure 10.1 The effect of the euro on labour-cost discipline has been positive in Germany but negative in Italy and Spain**

*Source:* Author's own research.

Despite the jobs summit and the euro, wage discipline took leave of absence, and that made both Spain and Italy highly uncompetitive. The EU unemployment initiatives had failed to take account of that possibility. They also forgot to take on the other dragon – the after-effect of a downturn. Wage inflation is not only destructive in good times, but is also responsible for soaring unemployment when adversity hits.

Spain provides an example. By December 2009, two and a half years after the start of the deep economic crisis of 2007–2011, its unemployment rate was just shy of 20 per cent versus about 8 per cent in Germany. *If* unemployment summits serve anything, *then* they should fully account for worst-case scenarios and come up with directives which help to avoid the worst by being more thoughtful in good times.

In addition, policy-makers should weigh up the fact that, of all age groups in the labour force, the must vulnerable are the 20–25-year olds and 50–55-year olds. Those more likely to face the effects of rising unemployment are at the extremes of the working people's distribution. Young people are at greater risk than their seniors of being made redundant, and companies are more inclined to sack elderly workers with poor qualifications.

Regarding older workers, people approaching retirement have also suffered a big blow in terms of the falling value of houses and equities – and many may not be able to complete the years necessary for retirement benefits. Therefore, together with the jobless young, they should arouse a particular concern that transcends politics.

As is evidenced by the above, to really confront the various faces of unemployment the EU 'summits' godfathers should use their imaginations to work out focused solutions. 'Wisdom is the daughter of experience,' said Leonardo da Vinci. But, among EU oligarchs, experience in solving employment problems – indeed, any difficult problems – is in short supply. There are two fallacies:

- Unemployment can be reduced by setting specific, but often meaningless, targets or *guidelines* in EU-speak.
- Budget deficits work towards reducing unemployment. That's the Keynesian thesis which time and again has proved to be wishful thinking.

These and other wrong-way risks are guiding the hands of a political leadership which has lost contact with reality and its base. Yet there have been clearly defined demerits for big budget deficits under Maastricht: if a country does not sufficiently trim its leverage, it will be eligible for sanctions. Cynics say that only fools believe in EU sanctions. Despite some huge and persistent deficits, this has not yet happened – almost all the big EU countries are swimming in red ink.

As for the first of the above two bullets, unlike budget deficits, few employment measures can be enforced by governments – short of ballooning their budgets and the national debt. It is the *private sector* that creates most new jobs, and the private sector searches for low labour-cost alternatives. It also has an aversion to students who go on strike before finding employment (Chapter 9) and hates the inflexibility of labour unions.

Tax-and-tax fiscal policies don't make matters any better. Another fallacy in the minds of bureaucrats and socialist politicians is that there exists a *third way* between adopting a free-market policy and suffering chronic arteriosclerosis. This imaginary *third way* would, in theory, be capable of:

- producing low unemployment,
- offering a great deal of job protection and
- reducing the unaffordable and unsustainable welfare benefits.

The killing of three flying birds with one well-placed stone is the 'solution' favoured by the French Left (and by the German *Linke*), while the Italians wait for a *miracolo* to come their way. 'There is no such thing as a miracle,' Dr. I.I. Rabi, the Manhattan Project physicist, once observed. 'Only happenings that we don't understand.'

Senseless rhetoric left aside, left, centre-left, centre-right and other EU political movements have done practically nothing to improve employment perspectives. This is neither a recent occurrence nor one encountered only in continental Europe. In Britain, the first Labour governments which were in office in 1924 and from 1929 to 1931 did little to help their supporters beyond raising unemployment benefit. Despite the strides made by the working-class movement,

- British Labour's principal achievement was better wages and shorter hours for those *in* jobs, and
- this was gained at the expense of those who were unemployed, because the miracle that was hoped for did not show up.

A similar miscalculation, coupled with lack of imagination in developing better employment conditions, has characterized socialist governments that took power in

Britain, France, Germany, Italy and everywhere else in Europe after World War II. Inertia has been the most widespread phenomenon, and inertia is contagious.

This is in stark contrast with more than five decades ago, when the Treaty of Rome was signed. France was enjoying *les trentes ans glorieuses*, 30 splendid post-war years. Italy was quickly gaining ground on its European neighbours. And West Germany was in the midst of its *Wirtschaftswunder* with:

- rapid growth,
- low unemployment and
- rapidly rising living standards.

The situation is totally different in 2010, and this not only because of the ongoing economic and banking crisis. Everybody is to blame for the failure to enact painful changes to make labour markets more flexible, trim overgenerous welfare benefits and inject new competition into product markets. As we saw in Chapter 9, with the example on Thatcher, to do all this means taking on trade unions and other vested interests – including the over-greedy bankers and other big company managers.

Major labour law changes, however, are politically painful; they are not the stuff for the second-raters who run many of the EU member states today. Surprisingly, not only long-haired socialists (who anyway live in the clouds), but also right-wing governments don't understand that the real option is between: A ±1 per cent economic growth and 8–9 per cent unemployment, on the one hand, and, on the other, a hard decision to make labour markets much more flexible, trim the many layers of welfare that have accumulated since the Great Depression, and enact bank regulation which puts a ceiling on speculation by the very few at the expense of the many.[8]

## 3. Using Recent Experience to Improve the Employment Model

Shaken by the competition which came on the heels of a massive influx of very low-cost products made in China, American and European companies have taken dramatic steps to radically cut labour costs. This has had evident effects on reducing unemployment, which became particularly dramatic because no measures were taken to position the Western labour force against the after-effects of globalization without limits, when there was still time to do so.

- Competition from countries with low-cost labour did not come onto the radar screen overnight.
- Not only were Western governments informed in advance, but they also had several decades to prepare their public for such competition – but little or nothing was done.

The first warning came from Japan in the 1960s. The second and stronger alarm bell rang in the early 1980s when deregulation brought to life the globalization wave

8 D.N. Chorafas, *Capitalism Without Capital*, Palgrave/Macmillan, London, 2009 and D.N. Chorafas, *Financial Boom and Gloom: The Credit and Banking Crisis of 2007–2009 and Beyond*, Palgrave/Macmillan, London, 2009.

which brought low-cost products to Europe and America from the so-called 'Asian tigers': Singapore, Taiwan, Thailand, Malaysia, Indonesia and South Korea. Skills were high in Singapore (followed by Taiwan), but its population was small compared to that of Indonesia and South Korea. The 'Asian tigers' were hard workers who:

- overleveraged themselves,
- went bust in 1997,
- but still survived.[9]

Then, the 1990s saw the entry of China into the global manufacturing market. This has been a totally different ballgame. With 1.4 billion people (who are both producers and consumers), unity of command, strong currency, a centrally administered strategic plan, mass production of engineers and very low-cost labour, the Chinese have proven that they can turn any other economy on its head.

- Their products are unmatched in cost-effectiveness, and
- to compete with *China price* and come up from under, both America and the EU have to trim labour costs by 65 per cent or more (according to some studies).

This trimming of salaries and wages is currently happening, and not only through outsourcing. An example is provided by the graduates of Lufthansa's Aircraft Maintenance School, one of the largest in the world. They have been offered employment contracts in one of the carrier's subsidiaries which pays one-third of Lufthansa's salaries for maintenance engineers. Deutsche Telekom has done something similar for surplus personnel whom it cannot fire – and these are only two examples.

A different case, also most revealing on what the future may hold in terms of salaries and wages for European and American workers and employees, is provided by Delphi Automotive. This former General Motors subsidiary was the largest supplier of car parts worldwide, with 180,000 employees. Delphi turned belly-up in mid-October 2005 filing under Chapter 11 for protection from creditors, and pundits said that this was a forerunner of bigger bankruptcy events.

Delphi's bankruptcy was not just 'bad luck'. Prior to it, its management made a last-ditch attempt to negotiate with the United Autoworkers Union (UAW) – with no results. As should have been expected, the fate of Delphi in 2005 was that of General Motors in 2008.

- Had the US government (not just the GM management) used Delphi as an alarm for restructuring, it would not have had to pour billions to save GM and Chrysler from falling into oblivion.[10]

Here, in a nutshell, is what Delphi demanded, which proved to be the signpost of a trend in labour contracts. First, immediate wage cuts, bringing the average wage in Delphi plants down to the equivalent of an unskilled entry-level job of $10 to $12 an hour. Lufthansa offered its Airfcraft Maintenance School graduates €9.50 per hour – which is about the same level.

---

9 Overleveraging in the 'tiger' economies led to the huge 1997 crisis in east Asia.

10 The same statement is valid about the governments of Germany, France and Sweden, and their car manufacturing industries.

Second, cuts in the many benefits of the hourly workers' pension plans, coupled with the complete replacement of the union retirees' healthcare plan by a single $10,000 payment to each person upon retirement. To appreciate the importance of this cost issue, the reader must keep in mind that, by and large in America, retirement and healthcare are paid by the company's budget and at the time of its bankruptcy Delphi had:

- a total business debt of $6 billion,
- but total pension and other post-retirement employee benefits underfunded by $14.5 billion – or 242 per cent higher than its business debt.

In Europe this load is on the shoulders of social security rather than on those of the employer, but most social security systems are bankrupt or nearly so. Therefore, the predicament of Delphi Automotive is a precedent that should be kept vividly in mind when talking about the overleveraged and overindebted social safety net.

Other requirements posed by Delphi management to the labour union in an eleventh-hour attempt to avoid bankruptcy included: elimination of cost-of-living pay increases (which are highly inflationary); the right to close, sell, or consolidate most of Delphi's US plants within three years; and elimination of the so-called *job bank* which is a Santa Claus benefit, yet universal in UAW contracts.

- The unaffordable *job bank* provides pay and other goodies to laid-off workers during the life of a contract, and
- its elimination would have axed 4,000 workers from these benefits, which they would have lost anyway as an after-effect of the bankruptcy.

UAW refused, and the rest is history. The labour union's decision was short-sighted and cost many more jobs, lots of worker pain, and greater loss of benefits than would have been the case had the offer been accepted. However, the UAW was right in maintaining that Delphi could not demand big sacrifices from the workers and at the same time *increase* the pay of 21 of its executives. This is an outrage which has been discussed in Chapter 8 in connection with the ongoing highly unwise destruction of the middle class in America and in Europe.

Interestingly enough, the rank and file was not total alienated by management's proposal. The way it has been reported in the press, a leaflet circulated to members by one UAW local unit declared, 'With that package, the UAW member would not be able to afford a vehicle that our products are assembled into.' *But*, the leaflet continued, 'If Delphi files for bankruptcy, the above proposal they made to the UAW will look better than the restructuring proposal it submits to courts.'[11]

This is precisely *the core of the problem* that governments, labour unions, wage-earners and salaried personnel must face in today's European and American workplace. Without deep cuts in labour costs and benefits, *China price* would wipe out the remaining industries in the US and Europe, particularly as many Western companies (GM included) have rushed to open shop in China. With this,

- consumer spending will dry up and

11 *Executive Intelligence Review*, 14 October 2004.

- bankruptcies will skyrocket, even after Western economies get out of the current economic crisis.

But everybody has to share the pain. It is simply unethical (and ineffectual) for the middle class to be penalized for what is not its fault, while bankers who crashed their institutions against the wall continue to gratify themselves with millions – instead of being brought to justice. On 24 June 2009 it was announced that virtually bankrupt Citigroup (kept alive through tens of billions of taxpayers' money) increased the salaries of its executives by 50 per cent.[12] It is revolting.

This is precisely what is meant by social injustice – but the Obama administration seems to have allowed it in total contrast to promises made prior to the November 2008 presidential election. That's a pity, because it means that its heralded conviction to create an egalitarian society is only smoke and mirrors, while its real attitude is no improvement on that of the Bush administration which preceded it.

Ethics aside, such an unbalanced approach to salaries and wages is also the road to hell – and not only because it diminishes the public's purchasing power. The whole model of the services-based Western economy of the late twentieth and early twenty-first centuries is tilting towards the downside.

The slump in America's services sector which started in April–May 2008 was still deepening by that year's end. The Institute for Supply Management's overall index and its indices for business activity recorded that new orders and employment all dropped to their lowest level since they were first compiled in 1997, but *services* had been particularly hard hit.

## 4. The Services Industry Enters a Zone of Turbulence

Dr Harold D. Koontz, my professor of business management at UCLA, taught his students that jobs can be best preserved if they belong to a well-managed viable enterprise with products that have market appeal. In the longer term, the risk lies in the fact that not all companies continue being well governed. When managements are weak in planning, organizing, staffing, directing and controlling, even apparently secure jobs become temporary.

Koontz was right. A basic ingredient of job security is sound management. Throwing money at the problem does not solve it, as the lavish amounts of taxpayers' money handed out to self-wounded banks, vehicle manufacturers and other companies demonstrate. Jobs disappear no matter how much capital the government gives away to provide life support to zombie firms – precisely because these firms are at the edge of the precipice.

The trend of rapid increasing unemployment in the US over nearly two years, shown in Figure 10. 2, makes this point. Induced by the crisis created by the lust and greed of the big banks, the rapid rise in unemployment had become so acute, particularly in the US, that one of the principal preoccupations of reasonable men and women in Washington was: 'Will the US economy founder?'

---

12 H. Duncan, 'Citigroup Staff Get 50 Per Cent Pay Rises to Beat Cuts in Bonus', *London Evening Standard*, 24 June 2009, at: http://www.thisislondon.co.uk/standard-business/article-23711445-citigroup-staff-get-50-per-cent-pay-rises-to-beat-cuts-in-bonus.do.

The response to this serious and unique crisis fed by superleveraging at all levels of society – from federal and local government to financial institutions, other companies and households and family levels has been more high leverage – this time by inflating the national debt. In addition, hidden behind the numbers which propelled the exponential curve in US employment is the fact that the industry worst hit by the economic crisis is services, and not only banking. This is serious because it suggests that:

- the 'messiah' of the Western economy is unwell, and
- those who said it was 'good news' that services rose to 80 per cent of employment in the US and 70 per cent in Europe are proven to be false prophets.

Two services industries are in particular distress: banking, the reason being the deleveraging of the bloated financial industry; and retail sales hit by the deleveraging of consumers. Even Christmas/New Year business was sharply down. In December 2008 retail sales fell by 2.7 per cent from the previous month, the sixth consecutive decline. By some estimates, American stores had their worst holiday shopping season in at least four decades.

In Europe the news from the service sector has been no better, and this did nothing to reassure people who irrationally feared the Polish plumber as the number one enemy of their job security (Chapter 7). The month-long 'work-for-free' scheme at British Airways is an example.[13] Britons are not alone in earning less. In Germany, under the government-subsidized *Kurzarbeit* (short-time working) system, short-time work is even more prevalent, with 1.25 million workers enrolled at the end of the first quarter of 2009.

From one country to the next, these schemes have had a common thread – lower labour costs – even if they differed in their conception and details. Another common ground they shared is the realization that the ability of the service industry to create more and more jobs is simply overestimated. There is a limit to the number of workplaces the services industry can create, and the risk is not just temporary unemployment but a wider destabilization. This advises against taking half-measures that:

- protect a company's human capital if the downsizing is short,
- but, if used over a prolonged period, weaken incentives for companies to restructure and for employees to recover their financial health.

Half-measures can also reduce hirings if and when the service industry's upswing comes. as For example, companies like MySpace are being outclassed by newcomers such as Facebook which are more efficient and productive in manpower than the incumbents. Therefore, they offer fewer jobs and also risk offering lower wages than those eliminated.

Few people have paid due attention to the fact that the boom in services employment during the last two decades may be a passing phenomenon – particularly at the higher end such as health services, university education and banking. As Part One brought to the reader's attention, in California the citizens rejected by a significant majority the

13 'British Airways' Staff Agree to Work for Free', *Bloomberg Businessweek*, 26 June 2009, at: http://www.businessweek.com/globalbiz/blog/europeinsight/archives/2009/06/british_airways_1.html.

proposal to balance the budget through taxation, which therefore obliged the governor to cut costs with a sharp knife. The two larger expense budget chapters, and by far, are:

- public health services and
- the University of California system

Both are services industries employing plenty of professionals. Things may be somewhat different at lower end of the services employment scale. For instance, an example from health services is hospices, places dedicated to caring rather than curing. Ironically, the latter find it difficult to fill the jobs they offer.

As our society ages, there has been something akin to a revolution in attitudes to care for people who are nearing the end of life, but few services industry workers care to do that job. They say that it is stressful to care for people suffering chronic disease of the heart or lungs, or succumbing slowly to dementia, general decay and other ills – and they crowd onto a narrow beam of service jobs where offers are limited.

(This is a wider social problem, not only an employment problem, but it is the latter that concerns us in this book. According to several estimates, by 2050 more than 25 per cent of the West's population will be over 65. At the moment that group makes up about 16 per cent, and only a quarter of them are over 80. But by 2050 the octogenarians will be a legion, comprising 40 per cent of the over 65s in countries like America, Europe and Japan).

The fact that the higher end of the services industry is entering a zone of turbulence of unknown proportions poses serious problems to governments, as they are totally unprepared for such a happening. By all likelihood this will accelerate the radical transformation under way, in which what used to be 'normal' contracts of employment, in the form of dependent full-time jobs for an unlimited period, are becoming less and less prevalent.

- *If* employment opportunities in the service industry are seriously reduced,
- *then* the increase in part-time jobs will be unstoppable, driven, to a significant extent, by a patchy demand for labour.

In turn, this will bring very a substantial need for adjustment by people, companies, governments and labour unions. Such an adjustment will turn current notions of labour contracts on their heads, in order to reflect changes in the underlying conditions in terms of offer and demand in the labour market. Adjustment of taxes and social security contributions will follow, unless economic policy-makers opt for persistent major imbalances in nation debt and for its twin – galloping inflation.

In conclusion, the crisis shaking the services industry, and its employment opportunities, is only now starting to become apparent. In all likelihood, this will lead to a radical *de facto* restructuring of the present broad range of forms of employment, which will either have to be met in terms of working patterns by a considerable increase in flexibility of labour deployment in the economy – or, alternatively, it will result in a mountain of structural unemployment. In addition:

- the problem of dequalification due to structural change will become acute, almost irrespective of rise or decline in the economy, and

- the insider–outsider conflict, which currently exists, will intensify, particularly if those who have a job (even a precarious one) press the politicians for greater workplace security – thereby locking out those who lack a job.

There is a chance that the resulting conflict will make many people angry against society, while the governments themselves become more unstable. Governments, labour unions and the electorate will face a brutal decision about whether to swim with the tide of history or against it, as economies are deeply shaken by the crisis.

In this environment, strategies that benefit union members at the expense of non-members will become anti-social. In the struggle to define a new model of labour, the biggest test may well be who will take up the role of the services industry as an employer – the way that industry did with manufacturing, and manufacturing with agriculture. 'The state' might be the answer. But when such a big employer does something like this, then Nazism, fascism and Stalinism knock at the door.

## 5. Affirmative Action is Throwing Money at the Problem

The wave of so-called *affirmative action* (AA)[14] has started in America, and its effects are murky at best. Since the beginning, discussions on AA's merits and demerits have raged at all levels of society and government, as well as in many forums. They have also been the concern of politicians, policy-makers and ordinary citizens.

In a way emulating Europe's inhibition with tackling ossified labour laws, the longer-term perception of affirmative action has been notably absent from most discussions. To the contrary, nobody can deny the presence of an angry backlash from both those who affirmative action is intended to help and people who paid the cost of AA, presented as the cost of:

- social justice,
- morality of action and
- democracy itself.

As told by a tenured full professor at a major research institution, 'When I recently received an award at work that virtually no women receive, I head a number of comments along the line of "You probably got it since they needed a woman".' [15] (Contrary to what many people think, affirmative action is not limited to promoting the minorities; it also promotes the majority, which happens to be women.)

There is also the fact that, as a long roster of cases demonstrates, affirmative action induces people – whether subject to social exclusion or poverty – to work less not harder, since *rent* takes care of them even if they put up no effort. At the same time, people with higher qualifications are passed over because positions are being reduced to make place for AA quotas. All this poses a critical question: why is AA even necessary? The answer is not self-evident.

14 Which is a misnomer.

15 *Communications of the ACM*, Vol. 38, No. 12, December 1995.

Excesses have led societies which initially did not question affirmative action to re-examine their position. For instance, minority hiring was not much of an issue in Britain, but in the mid-1990s it came under scrutiny in terms of both what was done and what was not done. In the latter case, a survey released in January 1995 by the British government's Commission for Racial Equality concluded that most big companies did little to assure equal opportunity in employment beyond verbal support for the idea.

- Many said they had no policy to spur minority hiring and no plans to create one, and,
- according to other opinions, forcing minority hiring is discrimination as British law bans race bias but sets no affirmative action criteria.

In terms of what they considered to be AA's excesses, critics said that in a technologically advanced society, only people with the skills in demand can find work. Job requirements in a knowledge society unavoidably increase the exclusion zone, but it is not the role of the state to featherbed minorities.

- To rise up from under, individuals must put up the effort, and
- only a fascist state run by a dictator and backed up by the military can order companies to do 'this' or 'that'.

When this happens it will be the ordinary people of all classes, and most particularly of the silent majority, who will be oppressed, and this oppression will be real. One can therefore understand why in 1996, when elected as Louisiana's new governor, Mike Foster ordered a halt to affirmative action programmes in state government. While acknowledging that his gesture was largely symbolic because most of Louisiana's affirmative action programmes were federally mandated or protected by state law, Foster stated:

- 'There was once a very good reason to do away with discrimination.
- [But] there is also a very, very good reason to do away with reverse discrimination'[16] (which is AA).

A year earlier, in 1995, affirmative action was on the way out in America's universities. The University of California's Board of Regents voted to end the controversial practice in their vast educational system. What the proponents of 'forced AA' failed to appreciate is that ultimately this action lowers (sometimes significantly) the quality of education.

An example of lowering of educational standards, because of silly measures by long-haired socialists, has been the abandonment of *numerus clausus* in European universities. Prior to World War II, and in the immediate post-war years, there were entry examinations to a university – which is absolutely normal because students must be qualified, and the number of available places is a fraction of the number of applicants. These exams allowed universities to select the best students, but they have been cancelled in the name of 'social justice' (read: injustice), and everybody unable to follow university studies can now subscribe (till they drop out) at taxpayers' expense.

---

16 *USA Today*, 12 January 1996.

Also in 1996, in America, a three-judge panel of the Fifth Circuit Court of Appeals, which covers Texas, Louisiana and Mississippi, declared unconstitutional the University of Texas Law School's elaborate AA system, which had already been revised several times since the early 1990s. The judges even rejected the use of affirmative action for 'the wholesome practice' of correcting racial imbalance in the student body.[17]

That case[18] involved four white students (three men, one woman) who in 1992 were denied admission to the highly selective law school, even though a number of black students with lesser qualifications were admitted. At the original trial, an Austin federal district judge agreed that the four white plaintiffs had been discriminated against. The judge ordered the University of Texas to:

- pay each of them the nominal sum of $1 and
- allow them to reapply without paying the usual fee.

The Fifth Circuit Court supported that view, noting that the Austin judge had largely based his ruling on Justice Lewis Powell's Supreme Court opinion in the original and most famous *reverse discrimination* case, *Regents of the University of California v. Bakke*, in 1978. 'To believe that a person's race controls his point of view is to stereotype him,' the Court of Appeals added.

The year 1996 saw a watershed of popular votes against the ills of so-called 'affirmative action'. By going to the polls on 5 November, Americans made decisions on more than the presidency and Congress. The citizens of California, where the state constitution permits the widespread use of referendums, also passed *Proposition 209*, which amounted to prohibition against discrimination, or preferential treatment, on grounds of gender or race.

Not only did Proposition 209 pass by a clear 54 to 46 per cent margin, but a majority of women and respectable proportions of California's ethnic minorities apparently voted in favour. The new law prevented the state government from deploying racial or sexual criteria in:

- hiring employees,
- awarding contracts or
- admission to higher education.

The issue, indeed the very definition, of affirmative action has long been controversial in California and in many other places across the US. Improperly known as 'positive discrimination', this is an unwelcome concept in a democratic society. It therefore comes at no surprise that many Americans became increasingly angry about AA:

- They believe that noble intentions have been perverted by politics, and
- their displeasure has fed through to the political system.

17 *The Economist*, 30 March 1996. The Texas Law School was giving preference to African-Americans and Hispanics, against other much better qualified candidates.

18 *Hopwood* v. *Texas*, 78 F.3d 932 (5th Cir. 1996).

Proposition 209 reverberated all over the US. The Golden State referendums have long been influencing other jurisdictions. The revolt against high taxation and the drive to limit politician's terms in office were both launched from the Pacific Coast. As the results of the referendums came in, law-makers in States of the Union noted the trend and changed their ways; if they did not, their voters did it for them.

Neither is this a matter of only race reverse discrimination. The concept underpinning AA dominates not one, but a horde, of so-called social programmes, including foreign aid. Milton Friedman, the economist and Nobel Prize winner, once noted the irony of trying to save poor countries from famine or communism by giving them money: 'The proponents of foreign aid have unwittingly adopted a basic premise of the Communist ideology that foreign aid is intended to combat,' Friedman suggested.[19]

According to William Easterly, an economist at New York University, the 'aid industry' remains a refuge for utopian social scientists whose boldness of vision is matched only by the poverty of their achievements. Easterly thinks that the now classical approach to helping the poor is seductive but dangerously wrong-headed. He also suggests that donors must be answerable to the people they claim to help.

If America was the first to take the road to AA, which has led to failure, other countries have followed on the wrong track. A 2006 report by Germany's IfW economic institute provides a example. It states that the €1 trillion ($1.4 trillion) in government aid poured into east Germany over the first five years of unification (1990–1995) has not only failed to kick-start its economy, but *has caused* the region's high unemployment. Dennis Snower, president of the Kiel-based IfW, also blamed the trade unions for pricing an entire generation of east Germans out of the labour market.

'After years of reunification, the east German labour market has yet to recover,' Professor Snower told the *Financial Times* in an interview. 'That is not in spite, but because of the massive financial transfers the region has received.'[20] Snower also made the point that after reunification, the West German trade unions played a key role in setting eastern wages at a level high enough to prevent easterners from emigrating to the west and threatening their members:

- Excessively generous unemployment benefits helped maintain these artificially high wages, causing unemployment to take root, and
- after all these years of lavish support by western Germany, eastern Germany has fallen into the classical joblessness trap where the unemployed never stop digging deeper their hole in the ground.

This is one more example of the fact that in every case where benefits are substituted for labour – whether in AA subsidies, aid or direct handouts – the result is disaster. In conclusion, not only has the so-called 'affirmative action' narrow limits, but it is also highly counterproductive and allows bad practices to take root as 'permanent social gains' – which is plain nonsense.

19 Milton Friedman, 'Foreign Economic Aid: Means and Objectives', in J. Bhagwati and R. Eckhaus, *Foreign Aid*, Harmondsworth: Penguin, 1970, p.77.

20 *Financial Times*, 16 March 2006.

## 6. Confronting the Growing Attraction of Benefits and of Self-made Unemployment

The message of section 5 was that 'affirmative action' and subsidies do not promote jobs and career opportunities. They kill initiative and therefore they kill jobs. The same is true of *permanent benefits* given to some sections of society because 'they need it' – even if this harms them.

The state supermarket has been a master in creating *self-made unemployment* which might look like a curious new term of uncertain meaning, but really carries a strong message. Some people have discovered how to make others (therefore the community as a whole) pay for their lives and pleasures. Since then:

- self-unemployment has become a profession, and
- its army of adherents, a fast-growing breed, is seeking benefits from society through any means it can muster.

The so-called 'social' (but in reality terribly *anti-social*) policies of various weak governments have created this unsupportable and irrational situation, which degrades our society and deprives people of their self-esteem. Today, the difference between the working poor and those who live on public 'assistance' is that the former decided to maintain some control over their lives because they have a sense of:

- responsibility and
- independence.

By contrast, the self-made unemployables exercise a detestable practice which can be found on both sides of the Atlantic and is condoned by the authorities. While some of the worse examples come from the EU, America is not alien to it as the whole concept underpinning unemployment assistance is twisted – and people have learned to play the system by being in and out of work.

The problem starts with the fact that unemployment benefits have been set well above minimum wages. American studies show that typically, after taxes, at a manual labour minimum wage a worker earns about $12,500 a year. By contrast, a welfare beneficiary makes $16,000 a year, including direct support, food stamps and day care for children. Hence,

- one earns more money by staying in the welfare line than by working on the assembly line, and
- this not only penalizes all of society, but permanent welfare is also one of the worse misfortunes that can hit a family, because the children, too, learn how to avoid work.

There are many reasons why the self-made unemployables see themselves as having an honourable profession. All of them revolve around the exploitation of loopholes in state benefit. to make up for their lack of educational standards, which tends to make financial self-reliance doubtful. Many of the kids who come out of this infernal machine of *state benefits*, particularly from families who rapidly produce more and more siblings, are behind the curve in:

- their upbringing,
- their learning and
- family discipline.

Their condition is compounded by the steady shrinking in the demand for unskilled labour in Western countries, and the person's unwillingness to abandon the wages of free subsistence and move ahead up society's ladder. The argument of a causal connection between poverty and benefits should be dismissed.

By contrast, there is the so-called *workfare argument*. Its principle states that unemployed people should do community work to qualify for their dole money. This is a very sound principle. The problem is that even governments that would like to take this line of action fall short of full-blooded workfare when it comes to compulsory work in return for benefits,[21] the recipients of which come under a variety of headings from stay-at-home mothers to the:

- the unemployed,
- the self-made unemployable and
- the pure cheats.

Among the latter, many capitalize on the wrong policy of giving benefits to young people to keep them off the streets – which started in the 1960s, when the number of job opportunities shrank once the destructions of World War II had been more or less repaired. This has created a generation of people for whom benefits became inseparable from their daily living.

In all fairness, much of the blame lies with governments and not only with people who seek benefits or ask the state to guarantee them lifelong employment. It is governments which, in their ineptitude, created this deplorable social situation that is difficult to correct, but should be changed. There is simply no guidance given to young people of the new generation who struggle between:

- the post-war job-for-life mentality, searching in vain for something offering such guarantees, and
- the inability to understand that seeking a job for life when there is none is a sure way to become self-unemployable.

Added to this is the fact that one of the defining economic shifts of recent times has been the increasing instability facing families. It is not only income inequality that has risen sharply since the 1970s (see Chapter 8), but also *income instability* which reflects the size of short-term income fluctuations. Studies show that short-term income volatility in America is 300 per cent higher than it was just three decades ago.

21 For instance, two British pilot projects (Project Work), one in Hull and the other in Maidstone in 1996, required the long-term unemployed to do 13 weeks of job training followed by 13 weeks of work as a condition of receiving benefit. That is an excellent initiative.

- Young people who are more flexible and better educated are better off, because they accept going from one short-term contract to another.
- By contrast, those who interrupt their studies to join unstoppable demonstrations become *de facto* self-unemployable, and they depend increasingly on benefits.

An article in the *International Herald Tribune* provided an example from the class of flexible young people described by the first bullet. Since he graduated with an architecture degree in 2000, Antonio Incorvaia held a dizzying number of jobs: graphic designer, television writer, Web editor and journalist for trade and pop culture magazines. At 31, he described himself as a 'serial trainee', but he kept on trying and opened up for himself a career as an author.[22]

Closely connected to the second bullet are the references from Chapter 9 to the anti-CPE demonstrations in Paris. These have been condemned both in France and abroad, but they also spread across borders. The students who terrorized the centre of Athens in 2009 were prodded by local opposition politicians to follow the 'French example'.

This has happened despite the fact that the French students had misunderstood their own interests, as comments made in Spain, Sweden, Britain and Germany document. Spain's *El Pais* ran a front-page article about the protests, titled 'More than a million French take to the streets to reject the youth employment plan'. Sweden's *Svenska Dagbladet* led with the headline 'Mass protests paralysed France', and gave only a simple summary of the background to events in Paris. Britain's *Daily Mail* ran an article on the protests under the headline 'Demo mobs spread anarchy across France'. In Belfast's *Telegraph*, the headline on the students' march read 'Gangs set Paris on fire in law protests'.

The German *Die Welt*, a centrist daily, accused the French student strikers of spreading 'the virus of reality denial'. Instead of welcoming an improvement to the labour market, the paper said, young people complained that the change did not immediately deliver the security they want. Reality, however, is worse than that. Not is only job security, once lost, not easily regained, but student strikers are also preparing for themselves an awful future.

Let's face it. Job instability is a major reason why young people are staying at home longer and have fewer children than before, but this does not mean that they have to adopt benefits as a way of life. This process of generational downgrading hurts society where it matters. The milking of public finances becomes worse as politicians focus more on the country's aging electorate, promising:

- higher pensions and
- better, but much more costly, healthcare.

That's the easy way. The difficult path is to take stronger positions on better education and first-time employment. Issues connected to the changing social structure and affecting young people should be given priority. For instance, because of lack of serious progress on pension reform, young people entering the labour force will have to pay higher taxes and receive lower pensions when they retire. That's not good news for the young generation, but no government cares to make that explicit (more on pensions in Part Four).

22 *International Herald Tribune*, 30 March 2006.

## 7. As Long as the European Labour Market Agonizes, There Will Be No New Employment Opportunities

The only conceivable way of stopping jobs from moving to countries with much lower wages is to redimension wages and slim down social benefits in western Europe, says Michel Camdessus, former president of the IMF and former CEO of Banque de France. This message has been brought to the public eye through a 2004 study made at the demand of the French government and aimed at reducing social costs and turning round a situation of rising unemployment.[23] Other proposals made by Camdessus are:

- Stop all the pre-retirement lay-offs.
- Initiate a programme of practical on-the-job experience.
- Authorize the retired to receive their pensions and work at the same time.

Camdessus also highlights the urgency of such measures, as over the last 30 years the working population has dwindled, youth unemployment is of the order of 24 per cent, and there is an unemployment rate of about 36 per cent of those over 50 – well prior to legal retirement age at 60.

These statistics are thought-provoking because, everything counted, they leave a quite small percentage of the population still working. In other terms, the European labour market agonizes.

The analysis presented by Camdessus suggests that the French economy is in the process of unravelling, and that by 2011 it will be growing by no more than 1.75 per cent. (In fact, in 2009 it had negative growth. This, however, was due to the ongoing global economic crisis.) The salient problem identified by the former governor of Banque de France is a lack of employment opportunities, but employment opportunities don't rise when the labour market is in agony.

Camdessus also shows that the active part of the population who must 'carry' the economy is very small because youth unemployment is high. In terms of a prescription for recovery he proposes the harmonization of France's labour laws and unemployment benefits with those of other EU countries, including the institution of laws necessary to force the unemployed to work, along with a reorganization of state agencies that deal with unemployment.

The second suggestion has been carried out, but not the first. Theoretically, it is not that easy to force the unemployed and early retirees into the job market, because governments don't like waking up sleeping dogs – and too many people, including the young, have got into the habit of being paid for doing nothing. But a few years ago Switzerland took a great initiative (in spite of socialist opposition) when a new law offered unemployed people the option to reject the first offer for a job, but:

- *if* they don't accept the second offer,
- *then* they are cut off from social assistance.

23 Michel Camdessus, 'A Beginning: Towards a New Growth for France', References made in *Executive Intelligence Review*, 5 and 12 November 2004.

Theoretically, but only theoretically, it looks like political suicide to restrict unemployment benefit because a second job has been rejected the unemployed individual. But in reality our society has promised too much which:

- it cannot afford and
- cannot deliver.

For the employed, Camdessus advocates a single labour contract, supported by a public employment service providing incentives to make possible the best deployment of the unemployed and underemployed. He also suggests that these measures should be cut in a way that improves the *mobility of labour*. (France is experimenting with the incentives scheme, but the general principle of labour mobility still has to see the light of day.)

The Camdessus report has been criticized by different parties (I personally think unfairly). The socialists said that it is against the *acquis sociaux* (endowments) and tries to dismantle them, while some right-wing politicians commented that it does not go far enough to counteract social inertia as well as embedded no-work habits.

Another reason that made the plan's critics pessimistic regarding its acceptance by politicians and the general public is that the optimization of employment at national scale would require dislocations and demographic transformations. In this, mobility of labour, which exists in America but not in Europe, is the cornerstone of success.

Everything counted, the most far-reaching of Camdessus's proposals, as well as the most controversial, concerned the issue of wage levels. The minimum wage is 'too high' said the former president of the International Monetary Fund, and this ensures that more and more jobs are outsourced abroad in countries featuring much lower wages.

This is a matter on which most experts agree. It is also an issue that divides, in terms of salaries and wages, western from eastern European countries within the EU. But it is not the only one that encounters above-average social resistance. Speaking from an American perspective, Alan S. Blinder, economics professor at Princeton University and former vice chairman of the Federal Reserve, adds that protectionist measures, too, are to blame because:

- they redistribute income from average citizen to those doing better than average, and
- they harm efficiency while taking sides in wealth distribution.

In conclusion, while a *new social model* is still trying to find its way, the *legacy social model* has become a drag on the economy, and the perception has grown that a lack of structural reforms is damaging the younger generation. Yet, several European governments are backtracking on reforms, and future weaknesses will certainly reflect such a lack of forward-looking policy, even the road ahead is more subtle than ideologically charged statements imply.

Without the smallest doubt, the new social model should restore the power of the middle class and also deal with the problem of managers – which has two aspects. The one is the quality of management shown through its deliverables; the other is its ethics. Only one-third of British companies are well-managed, a Goldman Sachs study has shown. Despite their sprawling number (or because of it), business schools have been unable to close that gap.

The question of ethics is both more difficult to track and more profound. Since ancient Greece, medical doctors have had their code of ethical behaviour, but business schools never adopted one. They tell their students that their sole mission as managers should be increasing shareholder value. That's awfully one-sided[24],because:

- it gives rise to terrible abuses and
- leaves social values by the wayside.

Managers who, through share options and bonuses ,profit handsomely from abusing their position say that a code of ethics is unnecessary, or even harmful. Crimes such as embezzlement may be punishable by law, but shareholders who feel that managers have not acted in their best interests know that suing them is an expensive and uncertain path. Managers pay the lobbyists with shareholders' money. A code of ethics might have put the brakes on looting shareholders and society at large.

24 Besides, as the 2004 to 2010 events documented, fat cats at the company's helm don't give a penny for shareholder value. They only care for their own bonuses and options.

# PART IV Pensions and the Social Safety Net

# CHAPTER 11 The Principle of Social Insurance

## 1. Bismarck's Welfare Model was Made for Yesterday's World

In 1889, 121 years ago, Otto von Bismarck, Germany's 'Iron Chancellor', introduced the first state pension for workers over 70. At that time, life expectancy for manual workers was 45 years, Germany was an upcoming industrial power, and by all accounts the cost to the state was contained.

This was the beginning of the *welfare state* which, over the following decades, developed into the *state supermarket*. Nowadays, people look to the government – and therefore to the taxpayers – as the source of pension, security, healthcare, education, unemployment benefits, protection from poverty, housing[1] and a growing shopping list of other entitlements.

The so-called social safety net, or *social insurance*, did not come overnight all over the world. Germany started it in 1889, but America's social security (which provides state pensions but not health insurance) came with the New Deal in 1935. Britain got its first state pension in 1908 (when Lloyd George instituted a pension of between one and five shillings a week for men of 70 years or older, on a means-tested basis), and healthcare in 1948 – through the very expensive and inefficient National Health Service (NHS).

This lag of 20 years for Britain and nearly half a century for America makes Bismarck the founder of 'welfare capitalism'. He was the person who passed the first package of social security laws – the brainchild of Gustav von Schmoller, the Iron Chancellor's one-man economic brains trust and a socialist. (Preoccupied with external conquest, Bismarck had delegated internal social policy to Schmoller.)

In his classic book, *Socialism*, Ludwig von Mises, the Austrian economist and mathematician, says that Bismarck's social security scheme was 'a more momentous pioneering on the way towards socialism than was (Lenin's) expropriation of the backward Russian manufacturers.'[2] It was also a balancing act – a choice between nascent social policy and armaments.

Schmoller had spent two decades working in the German social bureaucracy, including a term as chief of the 'Socialists of the Chair' (the *Kathedersozialisten*) and was the founder of the so-called 'Younger Historical School' of economists. That school provided the intellectual underpinning for Bismarck's social policies. It is, however, worth noting that, according to several historians:

- The driving force behind the efforts of both Bismarck and Schmoller was not altruism, but fear.

1 At least in France, where housing has become a 'right'.

2 Ludwig von Mises, *Socialism: An Economic and Sociological Analysis*, Jonathan Cape, London, 1936.

- Their fear was that the German proletariat would resort to revolution *if* something was not done to bring them into the mainstream of society.

Critics say that Bismarck's initiative and that of his imitators, before and after World War I, were shaped for yesterday's world, not that of today's and tomorrow's. In 1935 when President Roosevelt set up America's social security system, and in 1936 when Léon Blum, the French prime minister, instituted social security, the official pension age was 65; three years beyond the lifespan of the typical citizen. Therefore:

- In the late nineteenth/early twentieth centuries, state-sponsored retirement was designed to be a brief sunset to life, for a rather limited number of people.
- By contrast, in the twenty-first century not only is retirement for everyone, but it also runs as long as 20 years or more.

In European countries where people retire around 60, the average retirement lasts more than a quarter of a century. In America the official pension age is 66, but the average American retires at 64 and can then expect to live for at least another 16 years. On both sides of the Atlantic these statistics turn on their heads all calculations about financing retirement plans.

At the same time, the ratio of retired people to those working and contributing to social security has been totally destabilized because of demographics (more on this later in this chapter and in Chapter 12). The average spending on public pensions across the OECD for retirement purposes is now the equivalent of over 7 per cent[3] of GDP – or 3,500 per cent of what it cost in America back in 1935.[4]

Worse still, in some countries the current costs of retirement benefits to the common purse could double by 2050. To this wholesome amount should be added the cost of private pensions and extra spending on health and long-term care – which is enough to bankrupt even the richest economy.

The financial impact of these statistics is particularly depressing in Europe because its relative weight in the world economy is doomed to decline. This will further weaken its ability to fund welfare programmes whose roots go back to the nineteenth century and the ideological contests that followed the first Great Depression. But, even in America, the time has come for restructuring entitlements. In California, Arnold Schwarzenegger has made plain his desire to:

- chip away at what he described in July 2009 as 'unsustainable retiree pension formulas', and
- revisit promises 'that are overly burdensome on our state budgets'[5] – indeed, on the budget of every country on the globe.

Some economists say that the mistake made by Otto von Bismarck, Lloyd George, Franklin Roosevelt, Léon Blum and other heads of state was to base social security on the

3 To which should be added the public cost of health insurance, ranging from 8 per cent of GDP in continental Europe to about 15 per cent in the US.

4 At Roosevelt's time the cost of social security was 0.2 per cent of the then US GDP.

5 'Reforming State Employee Retirement Compensation', Office of the Governor Fact Sheet, 1 July 2009, at: http://gov.ca.gov/index.php?/fact-sheet/12836/.

working people's contribution rather than investing that money and make it grow. That's a half-baked critique, and not only because the concept of a private pension did not exist in 1889, 1908 or the mid-1930s.

- The experience of Chile with converting from public to private pensions and investing in equities has been close to disastrous.
- Private pension funds, which earlier in this century went long on equities and most unwisely entered 'alternative investments',[6] lost over 25 per cent of their wealth with the 2007–2011 economic crisis.[7]

It is no secret that all over the world private-sector pensions have been ravaged by the global financial crisis. Ireland's defined benefit schemes provide an example. They presently cover around 500,000 workers, but they no longer meet the minimum solvency standard set by the Irish pensions regulator. The industry forecasts that 40 per cent of these entities will be forced to close,[8] with great distress to the pensioners.

People relying solely on the basic state pension to see them through retirement (roughly half the working population) are not much better off because, as the ongoing deep economic crisis demonstrates, the government, too, may go bankrupt and become unable to meet to its obligations. According to some estimates, the cost of state pensions in Ireland will rise from 5.5 per cent of GDP to 15.5 per cent by 2050 – which is plainly unaffordable.

Neither is this situation 'typically Irish'. It prevails all over the Western world and is a direct result of decisions on state pensions reached back in 1935 and 1936, respectively in the US and France – precisely the *pay-as-you-go* system we have been discussing. Three-quarters of a century down the line, this solution which, in its time, seemed 'fair' is hitting the wall.

There is also the other side of the coin. American economists have estimated that if social security had not followed the *pay-as-you-go* principle, but instead had invested the special taxation money in equities since the beginning (that is, since 1935), it would have owned nearly every company on the stock exchange by now. And it would have become an unstable monster like Fanny Mae and Freddie Mac.

These statistics and economic opinions lead us to the conclusion that it is not Bismarck's original concept, but the effect of the mass society augmented by mismanagement which caused the social security process to fail. The principal fault lies with governments which adopted an increasingly one-dimensional view of citizens' pensions – being afraid of change, rather than managing it.

## 2. Devaluing the Individuals as 'Savers'

Retirement and pension plans are differ strongly among EU countries despite fairly similar social conditions and mortality rates. Some jurisdictions exhibit very early retirement, while others manage to keep 'silver' workers on the job (see section 6). It is difficult to say how many of these differences are driven by pension laws and how many by political expedience.

---

6 Which has been a cheat. See D.N. Chorafas, *Alternative Investments and the Mismanagement of Risk*, Macmillan/ Palgrave, London, 2003.

7 Some have been really dragged down by the size of their equity and leveraged alternative investments holdings.

8 *Financial Times*, 8 March 2010.

The fact that endowments keep on increasing makes it even more difficult to define how much a pensioner should cost the taxpayer. For instance, should it cost more or less than spending for a prisoner? As an example, California spends $49,000 a year on each prisoner, almost twice the US average.

Another question concerns quality of work. Should it or should it not be part of the retirement equation? There is wide variation in quality of work across EU countries. Everything counted, in terms of an honest year's deliverables, some member nations have poor work standards while others show high overall quality of work – which ultimately:

- is reflected in productivity,
- limits wage inflation and
- improves the country's ability to compete in the global market.

There is no evidence that the questions the preceding paragraphs have posed have been subjects of discussions at EU 'summits', and the same is true of the affordability and sustainability of the mare's nest of current entitlements. This is a pity, because the clock of the taxpayers' revolt (if not outright bankruptcy) is ticking.

Eager to please everybody with all sorts of goods, which the state supermarket cannot afford to offer, governments have reached the crossroads of a decision between increasing taxes and reducing entitlements. The time for ever more increases in retirement benefits and in healthcare is past. Governments cannot afford to be healthcare *and* retirement plans treasurers.

- Big spending,
- ineptitude and
- the mass effect

saw to it that instead of improvement there has been deterioration. What is at work today is not passive job insecurity, but active dissatisfaction. Working people are in fear of losing jobs that they need for livelihoods, and they are increasingly uncertain about their pensions as the overcrowded and overleveraged social security system goes up against the wall.

One way to face the future challenges *now*, not after it is too late, is to induce people to save – rather than buy on debt – which would permit them to have control over their retirement money and also reduce the state's pension commitments. A study by the French Institute Nationale de Statistiques has documented that *on average* a couple of pensioned people are better off financially than a working couple with two kids.

As we will also see in section 3, developing countries should not kid themselves by thinking that in terms of state-supported pensions, they will do better than today's industrial states. Apart the downsides already discussed, state-run welfare systems are also open to political manipulation. *Inter alia*, in recent years politicians in several countries have tried to keep down the official figures on the cost of endowments, but economists have managed to get startling statistics. One concerns pensioners aged 65 and over as a percentage of the labour force as of 2009:

- In Japan pensioners constitute 36 per cent of the labour force, and the forecast is that it will double to over 70 per cent by 2050.

- In Italy, these two crucial numbers are a little over 30 per cent, rising to nearly 60 per cent.

Germany follows closely on Italy's heels with a little over 30 per cent and 55 per cent; in France they are about 27 per cent and 42 per cent; in Britain, 26 per cent, and 39 per cent; and in America, not quite 20 per cent, and nearly 40 per cent. But look at three of the BRICS (Brazil, Russia, India, China):

- In Russia, pensioners at age 65 or over constitute roughly 17 per cent of the working population, but the projection for 2050 puts their share to almost 40 per cent (not too different a pattern from America's).
- In China, currently the first figure is 12 per cent, zooming up to 40 per cent in 2050 – worse than Japan, Germany and Italy as they now stand.
- In India, the current figure is less than 10 per cent, but will exceed 20 per cent in 2050 according to projections – higher than the American percentage in 2009.[9]

This having been said, it has must be pointed out that if the state supermarket is a prescription for failure, individual solutions – including private pensions and the various money funds – are by no means the sure way to success. No investment is risk-free and, no matter how you look at it, pensions are investments (see also the discussion on annuities in Chapter 12).

Such dismal statistics have led several Western governments to conclude that their pension and healthcare promises will soon become truly unaffordable. Therefore, some of them have embarked on reforms, but so far only timidly because they fear public reaction – as they fail to publicly explain that nineteenth-century-style social security is unsustainable.

- With an eye on the next election, politicians hardly rush to introduce unpopular measures that may not bear fruit for years – but they are unavoidable.
- In addition, the outline of the changes needed is uncertain because it has not been properly studied, particularly with emphasis on the longer term.

The only thing that is clear is that to avoid fiscal meltdown, public pensions and healthcare provision will have to be severely reined back. For the time being, precisely the opposite is being done as evidenced by Barack Obama's 'healthcare for all' package. This goes against logic which suggests that new policies need to be introduced with:

- the retirement age changed,
- healthcare costs shared and
- social taxes levied while endowments shrink.

What is true of the Western countries today will be true of developing countries tomorrow. Over a century ago, in the 1880s, planet Earth supported a billion people. Now there are more than six-and-a half billion of us, and while in Western countries birth rates are generally shrinking, in less developed countries birth rates are booming.

9 *The Economist*, 9 May 2009.

There is also a spectacular increase in longevity (Chapter 12). People live much longer. At the time of Jesus Christ the average life expectancy worldwide was 30 years or less. A century ago it was about 40 to 45 years. Now this has increased everywhere by another 15 to 20 years and, in the West, up to and beyond 80 years.

Moreover (with a few exceptions) infant mortality is more or less under control – in the West because of better nutrition, exercise and preventive medicine; in other countries as a result of economic and medical aid. Some projections say that in less than a quarter of a century a person of 65 may be physically comparable to a 45-year-old of today.

All this is creating a very different world than that of Bismarck, and his social medicine, which was *avant garde* in the late nineteenth century, but has become poisonous in today's mass society. The ability of a modern state, whose finances are overstretched, to support state supermarket policies has been declining at an accelerating rate. Pursuing a utopian goal has never been a prescription for success.

## 3. The Price of Unaffordable Promises and Claims

Promises oblige only those who listen to them, says Charles Pasqua, the French politician. Europeans are now paying the price of promises made by the generation that came out of World War II, which provided verbal assurance of secure, well-paid and full employment, good pensions, healthcare for everyone and plenty of other benefits that cannot be maintained in the longer run. Nobody seems to have examined whether the European economy could afford all these expenses.

*If* any such study was done, *then* its foundations were meagre and unsatisfactory. In 1945, when today's prevailing pension plans were framed, for each retired person there were four people working[10] (depending on the country) – that is, earning money and contributing to social security. Currently the ratio is 1 to 1.5 (also depending on the country) – and it continues to become slimmer.

There is no evidence that this trend may reverse in the EU, and, as it stands, the retirees to working people ratio is clearly affordable and unsustainable. Women no longer have enough babies to keep up the numbers. Moreover, the so-called 'baby-boom' generation, born after World War II, has begun to retire, which will make matters worse.

Because the ranks of those who used to finance it through their taxes are shrinking, the state supermarket's welfare model is known to be broken, but politicians have neither the vision nor the courage to change it. As the old Europe's population ages, the cost of providing generous state pensions under the current rules is insupportable.

- Big increases in tax rates will be needed to balance the books, and
- several studies show that these are much bigger than most politicians think voters will accept.

In addition, as will be recalled from Part Two, another characteristically European problem can also be blamed on the state supermarket: chronically high unemployment

10 This figure comes from western Europe. In 1950 the OECD countries had seven people aged 20–64 for every person aged 65 and over – a ratio of one to seven under the aforementioned metrics. Now it is one or a little more than one, except in OECD countries (like Mexico) where the birth rate has not yet collapsed.

which adds its weight on to the governments' budgets and, by extension, on to the national debt. As we have seen, most economists attribute it to a combination of employment-protection laws, and generous unemployment benefits.

- Ask voters if they prefer low taxes to high taxes and a vast majority will say 'low taxes'.
- Ask them whether they prefer big pensions or small pensions and a large majority will say 'big pensions'.

This is one of the trickiest political issues in any electoral campaign. No wonder that a succession of governments has chosen to ignore the pension problem, deterred by the complexity of the issue and by public opposition, particularly that of the trade unions which don't seem to understand that a one-way street leads to a dead end.

The alarm bells are ringing because the strains on the system are now so intense that governments may not be able to delay the needed overhaul forever. The 1 to 1.5 ratio of pensioners to those working means the social security deficit will grow and grow unless a package of measures is introduced that involves:

- cutting pensions,
- raising the retirement age or
- significantly increasing employees' contributions.

Instead of lowering the retirement age from 65 to 60, as some countries have said they want to do, they should raise it to 68, 70 and beyond. Banning mandatory retirement ages in the private sector, as America has done, is a sensible initiative, and the same is true of creating conditions in which people can retire more gradually (see section 5).

Half-measures don't work. Some recent increases of the retirement age to 67 or 68 have done no more than compensate for the rise in life expectancy. Out-of-the-box solutions should be welcome, but so far only Denmark has taken the step of indexing the pensionable age to life expectancy.

These references explain how tough it is for the state supermarket (and the politicians who have been promoting it) to make ends meet. Developing countries should take notice, because they are falling into the same trap by introducing phased pension schemes that:

- copy those of the West,
- are run by the state and
- pay for pensions from the money received from those in work.

Emerging countries can learn from the mistakes that EU states and America have made because, as far as future pensions are concerned, the challenges facing them are no different to those confronting the West. Investment options are by no means unlimited, and this is true of both pension funds and individual savers. The four main classes are:

- cash,
- bonds,
- equities (more risky than bonds) and
- other, even more risky investments.

Cash is depreciating year-on-year due to inflation (as is the nominal value of other investments). This is supposedly compensated by the interest paid on deposits, but when governments and central banks bring the interest rate down to nearly zero per cent (Federal Reserve, Bank of England) or even 1 per cent (European Central Bank), they severely penalize savers.

Fixed-income instruments (bonds) can be of several kinds. They are subject to market risk (a function of interest rates and currencies) and credit risk, depending on the authority issuing the bond. The latter broadly divide into sovereigns, private companies and other entities (some of which are government-backed).

The issuer may default. Walter Wriston, the former CEO of Citibank, said that countries don't go into bankruptcy. But Argentina went bankrupt in December 2001 and Ecuador followed some years later (these are only two examples among many). Companies and municipalities also default.

Investment advisors suggest that stock markets have a better return in the longer run. That may be true, but pension funds and other investors lost some 50 per cent of their capital in equities as the global stock markets crashed in 2008 and up to March 2009. 'More upside' in good times is followed by 'more downside' in cases of adversity.

Because of the risks they involve (including many opaque and poorly understood exposures), alternative investments[11] are neither for savers nor for pension funds. These include structured products (based on derivatives), index trackers, commodities, hedge funds, private equity and more. To them (as well as to equities) applies the saying that 'the best way to make a small fortune at Wall Street is to start with a big one'.

Large pension funds like Japan's Government Pension Investment (over $1 trillion), Norway's government pension scheme ($420 billion), the Netherland's ABP ($250 billion), California's CalPERS (nearly $200 billion), and America's Federal Retirement Thrift (also $200 billion) have investment managers theoretically able to weather storms. Still, when in 2008 the Californian housing market descended into the abyss and LandSource Communities Development, a housing partnership, fell into bankruptcy, CalPERS lost close to $1 billion.[12]

Big pension funds can afford these shocks and hope to recover the money lost in investments. This is more difficult with individuals, who may also confront other adversities. As an example, in the early years of the twenty-first century retirees worldwide have been facing increasing challenges:

- The value of their savings has shrunk because of falling interest rates and bond yields.
- The income from savings in banks has been slashed by the wrong policy of governments which taxes income from savings.
- The performance of largely mismanaged company retirements funds has been dismal.[13]

11 D.N. Chorafas, *Alternative Investments and the Mismanagement of Risk*, Macmillan/Palgrave, London, 2003.

12 Also, its private equity investments fell 31 per cent, while investments in public equities lost 28 per cent.

13 This has happened twice during the last decade. In the US, pensioners who have put their trust in equity funds saw their retirement income fall by 54 per cent between 1999 and 2002. In 1999 many investors were caught up in the euphoria of the technology bubble, and were overexposed to equities. And, with the 2007–2011 economic and banking crisis, many equity funds and pension funds lost a quarter or more of the wealth under their watch. Berkshire of Warren Buffett (a renowned investor) lost 25 per cent of its assets in the 2008 general debacle.

This, however, in no way means that one has to depend 100 per cent on the state; as already stated, social security in many Western countries is virtually bankrupt. In the aftermath of all this, according to some estimates, people should expect that if they depend on only one source for their pension, their potential retirement income will fall. The better alternative is to diversify the sources of one's income at retirement.

## 4. 'Equality and Security': A Modern Myth

'This couple, *Equality/Security*, is one of principal causes of the *French divorce*,' writes Alain-Gerard Slama. 'It cannot be maintained without the detriment of *freedom* – which must be the priority value in a democracy.'[14] Slama is right. Equality and security are modern myths. In addition, freedom has a variable geometry[15] while:

- equality has no clearly defined limits, and
- in a world of some 6.8 billion souls, with permeable borders,[16] economic security makes no more sense.

Under the prevailing conditions of globalization, and of the currently massive legal and illegal immigration, a welfare system can degenerate into *crony socialism*. In most EU countries, as well as in North America and elsewhere, this is precisely what has happened to the nanny state which, even if bankrupt, has found a way of becoming:

- unusually protective for those inside it and
- extraordinarily hard to crack for those who are not accepted as full members of a closed society.

One of the reasons for this bifurcation is that social insurability is too vague as a reference term, and it is interpreted in different ways by different people according to their desires. This makes difficult a good understanding of the insurance economics underpinning the state supermarket and blurs what should have been an in-depth debate on the dividing line between private and public economic contributions. It also became difficult:

- to map the limits of the welfare state within society, including demographic issues (Chapter 12), and
- compare, for reasons of optimization, the many ways in which different viewpoints can be debated, all the way to regulation.

The themes in these two bullets should be the subjects of careful analysis with a view towards the future, and of public discussion. This is not being done, and that is a pity, particularly in view of the fact that the dependency ratio of population aged 65 and

---

14 *Le Figaro Magazine*, 11 March 2006 (emphasis added)

15 An American judge expressed this beautifully when he said to the defendant who claimed to have exercised his Fifth Amendment freedom: 'Your freedom ends where your neighbor's nose begins.'

16 D.N. Chorafas, *Globalization's Limits: Conflicting National Interests in Trade and Finance*, Gower, Aldershot, 2009.

over as a percentage of the population aged 20 to 64 continues to increase. Everything counted, the best approach for governments would be to:

- admit the fact that 'equality and security' is a myth and
- make cuts in entitlement programmes the subject of an *open public debate* in which participants come up with concrete proposals, not empty words.

Some politicians have the courage to say so publicly. If Germany does not drastically ease burdens on employers, said then Economics Minister Günther Rexrodt back in 1994, 'we will become the world champions at exporting jobs rather than goods'.[17] Also, on 25 February 2004, testifying about the ballooning federal budget deficit Alan Greenspan, then chairman of the Federal Reserve, demanded a reduction in social security and Medicare benefits for workers at or near retirement age.[18]

Talking about what lies ahead for the American government, the Fed chairman further pointed out that 'we will eventually have no choice but to make significant structural adjustments in the major retirement programs'. He added that this should be done 'as soon as possible' on the grounds that the government was overcommitted in spending on:

- required benefits and
- health insurance.

'I think it is terribly important to make certain that we communicate to the people who are about to retire, what it is they are going to have to live with,' Greenspan stated, urging Congress to push up the retirement age for social security and Medicare, and to reduce the cost-of-living increases linked to inflation. (According to Dr Greenspan, Medicare is the main fiscal problem, partly due to the fact that advances in medical technology allow people to live longer, thereby increasing the level of spending for retiree healthcare.)

Left unchecked, expenses for healthcare, retirement and unemployment benefits become impossible to manage. The challenge they are posing is easier to handle in an economic climate of reasonably rapid growth, brief recessions and rising employment – as in Europe of the immediate post-World War II years.

- This state of affairs has disappeared forever, and
- today economists point to the rich social safety net as the key culprit undermining the EU's competitiveness.

From Britain to Greece and from Spain to Scandinavia, European leaders are facing rising budget deficits, deteriorating pension plans and lavish healthcare benefits. Therefore, they are under heavy pressure to find programmes that cost less and to encourage employment instead of widespread time on the dole.

For their part, private individuals are left to wonder what happened to all those promises of 'great prosperity', and why the *demons* of their societies were right. In his

17 *Business Week*, 24 January 1994.

18 *Executive Intelligence Review*, 5 March 2004.

book, *The Road to Serfdom*, F.A. Hayek, the economist,[19] described this process of believing in Santa Claus two-thirds of a century ago:

> *The people may have agreed on adopting a system of directed economy because they have been convinced that it will produce great prosperity... the goal of (state) planning (was) described by some such term as 'common welfare', which only conceals the absence of real agreement on the ends ... [but] then it will appear that the agreement on the desirability of planning is not supported by agreement on the ends the plan is to serve.*[20]

This is precisely the point that we have reached. There is general disagreement on the ends social insurance should pursue, and therefore what its plan should serve. Having put forward no common goal, including that connected to the pain of financing it, there is no way that all members and factions of society can move together in the same direction.

The *pay-as-you-go* principle, which in most industrial countries is the biggest source of finance for retirement income, is broken, but, as we saw in section 3, the alternatives have downsides which don't make them appealing as wholesome solutions. Nevertheless, as labour forces are starting to contract and the number of pensioners is rising, there is an urgent need for alternatives to be carefully studied in terms of:

- risk and
- return.

It is not just that the myth of 'equality and security' has been exposed. Even more important is the fact that the next generations will fall flat under the weight of the present generation's endowments. Some economists estimate that if nothing is done, the cost of state pensions in developed countries will almost double, from an average of 7.7 per cent of GDP now to more 15 per cent by 2050, while in Japan and some western European countries it could rise to well above 20 per cent.

Have the politicians who brought this disaster upon their countries been careless, incompetent, big-headed, theorists or believers in Louis XIV's dictum '*Après moi le deluge*'? The answer is a cocktail of these reasons. Otherwise, it is difficult to explain that *net* mandatory pension benefits (as a percentage of net median earnings) are 105 per cent in the Netherlands, 85 per cent in Spain, 72 per cent in Italy, 67 per cent in Sweden and so on[21] – while over and above that comes the coverage of sprawling health costs which have only one way to go – upwards.

## 5. Defined Benefits and Defined Contributions

Many people live under the fallacious assumption that whether we talk of pensions, healthcare or other entitlements, the nearest possible metaphor to a solution is manna from heaven. As the Bible suggests, manna is a gift from God; the sky has been friendly,

19 And disciple of Carl Menger

20 F.A. Hayek, *The Road to Serfdom*, Routledge, London, 1944.

21 *The Economist*, 27 June 2009.

and the needy (which means everybody) are benefiting from divine generosity distributed free as compensation for mankind's good deeds.

Nothing is further from the truth. Nobody but the recipients of the endowments pays for all these goodies, and they don't even get back all of their money, because plenty is lost due to inefficiency. Moreover, a more than negligible share is eaten up by administrative expenses (read: the bureaucracy). The state supermarket picks 'more and more' out of the pockets of its citizens.

When social security started in the mid-1930s in America, it was funded by a 2 per cent payroll tax; that has now ballooned to a two-digit figure. Later on, another 2.9 per cent went on Medicare, and this also took an upward path. Theoretically, it is politically difficult to keep raising taxes; practically, it is politically deadly to even talk of reducing 'benefits'. There seems to be just one recourse:

- changing the way the system handles other people's money, and
- redimensioning endowments and making their management more cost-effective.

The change which took place in regard to pensions in US private industry shows how radical the switch can be when the old model is no longer affordable. This has been a painful (for employees) but interesting experience, which can serve as eye-opener at a time when public pension schemes oscillate between unaffordability and rebirth.

Starting with the fundamentals, pensions have always been expensive to provide, whether financed by the taxpayer or a company. Still, in the 1950s and 1960s, when large corporations and their earnings were stable, an increasing percentage of American employees received generous pensions based on:

- their job tenure and
- their wage or salary histories.

The retirement pay-out of a *defined benefits* plan was guaranteed by the employer, in much the way that government guaranteed social security. But this type of private retirement coverage began to be phased out by the late 1980s. Employers baulked at the cost of defined benefit schemes, in which pensioners are paid a proportion of their final salaries. Many defined benefits plans have been closed down to new members or discontinued altogether.[22] (These are the so-called 'closed' schemes which, in Britain, outnumber 'open' ones by more than three to one.)

Ironically, governments learned nothing from this experience and, although they faced similar challenges, they continued with final-salary pension plans. Critics say that the first reason is that the public sector is too paternalistic and the second is that the true cost of social security pensions is not being properly estimated.

In the background of this criticism lies the fact that the public sector has not discovered the magic formula. Indeed, it faces the same costs as the private sector. Government

22 Alternatively, new legislation may allow them to be modified. Millions of workers could be poorer when they retire because of a government plan that would allow the terms of their pension schemes to be rewritten, said a news item in *The Times*. Behind it was the fact that the British pensions minister had confirmed that he is considering legislation that would make it easier for the trustees of private-sector defined benefit schemes to water down crucial member safeguards (*The Times*, 20 September 2010).

employees are living longer, just as private-sector workers are, and their wages are rising. The fact that the cost is being disguised has two consequences:

- Governments are building up a huge future liability that taxpayers will be required to meet.[23]
- Public employees are getting a much better deal than those of the private sector which has switched to *defined contribution* pension schemes.

In the 1990s and thereafter, heightened competition and an aging workforce led corporations to shed pension obligations in favour of optional defined contribution plans, in which the employee takes on the risk of market ups and downs. Unlike the traditional defined benefits pensions, the evolving new sort of company pensions could actually run out of money:

- if the retiree lives too long or
- if the stock market crashes and the debt instrument issuers default.

These are not hypotheses. According to some fairly well-documented accounts, the assets of American private pensions dropped by some $1.1 trillion, or 19 per cent – a big fall. Of course, Kirk Kerkorian lost $8 billion in the market upheaval, but still has $3 billion left; and Warren Buffett lost $10 billion, but this can hardly hurt as he was left with over $30 billion. Pensioners don't have that sort of cushion.

Critics of investments carrying significant market and credit risks point out that rather than guaranteeing retirement incomes, this approach benefits the stock market and fund managers – while, for pensioners, it leaves much to be desired. This criticism goes to the heart of private pension fund practices which have been often touted as a solution to the pension crisis. The pros are taking Chile's private pensions as an example, but its not-so-successful privatization of pension plans hardly qualifies for that purpose.

Down to basics, a golden rule of investment is the preservation of capital, as well as the appreciation of an age-old correlation: higher earnings are accompanied by higher risks – and risk is generally poorly managed all over the financial industry, including pension funds. If this were not the case, we would not have been in the mess of the 2007–20011 severe economic and banking crisis.

Few politicians, bankers and private citizens appreciate that poor risk management has fatal consequences among the financially weaker citizens. Even worse is the fact that schools don't teach the fundamentals of personal finance. Yet, there is little doubt that defined contributions is becoming the rule in private pensions, and this means that:

- people should be financially responsible for their own retirement, and
- they should have their own retirement plan because it is not a good idea to rely completely on either the state supermarket or a nanny company.

Being in charge of one's pension plan has two prerequisites. First, starting at a young age, employees and workers should begin to put aside money for retirement. And, second,

---

23 For instance, the Bank of England's funded a defined benefits pension scheme which slipped into deficit in recent years (*The Economist*, 11 July 2009).

they must learn how to manage their finances all the way to their pensions. This is evidently a tall order because neither the spirit of saving money nor the notion of risk management is taught at school or in the family – as should be the case.

In addition, workers in struggling companies have suddenly realized that their pensions are insecure even if these were 'final salary schemes'. A major underlying reason has been underfunding, based on the supposition that 'the worst will never happen' – which time and again proves to be a hopelessly inadequate dictum for those who wanted to build a decent pension.

In some ways emulating the government social security schemes, many firms are reckless in financing their pension plans. For instance, the hole in American car-makers' pension funds is more than twice as big as was thought. Back in 2003, a study by Goldman Sachs said that much, pointing out that deficits were understated by $40 billion because car companies' accounts assumed that there would be no future increase in pension benefits.[24] The bankruptcies of General Motors and Chrysler in 2009 proved Goldman Sachs right.[25]

Judged realistically for what they are, the choices in regard to public and private pensions are stark and, whether we talk of the US or the EU, politicians are not known to be busy in finding a radical solution that can replace the current crumbling pensions structures. They are more prone to enacting some modest adjustments which have short legs. 'You can do a lot of small things,' says a bureaucratic proverb. So much the better,

- *if* these small things have no consequences, and you know it in advance, and
- *if* those who hear about them believe that, at long last, politicians have found the courage to do 'something'.

Economists, too, are not known for having worked out a better solution to the pension problem, despite the torrent of Nobel Prizes. Most economists suggest the obvious: that the ultimate answer to the social security and other pension problems is stronger economic growth which brings greater wealth.

It needs no explanation that stronger economic development makes it easier to shoulder the burden of an aging population. The problem is that rapid economic growth is nowadays a characteristic of a few developing nations, not of the EU, America and Japan. Trying to jump-start the economy is a high-wire act, and such acts hurt when they fail.

## 6. Silver Workers: Instituting a Policy of Gradual Retirement

*Gradual retirement* essentially means partial or part-time retirement, which offers a transitional period between full-time employment and full retirement. In lieu of working full-time one day and fully retiring the next, one can reduce one's working hours according to graduated (and agreed) schedules while drawing part-time pay and some kind of state-subsidized partial pension.

---

24 *Financial Times*, 23–24 August 2003.

25 There has also been the case of Enron whose bankruptcy caused its employees to be hit by a triple whammy: they lost their jobs, their pensions and their savings invested in the stock of the company for which they worked.

In a way we are going full circle to a pre-Bismarck world, where work had no formal stopping point. In the opinion of a growing number of economists, preparations for this major transition should start now to ensure that when the inevitable takes place there is no massive social shock.

This concept of *silver professionals* and *silver workers* may well be the 'out-of-the box' solution to a major social problem, and therefore it is attracting much more than casual interest among open-eyed politicians and ordinary citizens. Interested parties include (in alphabetical order):

- European Foundation for the Improvement of Working Conditions
- European Parliament
- Geneva Association
- Geneva International Network on Ageing (GINA)
- International Labour Organization (ILO)
- International Social Security Association (ISSA)
- Organization of Economic Cooperation and Development (OECD)
- UN Economic and Social Commission for Europe

The bottom line is *proactive aging* which essentially means productive aging, and its benefits may be society-wide. Only those whom the state supermarket and its inordinate welfare policies have turned pensioners, twiddling their thumbs day after day will be insensitive to the concept of proactive aging.

In fact, there are practical, as well as purely economic, reasons for such a transition. People are living longer; according to some accounts, life expectancy has been rising by two or three years for every ten that pass, despite repeated forecasts that it was about to reach its limit (which is, however, true in some countries, such as Russia). And there are (also non-economic) benefits for both

- employees and
- employers.

For older employees, gradual retirement makes it possible for them to adapt their work to their changing abilities, reduces the stress from doing nothing, increases the satisfaction of being productive and offers the opportunity to benefit psychologically from continued membership of a work team. At the same time, it provides older workers with free time to develop other, more personal, activities and interests.

The argument that older people have low productivity and are unable to concentrate on their work is a non-starter. Not only is the correlation between age and intellect not equal to –1 (minus one), but also (sometimes) age and intellect move in unison. There is a fundamental difference between:

- a person's chronological age, measured since birth, and
- intellectual age, describing the state of physical and mental fitness.

In the modern world, particularly in developed countries, a person over 60 years of age is in a far better psychological and physical condition than people in the nineteenth century were at the age of 40. At 60, or even at 80, we can be much younger intellectually than we have ever been before. And, with few exceptions, the situation is improving.

Moreover, one must account for the difference between *fluid intelligence* and *crystallized intelligence*. Fluid intelligence (including the ability to adjust rapidly to new situations as well as numerical skills) might be reduced in middle age, although even this is by no means certain. Great thinkers, like Einstein, generally do their most innovative work before they are 40, but others, like Ralph Waldo Emerson, continue to be creative until they die at an advanced age.

An example of fluid intelligence is provided by the snap answer Bandar bin Sultan gave to President Reagan on 24 October 1983 when he became Saudi Arabia's ambassador to the US. (Bandar had briefly met Ronald Reagan in California in the Carter years.) The US president cut short the ambassador's presentation to exclaim:

'You know something? You came a long way. When I first met you, you were a young major in your air force and now you are an ambassador of your country to the United States of America.'

'Well, Mr. President [answered Bandar], you didn't do too shabbily yourself. When I first met you, you were an unemployed governor, and now you are president of the greatest country in the world.'[26]

In contrast to fluid intelligence, crystallized intelligence includes a wealth of knowledge, experience, verbal ability and more. Provided one remains active, this continues at much the same level or even improves with age. The real issue, therefore, is not that our society is crumbling under the weight of an aging population but:

- how we can best exploit our throw-away human resources, and
- how we can integrate them into a whole range of productive activities, in which the experience of the old and the energy of the young can help provide a better future.

Advantages include: gains in skills and expertise as new workers learn specific contributions from older workers who are retained within the firm. This amounts to: technology transfer; significant increases in job satisfaction whenever the firm is in a position to retain the older employee in interesting work; and better hand-holding with customers, as the latter find older workers friendlier and more helpful

Retailers like Wal-Mart have started hiring pensioners precisely for these reasons. In addition, skills shortages are already creating opportunities for specialists and workers who have been pushed into retirement by inflexible labour laws. A dearth of German engineers has caused companies to bring back silver workers. Thinking of the longer term, the extension of working life that gradual retirement makes possible is generating a new environment which, apart other benefits, counterbalances the uncertainties of pensions by providing income from flexible part-time work after retirement age. *Proactive aging* is a very useful concept, conveying the idea that:

- older people could continue to make an economic and social contribution, and
- do so in a manner that sustains their physical and mental health.

---

26 David B. Ottaway, *The King's Messenger*, Walter & Company, New York, 2008

The health benefits should never be underestimated. Some years ago a study found that senior bankers who retire die two years later, no matter what their retirement age. Nor is it an inspiring prospect to die while watching stupid TV shows. Work can keep people alive longer. Research documents that, other things being equal, people who remain at work have lower death rates than their retired peers – and they tend to be happier, too.

## 7. Healthcare: The Public Purse's Abyss

Otto von Bismarck was not only the great innovator in state pensions; he also believed that the ordinary worker 'is unsure if he will always be healthy and he can predict that he will reach old age and be unable to work. If he falls into poverty, and be that only through prolonged illness, he will find himself totally helpless.'[27]

Therefore, in 1883, six years prior to the pensions system, Bismarck introduced a health insurance law requiring companies and workers to contribute to the costs of healthcare. It is interesting to note that this concept of insurance against adverse health events was not totally alien, but until 1883 health insurance had been essentially a voluntary affair.

- In different European states private non-commercial organizations, like mutuals, had sold health insurance for centuries.
- By involving the state, however, Bismarck's social insurance scheme was a new departure.

During the elapsed years, which run into 13 decades, although private insurance still exists, the population's healthcare has been increasingly and largely financed by governments. This may be now changing.

Recently, private health insurance has had a state-induced revival in both Switzerland and the Netherlands. The Swiss have been keen to expand access to all citizens, while containing costs. The Dutch looked at private insurance as the best solution both in connection to consumer choice and in terms of innovation in delivery of healthcare.

By contrast, because they use other people's money (in essence the taxpayers' money), by and large public healthcare plans and programmes are widely abused. Governments are lenient in regard to these abuses, which are well-known. The public healthcare plans themselves are not tightly regulated – as should have been the case – and all this is breeding three scourges:

- soaring costs,
- inadequate quality and
- a paucity of innovation.

Along with pensions, of which it can be seen as an important supplement, healthcare is by all evidence a runaway endowment. It is also the most intractable of commitments

27 Quoted in *The Economist*, 20 February 2010.

made by the welfare state; yet populist politicians always find an excuse to increase its negative economic impact. There are five reasons for this statement:

1. Healthcare initiatives are a patchwork of add-ons and flaws.
2. Abuse by nearly every person benefiting from it is rampant (more on this later).
3. Ill-defined boundaries concerning what is insured and what is not feed both skyrocketing costs and abuse.
4. An aging population requires not only 'more', but also more expensive, healthcare.
5. Medical technology, as well as sophisticated medicines, inflates the bill footed by the state.

It comes therefore as no surprise that a rapidly growing number of EU governments think that healthcare reform is necessary for millions of families. The long-term fiscal and economic health of public finances depends on it. The challenge lies in how to address the forces that make the healthcare system unaffordable and inefficient, without creating a backlash by the electorate.

Starting with the fundamentals, healthcare costs are no one-chapter business on which a determined administration can bring its undivided attention with the aim of smothering them. Instead, they resemble an octopus whose appetite for funds is deep and whose tentacles expand in all directions. The biggest tentacles are:

- hospital treatment, which is the largest chapter representing nearly one-third of healthcare costs;
- pharmaceuticals, the next largest chapter, but representing barely half the cost of hospitalization;
- outpatient treatment, whose cost stands, on average, at slightly less than pharmaceuticals.

Other important, but less deadly, expenditures include:

- therapeutic treatment and aids (not AIDS);
- sickness benefits (often for a fake sickness);
- expenditures due to fraud and playing the healthcare system

Tolstoy once wrote that every unhappy family is miserable in its own way. In a similar manner, every country has to find its own solution in restructuring and downsizing healthcare. Uniform solutions are of no great use because patterns of sickness vary widely between and within countries. Hence, general statements are not very helpful, although some are nevertheless worth noting.

For instance, a British study has shown that poorer people are much more likely to smoke than richer people, and this exposes them more to lung cancer. (That's a change from the immediate post-World War II years when professionals and labourers were equally keen to use tobacco and suffer its after-effects.) Taking US healthcare as another example, and bearing in mind that this is the most mismanaged system of them all, there seems to be a rather broad agreement that there are two main reasons (fraud aside) why its costs have risen so alarmingly:

- Profits by providers and high administration expenditures cause health insurance costs to skyrocket.
- An uncoordinated fee-for-services delivery of healthcare encourages greater specialization, justifying higher fees and promoting extra expenditures

These extra services are largely unnecessary, but not all of them are irrational because of the fear of litigation. Many medical doctors in America are ordering additional tests to prevent malpractice claims. In fact, promoted by a swarm of lawyers, litigation is so embedded into the system that many people believe malpractice reform will *not* decrease medical costs:

- Doctors will continue to order the same number of tests that they previously ordered, and
- few will be willing to give up the legal protection as well as the income that these tests provide to them and to the medical profession at large.

No matter what Barack Obama and other government officials may be saying, it does not look as if the US will manage to put a leash on surging healthcare expenditures, which consume nearly16 per cent[28] of GDP. Healthcare costs continue to pick up steam and the search to control spending and lighten the massive burden that lies ahead is not giving convincing deliverables.

- *If* the deficient regulation of the financial industry is taken as a precedent,
- *then* Obama's universal healthcare plan has been heading for the high seas since its inception.

Dr Nelson Mohler, a retired American physician with great experience in medicine and pharmacology, says that Barack Obama's mistake has been not to attack first things first. He should have restructured the cost basis of health insurance and improved its deliverables, prior to extending it to 47 million people who lack health insurance in the US. As things now stand, the cost of exploding health costs will be paid by his grandsons and their generation.[29]

EU governments can learn important lessons for the future by studying what is happening with American healthcare costs today. One of these is that differences from state to state can be stark. Comparing Minneapolis to Miami, researchers found Medicare spending per patient in the final months of life was more than twice as high in Miami.[30]

- The average number of days per person spent in intensive care was nearly four times greater, and

28 This was only 14 per cent of GDP in the mid-1990s.

29 Quotation from a recent meeting with Dr Nelson Mohler.

30 Adjusted for illnesses, local prices, age, sex and other variables.

- billed doctors' visits both in and outside hospital varied by as much as 500 per cent.[31]

Every community seems to have its own culture and ideas on how to spend taxpayers' money on health services, yet there is no evidence that spending more money provides a better outcome in pure health terms. Rather, as an American study has found, what apparently affects Medicare spending is the level of local medical and clinical resources.

- The higher the number of hospital beds or specialists relative to the population,
- the greater the outlays for people in their final months of life are likely to be.

Technology, and not just clinical technology, has added to the costs. On 23 April 2006 CNBC hosted a panel on healthcare which included the health secretary of the Bush administration. The panellists' conclusion was to put all medical records on computers – because 'today everybody has a PC'.

There were no dissenting voices, which is surprising because as Alfred Sloan, a great manager, has pointed out, no valuable decision can be reached without dissent. Apart from the fact that wide-ranging computerization of medical records is an invasion of privacy, there is plenty of evidence that databases, PCs and smart cards add to healthcare costs:

- In France the use of chip-and-pin card was heralded as the solution to the problem of healthcare fraud. Today 50 million people qualify for it, but there are 60 million plastic cards in circulation and the most often used are those providing full health coverage – used by people who do not qualify for it.
- In Britain, in 2002, the National Health Service (NHS) started a king-size, database project supposed to make available instantaneously the medical records of 50 million patients. After eight years of trying, at a cost of £12 billion ($19 billion), this project failed to deliver.[32]

Neither should risks connected to privacy and costs associated with recovery (if at all possible) of lost computer-based records be discounted. A day after the aforementioned CNBC health panels, a medical doctor's car was stolen along with his PC and the medical records of his clients stored on it. He had no copy of them and made a plea on TV to have the PC returned.

It is also quite interesting that the TV panel, including the health secretary, also decided that by computerizing all medical records the government would save an impressive $180 billion. (That number was supposedly based on a study, but its wholesome size rather suggests that it came out of a hut.) Nobody on the panel objected that the $180 billion was too big a number to be true.

Savings are always overestimated; by contrast, risk and the doomsday are put on the backburner. At the end of the day, however, somebody must pay for healthcare

31 *Business Week*, 13 July 1998. Reference is made to a study by Jonathan Skinner of Dartmouth College, an economist, and John E. Wennberg of Dartmouth Medical School, a physician.

32 D.N. Chorafas, *Cloud Computing Strategies*, Auerbach/CRC, New York, 2010.

and its growing costs, while its downsizing (including its restructuring) is typically an afterthought.

## 8. De Tocqueville and the Morality of the Social Safety Net

The first seven sections of this chapter provided evidence that presidents and prime ministers of sovereign states have two mountain peaks to climb on their way to save their governments from bankruptcy. The first peak is convincing the electorate that there is a *solvency problem*. The second is making the case for a fairly radical *structural reform* of the social safety net, which will be painful for practically everybody.

It takes much more than good intentions and plans to cross these two milestones without leaving one's skin in the battle royal of vested interests. Even solutions that may seem to make good sense often prove to be unworkable politically. New enemies of the social safety net's redimensioning and rationalization pop up all the time. The more recent are:

- the growing reliance of individuals and families on debt[33] and
- their inability to accumulate savings for a rainy day (section 2).

Moreover, because democracies depend on a multi-party system, political polarization over the issue of structural reform impedes a meaningful dialogue with the electorate. This makes it even more difficult to make changes so that the social security system becomes more flexible and adaptable to the rapidly changing demographics (Chapter 12), with all that means in terms of *longevity risk* – which can unsettle the people's lives, the policies of insurance companies and the state social security structure.

In mid-2007 *The Economist* published some interesting statistics on 'total pension assets as percentage of GDP (based on 2006 figures) and the 'old age dependency ratio' expressed as the number of people over 65 as a percentage of the total labour force – based on a forecast for 2025. In terms of total pension assets as a percentage of GDP:

- The best off have been the Netherlands, Sweden and Switzerland with a rather comfortable ratio between 120 and 140.
- At mid-range, between 60 per cent and slightly over 80 per cent, clustered America, Australia, Britain, Canada and Japan.
- Interestingly enough, India and China (two of the BRICS) had nearly zero pension assets.

It is wise to keep that classification in mind when talking of the future of pensions in developing countries, including the more prosperous among them. It looks *as if* the top brass of the BRICS and other developing countries have not yet paid enough attention to future liabilities. The picture is, however, quite different in regard to old age dependency ratios, where the impact of the young generation of workers is felt:

- Best off is India, followed by China.

33 D.N. Chorafas, *The Management of Bond Investments and Trading of Debt*, Butterworth-Heinemann, London, 2005.

- The worst off is Japan.
- The Netherlands, Sweden and Switzerland fall in-between, followed by America, Australia, Britain and Canada.

With relatively low total pension assets and a high old age dependency ratio, Japan looks like a basket case. But Australia, Britain, Canada and America are not sitting pretty, because they are next in the firing line. Now is the time to do something radical to redress the situation – but this takes political skill and guts.

Critics say, not without reason, that politicians and so-called social scientists have learned nothing from past failures; therefore they keep on repeating them. Yet, the limits of the welfare state are no secret. They have been explained by Alexis de Tocqueville, the eminent nineteenth-century French political observer and scholar.

Tocqueville was a clear thinker who never entered into political machination, and said what he thought. Quite significant have been his observations made during his first visit to Britain[34] where he addressed the paradox presented by the vast number of 'paupers' that populated the country despite the fact that Britain:

- was at the forefront of the industrial movement and
- was generally regarded (at the time) as the wealthiest nation on Earth.

In Tocqueville's own words quoted from his *Memoir on Pauperism*:

> *Cross the English countryside and you will think yourself transported into the Eden of modern civilization – magnificently maintained roads, clean new houses, well-fed cattle roaming rich meadows … more dazzling wealth than in any other country in the world.*

All that sounds, indeed, great. But then he writes:

> *… look more closely at the villages; examine the parish registers, and you will discover with indescribable astonishment that one-sixth of the inhabitants of this flourishing kingdom are so poor as to be classified paupers or indigents.*[35]

What Tocqueville essentially did was to vilify his time's welfare state. He wasted little time in finding a culprit on which to lay the blame for these very contradictory social circumstances. What is responsible for the teeming strata of paupers, he said, was Britain's generous 'Poor Law' which we call today government-sponsored welfare – the state supermarket in person.

'The more prosperous a society is,' Tocqueville wrote, 'the more … [it] simulate[s] true necessity through habit and imitation … Among very civilized peoples, the lack of multitude of things causes poverty; in the savage state, poverty consists only in not

34 Alexis de Tocqueville also visited America and wrote a great deal about his observations, impressions and projections.

35 A. de Tocqueville, *Memoir on Pauperism*, trans. S. Drescher, Civitas, London, 1997, p. 17. Available at: http://www.civitas.org.uk/pdf/Tocqueville_rr2.pdf.

finding something to eat.'[36] Keep that in mind when you hear the government's Orwellian New Talk about spending other people's money 'to eradicate poverty'.

Why aren't individuals themselves getting more active to improve their condition rather than waiting for somebody else – the state's bureaucrats – to do it for them? 'Man', Tocqueville argues, '... has a natural passion for idleness. There are, however, two incentives to work: the need to live and the desire to improve the conditions of life. Experience has proven that the majority of men can be sufficiently motivated to work only by the first of these incentives.'[37] In different terms:

- *If* one provides guaranteed public charity to meet basic needs such as food, clothing, shelter and (why not?) vacations and entertainment,
- *then* one likewise takes away the primary motivation to work, creating in one go a lazy society and a moral hazard.

Tocqueville confirms this interpretation by writing: 'Any measure which establishes legal charity on a permanent basis and gives it an administrative form thereby creates an idle and lazy class living at the expense of the industrial and working class.'[38] Tocqueville's bones would have turned in his grave had he been able to hear that in the early years of the twenty-first century French leftists asked for and got from the government the right to housing.

*As if* he had thought about that eventuality and wanted to clearly express a dissenting opinion, Tocqueville suggested that the morality of society as a whole suffers when public charity is the norm:

> *If you closely observe the condition of populations among whom such legislation has long been in force, you will easily discover that the effects are not less unfortunate for morality than for public prosperity, and that it depraves men even more than it impoverishes them.*[39]

It would indeed be difficult to find more clear thoughts to condemn:

- the drift of the social safety net and
- its metamorphosis into a giant state supermarket.

The reader should notice that these are not only Tocqueville's ideas, although he was the first on record to put them in print. In an address to Congress in 1935, the very year social security US-style was born, President Franklin Delano Roosevelt himself warned that:

> *Continued dependence on relief induces a spiritual and moral disintegration fundamentally destructive to the national fiber. To dole out relief in this way is to administer a narcotic, a subtle destroyer of the 'human spirit'.*[40]

36 Ibid., p. 24.

37 Ibid., p. 27.

38 Ibid., p. 30.

39 Ibid.

40 State of the Union Address, 1935.

On both sides of the Atlantic politicians who cannot make up their minds which way to go in restructuring and slimming down the welfare state – pensions, healthcare and other entitlements – should heed Tocqueville's and Roosevelt's advice. They essentially said the same thing, albeit in different words.

# CHAPTER 12 Demographic Changes and Longevity Risk

## 1. Gulliver's Travels and Real Life

According to anecdotal evidence, thousands of people in America are now living past the age of 100. Their number will probably increase as research projects are currently underway whose goal is to find a way of switching off the aging process by manipulating the appropriate genes. Theoretically, this could make people near-immortal, although the advice given by George Bernard Shaw's: 'Do not try to live forever. You will not succeed' is always valid. In practice:

- in all likelihood, such people will feel miserable and
- they will also put a heavy burden on the social safety net.

But strange things can happen. In Jonathan Swift's *Gulliver's Travels*, the famous traveller discovered a different world where houses were built upside down. He also met a tribe of immortals, the Struldbrugs. Far from being wise and serene, these turned out as a very unhappy lot because they continued to age and suffer age-related ailments. Whenever they saw a funeral, they lamented and repined that:

- others had gone to a harbour of rest,
- whereas they themselves could never hope to arrive there.

We are all mortals and happy to be so. Countries holding the longevity record are not blessed because of it. They have an acute problem to solve, which promises to become more complex, challenging and expensive – not simpler and more manageable. Projections talk of life expectancy reaching the mid-90s by 2050, at least in Western countries.

> *Globally, the number of persons aged 60 or over is expected almost to triple, increasing from 739 million in 2009 to 2 billion by 2050. Furthermore, already 65 per cent of the world's older persons live in the less developed regions and by 2050, 79 per cent will do so.* [1]

This message in demographics, conveyed by a study by the Geneva Association, is one of the alarm bells announcing that delays in positioning ourselves against the forces of the future will end in catastrophe.

Another most interesting finding is that, in aging populations, the number of people of older ages is growing faster the higher the age range considered. For instance, while

1 The Geneva Association, 'Changes in Work and Retirement', *The Four Pillars*, No. 45, September 2009.

the number of people aged 60 or over is expected to triple, that of people aged 80 or over – the so-called *oldest-old* – is projected to increase by 400 per cent , and it may reach 395 million in 2050.

- At present, just about half of the *oldest-old* live in developing countries.
- However, that share is expected to reach 69 per cent in 2050, putting each country's social safety net under severe stress.

The science of *demographics* is not new, but recently it has received a great deal of attention. Theoretically, the study of demographics is that of numbers concerning reproduction per woman, births, deaths and trends in aging populations. In practice, this is a very near-sighted approach. The study of demographics is a far more sophisticated business:

- it begins with the breakdown of the family, which highly impacts on birth rates, and
- it carries on all the way to longevity analysis (section 4) and the renewal of generations.

Regarding the first bullet, in Europe, but also in the US where the breakdown of the family originally started, marriage is in terminal decline. Many children are being brought up by single mothers; the educational system (whose mission is to make men out of a mass of flesh and bone) is limping;[2] God is dead (particularly in Europe, among Christians); and society is falling apart as a result of all these happenings.

Of course, anxiety about the state of the family is nothing new. A constant of modern history is the perception of social decay, and, in this, the breakdown of family cohesion and values has seen long service. There is also the fact that people aspire to rapid material and financial progress. Studies about the correlation between what is called 'economic progress' and 'society's change' are unsurprising.

- Eggheads say that economic progress gives people opportunities they were hitherto denied.
- Others answer that this provokes social change which (almost always) lessens the constraints which previously existed.

The breakdown of social discipline, divided families, absence of strict rules of education and plenty of other reasons have a clear impact on society, all the way to birth rates. As birth rates fall, the size of Euroland's workforce declines. As the population ages, each worker has to support more retirees (Chapter 11). This means that:

- either public finances worsen,
- or taxes have to rise to close the gap and avoid bankruptcy of the national economy.

Unless productivity increases to compensate, which is unlikely as the services industry is becoming more and more predominant (see Part Two), precious points are subtracted

2 See the evidence provided in Part One.

from gross domestic product (GDP). Although work and retirement patterns vary among countries, what is said in these paragraphs describes the trend well enough.

Dry statistics don't tell even half of the demographics story. Much more is involved, as many factors are interlinked among themselves and with the economy. America provides an example of the difficulty in keeping a balance between the time spent working and time in retirement.

In the US, the *baby-boom* generation did not follow their parents' policies. The so-called *baby-boom echo* – the children of the baby-boomers – are not keen to have big families and birth rates have dropped as Figure 12.1 shows. That is also the pattern in Europe (albeit more pronounced), but not in developing countries.

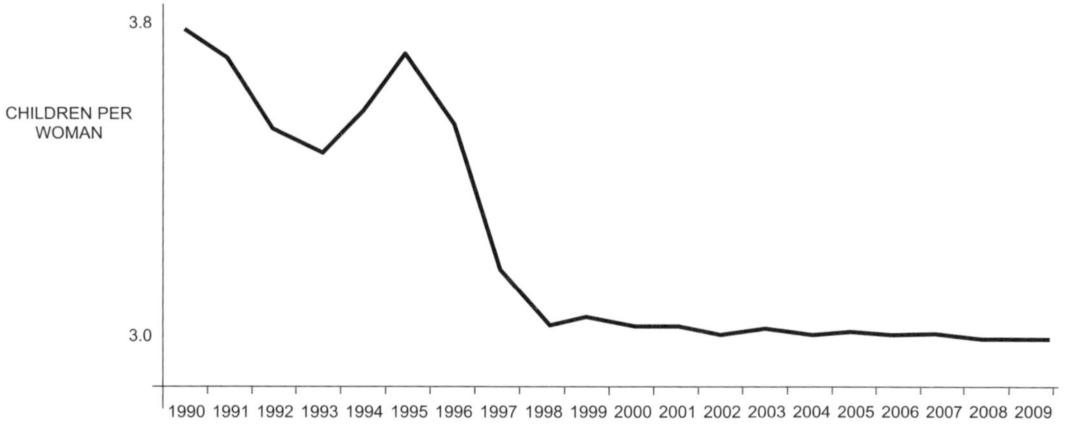


**Figure 12.1 Reproduction rate per family in the US, 1990–2009**

Practically everybody is afraid of Iran's nuclear weapon (in the making). But the fundamentalist revolution of the late 1970s plays on demographics for its expansionism (which is a better tool than the atomic bomb), and more than half of Iran's population is younger than 22 years old.

- The Iranian regime's problem is feeding mouths and high unemployment.
- It is not the ratio between those working and those in retirement, as in the West.

High, unaffordable birth rates are a difficult model of demographic challenges. Among Islamic nations (and some Catholic, too) even those who cannot afford large families have them nevertheless. The Palestinian population, for example, has one of the highest fertility and birth rates in the world, and, taking into account increased longevity, even if the birth rate falls, as projected, the population will continue to grow.

The *fertility rates* of Palestinian women in the West Bank and Gaza are among the highest in the global landscape, 5.6[3] and 6.9 children respectively for each woman of child-bearing age versus 0.5 in Italy's Piemonte. Some demographers estimate that by 2015 the Palestinian population will number over 5 million, and, with an influx of perhaps 600,000 returnees, the total population of the West Bank and Gaza could reach 6.5 million, by 2020.

3 A UNICEF estimate put this ratio at 5 in 2008. See: http://www.unicef.org/infobycountry/oPt_statistics.html.

This is simply unaffordable. Even today, with just over half of this population, Palestine is one of the most densely populated areas of the world, with more than 1,500 people per square mile. Given projected demographic growth, the density could reach 2,500 per square mile in just 15 years. That's the other side of the demographics equation which is swollen at its two extremes.

- In developed countries, birth rates are too low compared to life expectancy which is too high, and
- in less developed areas of the globe, birth rates reach for the stars, and, even accounting for low life expectancy, they are leaving a large unmanageable surplus.

Whatever the reasons for the first or for the second bullet, these fat legs of the distribution – too many old people in one side, too many babies in the other – turn the principles of proper management of demographics on their head. Something big, but negative, is going to happen, as Gulliver found in his travels in the land of Lilliput.

In conclusion, in thinking about demographics and the economy, as well as in projecting what the future may bring, it is wise to keep in mind that social structures, too, obey the laws of physics: when overloaded, they crack. Plenty of examples document this thesis – from family breakdown to the ever-increasing number of new mouths to be fed which (to the society producing them) are unaffordable and unmanageable.

## 2. Demographic Changes Mean More than Births and Deaths

In the late 1990s the International Monetary Fund conducted a study on *Aging Populations and Public Pension Schemes*, which attempted to quantify the fiscal burden as existing public pension schemes are affected by demographic changes.[4] The study accounted for the fact that practically all Western countries and some of the developing countries have aging populations, characterized by a growing proportion of the elderly compared to people actively working.[5] As we saw in section 1,

- this demographic shift is caused by lower fertility and increasing longevity, and
- their dual impact puts in question the claim that a birth rate of 2.1 per family is what is needed to maintain a stable relationship between the elderly and the potential labour force.

While the 2.1 birth rate is to be welcomed in terms of both quality of life and the environment, in regard to work-to-retirement it is one-sided because it leaves out of the equation many demographic factors that go well beyond statistics on births and deaths – and whose impact can weigh significantly on economic growth or decline.

For instance, the fact that quality of education is in free fall both in Europe and in America (see Part One) is having a tremendous impact on productivity and (most

4 S.K. Chand and A. Jaeger, *Aging Populations and Public Pension Schemes*, Occasional Paper 147, IMF, Washington, DC, 1996.

5 For instance, according to the Organization for Economic Cooperation and Development (OECD), nine of the ten fastest-aging populations in the world, based on current trends, are estimated to be in emerging markets.

importantly) on the stability of Western society – as well as on its ethics. Moreover, there is mounting evidence of harm caused to children by broken marriages and lone parenthood.

An example is provided by the collapse of the black American family. Statistics show that more than three out of five black American households with children are headed by a lone mother, usually young, poor and never married. In inner cities, the ratio exceeds four out of five. Ironically, this is not negative in terms of classical demographics, but it is bleak for overall demographic trends as it significantly affects:

- quality of life,
- children's education and
- the structure of society at large

'Two worlds with different demographics' that live side by side is a fact, and it is by no means clear who can reverse that trend. In a free society like ours, governments have no business imposing their moral choices on citizens. And scandals associated with various churches, like the boom in pederasty, have made sure that the church's moral prodding power has considerably waned.

But while the principle of individual freedom bars the state from intervening, at the same time it requires governments to take care where decisions about separation and single-parenthood influence the social safety net. Often, when a family breaks up, the husband's standard of living rises while that of his wife and children falls, sometimes even below the poverty line. Taxpayers' money is then used to support the remnants of the family to keep them floating above that line.

In several countries this role of the state as *Deus ex machina* impacts negatively on the demographics. An example is provided by France. *Allocations familiales* (support for larger families) were introduced after the haemorrhage of World War I, in which millions were killed for nothing on both sides of the divide: the Allies and the Central Powers. The *allocations* were invented to encourage families into making more children (probably as cannon fodder for the next World War).

After World War II, that system turned on its head. The French did not make more children, but generous *allocations familiales* (financed by the taxpayer) attracted large-scale immigration, some of which was illegal. As this included people from cultures where polygamous marriages and overlarge families were the norm, this resulted in a substantial number of children:

- being at risk of becoming school drop-outs;
- becoming involved in crime and disorder; and
- joining the ranks of future unemployables.

These dismal demographics of uncontrollable reproduction just for the sake of providing the procreator with pleasure and income are matched by the fact that more and more European and American families are made up of four generations instead of the classical two – or at least of three generations. With unemployment relatively high, in several European countries the more elderly provide a significant proportion of the family's income through their pensions.[6] Some economists project that:

- the four-generation family will become rather common, and
- children will get to know not only their grandparents, but also their great-grandparents.

This phenomenon of multi-generational families has mixed implications and social consequences More children will grow up with the support of older relatives and fewer young people will look for work, while people in their 60s will be called upon to care for 80- and 90-year-old parents facing the concern and (risk of) expenses, as the state's health support system breaks down (Chapter 11).

An example from the US, where the many-layered family has come into the social picture, can illuminate this issue. Think, for a start, about the rapid growth of the number of Americans who are 65 and older. Largely as a result of medical and public health advances, that group grew at a pace more than double the growth of the nation as a whole. And it continues to grow, just like it does in Europe – for instance, in England, France and Germany.

This scenario is intriguing for Euroland because in countries like France, Germany, Belgium and the Netherlands (at present) about 90 per cent of elderly people are white (or Caucasian to use the American term). But the proportion of older immigrants will eventually increase faster than that of their overall population, as women in immigrant communities become better educated and more assertive in resisting their husbands' procreation policies.

Nor does the complexity of demographics end at that point. A combination of an aging population and the increase in early retirement actively asked for by those currently working will inevitably lead many Western countries to market imbalances in the state pension structure which are difficult to put right. As will be recalled from Chapter 11:

- the funds coming into the system in the form of contributions are not sufficient to support the huge demand for pensions;
- therefore, demographers predict that (if the present trend continues) the social safety net will collapse in ruins when the number of pensioners outnumbers workers by 2030.

All these issues leave a footprint in the broader picture of demographics. Comfortable pensions, unemployment benefits, healthcare, medical progress, improved hygiene, better living standards and the absence of major pandemics are fine and dandy, but there are hidden costs linked to them, which should become public knowledge rather than being kept in the closet.

In mid-2009 a study by the International Monetary Fund noted that, in the longer term, the costs of the recent financial crisis (which indeed are huge) will be dwarfed by age-related spending. The IMF predicts that 'for advanced countries, the fiscal burden of the crisis will be roughly 10 per cent of the ageing-related costs'.

---

6 Ironically, many elderly people who are not beneficiaries of this four-generation set-up find themselves parked in old people's homes for the rest of their lives.

The lion's share of this torrent of sovereign debt will be extra spending on pensions, health and long-term care, while the present-day developing countries will also face turbulence because of *their* demographics. Developments related to public spending for an aged population are a serious business which has to be analysed and confronted *now*.

## 3. The Impact of Demographic Changes on Financial Well-being

Demographic changes responsible for the financing and solvency of the social safety net contribute a great deal to the political climate, because the larger part of the population is hostile to structural reform. In the US, for example, the rapidly growing numbers of people who are retired, or close to retirement, have created highly sophisticated and effective lobbying organizations that oppose any amendments to the goodies provided by the state supermarket.

Yet, it is beyond doubt that both the current situation and the prevailing trend are unaffordable and unsustainable. As sections 1 and 2 showed, in America and Europe the scale of the demographic challenge is immense and, as such, requires close examination through:

- fundamental study,
- comparison of means and ends, and
- wide public debate.

In 2001 heads of state participating in a meeting of the European Council, held in Stockholm, decided to regularly examine the long-term outlook for public finances – with particular emphasis on the strains caused by demographic developments. To perform this function the Council instituted the Ageing Working Group (AWG), which comprises:

- staff from international institutions and
- representatives of national ministries of finance and social affairs (among others).

In April 2009 the AWG published its projections up until 2060 on age-related government expenditure growth in EU member states.[7] One of the most interesting findings was the disproportionately large expansion in spending on old age, healthcare and long-term care in relation to GDP growth[8] – which essentially documents the worries expressed in Chapter 11 and first two sections of this chapter.

Another interesting finding of the AWG study is that total age-related public spending to GDP is expected to rise unevenly in Euroland. Economists suggest that countries with high dependency ratios and twisted demographics cannot avoid weaker economic growth and poorer investment returns as the returns on assets (physical and financial) tend to be related to output growth over the longer term. There is also a correlation

7 European Commission and Economic Policy Committee (AWG), *The 2009 Ageing Report: Economic and Budgetary Projections for the EU-27 Member States (2008–2060)*, Official Publications of the European Union, Luxembourg, 2009. Available at: http://ec.europa.eu/economy_finance/publications/publication14992_en.pdf.

8 Moreover, it should be noted that the macroeconomic scenario underlying the aging cost projections was finalized in 2008 and does not incorporate the impact of the 2007–2011 economic crisis which will have worsened the figures.

between demographics and savings. Economic theory tends to use age-related life cycles as a yardstick.

- Young people borrow.
- Middle-aged save.
- The elderly run down their savings.

When a large proportion of the population is middle-aged, savings are higher. But as the middle-aged join the elderly population, the supply of savings diminishes. A rising dependency ratio could deprive the West of needed capital for investments. This concern might be eased by the retirees' willingness (or need) to continue working at least part-time (see Chapter 11).

(A counterbalance to this is that, at least in Europe, the proportion of people aged 80 and over has grown even faster: from 1 per cent in 1950 to 4 per cent today – and this figure is set to rise to 10 per cent by 2050. North America and Asia are expected to follow similar trends.)

There are also reasons to believe that demographic changes will have an indirect impact on business activity. According to sociologists, aging societies become rather sclerotic; entrepreneurship and innovation dwindle, fewer risks are taken and demand for innovation slows. This bends the growth curve by:

- affecting investment returns and
- putting extra weight on retirement and healthcare financing.

Within the realm of the examples above, economic theory suggests that to protect their financial staying power, retirees should allocate a substantial portion of their savings to immediate annuities, to assure themselves against longevity risk (section 4). The problem is that people generally tend to underestimate their life expectancy. In Britain, men underestimate their life expectancy on average by 4.6 years and women by six years. In America roughly 40 per cent of pre-retirees underestimate their life expectancies by five or more years.[9]

The ability to correctly estimate one's own life expectancy is sometimes called *demographic literacy*. As the above statistics show, this is a rare skill. Typically, people misjudge their post-retirement needs in two ways: overestimating their ability to guess correctly and substantially underestimating their life expectancy. This has an evident impact on savings. In addition, committing to a serious savings plan (or insurance product) requires self-discipline, which is not frequently found.

Usually, current consumption often takes priority over savings. Precisely because people procrastinate when faced with the need to position themselves against longevity risk, governments have to produce inducements to save rather than promote consumption. In addition, it has become most urgent for countries to:

- curtail access to early retirement schemes and
- control future public spending pressures more effectively.

9 Swiss Re, *Sigma*, No. 4, 2008.

As the preceding paragraphs reveal, there are multiple financial effects associated with an aging population. As people in America, Europe and Japan grow older, bank accounts in these nations, where most of the world's wealth has been created and held in the past, are likely to grow slowly, if at all. The drying up of capital will worsen as populations age.

Curiously enough, it is not generally appreciated that the slowdown in global savings and decline in projected financial wealth creates a vicious circle by depressing investments and slowing economic growth. It also induces significant changes in the structure and behaviour of financial markets, including the pricing of assets. As the European Central Bank's 2004 *Annual Report* pointed out,[10] households of different generations typically:

- hold different amounts of financial assets and
- choose assets with different risk profiles for their investments.

This impacts on investment choices and therefore on asset prices. Since long-run demand for housing depends, at least partly, on the number of households in an economy, demographic changes also affect real estate prices. Pension reforms, too, particularly concerning their private funding, impact on financial markets as the role of institutional investors, like pension funds and insurance companies, increases.

According to a European Central Bank study, the possible effects of demographic change on financial markets can be quantified through simulation. Using models based on life-cycle theory, ECB researchers found that an ageing population implies a decrease in financial asset prices (both equities and bonds) and an increase in the required equity premium when the currently active population retires. Other studies, however, maintain that there is a bifurcation: equity prices tend to decrease, but bond prices tend to increase.

Economic studies have also concentrated on the age divide in perceptions of the current social safety net system. One of these was a survey conducted by the American Financial Services Forum which found that a majority of people under the age of 50 thought that social security would meet only a minor portion of their retirement needs, while 60 per cent of people over 65 saw it as a major source of their income. Overall:

- scepticism about social security increased with younger generations, and
- three out of four Americans aged 18–34 do not expect social security to provide a major source of their retirement income.

This, of course, contradicts the population's growing reliance on debt and its associated inability to accumulate significant savings – which prevails both in the US and in Europe. According the Federal Reserve's, 2004 *Survey of Consumer Finances* debt as a percentage of total assets rose to 15 per cent in 2004 from 12.1 per cent in 2001.[11] In 2004 American consumers were feeling wealthier because the value of their homes was going up. The bubble burst in 2007.

---

10 European Central Bank, *Annual Report 2004*, ECB, Frankfurt-am-Main, 2005. Available at: http://www.ecb.eu/pub/pdf/annrep/ar2004en.pdf.

11 *Federal Reserve Bulletin*, 2006, Table 11, p. A26, at: http://www.federalreserve.gov/pubs/bulletin/2006/financesurvey.pdf.

It needs no explaining that, in terms of retirement incomes, shrinking assets will leave people with debts. People will also have to pay interest on this debt out of their pensions rather than supplementing their pensions with interest from their savings.

## 4. Longevity Risk and its Hedging

Section 3 brought to the reader's attention the fact that the ability to guestimate one's own longevity is limited. This is true not only of ordinary citizens, where wishful thinking may play a role, but also of professionals, such as actuaries. This leads to *longevity risk*, defined as a double danger:

- Retirees may bleed their pension scheme dry by living well beyond the 'average' life cycle prescribed by actuarial tables, and
- retirees with greater longevity may find themselves with inadequate financial resources as pension plans wane, insurers go bankrupt, or social security payments don't keep up with inflation.

In connection to the first bullet, longevity risk has become a major concern to insurance companies offering annuities, as well as pension funds and other schemes, because it affects their solvency. The way an article in the *Financial Times* had it, a survey by Aberdeen Asset Management of 76 British pension entities found that longevity risk is now perceived as the second largest exposure facing insurance and other organizations guaranteeing payments to retired people. In the number one position is investment risk.[12]

The risk that people will live longer than expected weighs heavily on both pension plans and insurers providing annuities. Another negative is the industry track record of systematically underestimating gains in life expectancy, resulting in a bigger bill for benefits providers. Estimates that saw the light in business publications bring two facts to attention:

- In British defined benefit schemes, at age 65 every additional year of life expectancy pushes up the present value of pension liabilities by 3 per cent.[13]
- The pending rules governing European insurers known as Solvency 2 will oblige annuity providers to hold more capital against unhedged longevity risk, weighing on pension plans and insurance entities.

Concern about longevity risk is further highlighted by the shift from defined benefit to defined contribution plans (Chapter 11). As an investment exposure, it constitutes a greater danger than interest rate or inflation risk. In addition, while there are ways of hedging out the other key risks, approaches able to militate longevity risk are not quite effective.

Even more unsettling to those concerned is the fact that longevity risk is increasing as people tend to live materially longer than expected. Because countless individuals,

12 *Financial Times*, 2 March 2009.

13 *The Economist*, 6 February 2010.

employers, pension funds, insurers and governments are exposed to it, searches for ways and means of controlling risk are under way. According to some experts, derivatives present an answer in terms of developing a liquid longevity risk market.

- Derivatives enable insurers to create innovative retirement solutions for individuals and institutions.
- They could provide a way for market players to price longevity risk.

For instance, options have been used with a certain amount of success for hedging purposes.[14] Analytical studies target the long tail of a longevity risk distribution, develop worst-case scenarios and try to unload the plausible, but unlikely, events with the greater potential impact on to third parties. Another possible vehicle for trading longevity risk is the longevity bond with long maturity.

Still another way of hedging is longevity swaps in which investors take the risk of paying for longer-living pensioners in return for an agreed stream of cash from the seller. (In 2009 Babcock International became the first company to complete a longevity swap with Credit Suisse.)

All told, the market for trading longevity risk is still in an early state of development, and new approaches are being brought forward. On 1 February 2010 several banks and insurers launched the Life and Longevity Markets Association (LLMA). This is a London-based trade body aiming to spur the development of a liquid longevity market. According to some estimates, the total British exposure to longevity risk may exceed £2 trillion.[15]

Derivative financial instruments, however, present a mare's nest of risks which are often poorly understood, even by professionals. Capital market solutions for longevity risk are still in their infancy and, in general, they have not been properly studied so far in terms of:

- instrument pricing[16] and
- exposure assumed by investors.

An example from the domain of longevity risk is the *longevity swap*, in which the buyer makes regular payments, based on agreed mortality assumptions, to a seller (insurer). In return, the seller pays varying amounts depending on realized mortality rates within the scheme. (The structure is akin to an interest rate or inflation swap.)

Any hedging solution involving third parties must account for credit risk associated with hedging instruments. Practically all over-the-counter (OTC) deals involve counterparty exposure. This could be minimized *if* the trade transits through a clearer rather than being done over the counter or a standardized longevity index is created (a concept that has remained elusive so far).

The pros say that an advantage of OTC deals, not only for hedging longevity risk but in the general case, is that such contracts are custom-made. This serves in the realm of the

---

14 D.N. Chorafas, *An Introduction to Derivative Financial Instruments*, McGraw-Hill, New York, 2008.

15 Critics suggest that longevity swaps will most likely follow the trajectory of credit default swaps (CDSs), including the instability they brought to the market as exposure reached for the stars. D.N. Chorafas, *Financial Boom and Gloom. The Credit and Banking Crisis of 2007–2009 and Beyond*, Palgrave/Macmillan, London, 2009.

16 D.N. Chorafas, *Risk Pricing*, Harriman House, London, 2010.

subject under discussion because lifespans are not behaving in a normal (read: expected) manner – nor are they increasing at the same rate. Smokers, drinkers and workers in hazardous jobs die earlier than others. Hence there is a point in estimating:

- how long a scheme's members and
- their dependants are likely to live.

Theoretically, this permits the hedging to be priced according to assumed exposure. In practice, the general tendency is to underrate risk, which biases the pricing of financial instruments. Given that an insurance policy may continue until the last member's dependant dies, many estimates turn out to be overoptimistic as nobody can really tell what will happen to lifespans so many years down the line.

Older approaches provide an example of risks being assumed. In France, a type of tradable longevity risk is the *viager*. A person or company pays the owner of real estate a fraction of the going market price to buy the property, plus an annuity as long as the seller lives. The deal may be a bargain if the former owner dies in a few years, but can end up by costing more than the original market price of the house if he or she lives another 20 years or more.

The existence of precedents in longevity risk trades is important inasmuch as it provides data that assists in developing and testing insurance mechanisms for hedging purposes. Typically, such schemes are activated when longevity risk goes beyond a pre-set reference level – but their wider use requires vehicles whose return distribution differs from that of existing asset classes.

So far, the contribution of existing financial instruments to the control of longevity risk has not been outstanding. In addition, as the 2007–2011 economic and banking crisis has demonstrated, hedging plans thought to be a kind of insurance hide major exposure in the longer term.

- Theoretically, risk transfer solutions based on innovative financial products suited to retiree preferences offer attractive hedging opportunities.
- In practice, the medicine may turn out to be worse than the disease. Credit default swaps (CDSs), after all, were risk transfer mechanisms but they ended by becoming runaway risks.

New instruments have to be carefully studied in terms of their short-, medium- and long-term aftermath – keeping well in mind that the wealth of a pension plan becomes *inversely correlated* with the well-being and health of its adherents. This negative correlation and its effects bring into perspective two levels of reference:

- individual and
- aggregate longevity risk

With individual longevity risk, each person hedges his or her individual uncertainty regarding how long he will live. The classical way of doing so is by buying life annuities. The insurance industry has also developed other products, some of which may be seen as aligned with consumer preferences. For instance, variable annuities with guarantees help retirees link their pension income to an investment sector they may prefer, such as equities, while up to a point (but only up to a point) offering protection from adverse stock market developments.

Other insurance products that aim to provide a certain protection against health risks also exist. However, providers of pensions, annuities and protection schemes are exposed to aggregate longevity risk, or the risk of a population living longer – which is much more difficult to manage.

As lifespans lengthen, it becomes critically important to develop thoroughly studied ways and means able to position providers (governments, pension plans, insurance companies, annuity sellers) against aggregate longevity risk. There is a crying need to confront the likelihood of a systematic increase in life duration for the population as a whole. The undiversifiable nature of this exposure defies traditional risk management approaches and poses myriad challenges. Already:

- The amount of longevity risk on the books of insurers and pension providers is believed to be large and growing.
- To protect themselves against an explosive growth, insourcers encouraged the redistribution of longevity risk through capital markets, but the 2007–2011 economic crisis upset these plans.

Nevertheless, there is no lack of writers of hedging schemes with an appetite for risk, including banks and insurance companies. For example J.P. Morgan launched a derivative contract to allow pension providers to hedge against an increase in lifespans greater than that predicted by a longevity index. Other schemes ask for collateral to be posted on a regular basis, their downsides being that they are based on the specific longevity experience of a given pension plan and/or they are quite illiquid.

Insurers also maintain that governments have a role to play in promoting conditions conducive to the development of private-market solutions to longevity risk. But governments have neither the skills nor the inclination to do so, particularly after the highly costly salvage of mismanaged banks and insurers in 2008 and 2009.

## 5. Longevity, Social Costs and Life Insurance

While the concern about longevity risk is relatively recent, that of longevity's impact on social costs dates back to the 1980s. A study published in the February 1995 issue of the *Population and Development Review*, brought attention to the fact that longevity for those in their 80s and 90s has already increased significantly and will probably continue to do so. If so, the study said, this is a trend with major social and economic implications.

Since then, 15 years' experience of demographic trends and social costs has demonstrated that the researchers were right. Not only have the death rates of the very old been declining at an accelerating pace, but also, in a number of Western nations, the effects have been felt in financial terms.

- *If* this accelerated trend continues,
- *then* the '80-plus' population may far exceed current estimates.

Not long ago a French study projected that in 2050 there will still be 64 million French people, but with a totally different age distribution to the one prevailing today, and carrying greatly increased social costs. About 30 per cent of French citizens will be 60 years or older, and a big chunk of these (nearly 10 per cent of the total) will be over 80.

The good news is that such a huge mass of senior citizens would need to be served. The French study estimated that 400,000 jobs will need to be created, and its authors are pessimistic on whether these can be filled. Even today, when the demand is much smaller, people prefer to be unemployed than serve the elderly (see also Part Two).

The bad news is that the cost to the national economy (if a distinct national economy exists at that time), will be unbelievable. In addition, it will be wrong to continue measuring material standard of living by GDP per head, because that huge chunk of 30 per cent of the population will contribute nearly nothing to GDP in terms of the way it is computed today.

Other researchers have examined the social costs of longevity in healthcare (Chapter 11) and brought attention to the fact that since World War II there has been a trend of collecting benefits rather than contributing to the common purse. Sooner rather than later, insurance policy and public law will have to be revisited – restricting rather than expanding healthcare coverage in the way the Obama administration endeavoured to do in 2009.

Based on research findings, a growing number of critics of the current drift in public finances argue that the US, Canada and nations of the European Union have become lands of *perpetual dependants*. American economists point out that if one includes Medicare, Medicaid, social security and other means of getting assistance through entitlements, fully 51 per cent of American families already receive some form of federal payment.

Because entrenched benefits tend to grow as politicians vote for more free goodies for the electorate, the financial aftermath is worse than originally thought in terms of public deficits. Eventually, the facts of life will see to it that social security benefits have to be cut substantially through changes in the way in which costs are shared. As mentioned in Chapter 11, a growing number of economists suggest that:

- the time when the Western countries retirees were thriving on a largely out-of-control system has now passed, and
- the odds are that the working population will be faced with higher taxes and renewed inflation, unless governments finally decide to take charge of financial matters.

Since the policies of EU governments concerning the state supermarket are uneven and uncoordinated, and the results produced by the free market in Britain and America are not necessarily the paradigm of a rock-solid solution, two mandatory measures are worth examining:

- life insurance amended by annuities and
- the policy on private health insurance, as practised in Switzerland.

The reader should know that life insurance pre-dates health insurance by thousands of years. The practice started at about 2500BC when stone masons in lower Egypt formed a formal fund to provide support in case of its members' deaths.[17] Currently, many insurers

17 'Swiss Re', *Sigma*, No. 4, 2004.

believe that the core competency should be the management of retirement savings. In this market:

- monoline life insurers and pension funds are in direct competition, but
- with both vehicles, savers are assuming significant credit risk and market risk.

Part of the market risk is a significant amount of derivatives exposure. Tight supervision of life insurers to avoid repetition of the type of gambles taken by AIG which led to its bankruptcy is often talked about but not yet practised. The credit risk for each insured person is that the life insurer may go bankrupt before discharging its obligations.

Alternatively, confronted with financial difficulties, the life insurer may try to downsize the obligations it has assumed. In July 2000, Britain's Equitable Life, the world's oldest mutually owned life insurer, lost a court case brought by pensioners to force it to meet guaranteed annuities. The insurer said this decision would cost it £1.5 billion ($2.4 billion) and, being unable to afford this sum, put itself up for sale.

Theoretically, these problems should discourage taking out life insurance policies, participating in pension funds or buying health insurance. In practice, market risk and counterparty risk are part of daily life whether one acknowledges it or not. The state itself and/or its pension system may go bankrupt, or the state may loot the private pension schemes to help itself to their money, as happened in Argentina in early 2009.

The negative effects of the *nanny state* produced by years of drift towards more and more unaffordable and unsustainable entitlements can be best appreciated by what is happening in the EU. A short while ago, a study found that the welfare state in Europe is so heavily entrenched and pays out so lavishly, that if anyone becoming an entrepreneur will probably have to:

- accept earning less than unemployment insurance at the outset,
- be tireless in filling out forms for value added tax (VAT) and employee benefits, and
- subject himself or herself to many controls, as well as suffer from contradictory laws, irrational regulations and a vindictive bureaucracy.

Therefore, it is time to rethink what is the cost of all that, who pays at the end of the day, and what the state supermarket should and should not do in connection with the welfare of ordinary citizens and their freedom of action. Social spending has to be financed, but the government's action must reach a much higher standard of professionalism, avoiding the uncoordinated use of poorly qualified staff, which occurs in so many socially-oriented activities.

President Reagan once said that the most terrifying words in the English language are: 'I'm from the government and I'm here to help.' People who have studied the current situation and have projected well into the future have concluded that governments can no longer afford to continue their high-gear spending pattern which has produced more commitments than can possibly be kept.

For their part, the citizens of the EU and North America should understand that they can no longer live with the comfortable conviction that ultimately everyone is entitled to everything in life – and, most particularly, to getting from the government much more than they contribute to the common good. The moment of truth has arrived, even if second-rate politicians find it difficult to inform the public.

Indeed, not just yesterday but for some time, clear-eyed economists have suggested that the only way of restructuring the national debt is by cutting welfare. The mechanics that command deficit financing must be radically changed; otherwise, red ink will continue to flow without restraint, diminishing the standard of living of coming generations. The problem is that most cuts in entitlements and other social programmes offend the electorate which has become accustomed to handouts over the years.

## 6. What Can be Learned from the Human Development Index

It might be argued that a discussion on the Human Development Index (HDI) is out of place in the context of demographics and their impact on politics and social costs. This argument, however, would be rather near-sighted, sustainable only if one looks at demographics as numbers. By contrast, it would fall flat within the larger context which has been chosen (and followed) since section 1. We will see why.

The Human Development Index (HDI) was established by the UN Development Programme (UNDP), and some people consider it to be an entirely admirable endeavour (I don't share that excitement, but still it is not something that should be discarded). The UNDP agency has focused on three broad dimensions of development:

- health,
- education,
- material standard of living.

*Health* is measured by taking life expectancy at birth, subtracting 25 years, then dividing by 60. This score, which has a one-third weighting in the final rating, looks as if it has been a sort of compromise – but it can be lived with.

*Educational* development is measured as a joint result of adult literacy and the opportunity to become literate (which is subjective). The education index is derived from the adult literacy rate and average number of schooling (in years). Because quality of education varies widely, this has been criticized as a debatable yardstick, but this text only tries to explain the UNDP metrics, not to revamp them.

The UNDP measures *material standard of living* as GDP per head at purchasing power parity (PPP) – which is another debatable notion. Because differences in GDP are much larger than differences in life expectancy, the UN Human Development Index uses the logarithm of GDP.

The UNDP gives equal weight to each of the aforementioned three components to come up with a rating measure. While, as stated, none of these component parts is perfect, by accepting the Fermi paradox (which states that, in the long run, pluses and minuses tend to average out), one can look at the UN Human Development Index as a usable (albeit) relative reference scale.

The interesting part of it is that it is a first attempt to give every country a score between zero and one, based on its citizens' combined *health*, *education* and *income*. That is the basic reason why the HDI has been included as one of this chapter's topics.[18] Health could serve as proxy for longevity.

To provide some level ground in the globalized economy, the UNDP has adjusted the income basis according to a law of diminishing returns. If one poor country has twice the GDP per capita of another, that produces a much larger difference in their index scores than it does for one rich country having twice the GDP of another rich country.

As all this shows, within a certain degree of approximation, the HDI helps in comparing different nations' level of development in more than mere money income terms. All things considered, although the HDI is far from perfect,

- it can display the gap between richer and poorer countries starkly, and
- it could lead to an interesting comparison in terms of the three channels of spending which add up to the final score.

Healthcare and pensions (as well as wages and salaries for those currently working) sustain longevity. Money spent on upgrading the means of schooling shows up in the adult literacy rate (if these resources are wisely spent). Adjusted for purchasing power parity, real GDP per capita provides a basis for judging how rich or poor the average citizen of a country tends to be.

In the statistics I could find in terms of life expectancy at birth (in years) the top five countries have been Japan (with a score of nearly 79), Switzerland and Sweden (at 77.4 each), the Netherlands (77.2), Norway (77.1), Canada (77), France (76.4), America (75.9), Britain (75.7) and Germany (75.2).

The longevity index dropped below 50 with the last states in the list, three of which are in Africa (Burkina-Faso, Sierra Leone, Guinea) and one in Asia (Afghanistan). Guinea, which finds itself at the very bottom of the classification, has an index of life expectancy at birth of 43.5 (just 55 per cent Japan's).

By all evidence GDP per capita plays a crucial role as it correlates strongly with longevity. However, while the PPP in statistical tables presenting GDP per capita is expressed in dollars, and exchange rates are volatile, it makes little sense to quote numbers which will be obsolete anyway sometime down the line. In terms of per capita counted in their own currencies,

- The top ten countries are (in alphabetical order): America, Britain, Canada, France, Germany, Japan, Netherlands, Norway, Sweden and Switzerland.
- The longevity of this group varies between 75.2 and 78.6, resulting in about 2 per cent approximation from their mean if one discards the range. It is proper, then, to say that higher income correlates with a longevity of over 75 years.
- The bottom ten countries in GDP per capita divide into two groups: those with a GDP per person of over $1,000 per year and those below that level.

Countries with a per capital PPP income between $1,000 and $2,200 feature a longevity between a little above 50 years and somewhat over 60 years. They include (in alphabetical order): Egypt, India, Indonesia, Nigeria and Pakistan.

18 There is also a 'misery index', created by Arthur Okun in the US, based on illiteracy, unemployment and a couple of other factors. The HDI is better because it takes a positive attitude – reflecting a level that developing nations should aspire to reach.

With one exception (Sierra Leone, which features a GDP per capita per year of slightly over $1,000) the countries in the second group – Afghanistan, Bangladesh, Burkina-Faso, Guinea, Sierra Leone – have a GDP per capita below $1,000. Life expectancy in these countries (including Sierra Leone) ranges between 42 and 51.8 years. There is, indeed, a correlation between life expectancy at birth and income.[19]

That's life. It also testifies to the fact that countries which do nothing to bring their birth rates down to below 2.1 per woman – or even below that, to whatever is their level of affordability and sustainability – condemn themselves to remain poor, hungry and uneducated. Global resources are limited, or at least finite, and one should not expect to live on charitable handouts forever.

- *Either* the use of available resources is properly planned and managed to attain wanted results,
- *or* these resources are wasted through a galloping birth rate accompanied by high infant mortality, exposure to illnesses (including malaria and AIDS), plain illiteracy, lack of employment and illegal immigration.

The great part of the difference between *Homo sapiens* and other animals is made up by education and, in education, the word 'crisis' crops up a lot – not just in Africa, but in America and Europe as well. Now is the time to take measures to avert an educational crisis. Half-baked approaches like shaving off a year from high-school studies, unwisely decided by the EU, will not do. Their only result is that of reducing the level of literacy of the young generation, which is already suffering badly from another unwise decision – that of severely trimming the emphasis on teaching mathematics.

As far as I am aware, there are no statistics that I know of on how much it would cost to 'buy more' schooling or life expectancy – a basic reason probably being that costs associated with both items can vary widely from one country to the next. However, a June 2009 statement by the State of California provides a hint. California confronts virtual bankruptcy and it urgently needs to trim the budget. That mid-2009 report stated that the two largest expense items have been:

- healthcare and
- education (particularly connected to the University of California system).

With these two big-ticket items the level of the government budget, and therefore of public debt, is bound to rise sharply. As we have already seen through many examples, from pensions to healthcare and aging, none of the national programmes in the main developed countries is sustainable. Therefore, these countries will have to cut spending, and this will probably have an impact on longevity.

19 It is interesting, as well, to observe that these countries have a high birth rate and high infant mortality. In short, they are awfully mismanaged. In this 'modern age' hunger is not an accident. It is the result of failure to exercise family planning, limiting birth rates to what the economy can afford, and working hard to feed the new mouths.

# 7. Findings of the Demographic Fitness Index

One of the ironies with longevity is that it has become a measure of social progress. But, at the same time, everyone knows that the result of an aging population is not only that pensions and healthcare eat up an ever larger share of government spending, but also that it has a direct aftermath in the workplace which can be eased but not waived by switching to a policy of employing silver workers (see Chapter 11).

Nor will illegal immigrants from Burkina-Faso, with 0.1 years of schooling, solve the problems confronted by a knowledge society. Companies are waking up to the demographic challenge of an aging and shrinking workforce, and their concerns run deep. Several have started to analyse their internal age structure and skills deficits. Some say they plan to hire more employees aged 50 and over.

The reference made in the preceding paragraph is a key finding of the *European Demographic Fitness Survey* conducted among 2,518 companies in Britain, France, Germany, Italy and Spain, and published in January 2008.[20] This survey measured, on a scale of 100 to 400 points of the Demographic Fitness Index (DFX, explained in the following paragraph), the preparedness of companies to cope with the demographic crunch – and it revealed that much remains to be done in facing the challenge. For instance, European companies averaged only 182 points.[21]

First established by the Adecco Institute[22] in 2006 to help companies adapt to the aging of their workforce, the Demographic Fitness Index, resulted from the second *Demographic Fitness Survey*. Basically, it measures five variables influencing a company's ability to successfully cope with an aging workforce:

- career management,
- lifelong learning,
- knowledge upkeep,
- health management and
- ability to diversify.[23]

Other surveys have focused on the aging workforce itself, and responses being received are documenting the hypothesis that the world's population is financially underprepared to cope with retirement. Financial issues are topping the list of worries. Some 60 per cent of the world's pre-retired adults are not sure that they have saved enough for retirement, while just under 50 per cent of the world's retired adults wish they had done something earlier to provide enough for their retirement. According to Aviva, the British insurance company,

- only three in ten British citizens are currently saving for retirement, compared with almost a half of Americans and three out of four Hong Kong citizens, and

20 Adecco Institute, *The European Demographic Fitness Survey 2008: Demographic Fitness of Companies in Rough Economic Waters*. Available at: http://institute.adecco.com/Research/Articles/Pages/DFX2008_EU.aspx.

21 Results by EU country, where the survey was conducted, were surprisingly homogeneous. Britain and Germany led the group with 186 index points each, followed by Italy, Spain and France which averaged around 180 points.

22 Adecco is a Swiss employment agency operating worldwide.

23 The Geneva Association, *The Four Pillars*, No. 42, March 2008.

- six in ten pre-retirees across the world are underprepared for the financial rigours of retirement, prompting real concerns of a global pension crisis in the next 10–15 years.

This is a double whammy. People generally want to retire early and many do so, but they are unprepared for it. At the same time, companies face a lack of skills. Survey findings indicate that people are unprepared for retirement despite the fact that the financial weaknesses of state pensions have become more or less common knowledge. This contradicts earlier assumptions that:

- greater exposure to financial news and
- the globalization of markets has increasingly thrust upon individuals greater responsibility for their financial future.

Many theorists have opined that the ability to invest appropriately to meet one's individual requirements has been a major benefit of globalization and the single most important determinant of a person's ability to maintain his or her current standard of living during retirement years. In America many companies have used this argument in justifying to new hires their movement from defined benefit plans to defined contribution plans (see Chapter 11).

The real reason for the switch is that in an economy of slow or no growth defined benefit solutions are unaffordable (the wreckage of social security bears witness to that statement). On the other hand, the change from defined benefits to defined contributions transfers the risk of future underperformance of capital markets and other investments to the individual – who is ill-prepared to confront them.

In addition, thinking only of retirement challenges is definitely the wrong approach. The able management of human resources requires that all five variables conditioning the Demographic Fitness Index are accounted for, including a new one: the changed demographics in an aged society. Anything short of a holistic approach to the challenge of human resources is totally unconvincing.

There is, of course, little doubt that a holistic picture is complicated by the many ways in which legal and social issues, such as obsolete labour laws and the public's attachment to them, enter into career and investment decisions. Moreover, left to their own devices, very few people are able to interpret the opportunities, risks and whims of markets. Pension fund managers could do that (at least theoretically), but the quality of their performance is far from being consistently first-class.

As for the average citizens, when they look at their retirement nest egg, they find it difficult even to understand the financial jargon. What does it mean that portfolios thought to be diversified may no longer be so? Where have the benefits of diversification gone? What is meant by non-correlated assets? How do these affect risk and return? What is meant by risk and return in the first place?

- *If* the ordinary citizen does not know the depth of the risk and return argument,
- *then* he or she can be taken to the cleaners by any unscrupulous vendor of financial products *à la* Madoff.

Summing up the points made in this and preceding chapters, the more sophisticated the economic and financial side of society becomes, the more the average citizens find themselves at disadvantage. Queries also come up in regard to healthcare, which has started to become globalized. These range from the coverage of treatment expenses for surgical operations done abroad by national healthcare services (Medicaid/Medicare in the US, the NHS in Britain, Social Security in continental Europe) to:

- the quality of medical services received abroad and
- medical liability if something goes wrong.

Globalization and innovation don't affect only financial investment issues, although constant innovation in banking products, as well as access to increasingly obscure derivative instruments,[24] do present tough problems of choice and of steady oversight. And it is not only the financial investment horizon which has grown by leaps and bounds. Until not long ago, education and healthcare were not seen as *investments* – but that's what they have recently become.

In conclusion, planning for the future and for retirement is not just a matter of assuring enough money for bread, butter, rent and utilities. It also involves a host of other items related to consumption (such as vacations) and the aforementioned investments. People planning to supplement what the state supermarket is providing must appreciate that this will more or less be based on financial markets. Hence, they should understand and appreciate:

- the risks involved, including those associated with social security and pension funds, and
- that watching over the nest egg imposes many more considerations than simply following the daily news or relying on promises by politicians.

Any investment plan which does not fit the requirements of its owner is fundamentally unsatisfactory. Current social and financial conditions teach us that planning for the longer term makes far more sense than basing one's future on short-term events which may create more excitement, but hide the need for thinking about the future.

Every day is a learning experience in our life, and we must put what we learn into practice. If we don't, we will only have ourselves to blame.

24 D.N. Chorafas, *An Introduction to Derivative Financial Instruments*, McGraw-Hill, New York, 2008.

# Index